A GUIDE TO THE
# VOLUNTEERS
## OF
## ENGLAND
## 1859-1908

# A GUIDE TO THE VOLUNTEERS OF ENGLAND

## 1859-1908

by Ray Westlake

The Naval & Military Press

For Claire
My Guide in all Things

*Published by*

**The Naval & Military Press Ltd**
Unit 5 Riverside
Bellbrook Industrial Estate
Uckfield, East Sussex
TN22 1QQ England

Tel: +44 (0) 1825 749494
www.naval-military-press.com

# CONTENTS

# INTRODUCTION

The intention of this work is to put on record the various light horse, mounted rifles, artillery, engineer and rifle volunteer corps that were created throughout England as a result of the formation in 1859 of the Volunteer Force.

Listed under the counties in which they were raised and numbered are the corps that were accepted by the War Office, each having its formation date and location. Any changes in designation, organisation, disbandments or amalgamations have been recorded through to 1908 and transfer to the Territorial Force. In cases where more than one unit held the same number this has been indicated as, e.g., 1st (1859-1880) or 2nd (1880-1908). Cadet units were formed by some corps, and these have been dealt with within the records of the unit to which they were affiliated.

The official formation date of a corps is that on which its offer of service was accepted by the Secretary of State for War. However, in the vast majority of cases these 'letters of acceptance' cannot be traced and here the date of the commission issued to the unit's first officer has been used. These, in most cases, only differ from the acceptance date by a few weeks, or even days.

When a corps becomes part of another its subsequent records, where known, will be covered within those of the unit into which is has been 'absorbed', 'merged', 'consolidated' or 'amalgamated'.

The location given ('formed in' or 'raised in') for each corps is that of its headquarters. Recruiting, however, was often carried out in the surrounding areas and detachments of the main corps were also to be found in nearby towns and villages. In cases where a corps consisted of more than one battery of company the location given is again that of its main headquarters. Battery and company locations, if different from those of corps headquarters are, where known, given.

It will be seen that the corps of several of the smaller counties were to be included in the administrative formations of others. The development of these units will be recorded under their own county until such times that, due to consolidation, they lose their county number and become a lettered (numbers were sometimes used prior to 1880) battery or company within the new formation. From this point subsequent changes (when known) are noted in the records of the county to which the new corps belongs. An example of this is Radnorshire whose rifle volunteer corps were included in the 1st Herefordshire Admin Battalion. When this battalion was consolidated as the new 1st Herefordshire RVC in 1880, the 1st and 2nd Radnorshire lost their individual numbers and county reference and from then on were know as 'I' and 'K' Companies of the 1st Herefordshire RVC. Therefore, any further changes regarding these companies will be seen under 1st Herefordshire. On occasion, consolidated admin formations included more than one county name within its title. For example, in 1880 the Clackmannanshire Admin Battalion, which also included corps from Kinross, became the 1st Clackmannan and Kinross RVC. From here on the post-1880 records of the last named county will be dealt with in those of the first.

As previously mentioned only corps recognised by the War Office have been included. In addition to these a number were formed only to have their offer of service reach no further than the office of the county lord lieutenant. Such units were often in the process of training—even uniformed and badged—but for various reasons did not gain official recognition. These, therefore, are beyond the scope of this book.

# THE VOLUNTEER FORCE 1859–1908

## Reasons for Formation

It was most probably the Duke of Wellington who was responsible for the formation in 1859 of the Volunteer Force. In a letter to Sir John Burgoyne in 1847 the Duke had made clear his concern regarding this country's national defences. He, at the age of seventy-seven, did not share the general opinion of the Government that the United Kingdom was safe from attack. It was true that Britain had, since Waterloo, been free from troubles in Europe. And indeed, the several campaigns fought abroad were also far enough away not to render necessary the formation of additional forces to defend these shores. The Duke, however, did not think it sensible to sit back in what he believed was a false sense of security. 'It was time', he said, 'to make provisions for the defence of the country and to take all precautions against invasion. I hope,' he went on, 'that the Almighty may protect me from being witness of the tragedy which I cannot persuade my contemporaries to take measures to avert.'

If, as in the days of Napoleon I, home defence was to be supplemented by volunteers, the Duke's fears were quite understandable. True, there was a small number of yeomanry troops but, at the time of his letter to Sir John only two units, as far as infantry were concerned, were then in existence. These were the Honourable Artillery Company (later not to be included in the Volunteer Force) and the Royal Victoria Rifles (RVR) who became the 1st Middlesex RVC.

In agreement with the Duke, Barrister and one time High Sheriff of Radnor, Captain Hans Busk of the RVR later circulated copies of the Duke's 1847 letter. Busk's corps had, by 1858, dwindled to just fifty-seven effective men. But, and as a direct result of the action taken, the RVR by the middle of 1859, would muster no less than 800.

At the same time as Captain Busk was working on behalf of the RVR, others in the country were intent on organising a Volunteer Force nationwide. A corps had already been sanctioned at Exeter in 1852 and by 1855 the formation of one in Liverpool was well under way. It was not until 1859, however, that the main surge of volunteers came forward.

## Acceptance by the Government

At first the government of the day was not overly keen on seeing the creation of a part-time army. The idea of 'amateur soldiers' was not appealing, and it was also thought that the establishment of such a system would interfere with the recruiting of the Regular Army. The War Office, however, finally gave way and on 12 May 1859 sanction to form volunteer corps throughout the country was given—this authorisation being conveyed in a Circular addressed to the lord lieutenants of counties who were asked to submit any plans they might have.

Formation of volunteer corps was to be under the provisions of Act 44, George III, cap. 54, dated 5 June 1804. The main provisions of the 1804 Act were summarized in the 12 May Circular: officers' commissions should be signed by the lord lieutenant, volunteers could be called out in the case of actual invasion or rebellion, while under arms members of the corps should be subject to military law and while on active service no volunteer could quit his corps. He could, however, at other times leave after giving fourteen days' notice.

## Numbering and Precedence

It was a Memorandum of 13 July that the subject of precedence was settled. Each arm of the Volunteer Force was to rank more or less along the lines of the Regular Forces. At the time of the Memorandum, rifle volunteer corps (the infantry) were to rank after artillery volunteer corps as these were the only two arms then in existence. Within a short time, however, others were created and the eventual precedence list among the several volunteer arms read as follows: Light Horse, Artillery, Engineers, Mounted Rifles and Rifles.

The precedence of a corps within its county was indicated by the number allotted to it by the Secretary of State for War. The procedure here was that when the lord lieutenant received an application for the formation of a corps, he would then date it and forward the offer of service on to the War Office. When the Secretary of State for War had satisfied himself that the proposed unit had fulfilled the necessary conditions, he would, according to the date entered on the application by the lord lieutenant, allot the corps its number. The next step was to inform the corps of its acceptance of service by HM the Queen. It is the date of the letter bearing this information that determined an official date of formation. As a rule, these dates coincide with the precedence number assigned. On occasion, however, a number was allotted; but due to some special circumstances where reference had to be made to the corps concerned because of some informality in its offer of service, the acceptance date was held up. Very soon after the acceptance of the corps and the assignment of its number, the gazetting of officers was proceeded with.

## Infantry

Easily the highest in number, infantry volunteer units were styled as rifle volunteer corps, retaining this style until 1891 when a slight change was made to volunteer rifle corps. At the beginning of 1860 it was realised by the War Office that due to the unforeseen number of independent companies being formed, some kind of higher organisation was necessary. In a Circular issued to lord lieutenants of counties dated 24 March, suggestions for companies to merge, either as consolidated or administrative battalions, were put forward.

A consolidated formation, the Circular explained, 'applies to a battalion whose constituent companies are drawn from the same town or city.' When such a battalion was formed the corps involved were to lose their individual numbers and continue service either as a numbered or lettered company. It was also laid down that after consolidation the new, now larger, corps would thereafter be known by the number previously held by its senior company.

The administrative battalion, in the main, catered for corps situated in rural areas. In this case each battalion was designated, e.g. 1st Administrative Battalion of Shropshire Rifle Volunteers, and was allotted its own staff and headquarters. The corps included in an admin battalion, unlike those that had consolidated, remained distinct and financially independent units and were permitted to retain their county numbers and titles. 'The object of the formation of an Administrative Battalion', according to a Memorandum dated 4 September 1860, 'is to unite the different corps composing it under one common head, to secure uniformity of drill among them, and afford them the advantage of the instruction and assistance of an adjutant; but it is not intended to interfere with financial arrangements of the separate corps, or with the operation of the respective rules, or to compel them to meet together for battalion drill in ordinary times, except with their own consent.' In counties where there were insufficient corps to constitute a battalion, these were permitted to join that of one of its neighbours. Admin battalions were also permitted to consolidate at any time should they choose to do so.

By General Regulations and Instructions of 2 July 1873, the United Kingdom was divided into seventy infantry sub-districts. Each was designated as a 'Sub-District Brigade' and to it were allotted for recruiting purposes: two line battalions (the regulars), along with the militia (the reserves) and volunteers of a certain area. These were to be the first steps to the closer association of the Volunteer Force with the Regular Forces.

Although the proposals of the committee set up in 1878 under the presidency of Viscount Bury (Parliamentary Under Secretary of State) to look into the organisation of the Volunteer Force did not include any material changes in its composition, consolidation of all existing administrative battalions was, however, recommended. It therefore followed that during 1880 this recommendation was carried out and all remaining admin formations were consolidated. By the practice laid down in 1860, the corps contained within each battalion lost their independent status and became lettered companies of the new large corps. At first the new formations took on the number of its senior corps as before, but in counties that had more than one battalion this created a run of numbers with many gaps.

By June 1880, however, a general renumbering within each county had commenced and corps were subsequently numbered from 1st on. Only Suffolk, who in 1880 had its rifle volunteer corps organised into two battalions, chose to retain the original numbers (1st and 6th) adopted at the outset. To avoid confusion, I have referred to all post-1880 corps by their eventual number.

The Army Reorganisations of 1881 saw the old Sub-Districts formed into territorial regiments, better known, perhaps as 'county regiments'—Devonshire Regiment, Somerset Light Infantry, Essex Regiment, etc. In then came the former numbered 'Regiments of Foot' as 1st and 2nd battalions, the old Militia following on as 3rd, 4th, etc. The Volunteer Corps however, who were now to constitute 'Volunteer Battalions' of the new regiments, were to be numbered in a separate sequence. This change in designation, however, was carried out over a period of time with each battalion being notified in General (later Army) Orders. The 1st, 2nd and 3rd Somersetshire RVC would be the first to adopt the new style when under General Order 261 of October 1882 they became respectively the 1st, 2nd and 3rd Volunteer Battalions Prince Albert's (Somerset Light Infantry). It was by no means all corps that assumed the new 'VB' designations and several, whilst taking their place in their regiment's volunteer line-up, chose to retain their RVC titles. These, however, were required to change, e.g., from 1st Shropshire Rifle Volunteer Corps to 1st Shropshire Volunteer Rifle Corps in 1891.

The higher organisation of the volunteer infantry into brigades commenced in 1888. Nineteen were created under Army Order 314 of July, these to be followed by a further twelve in September (Army Order 408). The number of battalions forming each brigade varied from just three in one case, to seventeen in another. In 1890 (Army Orders 207 and 395) additional brigades were formed and at the same time battalions were distributed on a more even basis. The next change affecting volunteer infantry brigades occurred in 1906 when under Army Order 130 the total was brought up to forty-four.

In 1900, and under a Special Army Order dated 2 January, volunteer battalions were called upon to raise companies for active service in South Africa. For each regular battalion serving in the war one company was to be raised from its affiliated volunteers. These were to consist of 116 all ranks who, in order to surmount the difficulties of the Volunteer Act, had to enlist into the Regular Army for a period of one year or the duration of the war. Such companies were designated, e.g. 1st Volunteer Service Company King's (Shropshire Light Infantry). A separate organisation known as the City Imperial Volunteers was also formed within the London area, this taking in the volunteers from most of Middlesex as well as the capital. As a result, volunteer corps, or volunteer battalions, as the case may be, received a 'South Africa' battle honour. A date was also included, e.g. '1900-02', but this varied according to the period of time the volunteer contingents had actually served. In the text, if not mentioned, it may be assumed that all volunteer corps were represented in South Africa.

## Artillery

Artillery units were styled Artillery Volunteer Corps and followed the same pattern as the infantry above regarding administrative formations (brigades in this case) and consolidation. In 1882 artillery corps were affiliated to nine out of the eleven territorial divisions of artillery that were formed that year under General Order 72 of 1 April. Shortly after, some corps were re-designated, the new titles reflecting to which division it belonged. For example, the 1st Hampshire Artillery Volunteer Corp became the 1st Volunteer (Hampshire) Brigade, Southern Division, Royal Artillery. Those that did adopt the new styling did so over a period of time, the changes being notified in General (later Army) Orders.

When the three division system was introduced in 1889 the titles of all units again became e.g. 1st Shropshire Artillery Volunteer Corps. Some, however, once again chose to indicate their affiliation by adding e.g. (Southern Division, Royal Artillery) after the main title. With effect from 1 June 1899 the Royal Regiment of Artillery was rearranged into mounted and dismounted branches—the Royal Field Artillery and Royal Garrison Artillery. The volunteers became part of the latter and those showing divisional affiliations within their titles charged to e.g. (Southern Division, Royal Garrison Artillery). All Artillery Volunteer Corps were restyled as Volunteer Artillery Corps by December 1891.

Position batteries were introduced to volunteer artillery in May 1888 under Army Order 209 of 1 May. These batteries, which were intended to provide an element of semi-mobile field artillery to work with infantry brigades, were formed from the personnel of two existing garrison batteries. Under Army Order 234 of 1 November 1891 all batteries, with the exception of position, were restyled as companies. The manning of position batteries by garrison companies was to lead to a great deal of confusion so in 1892 (Army Order 218) position batteries were made independent and numbered within their corps from No 1 onwards. The remaining garrison companies were then numbered on from the position batteries. Position batteries were re-designated as Heavy by Army Order 120 of May 1902. Where corps consisted entirely of position/heavy batteries the words 'Position Artillery' then 'Heavy Artillery' was added in the Army List. This, however, formed no part of the unit designation.

## Engineers

Engineer units were styled Engineer Volunteer Corps and like the infantry (rifles) were sometimes grouped into administrative battalions, these also being ordered to consolidate in 1880. In 1888 the general styling of engineers was changed to Engineer Volunteers, Fortress and Railway Forces, Royal Engineers. This was changed to Volunteer Engineers, Fortress and Railway Forces, Royal Engineers in 1891 and finally to Royal Engineers (Volunteers) in 1896.

Companies trained in the duties of submarine miners were first introduced to engineer volunteer corps in 1883/84. In 1886, however, it was decided by the War Office that it was not, due to the higher standard of training required, entirely convenient for these to be administered by the units in which they were originally formed. Also, in 1886 it was proposed that additional companies should be created and, together with those already maintained by existing corps, be formed into independent units.

In the Army List for September 1886 under the heading 'The Volunteer Submarine Miners' six divisions were listed as follows: Severn, Humber, Tees, Falmouth, Forth and Tay. Of these, five were new units, Severn having been formed by the Submarine Mining companies of the 1st Gloucestershire EVC.

By March 1888 all remaining submarine mining companies were withdrawn from the parent corps and made independent. The Army List for that month showed: Tyne, Severn, Clyde, Humber, Tees, Forth, Tay and Mersey. Missing from the previous list is Falmouth, but this was added in the Army List for July 1888. In 1907 the abolition of submarine mines in defended ports was ordered by the War Office. As a result, submarine mining units were each reduced to a number necessary to work the electric lights of gun defences and thereafter were known as 'Electrical Engineers'.

## Cavalry

Distinct from the Yeomanry, the several mounted units of the Volunteer Force were styled either as light horse volunteers or mounted rifle volunteers.

## Territorial Force 1908

Under the Territorial and Reserve Forces Act of 1907, the Volunteer Force ceased to exist on 31 March 1908. On the following day, 1 April, the Territorial Force (TF) was born and the old volunteers invited to enlist. The change was not a popular one with the volunteers as the new system often necessitated the reorganisation, and in some cases, disbandment of many of the existing companies. Some infantry battalions were even required to convert to artillery or some other arm of service. The new force was soon established, however, and the majority of units were to transfer en bloc. The new TF battalions were, unlike the former volunteer battalions, who had their own sequence, numbered on from the Special Reserve.

## Cadet Corps

Cadet units, which were to be formed in connection with volunteer corps or administrative battalions, were first sanctioned in Volunteer Regulations for 1863, article 279 directing that any cadet corps raised should consist of boys twelve years of age and upwards, these to be officered by gentlemen holding honorary commissions only. There were, however, numerous units formed prior to 1863—such organisations as the Shrewsbury School Drill Company are known to have exited as early as 1860. Cadet corps were normally organised into companies of not less than thirty boys. These were then affiliated to individual corps or administrative battalions and took precedence with them when on parade.

Recruiting of boys for cadet corps was, in the main, concentrated among the public schools of the day. Youths from all walks of life, however, were involved and many units were to be formed from the junior staff of factories, warehouses and large businesses—the Postal Telegraph Messengers Cadet Corps from the Derby Post Office, for example.

In June 1886 authority was given for the formation of cadet battalions consisting of four companies. These, although linked to a line regiment, were completely independent of any volunteer corps.

The contribution made by public schools to the Volunteer Movement is well known. Not only did they raise cadet corps, but some schools such as Eton, Harrow and Rugby also provided volunteer corps in their own right. In 1908, and upon the formation of the Territorial Force, all cadet corps formed by schools were invited to join the newly created Officers Training Corps. The vast majority did so and from then on came under the direct authority of the War Office. At the same time all affiliations to volunteer corps (now Territorial Force units) ceased. The non-school corps, and those schools choosing to remain part of the Territorial Force, were from 1908 recorded in the Army List under the heading 'Cadet Companies and Corps'. This section, which appeared immediately after the OTC, was not seen after 1913, by which time all units receiving recognition by the TF had been included once again with their parent unit.

# THE ENGLISH VOLUNTEERS BY COUNTY

# Bedfordshire

## Engineer Volunteers

**1st**—In 1888 a cadet corps was formed at Bedford Grammar School by one of its masters—retired German Army Engineer officer Captain G J R Glünicke—who placed the unit in the care of the 2nd Tower Hamlets EVC. The school moved from its location on St Paul's Square in the town centre to a site adjoining De Parys Avenue in 1891. Captain Glünicke, who lived close by on the west side of the avenue, was also responsible for the formation on 4 May 1900 of the adult 1st Bedfordshire EVC—a corps with an establishment of four companies under his command. Soon attached was the Bedford Grammar School contingent, followed by the cadet corps located at Bedford County School (formed 12 December 1900) and Bedford Modern School which joined in 1904. The latter, authorised on 18 April 1900, had hitherto been attached to the 3rd Volunteer Battalion of the Bedfordshire Regiment. Territorials: East Anglian Divisional Engineers. All three cadet corps became contingents of the Junior Division, Officers Training Corps, the County School being renamed as Elstow School.

## Rifle Volunteers

All rifle corps formed were placed into the 1st Admin Battalion which in 1880 provided the new 1st Corps.

**1st (1860-1880)**—Formed 27 February 1860 as one company at Bedford with former Rifle Brigade officer William Crosbie as captain. Increased to two companies in 1878 and became 'A' and 'B' Companies of the new 1st Corps in 1880.

**1st (1880-1908)**—The 1st Admin Battalion was formed in August 1860 with headquarters at Bedford, transferring to Toddington in 1866, then to Woburn in 1870. The battalion was consolidated in 1880 as the new 1st Corps with nine companies: 'A' Bedford (late 1st Corps), 'B' Bedford (late 1st Corps), 'C' Toddington (late 2nd Corps), 'D' Dunstable (late 4th Corps), 'E' Ampthill (late 5th Corps), 'F' Luton (late 6th Corps), 'G' Luton (late 6th Corps), 'H' Shefford (late 7th Corps), 'I' Woburn (late 8th Corps).

Designated 3rd Volunteer Battalion Bedfordshire Regiment in 1887 and by July 1894

**Bedfordshire Rifle Volunteers pouch-belt plate.**

company locations were: Bedford (2), Dunstable, Ampthill, Luton (3), Shefford and Biggleswade. The Bedford Modern School Cadet Corps was affiliated in 1900 but was transferred to the 1st Bedfordshire Royal Engineers (Volunteers) in 1904. *Territorials:* Four companies of the 5th Battalion Bedfordshire Regiment.

**2nd**—Formed at Toddington on 1 March 1860 with former Bedfordshire Militia officer William C Cooper as captain. Became 'C' Company of the new 1st Corps in 1880.

**3rd**—None recorded.

**4th**—Formed at Dunstable with Arthur Macnamara as captain, local solicitor William Medland as lieutenant and William Eames, ensign. All three held commissions dated 24 April 1860. Became 'D' Company of the new 1st Corps in 1880.

**5th**—Formed at Ampthill on 26 April 1860. The commanding officer, Captain Brooks, had previously held the rank of Major in the Bengal Light Cavalry. Became 'E' Company of the new 1st Corp in 1880.

**6th**—Formed at Luton with Captain John S Crawley in command on 16 May 1860. Increased to two companies and became 'F' and 'G' Companies of the new 1st Corps in 1880. In the north transept of St Mary's Church, among some fifteenth- and sixteenth-century brasses, Captain Crawley's family arms appear on a stone shield.

**7th**—Formed at Biggleswade with Captain Robert Henry Lindsell, Lieutenant Frederick Hogge and Ensign Frederick Gresham holding commissions dated 11 September 1860. Robert Lindsell had previously held the rank of lieutenant-colonel in the 28th Regiment of Foot and was present at the battles of Alma, Inkerman and the siege of Sebastopol during the Crimean War. Headquarters moved to Shefford in 1871 and 7th Corps became 'H' Company of the new 1st Corps in 1880.

**8th**—Formed at Woburn from workers on the Duke of Bedford's estate on 18 September 1860. Became 'I' Company of the new 1st Corps in 1880.

**9th**—Formed at Bedford from employees of Howard's Britannia Agricultural Implements factory. Ensign William Henry Lester was the first to be commissioned on 16 May 1864, with Lieutenant Charles Johnson following on 24 May and Captain Henry H Green on 6 June. James Howard, one of the directors of the Britannia works, was commissioned as captain on 16 January 1865 and took command. The corps was later disbanded and last seen in the Army List for November 1872.

# Berkshire

**Rifle Volunteers**

The county provided one admin battalion, which included all corps, and in 1873 was consolidated to form a new 1st corps. Two numbered sub-divisions appeared in the early Army Lists, the 1st and 2nd subsequently being numbered as 2nd and 3rd Corps respectively.

**1st (1860-1873)**—Formed with headquarters at Reading on 10 September 1859 and soon comprised three companies under the overall command of Major Commandant Robert James Loyd-Lindsay, former lieutenant colonel Scots Fusilier Guards and winner of the Victoria Cross at the Crimea. Loyd-Lindsay later took command of the 1st Admin Battalion, the three 1st Corps companies after that being commanded by Captains Sir Claudius S Paul Hunter, Charles Stephens and William Martin Atkins. The Borough Museum at Reading are in possession of a photograph which shows three officers of the 1st Corps—Loyd-Lindsay, Sir Paul Hunter and William Atkins. Reproduced in Volume 38 of the *Journal for the Society of Army Historical Research,* the group is referred to as 'three officers of the Wantage and Vale of White Horse Companies'. The 1st Corps became 'A', 'B' and 'C' Companies of the new 1st Corps in 1873.

Noted among the main industries of Reading is biscuit making. Oscar Wilde is on record as having visited the Huntly & Palmers factory in 1892. He would make another visit to Reading three years later, but for a less enjoyable reason. Indeed, workers from Huntly & Palmers are known to have served in the Volunteers, many, no doubt, taking part in the parade that saw the December 1886 unveiling in Forbury

Gardens by Robert Loyd-Lindsay (by then Lord Wantage, VC) of the 'Maiwand Lion'. Apparently the largest lion statue in the world, this magnificent beast commemorates those of the 66th (Berkshire) Regiment who laid down their lives during the Afghan Campaign of 1879-1880.

**1st (1873-1908)**—The 1st Admin Battalion of Berkshire Rifle Volunteers was formed with headquarters at Reading in June 1860. Robert Loyd-Lindsay VC of the 1st Corps took command. When the battalion was consolidated as the new 1st Corps in 1873 the combined strength of the eleven independent corps then in existence totalled thirteen companies. Headquarters remained at Reading and the reorganisation went as follows: 'A' Reading (late 1st Corps), 'B' Reading (late 1st Corps), 'C' Reading (late 1st Corps), 'D' Windsor (late 2nd Corps), 'E' Newbury (late 3rd Corps), 'F' Abingdon (late 4th Corps), 'G' Maidenhead (late 5th Corps), 'H' Sandhurst (late 7th Corps), 'I' Faringdon (late 8th Corps), 'K' Wantage (late 9th Corps), 'L' Winkfield (late 10th Corps), 'M' Wallingford (late 11th Corps), 'N' Windsor Great Park (late 12th Corps).

Mention is made in a work privately produced in 1959 to commemorate the centenary of the 4th Battalion Royal Berkshire Regiment of an 'O' Company being present at Annual Camp in 1874. According to the book, this company had been formed by the 'cadets of Coopers Hill College' [presumably the Royal Indian Engineering College]. However, there is no record of a cadet company having been formed there and the Army List shows no indication that an increase in establishment had taken place. The corps was re-designated 1st Volunteer Battalion Berkshire Regiment in 1882—the title 'Royal' not being conferred upon that regiment until three years later in 1885. A Mounted Infantry Company was formed in 1886, the total number of companies amounting to fifteen by April 1897.

Some 137 members of the 1st Volunteer Battalion served in the Boer War, the first contingent under Major A F Ewen and Lieutenants R J Clarke and W P Alleyne, being inspected by Queen Victoria at Windsor in the last week of February 1900 before leaving for South Africa. Upon arrival, the first duty given to the Berkshire men was to provide an escort to a convoy going to Bloemfontein. Joined by a second draft under Lieutenant F A Simmonds, the volunteers, now serving alongside regulars from their county regiment, were placed under the command of General Sir Ian Hamilton at Pretoria. Action was seen on 2 August: Lord Robert's despatch of 10 October 1900 noting that 'on approaching Uitval Nek, Hamilton found it strongly held by the enemy, whom he engaged in the front with a portion of Cunningham's brigade, while two companies of the Berkshire Regiment

gallantly escaladed the steep cliff overlooking the pass from the east'. The enemy were cleared from the area, the loss to the attackers including Private Lee of the Volunteer Company who was killed. In the same action Private William House of the 2nd (Regular) Battalion received the Victoria Cross. Guarding lines of communication, escort and garrison duties followed, six of the volunteers during this period being lost due to disease.

Several cadet corps were formed and affiliated to the battalion—mention has already been made of one possibly existing at Coopers Hill. Those that did appear in the Army List, and had officers commissioned to them, were the Wellington College Cadet Corps (formed in 1882) Bradfield College, which appeared in 1884, and a unit raised in the East Berkshire parish of Cookham Dean in 1900—the latter gone from the Army List, however, by July 1902. The last return made by the battalion prior to joining the Territorial Force in 1908 showed a total

**1st Volunteer Battalion Royal Berkshire Regiment.**

strength of 1,078 all ranks. *Territorials:* 4th Battalion Royal Berkshire Regiment. Both Wellington and Bradfield Colleges became contingents of the Junior Division OTC.

**2nd**—Formed as the 1st Sub-division at Windsor on 27 October 1859 and increased to a full company by the beginning of the following year. The original officers held commissions dated 12 January 1860. Became 'D' Company of the new 1st Corps in 1873. At Windsor in 1881, the Albert Institute was opened with its reading rooms and lecture hall, and on Castle Hill, in Jubilee year, the volunteers held the ground at the unveiling of Queen Victoria's statue. A great model for them, as far as drill and smartness were concerned, was the several Guards regiments, one of which was always stationed in the town. Headquarters of the company were in Church Lane.

**3rd**—Formed at Newbury as the 2nd Sub-division on 14 December 1859. Later increased to the strength of a full company and shown as 3rd Corps in the Army List for the first time in March 1860. The Newbury Volunteers became 'E' Company of the new 1st Corps in 1873.

**4th**—Formed as one company at Abingdon on 23 February 1860. Became 'F' Company of the new 1st Corps in 1873.

**5th**—Formed at Maidenhead with Captain Robert Vansittart, Lieutenant Edward Sawyer and Ensign Henry Micklem commissioned on 24 February 1860. Robert Vansittart had previously held the rank of lieutenant-colonel in the Coldstream Guards. Became 'G' Company of the new 1st Corps in 1873.

**6th**—Formed at Wokingham on 14 May 1860. The corps disappeared from the Army List in March 1865 having not exceeded the strength of a half company.

**7th**—Formed as half company at Sandhurst with Lieutenant William Walker and Ensign Edward de la Motte commissioned on 25 August 1860. William Walker had previously served as an officer with the 69th (South Lincolnshire) Regiment. Increased to a full company in 1872 and became 'H' Company of the new 1st Corps in 1873.

**8th**—Formed as a half company at Faringdon on 21 September 1860, increasing to a full company by March of the following year. Became 'I' Company of the new 1st Corps in 1873.

**9th**—Formed as one company at Wantage on 24 October 1860. The corps did not join the 1st Admin Battalion until 1863 and became 'K' Company of the new 1st Corps in 1873.

**10th**—Formed as one company under the command of Captain George Dennistoun Scott on 1 March 1861. Headquarters was first given in the Army List as Woodside, the family seat of Captain Scott, but by July, Winkfield is listed. The 10th Corps did not join the 1st Admin Battalion until 1863 and became 'L' Company of the new 1st Corps in 1873.

**11th**—Formed as one company at Wallingford on 13 February 1861. Did not join the 1st Admin Battalion until 1863 and became 'M' Company of the new 1st Corps in 1873.

**12th**—Formed as a half company in the Spring on 1861, headquarters of the 12th Corps are given as Windsor Great Park. The first officer to be enrolled was former major general in the Regular Army, Francis Hugh Seymour who received his commission as lieutenant on 9 May 1861. Became 'N' Company of the new 1st Corps in 1873.

# Berwick-upon-Tweed

## Artillery Volunteers

**1st**—Formed on 27 February 1860 and disbanded with effect from 31 March 1908.

## Rifle Volunteers

**1st**—Formed on 28 March 1860. In the following November the corps was included in the 1st Northumberland Admin Battalion and in 1880 became 'G' Company of the new 1st Northumberland and Berwick-upon-Tweed RVC.

# Buckinghamshire

## Rifle Volunteers

The county's 1st Admin Battalion became the new 1st Corps in 1875. Two numbered sub-divisions (1st and 3rd) appear in the early Army Lists which subsequently formed the 1st and 2nd Corps respectively. Possibly the half company raised at Buckingham, the eventual 3rd Corps, filled the 2nd Sub-division slot. However, no such designation appeared in the Army List.

**1st (1859-1875)**—Formed at Great Marlow as the 1st Sub-division by Mr T Owen Wethered of Marlow and sworn in on 8 December 1859. The first officers: Lieutenant George Henry Vansittart of Bisham Abbey and Ensign T Owen Wethered, were all three commissioned on 16 December. Shown in the Army List as 1st Corps for the first time in April 1860 and became part of the new 1st Corps in 1875.

**1st (1875-1908)**—The 1st Admin Battalion was formed with headquarters at Aylesbury in July 1862. Great Marlow became headquarters in 1872 and in 1875 the battalion was consolidated to form the new 1st Corps which first appeared in the Army List for April. There were five companies: Great Marlow (late 1st Corps), Buckingham (late 3rd Corps), Aylesbury (late 4th Corps), Slough (late 5th Corps), Eton College (late 8th Corps).

New companies were later formed at High Wycombe, Buckingham and Wolverton—No 6 Company at Wolverton was recruited in the main from men employed at the London and North Western Railway Carriage Works and the volunteers at High Wycombe were from the staff of a local chair manufacturer. In 1876 a cadet corps was also provided by St Paul's College at Stony Stratford which, however, disappeared from the Army List in May 1883. The Eton College personnel were detached to form a new 2nd Corps in 1878.

It became a volunteer battalion (without change of title) of the Oxfordshire Light Infantry in 1881, the companies in 1897 being redistributed: two at High Wycombe (still mainly chair-makers), one-and-a-half at Wolverton (LNWR carriage works), half at Buckingham and one each at Marlow, Aylesbury, Slough and Stony Stratford. A ninth company was added in 1900. *Territorials:* The Buckinghamshire Battalion Oxfordshire Light Infantry.

**2nd (1860-1872)**—Formed at High Wycombe as the 3rd Sub-division with Lieutenant Henry H Williams commissioned on 6 March 1860. Shown in the Army List as 2nd Corps for the first time in April 1860. The corps was not seen listed after September of the following year. Re-formed, however, as 8th Corps under the command of Lieutenant-Colonel W C Pratt of the Royal Bucks Militia—the new officers having commissions dated 22 November 1861. Renumbered as 2nd again from December 1861 but disbanded in 1872.

**2nd (Eton College) (1878-1908)**—Formed as 8th Corps at Eton College in May 1867 with a cadet corps attached. Commanding Officers' commissions for both units: Captain Samuel Thomas George Evans (8th Corps) and Hon Captain Rev Edmond Warre (cadets), being dated 22 January 1868. Became part of the new 1st Corps in 1875. In June 1878, however, it was decided to removed the Eton College elements and form the companies into an independent corps designated 2nd Buckinghamshire (Eton College) RVC. Designated 4th (Eton College) Volunteer Battalion Oxfordshire Light Infantry in 1887, but reverted to its former title, 2nd (Eton College), in 1902. Establishment was increased from four to five companies in 1900.

**Glengarry badge, 1st Buckinghamshire Rifle Volunteer Corps.**

13

*Territorials*: In 1908 the Eton College Volunteers transferred to the Territorial Force as a contingent of the Junior Division OTC.

**3rd**—Formed at Buckingham as a half-company and shown in the Army List for the first time in March 1860. No officers appear until June, however, and then with commissions dated 11 May: Lieutenant the Hon. Percy Barrington (afterwards Viscount Barrington) and Ensign Robert A Fitzgerald. Absorbed the 7th Corps at Winslow in 1863 and became part of the new 1st Corps in 1875.

**4th**—Formed on 25 March 1860 at Aylesbury with Captain the Hon Florence G H Irby (afterwards Lord Boston) in command. Became part of the new 1st Corps in 1875.

**5th**—Formed at Slough on 20 July 1860 under the command of Captain R Bateson-Harvey (afterwards Sir and Member of Parliament) of the Bucks Yeomanry. Became part of the new 1st Corps in 1875.

**6th**—Formed at Newport Pagnell as 7th Corps with Samuel Newman commissioned as ensign on 14 September 1860. Renumbered 6th by January 1861. Disbanded later and last seen in the Army List for June 1864.

**7th (1860-1861)**—See 6th Corps.

**7th (1861-1863)**—Formed at Winslow with Thomas Newman commissioned as ensign on 17 May 1861. Absorbed into the 3rd Corps at Buckingham in 1863.

**8th**—Two corps held this number, see 2nd Corps and 2nd Corps (Eton College).

# Cambridgeshire

## Mounted Rifle Volunteers

**1st**—Formed at Newmarket 10 August 1860 and disbanded in April five years later. Although granted an establishment of one company, no captain was ever appointed, Lieutenant Charles W Townsley holding command from formation until disbandment.

**2nd**—Formed at Cambridge in May 1860 with Captain Henry W Pemberton in command. Disbanded in July 1863.

## Rifle Volunteers

Two admin battalions existed in Cambridgeshire, the 2nd being formed with headquarters at Cambridge in November 1862 and including the town's 1st and 8th Corps. From November 1863 the 17th Essex RVC was also included. In 1872 the 2nd Admin was broken up and the 1st Cambridge Corps, together with 17th Essex, were transferred to 1st Admin Battalion. One numbered sub-division was formed which became the 4th Corps.

**1st (1860-1880)**—Steps to raise a RVC in Cambridge were first taken at a meeting held at the Guildhall in May 1859. Subsequently a Rifle and Drill Club was formed, and it would be this that, once official recognition had been gained from the Government, became the 1st Cambridgeshire RVC of one company. The commissions of its first officers: Captain W P Prest, Lieutenant Frederick Barlow and Ensign Albert Decimus Claydon, were dated 16 January 1860. Francis R Hall joined them as surgeon and Charles H Crosse as chaplain in the following month. On 26 May 1860 the *Cambridge Chronicle* reported that on the previous day Colours had been presented to the 1st Corps by the ladies of Cambridge on Parker's Piece. In May 1862 a second company was added, and in addition, Nos 3 and 4 were authorised after the 8th Corps, also at Cambridge, was absorbed in 1864. Became 'A' to 'D' Companies of the new 1st Corps in 1880. Brief notes regarding the origins of the 1st Cambridgeshire RVC appear in *The Cambridgeshires 1914-1919*, Major G B Bowes, TD pointing out that the officers of the battalion were mostly drawn through two generations from well-known Cambridgeshire families. Large employers such as the Cambridge University Press— which for years provided a full company—the Colleges, Post Office, railway and timber yards of Wisbech, all contributed towards the ranks, as did the small-holders of the Fens, together with the clerks, shop assistants and mechanics of local firms.

**1st (1880-1908)**—The 1st Admin Battalion was formed with headquarters at March towards the end of 1860. Captain Frederick D Fryer of the 2nd Corps took command, his commission as Major being dated 7 December 1860. To the battalion were added the 2nd, 4th, 5th, 6th, 7th and 10th Cambridgeshire Corps. The 1st Cambridgeshire, 17th Essex and 1st Huntingdonshire RVC were also included in 1872. The battalion was consolidated as 1st Cambridgeshire RVC with the sub-title 'Cambridge, Essex and Hunts' reflecting its three-county association in 1880. Headquarters were placed at Cambridge and there were ten companies: 'A', 'B', 'C' and 'D' Cambridge (late 1st Cambridgeshire), 'E' Wisbech (late 2nd Cambridgeshire), 'F' Whittlesea (late 4th Cambridgeshire), 'G' March (late 5th Cambridgeshire), 'H' Ely (late 6th Cambridgeshire), 'I' Saffron Walden (late 17th Essex), 'J' St Neot's (late 1st Huntingdonshire).

General Order 181 of December 1887 notified a change in designation to 3rd (Cambridgeshire) Volunteer Battalion Suffolk Regiment. In 1889 the Hunts Company ('J') was disbanded. Three cadet corps were affiliated to the 3rd Volunteer Battalion: Leys School in Cambridge forming a company in 1900, followed by the Perse School (also in Cambridge) in 1905. The last formed was by the Cambridge and County School in 1906. On Sunday 29 March 1908 the Colours presented to the original 1st Corps in May 1860 were committed to the keeping of the vicar and churchwardens of Great St Mary. Two days later the Territorial Force came into being and as the 1st Cambridgeshire RVC stood down, the Cambridgeshire Battalion Suffolk Regiment was born, an unpopular title which soon changed to the Cambridgeshire Regiment. At the same time Leys and Cambridge and County Schools became contingents of the Junior Division OTC.

**2nd (1860-1880)**—Formed at Wisbech with Captain Frederick D Fryer, Lieutenant Francis Jackson and Ensign Richard Young commissioned on 2 January 1860. Became 'E' Company of the new 1st Corps in 1880.

**2nd (Cambridge University) (1880-1908)**—Grateful we must be to Hew Strachan who, in *History of the Cambridge OTC*, did much to simplify the complicated company structure of the Cambridge University Corps. Official approval and acceptance of a corps of rifle volunteers raised within Cambridge University was received by the Vice Chancellor in December 1859. An establishment of five companies was sanctioned and on 10 January of the following year the first officers were gazetted to the 3rd Cambridgeshire (Cambridge University) RVC—in command was Major James Baker of the 8th Light Dragoons. Six companies were in existence by March, all formed from members of the university and organised on the following basis: No 1 (formed from Gonville and Caius, Clare, Christ's, Corpus Christi, Emmanuel, Queens', Jesus and Sidney Sussex Colleges), No 2 (formed from St John's College), No 3 (formed from King's, Magdalene, Peterhouse and Trinity Hall Colleges), Nos 4, 5 and 6 (formed from Trinity College).

In 1864 personnel from St Catharine's and Pembroke Colleges were included in No 1 Company while those from Clare transferred to No 3. Sidney Sussex was also included in No 3 the following year and in November 1867 the six companies were lettered 'A' to 'F' with the following reorganisations: 'A' (now formed by Pembroke, Corpus

**4th Volunteer Battalion Suffolk Regiment.**

**Cambridge University Rifle Volunteer Corps.**

Christi, Queens', St Catharine's and Downing), 'B' (by St John's), 'C' (by Clare, Gonville and Caius, Trinity Hall, King's and Sidney Sussex), 'D' (by Jesus, Christ's, Emmanuel and Magdalene), 'E' and 'F' (by Trinity).

The 3rd Corps was renumbered as 2nd (Cambridge University) in 1880 and designated as 4th (Cambridge University) Volunteer Battalion Suffolk Regiment under General Order 181 of December 1887. During 1893-94 the company structure was changed yet again: 'A' (now from Peterhouse, Pembroke, Queens', Corpus Christi and St Catharine's), 'B' (from St John's), 'C' (from Gonville and Caius), 'D' (from Christ's, Emmanuel, Jesus and Magdalene), 'E' (from Trinity), 'F' (from Clare, Trinity Hall, King's, Sidney Sussex and Selwyn).

St John's became part of 'A' Company in 1896 and at the same time Pembroke became 'B' and Downing part of 'A'. Permission to increase the establishment to eight companies was granted during the early part of 1900, the change requiring the regrouping of the colleges as follows: St John's was removed from 'A' Company to form the new 'G', while at the same time Christ's, Magdalene, Sidney Sussex and Selwyn were taken from 'D' and 'F' to form 'H'. Under Army Order 56 of April 1903 His Majesty the King was graciously pleased to approve the new title of 'The Cambridge University Volunteer Rifle Corps', this being held until transfer to the Senior Division of the OTC in 1908.

**3rd**—See 2nd Corps (1880-1908).

**4th**—Formed at Whittlesea on the Fens with Lieutenant Edward Loomes and Ensign William Harris Bowker commissioned on 17 January 1860. Known as the 1st Sub-division until March and became 'F' Company of the new 1st Corps in 1880.

**5th**—Formed as one company at March with Captain Robert C Catling, Lieutenant Robert Dawbarn, Jun and Ensign William O Pratt commissioned on 13 June 1860. Became 'G' Company of the new 1st Corps in 1880.

**6th**—Formed at Ely with Captain Everard Calthrop, Lieutenant Henry W Marten and Ensign Charles T Harlock commissioned on 11 July 1860. Also attached to the corps were the Rev William E Dickson, MA, as chaplain, and Robert Muriel who was surgeon. Became 'H' Company of the new 1st Corps in 1880.

**7th**—Formed as a sub-division at Upwell with Lieutenant William L Ollard and Ensign William Elworthy commissioned on 7 September 1860. Also attached to the corps was John Hemming as surgeon. The corps was increased to a full company in 1864, but over the next years interest began to wane and in consequence the 7th Cambridgeshire RVC was disbanded and last seen in the Army List for December 1872.

**8th**—Formed as one company at Cambridge with Captain George Leapingwell, Lieutenant Charles J Clay and Ensign Josiah Chater commissioned on 6 November 1860. Also attached to the corps were the Rev A V Hadley, MA as chaplain, and James Carter as surgeon. Absorbed into the 1st Corps as its Nos 3 and 4 Companies in 1864.

**9th**—Formed as a sub-division at Newmarket with Ashley Patson Cooper as lieutenant and James Neal York, ensign. Both officers held commissions dated 15 January 1861 and in April they were joined by Samuel Gamble who became surgeon. The corps was shown in the Army List for July 1862 as being 'united' with the 1st Suffolk Admin Battalion and in the following month was removed from the Cambridgeshire list having been absorbed into the 20th Suffolk RVC. The town is part in Cambridgeshire and part in Suffolk.

**10th**—Formed at Soham with Richard Cockerton as lieutenant and James Westley, ensign. Both officers held commissions dated 28 January 1862. The corps was later disbanded and not shown in the Army List after October 1865.

# Cheshire

## Artillery Volunteers

The 1st Admin Brigade of Cheshire Artillery Volunteers was formed with headquarters in Chester during June 1860. In addition to the several Cheshire corps, the Army List for November 1863 indicates that both the 1st Shropshire and 1st Staffordshire AVC had been included followed in June 1865 by the 1st Worcestershire. All three, however, were removed by August 1869 and grouped together as the 1st Shropshire Admin Brigade. Other artillery volunteer corps from outside Cheshire to join the brigade were, from 1873, the 1st and 3rd Anglesey and 1st Carnarvonshire. The 1st Anglesey was disbanded in 1875 and in 1878 the 3rd was renamed 2nd Carnarvonshire. The 1st Isle of Man AVC also joined in 1873, but the corps was disbanded in 1875. The brigade was consolidated to form the new 1st Cheshire and Carnarvonshire AVC in 1880.

**1st (1859-1873)**—Formed at Birkenhead on 30 December 1859 and disbanded 1873.

**1st Cheshire and Carnarvonshire**—Formed in 1880 by the consolidation of the 1st Cheshire Admin Brigade. Headquarters were placed in Chester and the batteries were organised: Nos 1, 2 and 3 Chester (late 2nd Corps), No 4 New Brighton (late 4th Corps), No 5 Seacombe (late 3rd Corps), Nos 6 and 7 Bangor (late 2nd Carnarvonshire), No 8 Carnarvon (late 1st Carnarvonshire). In 1886 an unsuccessful attempt was made to include 'The Earl of Chester's' sub-title previously held by the 2nd Cheshire AVC into that of the new 1st. In 1904 the Carnarvonshire batteries were withdrawn to form their own unit, appearing in the Army List as 1st Carnarvonshire from July. *Territorials:* Nos 6 and 7 Companies of the Lancashire and Cheshire RGA and the 3rd Welsh Brigade RFA which contained the 1st and 2nd Cheshire Batteries.

**2nd**—Formed at Chester on 8 February 1860 and in 1870 was allowed to include 'The Earl of Chester's' in its title. Provided Nos 1, 2 and 3 Batteries of the new 1st Corps in 1880.

**3rd**—Formed at Seacombe on 10 February 1860 and provided No 5 Battery of the new 1st Corps in 1880.

**4th**—Formed at New Brighton on 15 February 1860 and provided No 4 Battery of the new 1st Corps in 1880.

**5th**—Formed at Birkenhead on 1 March 1860 and was disbanded in 1869.

## Engineer Volunteers

**1st**—Formed at Birkenhead on 10 May 1861, the 1st Cheshire EVC for a short time during 1864 was shown in the Army List as being attached for admin and drill to the 1st Lancashire Corps. The 1st Flintshire being attached for the same reasons to the Birkenhead unit from 1897. *Territorials*: 1st Cheshire Field Company of the Welsh Divisional Engineers.

**2nd**—It was not until 1 April 1887 that a 2nd Corps was formed. This time in the railway town of Crewe, its six companies being entirely manned by employees of the London & North Western Railway Company. Important to the town since it arrived in 1843 was the railway, its locomotive and carriage works employing some 7,000. Walter Richards in *His Majesty's Territorial Army* (Virtue & Co., London, 1910-11) notes that the 2nd Cheshire EVC was a 'popular' one, and throughout its existence notable for its high standard of efficiency. A fact abundantly evident by the performance of the Service Companies sent out from Birkenhead to South Africa in 1900 to serve alongside the regular army's Royal Engineers. In fact for a time, while working on the railway between Pretoria and the Portuguese border, Captain J L McLean of the 2nd Service Company

**1st Cheshire Engineer Volunteer Corps.**

17

was put in command of 31st Company, RE. *Territorials:* Unique within the Territorial Force, the Cheshire Railway Battalion.

## Rifle Volunteers

Five admin battalions were formed which in 1880 became the 1st to 5th new corps. The Boer War Memorial in Queen's Park, Victoria Avenue, Crewe, includes the names of fifty men that served with the several Volunteer Service Companies in South Africa.

**Officers' helmet, 1st Cheshire Rifle Volunteer Corps.**

**1st (1859-1880)**—Formed as one company with headquarters at Birkenhead, the first appointed officers being Captain John Cadell, Lieutenant Henry John Ward and Ensign John James Conway. All three held commissions dated 25 August 1859. Joined the 1st Admin Battalion and became 'A' Company of the new 1st Corps in 1880.

**1st (1880-1908)**—The 1st Admin Battalion was formed at Birkenhead towards the end of 1860 with Lieutenant-Colonel Vincent Ashfield King from the 2nd Corps in command. Included were the 1st, 2nd, 3rd, 4th, 11th, 14th, 30th, 34th and 35th Cheshire RVC. The battalion was consolidated as the new 1st Corps in 1880. Headquarters were placed at Oxton and the battalion's eight companies were located: 'A' Birkenhead (late 1st Corps), 'B' Oxton (late 2nd Corps), 'C' Egremont (late 3rd Corps), 'D' Bebington (late 4th Corps), 'E' Neston (late 11th Corps), 'F' Hooton (late 14th Corps), 'G' Tranmere (late 30th Corps), 'H' Bromborough (late 35th Corps).

General Order 181 of December 1887 directed the change in designation from 1st Cheshire RVC to 1st Volunteer Battalion Cheshire Regiment. New companies were formed at Birkenhead, Liscard and Heswall by 1900 and to answer the call for volunteers to go out to South Africa, ninety-six from the battalion would see active service, three of whom being killed in action. Called the 'Greys', from the colour of its uniform, the 1st Volunteer Battalion transfer to the Territorial Force in 1908 as 4th Battalion Cheshire Regiment.

Several cadet units were formed and affiliated to the battalion, the first to appear in the Army List being that raised by Wirral College in 1892. Both Mostyn House School at Parkgate and the West Kirby School provided companies the following year, the Wirral College corps, however, being disbanded in 1884 followed by West Kirby in 1900. In 1903 Liscard High School, Wallasey Grammar, and the New Brighton High School all appear in the Army List as having formed units. But by April 1904 all three had disappeared having had no officers appointed.

**2nd (1859-1880)**—Formed as one company at Oxton with Captain Vincent Ashfiled King as captain and William Horner, lieutenant. Both held commissions dated 30 August 1859, Ensign John Usher Cunningham joining them on 20 January 1860. When Captain King was appointed as commanding officer of the 1st Admin Battalion, William Horner replaced him as captain (commission dated 31 December 1860) and to replace him, James Roper came in as lieutenant. About the same time Joseph Godden (commissioned 15 February 1861) became surgeon to the corps. Joined the 1st Admin Battalion and became 'B' Company of the new 1st Corps in 1880.

**2nd (Earl of Chester's) (1880-1908)**—Chester was the headquarters of the 2nd Admin Battalion which included the 6th, 7th, 23rd and 24th Corps. Captain Richard Brooke of the 6th Corps was appointed as lieutenant-colonel in

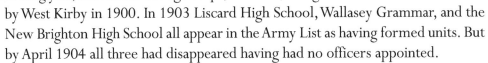
***2nd (Earl of Chester's) Rifle Volunteer Corps.***

command with a commission dated 30 October 1860. The battalion was consolidated in 1880 as the 2nd Cheshire (Earl of Chester's) RVC with nine companies: 'A' to 'E' Chester (late 6th Corps), 'F' and 'G' Runcorn (late 7th Corps), 'H' Weaverham (late 23rd Corps), 'I' Frodsham (late 24th Corps).

General Order 181 of December 1887 directed the change in designation from 2nd Cheshire RVC to 2nd (Earl of Chester's) Volunteer Battalion Cheshire Regiment. Two new companies were formed in 1900. Just prior to transfer to the Territorial Force in 1908 as headquarters and four companies of 5th Battalion Cheshire Regiment, the returned strength of the 2nd Volunteer Battalion stood at 1,081 all ranks.

**3rd (1859-1880)**—Formed as one company at Wallasey with William Chambres as captain, James Harrison, lieutenant and George Edmund Lance, ensign. All three held commissions dated 5 September 1859. Headquarters moved to Egremont in 1880 and in same year 3rd Cheshire RVC, as part of the 2nd Admin Battalion, became 'C' Company of the new 1st Corps.

**3rd (1880-1908)**—Formed towards the end of 1860 with Lieutenant-Colonel Thomas W Tatton in command (commissioned 1 November 1860), headquarters of the 3rd Admin Battalion were at first placed at Altrincham and the corps included in it, the 12th, 15th, 22nd, 25th, 26th, 28th and 32nd. The battalion moved to Knutsford in 1864 and in 1880 was consolidated as the new 3rd Cheshire RVC with eight companies: 'A' and 'B' Altrincham (late 12th Corps), 'C' Knutsford (late 15th Corps), 'D' Northwich (late No 1 Company of the 22nd Corps), 'E' Winsford (late No 2 Company of the 22nd Corps), 'F' Cheadle (late 26th Corps), 'G' Sale Moor (late 28th Corps), 'H' Lymm (late 32nd Corps).

The 3rd Corps was designated as 3rd Volunteer Battalion Cheshire Regiment in 1887, the change being notified in General Order 181 of December, and at the closing of the Volunteer Force its total strength stood at 736 all ranks. *Territorials:* Four companies of the 5th Battalion Cheshire Regiment.

**4th (1859-1880)**—Formed as one company at Bebington with Captain Frederick Pembroke Jones, late of the 4th Dragoon Guards, and Ensign William Stock Bower commissioned on 10 September 1859. The position of lieutenant would remain vacant until the Spring of 1860 when Ensign Bower was promoted, and his place taken by E Wrangham Bird who was commissioned on 15 May 1860. At the same time a surgeon joined the corps in the form of G T Roper, MD. The Army List shows an increase to two companies in 1862, all three new officers holding commissions dated 10 March, and in March 1863 headquarters of the 4th Corps are given as Rock Ferry just a mile or so from Bebington on the Birkenhead road. It would now seem that No 2 Company was withdrawn and made independent—its officers, as from Monthly Army List for April 1863, now being listed under a new formation, the 35th Cheshire RVC at Bromborough. The 4th Corps remained at Rock Ferry until September 1864, but in the Army List for the following month there is no mention of a 4th Corps at all. November 1864, on the other hand, shows a new 4th Corps, once again at Bebington and with three completely new officers—Captain John Mayer, Lieutenant John Mathews, Jun and Ensign Alfred S Walford—all with commissions dated 5 November 1864. As part of the 1st Admin Battalion, the 4th Cheshire became 'D' Company of the new 1st Corps in 1880.

**4th (1880-1908)**—Headquarters of the 4th Admin Battalion were at Stockport and to the several Cheshire corps included (9th, 13th, 17th, 18th, 19th, 20th, 21st, 29th and 31st) were added the 23rd Derbyshire RVC in 1876. Captain Francis D P Astley of the 13th Corps was appointed as lieutenant-colonel in command, his commission being dated 5 November 1860. The battalion was consolidated as the new 4th Cheshire RVC in 1880 with thirteen companies: 'A' to 'C' Stalybridge (late 13th Corps), 'D' Stockport (late 17th Corps), 'E' Stockport (late 18th Corps),

**4th Cheshire Rifle Volunteer Corps.**

**1st Cheshire Engineer Volunteer Corps.**

'F' Stockport (late 19th Corps), 'G' Stockport (late 20th Corps), 'H' Stockport (late 21st Corps), 'I' Stockport (late 29th Corps), 'K' Hyde (late 31st Corps), 'L', 'M' and 'N' Glossop (late 23rd Derbyshire Corps).

General Order 181 of December 1887 directed the change in designation from 4th Cheshire RVC to 4th Volunteer Battalion Cheshire Regiment and at the close of the Volunteer Movement the last return of the battalion gave a combined strength of 1,066 all ranks. *Territorials:* 6th Battalion Cheshire Regiment.

**5th (1859-1880)**—Formed as one company with headquarters at Congleton, the original 5th Corps officers were: Captain Sir Charles Watkin Shakerley, Bt, of Somerford Park, Lieutenant Francis Henry Randle Wilbraham and Ensign Arthur Isaac Solly. All held commissions dated 15 September 1859. Joined the 5th Admin Battalion and became 'A' and 'B' Companies of the new 5th Corps in 1880.

**5th (1880-1908)**—Captain of the 5th Corps, Sir Charles Watkin Shakerley, Bt, was commissioned as lieutenant-colonel of the 5th Admin Battalion on 15 November 1860. Headquarters were at Congleton and included in the battalion were the 5th, 8th, 16th, 27th, 33rd and 36th Cheshire RVC. When the battalion was consolidated in 1880 it was to include four companies provided by the 36th Cheshire at Crewe. The Crewe corps, however, was disbanded just before the merger and the eventual establishment of the new 5th Cheshire RVC was nine companies: 'A' and 'B' Congleton (late 5th Corps), 'C', 'D', 'E' and 'F' Macclesfield (late 8th Corps), 'G' Sandbach (late 16th Corps), 'H' Wilmslow (late 27th corps), 'I' Nantwich (late 33rd Corps).

By October 1880 the Army List indicated a ten-company establishment, the addition being commanded by a former lieutenant of the 27th Wilmslow Corps. General Order 181 of December 1887 directed the change in designation from 5th Cheshire RVC to 5th Volunteer Battalion Cheshire Regiment. The strength of the battalion just prior to transfer to the Territorial Force in 1908 as 7th Battalion Cheshire Regiment, being returned as 868 all ranks.

**6th (The Earl of Chester's)**—Formed as one company with headquarters at Chester, the original officers being: Captain Richard Brooke, who had previously served with the 1st Life Guards, former Honourable East India Company officer, Lieutenant John Ireland Blackburne, both with commissions dated 25 November 1859, and Ensign Francis H Barker who was not gazetted until 24 February 1860. Also, at Chester was the 10th Cheshire RVC which in June 1860 joined the 6th Corps as its No 2 Company. A popular corps in the Chester area, the first officer to No 3 Company was commissioned on 10 August 1860 and to No 4 on 20 July 1869. In the following year the additional title 'The Earl of Chester's' was authorized and in 1879 yet another company made its way onto the establishment. As part of the 2nd Admin Battalion, 6th Cheshire RVC became 'A' to 'E' Companies of the new 2nd Corps in 1880. The Drill Hall was in Volunteer Street, Chester.

**7th**—Formed as one company with headquarters at Runcorn, the original officers of the 7th Corps were Captain Arthur Brooke, Lieutenant Phillip Whiteway and Ensign John Brundrit. All three held commissions dated 30 November 1859. Henry Wilson joined as surgeon in April 1860, and in the Spring of 1866 a second company was added. As part of the 2nd Admin Battalion, 7th Cheshire RVC became 'F' and 'G' Companies of the new 2nd Corps in 1880.

**8th**—Formed as one company with headquarters at Macclesfield, the original officers of the 8th Cheshire RVC were Captain Samuel Pearson, Jun, a former officer with the 1st Dragoon Guards, Lieutenant Charles Edward Proctor and Ensign George Edward Adshead. All three held commissions dated 5 January 1860. John Mayer joined as surgeon to the corps in March 1860. The first officers were commissioned to a second company on 25 April 1860, a third on 5 June 1862 and to a fourth in 1876. As part of the 5th Admin Battalion, 8th Cheshire RVC became 'C' to 'F' Companies of the new 5th Corps in 1880. The Volunteer Drill Hall was built in 1872.

**9th**—Formed as one company at Mottram with Captain Alfred K Sidebottom, Lieutenant William Bayley, Jun and Henry Algernon West commissioned on 10 February 1860. Edward Sidebottom joined as surgeon to the corps in May 1860. Interest later fell off and the corps, which had been part of the 4th Admin Battalion, made its last appearance in the Army List for February 1861.

**10th**—Formed as one company at Chester with Captain Phillip S Humberston, Lieutenant Henry French and Ensign Edward Dixon commissioned on 25 February 1860. Joined the 2nd Admin Battalion and was absorbed into the 6th Corps as its No 2 Company in June 1860.

**11th**—Formed as one company at Neston with Captain Henry M Edwards, Lieutenant Hugh Craig, Ensign Horatio Lloyd and Surgeon David Russell, MD commissioned on 28 February 1860. Joined the 1st Admin Battalion and Became 'E' Company of the new 1st Corps in 1880.

**12th**—Formed as one company at Altrincham with Captain Hugh Fleming, Lieutenant Alfred Neild and Ensign Stephen Robinson commissioned on 1 March 1860. They were joined in May 1860 by Newcomb Rogers who became surgeon. Joined the 3rd Admin Battalion, absorbed the 25th Cheshire RVC at Timperley as its No 2 Company in 1866, and became 'A' and 'B' Companies of the new 3rd Corps in 1880.

**13th**—Formed as one company at Dukinfield with Francis Dukinfield P Astley as captain; Charles James Ashton, lieutenant, Thomas B Hall, ensign and Alfred Aspland, surgeon. All four held commissions dated 20 February 1860. This corps was raised by the Astley family and was known unofficially as the 'Astley Rifles'. In November 1860 Captain Astley was appointed as lieutenant-colonel in command of the 4th Admin Battalion and at the same time his place was taken in the 13th Corps by Charles Ashton who was promoted captain on 5th November. Ten days later the first officers of No 2 Company were commissioned and in March 1869, those of No 3. Headquarters moved to Newton Moor near Hyde in 1863 and then to Stalybridge in 1873. As part of the 4th Admin Battalion, the 13th Cheshire RVC became 'A' to 'C' Companies of the new 4th Corps in 1880.

**14th**—Formed as one company at Hooton with William Hope Jones as captain, Lancelot Dixon, lieutenant, George Gray Glen, ensign and Alexander R Lingard, surgeon. All four held commissions dated

3 March 1860. Joined the 1st Admin Battalion and became 'F' Company of the new 1st Corps in 1880.

**15th**—Formed as one company at Knutsford with John Pennington Legh as captain, David R Davies, lieutenant and Joshua Jackson, Jun, ensign. All three held commissions dated 5 March 1860. In the following July Edward M Gleeson was appointed as surgeon. Joined the 3rd Admin Battalion and became 'C' Company of the new 3rd Corps in 1880.

**16th**—Formed as one company at Sandbach with Edmund J Tipping as captain, Aaron C Howard, lieutenant and Henry S Armitstead, ensign. All three held commissions dated 7 March 1860. Joined the 5th Admin Battalion and became 'G' Company of the new 5th Corps in 1880.

**17th**—Formed as one company at Stockport with Henry Coppock as captain, David McClure, lieutenant and John McClure, ensign. All three held commissions dated 10 March 1860, Doctor William Rayner, MD joining them as surgeon to the corps in August 1860. As part of the 4th Admin Battalion, 17th Cheshire RVC became 'D' Company of the new 4th Corps in 1880. The 17th Cheshire RVC was the first of six corps to be raised at Stockport.

**18th**—Formed as one company at Stockport with John Thomas Emmerson as captain, William L Eskrigge, lieutenant and Alexander W Thorneley, ensign. All three held commissions dated 12 March 1860 and Doctor William H Medd joined them as surgeon in October 1860. Joined the 4th Admin Battalion and became 'E' Company of the new 4th Corps in 1880.

**19th**—Formed as one company at Stockport with Samuel W Wilkinson as captain, George A Ferneley, lieutenant and Henry Smith, ensign. All three held commissions dated 15 March 1860. John T Pearson was appointed surgeon in September 1860. Joined the 4th Admin Battalion and became 'F' Company of the new 4th Corps in 1880.

**20th**—Formed as one company at Stockport with Thomas H Sykes as captain, Godfrey Barnsely, lieutenant and Thomas Dixon Hill, ensign. All three held commissions dated 20 March 1860. Joined the 4th Admin Battalion and became 'G' Company of the new 4th Corps in 1880.

**21st**—Formed as one company at Stockport with Cephas John Howard as captain, Walter Hyde, lieutenant and John Turton, ensign. All three were commissioned on 22 March 1860. Joined the 4th Admin Battalion and became 'H' Company of the new 4th Corps in 1880.

**22nd**—Formed as one company at Northwich with Thomas H Marshall as captain, William S Bradburne, lieutenant and Christopher Cheshire, ensign. All three held commissions dated 26 March 1860. Doctor Thomas G Dixon joined them as surgeon to the corps in the following July. Joined the 3rd Admin Battalion, a second company was added at Winsford in 1877, and became 'D' and 'E' Companies of the new 3rd Corps in 1880.

**23rd**—The first officer to be appointed to the 23rd Corps of one company at Weaverham was Captain John Bolton Littledale who received his commission on 28 March 1860. He was joined by Lieutenant William Jones and Ensign William C Miller in the following June. As part of the 2nd Admin Battalion, 23rd Cheshire RVC became 'H' Company of the new 2nd Corps in 1880.

**24th**—Formed as one company at Frodsham with Captain Charles H Hitchen, Lieutenant Frederick W Jackson, Ensign Thomas F Linnell and Surgeon John Jones commissioned on 30 March 1860. Joined the 2nd Admin Battalion and became 'I' Company of the new 2nd Corps in 1880.

**25th**—Formed as one company at Timperley with Captain Alfred Lyon, Lieutenant Ashton M Gardiner and Ensign Robert K Gardiner commissioned on 2 April 1860. A No 2 Company was later added with officers holding commissions dated 15 October 1860. It would appear from the Army List that interest in the 25th Corps waned around 1865, the several vacancies appearing then among the officers not being filled. The corps, which had been part of the 3rd Admin Battalion, made its last appearance in July 1866 and what was left of it absorbed into the 12th Cheshire RVC as its No 2 Company.

**26th**—Formed as one company at Northenden with Thomas W Tatton as captain, George Peel, lieutenant and Francis Hampton, ensign. All three held commissions dated 4 April 1860. Joined the 3rd

Admin Battalion, moved headquarters to Cheadle in 1862, and became 'F' Company of the new 3rd Corps in 1880.

**27th**—Formed as one company at Wilmslow with Captain Edward H Greg, Lieutenant John Railton and Ensign Edwin C Hopps commissioned on 5 April 1860. Joined the 5th Admin Battalion in June 1861 and became 'H' Company of the new 5th Corps in 1880.

**28th**—Formed as one company at Sale Moor with Alfred Watkin as captain, John Cunliffe, lieutenant, James Frodsham, ensign and John H Larmuth who was appointed surgeon. All four held commissions dated 7 April 1860. Joined the 3rd Admin Battalion and became 'G' Company of the new 3rd Corps in 1880.

**29th**—Formed as one company at Stockport with John M Lingard, who had previously served with the 1st Royal Cheshire Militia, as captain, Thomas Steen, lieutenant and John G Graham, ensign. All three held commissions dated 10 April 1860. Joined the 4th Admin Battalion and became 'I' Company of the new 4th Corps in 1880.

**30th**—Formed as one company at Tranmere with Hugh H Nicholson as captain and William Brockie, lieutenant. Both held commissions dated 30 April 1860. They were later joined by Ensign John Mosford who was gazetted on 20 August 1860. Joined the 1st Admin Battalion and became 'G' Company of the new 1st Corps in 1880.

**31st**—Formed as one company at Hyde with Captain Thomas Mottram, Lieutenant Alfred Thornely and Ensign Frank Thornely commissioned on 15 August 1860. Thomas C Lear joined them as surgeon to the corps in the following October. Joined the 4th Admin Battalion and became 'K' Company of the new 4th Corps in 1880.

**32nd**—Formed as one company at Lymm with V Fox as captain, Charles F Bennett, lieutenant, Thomas Draper, ensign and William Brigham, surgeon. All four held commissions dated 10 September 1860. Joined the 3rd Admin Battalion and became 'H' Company of the new 3rd Corps in 1880.

**33rd**—Formed as one company at Nantwich with Captain Samuel C Starkey and Lieutenant John J Garnett commissioned on 5 November 1860. The ensign position was not filled until 1863 when Charles Stuart Brooke was commissioned on 25 August. Joined the 5th Admin Battalion and became 'I' Company of the new 5th Corps in 1880.

**34th**—Formed as one company at Upton with Captain William Inman, Lieutenant Thomas Bland Royden and Ensign William Hewitt commissioned on 5 June 1861. Joined the 1st Admin Battalion. Interest in the corps fell off around the middle of 1863, the captain position being vacant for almost a year before disbandment came in October 1864. There are several Uptons in Cheshire, but given its association with the 1st Admin Battalion, that of the 34th Corps is most likely to be the parish and village about four miles to the west of Birkenhead.

**35th**—Formed at Bromborough from No 2 Company of the 4th Corps with Captain William Henry Hatcher, Lieutenant John Henry Day and Ensign Charles Alexander Payne commissioned on 25 February 1863. Joined the 1st Admin Battalion and became 'H' Company of the new 1st Corps in 1880.

**36th**—Formed as two companies at Crewe with company commanders Captain Francis William Webb, commissioned on 20 January 1865, and Captain John N Spencer who was gazetted on 21 January 1865. Joined the 5th Admin Battalion. The 36th Cheshire was always a strong corps; two new companies were formed in the 1870s, but plans for it to join the new 5th Corps in 1880 were cancelled and instead the four Crewe companies were disbanded.

**1st Cadet Battalion Cheshire Regiment**—Formed with an establishment of four companies at Northenden, the first officer being commissioned on 2 December 1901. The battalion transferred to the Territorial Force in 1908, gaining recognition on 29 June 1910.

# Cinque Ports

## Artillery Volunteers

The 1st Admin Brigade was formed with headquarters at Dover in August 1862 and consolidated as the new 1st Corps in 1880.

**1st (1860-1880)**—Formed at Dover on 6 January 1860, this corps was recorded in the Army List as 3rd from April 1860 and then from August as No 1A. It was re-designated as 1st Corps in October 1870. Provided Nos 1 and 2 Batteries of the new 1st Corps in 1880.

**1st (1880-1908)**—Formed in 1880 by the consolidation of the 1st Admin Brigade. Headquarters remained at Dover and the batteries were organised: Nos 1 and 2 Dover (late 1st Corps), No 3 Folkestone (late 2nd Corps), Nos 4 and 5 Ramsgate (late 3rd Corps), No 6 Sandwich (late 4th Corps), No 7 Deal (late 5th Corps), Nos 8, 9 and 10 Hastings (late 6th Corps), No 11 St Leonards (late 7th Corps), No 12 Margate (late 8th Corps), No 13 Ninfield (late 9th Corps), No 14 Pevensey (late 9th Corps). There was also a half-battery at Margate which was provided by the former 8th Corps.

By General Order 77 of June 1887 the 1st Cinque Ports AVC was re-designated as 4th Volunteer (Cinque Ports) Brigade Cinque Ports Division Royal Artillery. This was changed, however, to 1st Cinque Ports (Eastern Division Royal Artillery) in 1889. In the following year part of the corps from around the St Leonards area was removed to form the 2nd Cinque Ports Corps which appeared for the first time in the Army List for May 1890. *Territorials:* 3rd Home Counties (Cinque Ports) Brigade RFA which included the 1st, 2nd and 3rd Kent Batteries and the 3rd Home Counties Ammunition Column.

**2nd (1870-1880)**—Formed at Folkstone on 7 November 1859 as the 3rd Kent AVC. In the Army List for April 1860 the corps appears as the 1st Cinque Ports and then from August as No 1B. The battery became 2nd Corps in October 1870. Provided No 3 Battery of the new 1st Corps in 1880.

**2nd (1890-1908)**—Formed 1890 by the withdrawal of the 1st Corps volunteers from the St Leonards area. The new corps also included Eastern Division Royal Artillery in its full title and in 1900 its six garrison companies were organised into three position batteries. *Territorials:* 5th Sussex Battery and 2nd Home Counties Ammunition Column of the 2nd Home Counties Brigade RFA.

**3rd**—First appeared in the Army List as 2nd Corps at Ramsgate having been formed on 2 January 1860. Was listed as No 1C in August 1860 and then as 3rd Corps from October 1870. Provided Nos 4 and 5 Batteries of the new 1st Corps in 1880.

**4th**—Formed as 2nd Corps at Sandwich on 13 February 1860. Renumbered as 4th in the following April, 2nd in August and 4th again in October 1870. Provided No 6 Battery of the new 1st Corps in 1880.

**5th**—This battery first appeared in the Army List as 3rd Corps at Walmer having been formed 6 February 1860. It was renumbered as 5th in April of that year, 3rd in the following August and from October 1870 was known as 5th Corps. Provided No 7 Battery of the new 1st Corps in 1880.

**6th**—Formed at Hastings on 20 February 1860 and was first shown in the Army List as 4th Corps. From April 1860 the corps was shown as 6th but from August was once again listed as 4th. A further change was in October 1870 when it again became 6th. A cadet corps was formed and affiliated in March 1864, but this was later broken up and disappeared from the Army List during 1868. Provided Nos 8, 9 and 10 Batteries of the new 1st Corps in 1880. Interestingly the 6th Corps once had a 4th Battery which was raised at Rye in 1861

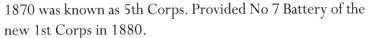

**Officers' pouch badge, Cinque Ports Artillery Volunteers.**

24

from former members of the recently disbanded Rye section of the 3rd Cinque Ports Rifle Volunteer Corps which wore a naval-type uniform which included sailors' caps. It was, however, disbanded in 1876 when, following a carbine shooting competition between themselves and the Hastings Battery in which they lost, the team refused to march ten miles back home and instead caught the train in defiance of their captain.

**7th (1860)**—Formed at Hythe on 17 December 1859 and was first known as the 1st Section of Cinque Ports Artillery Volunteers. Appeared as 7th Corps for the first time in April 1860, but this was changed to 5th by the following August. The strength of the corps did not reach more than a half-battery and subsequently it was disbanded in 1867.

**7th (1870-1880)**—On 23 October 1867 a new 5th Corps was formed at St Leonards, it being re-designated as 7th Corps in October 1870. Provided No 11 Battery of the new 1st Corps in 1880.

**8th**—Formed as 6th Corps at Margate on 26 June 1861 and renumbered 8th in October 1870. Provided No 12 Battery of the new 1st Corps in 1880.

**Bombardier, 7th Cinque Ports Artillery Volunteer Corps.**

**9th**—Formed at Pevensey on 9 April 1866 and until October 1870 was known as the 7th Corps. A second battery was raised at Ninfield in 1874. Provided Nos 13 and 14 Batteries of the new 1st Corps in 1880.

## Rifle Volunteers

An admin battalion for the Cinque Ports area first appeared in the Army List for October 1860. In December 1861 two battalions are listed, three corps from Sussex now included with the 1st. The 2nd Admin Battalion, however, was broken up in 1874, its corps either being absorbed in to the 5th Kent RVC or added to Kent's 4th Admin Battalion. When consolidation came in 1880, the 1st Cinque Ports Admin Battalion became the new 1st Cinque Ports RVC. Two numbered sub-divisions (1st and 3rd) existed which in due course became the 4th and 6th Corps.

**1st (1859-1880)**—Formed at Hastings with Captain the Hon George Waldegrave, Lieutenant Vandaleur B Crake and Ensign James Rock, Jun. All three held commissions dated 17 December 1859 and they were joined by John Savery as surgeon to the corps in September 1860. Joined the 1st Admin Battalion. The corps had been raised out of the Hastings Rifle Club which, in all but name, was the successor of the old Cinque Ports Volunteers of c1789. Absorbed the 9th Corps at Rye, together with the 16th, 17th and 20th Sussex RVC at Battle, Etchingham and Uckfield respectively in 1876 and became 'A' to 'C' Companies of the new 1st Corps in 1880.

**1st (1880-1908)**—The 1st Admin Battalion of Cinque Ports Rifle Volunteers was formed with headquarters at Hastings towards the end of 1860. At first all corps were included, but just the 1st and 9th remained after the formation by December 1861 of the 2nd Admin Battalion. About this time the 16th, 17th and 19th Sussex Corps were also included, followed by 2nd and 4th Sussex in 1863 and the 20th Sussex in 1870. The 19th Sussex, however, was removed in 1868, the 2nd Sussex in 1870 and in 1876 the 16th, 17th and 20th Sussex were absorbed into the 1st Cinque Ports Corps. The Battalion was then consolidated as the new 1st Corps in 1880, the bracketed Cinque Ports and Sussex also forming part of the title. Headquarters were placed at Hastings and the company disposition was as follows: 'A' Hastings (late 1st

**Pouch-belt plate, Cinque Ports Rifle Volunteers.**

Cinque Ports), 'B' Battle (late 1st Cinque Ports), 'C' Ticehurst (late 1st Cinque Ports), 'D' Lewes (late 4th Sussex).

Became a Volunteer battalion of the Royal Sussex Regiment in 1881, but no change in title was ever conferred. 'E' Company was formed at Rye in 1885, 'F' at Hastings in 1887, 'G' Crowborough and 'H' at Ore in 1890, 'I' Hastings and 'K' Ore in 1900. Eastbourne College provided a cadet corps in 1896. *Territorials:* 5th (Cinque Ports) Battalion Royal Sussex Regiment, the Eastbourne College Cadet Corps becoming a contingent of the Junior Division, OTC.

**2nd (1859-1860)**—See 3rd Corps.

**2nd (1860-1874)**—Formed at Ramsgate as the 2nd Kent RVC with Captain George Augustus Young, Lieutenant George F Burgess and Ensign Owen F Daniel commissioned on 18 September 1859. Doctor James Thomas Hiller was also appointed as surgeon, and later, in March 1860, the Rev George W Sicklemore, vicar of St Lawrence's, Ramsgate, became chaplain to the corps. Ensign Daniel had been a lieutenant in the Royal Navy and had served with the Baltic Fleet during the Crimean War. The trades and professions of those that enrolled into the corps are recorded in Charles Igglesden's book *History of the East Kent Volunteers* and include a brewer, several painters and decorators, a licensed victualler, hotel keeper, labourer, plumber, tailor, baker, an engineer, famer, several grocers, a carver, guilder and a cabinet maker. The 2nd Kent was re-designated as 2nd Cinque Ports RVC in April 1860. It joined the 1st Admin Battalion, transferring to 2nd Admin by the end of 1861, then was absorbed into the 5th Kent RVC as its 'A' Company in 1874.

**3rd**—The services of a company of rifle volunteers formed from the Rye and Tenterden areas (a half company each with headquarters at Rye) were accepted on 1 December 1859, its officers: Captain William Mackinnon, Lieutenant Edwin Dawes Saunders, Ensign Francis Bellingham and Surgeon C N Davies, being commissioned on 4 January 1860. The corps was originally numbered as 2nd but due to the transfer of the 2nd Kent RVC to Cinque Ports in April 1860 was restyled as 3rd.

Joined the 1st Admin Battalion. The Rye portion of the corps was later to suffer a setback when, due to its commanding officer's lack of interest, it began to break up. Some members in 1861 were to join the 6th Cinque Ports Artillery Volunteer Corps at Hastings, while those that chose to continue as riflemen enrolled into the 1st Cinque Ports RVC, also at Hastings. Subsequently, by September 1861, the 3rd Corps appears in the Army List as being located at Tenterden, the List for the following December showing the corps as having been placed into the 5th Kent Admin Battalion. Became 'G' Company of the new 5th Kent Corps in 1880.

**4th**—Formed at Hythe with Henry Bean Mackeson as lieutenant and James Watts, Jun as ensign. Both held commissions dated 13 February 1860. Later, the vicar of Hythe, the Rev Brenchley Kingsford, was appointed as chaplain to the corps. The Hythe Volunteers were known as 1st Sub-division until April when numbered as 4th Corps. Henry Mackeson was from the brewing family which were strong supporters of the Volunteer Movement. One relative had been a member of the old Deal Volunteers of 1804, and others would follow in the footsteps of Henry Mackeson and serve in the Hythe company. James Watts was a member of the legal profession. Joined the 1st Admin Battalion, transferring to 2nd Admin Battalion by the end of 1861, then to 4th Kent Admin Battalion in 1874. Absorbed into the 5th Kent RVC as 'D' Company in the same year. For some time, the 4th Corps was allowed to store its weapons at the School of Musketry in Hythe, but the authorities there were not too keen on this idea so a room loaned by the London and County Bank in Bank Street was taken into use. There would be yet another move, this time just across the road from the bank to premises owned by Henry Mackeson, which would serve as company headquarters until 1882.

**5th**—The 5th Cinque Ports RVC was formed as a result of a meeting held at the Old King's Arms Assembly Rooms in Folkestone. Charles G Percival was appointed to as captain, Angus Mackay Leith as lieutenant and Theodore H N Walsh, ensign. All three were gazetted on 30 March 1860. Later the Rev Alfred Gay became chaplain to the corps, Charles E Fitzgerald taking up the post of surgeon. Joined the 1st Admin Battalion, transferring to 2nd Admin Battalion by the end of 1861, then to the 4th Kent Admin Battalion in 1874. Absorbed into the 5th Kent RVC in the same year as its 'F' Company.

**6th**—Formed at Deal with Julius R Backhouse, CB, who had previously served as a colonel in the Bengal Artillery, commissioned as lieutenant on 20 April 1860. He was later joined by Ensign Lamprey Karney and Surgeon Frederick T Hulke who were both gazetted on 9 May. The Deal corps was known as 3rd Sub-division until April. Joined the 1st Admin Battalion, transferring to 2nd Admin Battalion by the end of 1861. Disbanded later and is last seen in the Army List for December 1863.

**7th**—Formed at Margate as one company with Charles James Cox, who resided at Fordwich, as captain, James Standring, a Margate wine merchant and member of the town council as lieutenant, and William Price who was appointed as ensign. All three officers held commissions dated 22 March 1860. A glance at the first muster roll shows how the occupations of the volunteers in this, and many other corps, varied. They included a hotel keeper, tobacconist, wine merchant, Private H Chexfield who was the superintendent at the Royal Infirmary, a solicitor's clerk, fruit seller, music seller, someone who made billiard tables, tailors, a ticket collector on the railway, hairdresser, bookseller, several builders, a butcher and a photographer.

Joined the 1st Admin Battalion, transferring to 2nd Admin Battalion by the end of 1861. Detachments were formed at St Peter's and Birchington in 1866, but these were short lived and disappeared in 1873. Headquarters of the Margate company were at first placed at the Town Hall, but later moved to the Civil and Military Club in New Inn Yard, and after that to Hawley Street. Absorbed into the 5th Kent RVC as its 'G' Company in 1874. Opened in Margate by the Duke of Connaught on 10 July 1875 was the Deaf and Dumb Asylum, the Margate Volunteers providing a guard of honour on the occasion.

**8th**—Formed at Dover with proprietor of the *Dover Chronicle,* Joseph G Churchward as captain and local solicitor George Fielding, lieutenant. Both held commissions dated 30 July 1860. Late in 1861 the first ensign to be appointed to the corps was W B Churchward, the son of his commanding officer, and in August of that year the vicar of Trinity Church, the Rev A J Woodhouse, joined as chaplain, and local practitioner, Doctor W Corke became surgeon. The original headquarters occupied by the 8th Cinque Ports RVC were in Snargate Street on property owned by the Chatham and Dover Railway Company. In 1866 Castle House in Dolphin Lane was taken over, which served the corps until moving to Northampton Street in 1876.

Joined the 1st Admin Battalion, transferring to 2nd Admin Battalion by the end of 1861, and was absorbed into the 5th Kent RVC as its 'K' Company in 1874. At Dover the Town Hall was opened in 1883 and the new Promenade Pier on Whitson Monday ten years after that. This was also the year when the Volunteers were among those that provided the guard of honour on the occasion of the Prince of Wales laying the foundation stone of the new Commercial Harbour.

**9th**—When the Rye portion of the 3rd Corps was broken up in 1861 those members wishing to continue as riflemen were transferred to the 1st Corps at Hasting, the detachment thereafter being known as the Rye Sub-division. At the same time (see Monthly Army List for September 1861) a 9th Cinque Ports RVC appears as having been formed at Rye and included in 1st Admin Battalion. According to a booklet published in 1954 entitled *The Story of the Rye Volunteers*, Rye attended the 'Great Review' at Brighton on 21 Apr. 1862 as 9th Corps. No officers, however, appear in the Army List under this heading which was removed in November 1862. Rye once again appears as providing a 9th Corps in January 1865. This time two officers—Captain John Frewen and Ensign William Henry Crowhurst—are listed with commissions dated 12 December. This new corps was in fact formed by the old Rye elements of 1st Corps. Disbandment yet again in 1876, the personnel returning to the 1st Corps.

**10th**—A 10th Corps at New Romney is shown in the Army List for August 1862. No officers were appointed, however, and the corps is not seen after April 1864. In January of the following year the 10th reappears, this time with Lieutenant Henry Stringer and Ensign Henry Cobb both holding commissions dated 22 December 1864. The new sub-division held its first drills, sometimes at Lydd or in the neighbouring village of Ruckinge. Headquarters were at the Assembly Rooms, New Romney, and firing ranges were originally on land that became the Littlestone Golf Links, then later at Lydd. Joined the 2nd Admin Battalion, transferring to the 4th Kent Admin Battalion in 1874, and was absorbed into the 5th Kent RVC as its 'L' Company the same year.

# Cornwall

## Artillery Volunteers

The 1st Admin Brigade was formed on 24 May 1860 with headquarters at Bodmin, the sub-title The Duke of Cornwall's Artillery Volunteers appearing in the Army List from July 1861. The brigade was consolidated as the new 1st Corps in 1880.

**1st (1859-1880)**—Formed at Padstow on 27 September 1859 and became No 1 Battery of the new 1st Corps in 1880.

**1st (1880-1908)**—Formed by the consolidation in 1880 of the 1st Admin Brigade. Headquarters remained at Bodmin and the ten batteries were organised as follows: No 1 Padstow (late 1st Corps), No 2 Looe (late 2nd Corps), No 3 Fowey (late 3rd Corps), No 4 Charlestown (late 4th Corps), No 5 Par (late 5th Corps), No 6 Polruan (late 7th Corps), No 7 Hayle (late 8th Corps), No 8 Penzance (late 10th Corps), No 9 Marazion (late 12th Corps), No 10 St Just (late 13th Corps). Under General Order 106 of September 1886 the corps was re-designated as 3rd Volunteer (Duke of Cornwall's) Brigade Western Division Royal Artillery. This was, however, changed to 1st Cornwall (Duke of Cornwall's) Artillery Volunteer Corps (Western Division Royal Artillery) by Army Order 443 of November 1889. Headquarters were moved from Bodmin to Falmouth in 1888. *Territorials:* The Cornwall (Duke of Cornwall's) RGA.

**2nd**—Formed at Looe on 17 October 1859 and became No 2 Battery of the new 1st Corps in 1880.

**3rd**—Formed at Fowey on 25 November 1859 and became No 3 Battery of the new 1st Corps in 1880.

**4th**—Formed at Charlestown on 30 October 1859 and became No 4 Battery of the new 1st Corps in 1880.

**5th**—Formed at Par as the 1st Section of Cornwall Artillery Volunteers on 23 December 1859. Became 5th Corps in March 1860 and in the following July absorbed the 6th Corps at Par Harbour. Provided No 5 Battery of the new 1st Corps in 1880.

**6th**—Formed with headquarters at Par Harbour on 4 February 1860 and was first know as the 2nd Section of Cornwall Artillery Volunteers. Renamed 6th Corps in June 1860 but was absorbed into the 5th during the following month.

**7th**—Formed at Polruan on 27 February 1860 and became No 6 Battery of the new 1st Corps in 1880.

**Arthur A Davis, Hon Assistant Surgeon, 3rd Cornwall Artillery Volunteer Corps.**

**8th**—Formed at Hayle on 2 April 1860 and became No 7 Battery of the new 1st Corps in 1880

**9th**—Formed with headquarters at the Fowey Consols Mine on 2 April 1860. This corps consisted entirely of mine workers and was disbanded late in 1863.

**10th**—Formed at Buryan on 5 November 1860, headquarters moving to Newlyn in 1868 then to Penzance in 1877. Became No 8 Battery of the new 1st Corps in 1880.

**11th**—Formed at St Ives on 8 November 1860 and disbanded in 1878.

**12th**—Formed at Marazion on 3 April 1861 and became No 9 Battery of the new 1st Corps in 1880.

**13th**—Formed at St Just on 26 September 1862 and became No 10 Battery of the new 1st Corps in 1880.

## Engineer Volunteers

**Falmouth Division Submarine Miners**—Formed in 1888 with its first officers commissioned 23 June. Disbanded 1891.

## Rifle Volunteers

Two administrative battalions were formed to accommodate the twenty-two individual numbered corps formed within the county. In 1880, these were consolidated to form the new 1st and 2nd Cornwall RVC. One numbered sub-division appeared in the early Army Lists, this later being numbered as 10th Corps.

**1st (1859-1880)**—Formed at Penzance with George Borlase Tremenhere as captain, Henry Dobree, lieutenant and Thomas Cornish, ensign. All three officers held commissions dated 10 September 1859. Joined the 1st Admin Battalion and became 'A' Company of the new 1st Corps in 1880.

**1st (The Duke of Cornwall's) (1880-1908)**—The 1st Admin Battalion was formed with headquarters at Penzance by May 1860, the additional title of The Duke of Cornwall's Rifle Volunteers was later granted and appears for the first time in the Army List for December 1861. Included in the battalion were the several corps from the western portion of the county: 1st, 2nd, 3rd, 7th, 8th (later renumbered as 21st), 11th, 12th, 15th, 17th, 18th and 20th Corps. The battalion was consolidated in 1880 as 1st (The Duke of Cornwall's) RVC with eleven companies: 'A' Penzance (late 1st Corps), 'B' Camborne (late 2nd Corps), 'C' Falmouth (late 3rd Corps), 'D' Helston (late 7th Corps), 'E' Truro (late 11th Corps), 'F' Truro (late 12th Corps), 'G' Hayle (late 15th Corps), 'H' Redruth (late 17th Corps), 'I' Trelowarren (late 18th Corps), 'J' St Just-in-Penwith (late 20th Corps), 'K' Penryn (late 21st Corps)

Headquarters were moved from Penzance to Falmouth in 1881. The corps was designated as 1st Volunteer Battalion Duke of Cornwall's Light Infantry in 1885 and headquarters moved again, this time to Truro, in 1902. Volunteers from the battalion served in South Africa during the Boer War. On 30 May 1901, Captain George Percy Bickford-Smith died at Heilbron from wounds received in action. From Trevarno, he had joined the battalion in 1893, being promoted to captain on 27 June 1900. Two new companies were sanctioned in 1900 and transfer to the Territorial Force in 1908 was as 4th Battalion DCLI.

**2nd (1859-1880)**—Formed at Camborne with John Solomon Bickford as captain, Thomas Hutchinson,

**Cap badge, 1st Volunteer Battalion Duke of Cornwall's Light Infantry.**

lieutenant and Walter Pike, ensign. All three officers held commissions dated 17 October 1859. Joined the 1st Admin Battalion and became 'B' Company of the new 1st Corps in 1880.

**2nd (The Duke of Cornwall's) (1880-1908)**—The 2nd Admin Battalion was formed with headquarters at Bodmin by May 1860, the additional title of The Duke of Cornwall's Rifle Volunteers was later added and appears for the first time in the Army List for December 1861. Included in the battalion were the corps from the eastern portion of the county: 4th, 5th, 6th, 9th, 10th, 13th, 14th, 16th, 19th and 22nd. Consolidated in 1880 as 2nd (The Duke of Cornwall's) with nine companies: 'A' Liskeard (late 4th Corps), 'B' Callington (late 5th Corps), 'C' Launceston (late 6th Corps), 'D' St Austell (late 9th Corps), 'E' Bodmin (late 10th Corps), 'F' Wadebridge (late 13th Corps), 'G' St Columb (late 16th Corps), 'H' Camelford (late 19th Corps), 'I' Saltash (late 22nd Corps).

Designated as 2nd Volunteer Battalion Duke of Cornwall's Light Infantry in 1885 and 'J' Company was added at Bude in 1900. Volunteers served alongside the Regulars of 2nd DCLI in South Africa. Lieutenant Edward G Cowlard, second son of C L Cowlard, Clerk of the Peace for Cornwall, died from enteric fever at Springfontein on 5 March 1901. Educated at Marlborough College, his name can be seen on a memorial in the chapel there. Transfer to the Territorial Force in 1908 was as 5th Battalion DCLI.

**3rd**—Formed at Falmouth with former 2nd Dragoons officer George Reid as captain, Marshall Valentine Bull, late of the 10th Regiment of Foot, as lieutenant and Henry A Sleeman, who had served with the 16th Light Dragoons, ensign. All three officers held commissions dated 28 October 1859. Joined the 1st Admin Battalion and became 'C' Company of the new 1st Corps in 1880.

**4th**—Formed at Liskeard with John Samuel Hawker as captain, Christopher Childs, lieutenant and John Sobey, ensign. All three officers held commissions dated 13 December 1859. Joined the 2nd Admin Battalion and became 'A' Company of the new 2nd Corps in 1880.

**5th**—Formed at Callington with John Kempthorne as captain and John Peter, Jun, ensign. Both held commissions dated 3 January 1860. Joined the 2nd Admin Battalion and became 'B' Company of the new 2nd Corps in 1880.

**6th**—Formed at Launceston with Lieutenant William Day Hanson commissioned on 10 January 1860. Joined the 2nd Admin Battalion and became 'C' Company of the new 2nd Corps in 1880.

**7th**—Formed at Helston with Thomas Phillips Tyacke as captain, Frederick Vivian Hill, lieutenant and George Reid, ensign. All three officers held commissions dated 25 January 1860. Joined the 1st Admin Battalion and became 'D' Company of the new 1st Corps in 1880.

**8th**—An 8th Corps is shown in the Army List as having been formed at Penryn with three officers: Captain William Herbert Mansell, Lieutenant Francis Gilbert Enys and Ensign William Francis Phillpotts all holding commissions dated 2 February 1860. The corps is not shown in October but reappears again in December only to disappear altogether in January 1861. A new corps at Penryn, this time with different officers, appears at the same time numbered as 21st.

**9th**—Formed at St Austell with Henry Hawkins Tremayne as captain, Edmund Carlyon, lieutenant and John Coode, ensign. All three officers held commissions dated 14 February 1860. Joined the 2nd Admin Battalion and became 'D' Company of the new 2nd Corps in 1880.

**10th**—Formed at Bodmin on 24 December 1859 and known as the 1st Sub-division until March 1860. Now a full company, its first officers were Captain Francis John Hext, Lieutenant Edmunds G Hamley and Ensign Preston James Wallace. All three held commissions dated 6 March 1860. Joined the 2nd Admin Battalion and became 'E' Company of the new 2nd Corps in 1880.

**11th**—Formed at Truro with Lieutenant Francis Hearle Cock and Ensign Edwin Parkin commissioned on 13 February 1860. Joined the 1st Admin Battalion and became 'E' Company of the new 1st Corps in 1880.

**12th**—Formed at Truro with James Henderson as captain, Arthur Williams, lieutenant and Thomas R Foster, ensign. All three officers held commissions dated 13 February 1860. Joined the 1st Admin Battalion and became 'F' Company of the new 1st Corps in 1880.

**13th**—Formed at Wadebridge with William R Crawford Potter as captain, Richard J M E Symonds, lieutenant and Richard G Pollard, ensign. All three officers held commissions dated 7 April 1860. Joined the 2nd Admin Battalion and became 'F' Company of the new 2nd Corps in 1880.

**14th**—Formed at Calstock with Edward Willyams as captain, William G Gard, lieutenant and John M Sellers, ensign. All three officers held commissions dated 15 March 1860. Joined the 2nd Admin Battalion, the corps being later disbanded and not shown in the Army List after November 1860.

**15th**—Formed at Hayle, the first officer to receive a commission being Lieutenant Samuel Hosken on 2 May 1860. Joined the 1st Admin Battalion and became 'G' Company of the new 1st Corps in 1880.

**16th**—Formed at St Columb with Edward B Willyams as captain, George B Collins, lieutenant and Edward B Whitford, ensign. All three officers held commissions dated 2 April 1860. Joined the 2nd Admin Battalion and became 'G' Company of the new 2nd Corps in 1880.

**17th**—Formed at Redruth with John Haye as captain, William M Grylls, lieutenant and James H Dennis, ensign. All three officers held commissions dated 7 April 1860. Joined the 1st Admin Battalion and became 'H' Company of the new 1st Corps in 1880.

**18th**—Formed at Helston with John Tyacke as captain, James P Tyacke, lieutenant and John B Kempthorne, ensign. All three officers held commissions dated 2 June 1860. A glance at the first muster roll of the 18th Corps shows that almost half of the members were farmers. Joined the 1st Admin Battalion towards the end of 1861, headquarters moved to Trelowarren (the seat of the Vyvyans close to Mawgan-in-Meneage) in 1864, and in 1880 the 18th became 'I' Company of the new 1st Corps.

**19th**—Formed at Camelford with Lieutenant William S Rosevear and Ensign William S Hawker, commissioned on 26 July 1860. Joined the 2nd Admin Battalion and became 'H' Company of the new 2nd Corps in 1880.

**20th**—Formed at St Just-in-Penwith with Captain Samuel Borcase, a former major in the Cornwall Rangers Militia, commissioned on 14 August 1860. Joined the 1st Admin Battalion and became 'J' Company of the new 1st Corps in 1880.

**21st**—Formed at Penryn with Lieutenant William Lanton and Ensign George A Jenkins commissioned on 1 December 1860. Joined the 1st Admin Battalion and became 'K' Company of the new 1st Corps in 1880.

**22nd**—Formed at Saltash with Captain Benjamin Snell in command holding a commission dated 23 February 1865. Joined the 2nd Admin Battalion and became 'I' Company of the new 2nd Corps in 1880.

# Cumberland

## Artillery Volunteers

The 1st Admin Brigade of Cumberland Artillery Volunteers was formed with headquarters at Carlisle on 10 July 1860 and was consolidated as the new 1st Corps in 1880.

**1st (1860-1880)**—Formed at Whitehaven on 7 May 1860 and became No 1 Battery of the new 1st Corps in 1880.

**1st (1880-1908)**—Formed by the consolidation of the 1st Admin Brigade in May 1880. Headquarters remained at Carlisle and the batteries were organised as follows: No 1 Whitehaven (late 1st Corps), No 2 Carlisle (late 2nd Corps), No 3 Maryport (late 3rd Corps), No 4 Carlisle (late 2nd Corps). *Territorials:* 1st and 2nd Cumberland (Howitzer) Batteries and Ammunition Column of the 4th East Lancashire (Howitzer) Brigade RFA.

**2nd**—Formed at Carlisle on 15 February 1860 and became Nos 2 and 4 Batteries of the new 1st Corps in 1880.

**3rd**—Formed at Maryport on 28 April 1860 and became No 3 Battery of the new 1st Corps in 1880.

**4th**—Formed at Workington on 5 March 1860 and made its last appearance in the Army List for January 1866.

**5th**—Formed at Harrington on 11 May 1860 and disbanded in 1876.

## Engineer Volunteers

**1st**—The only engineer corps to be formed within the county was raised at Cockermouth on 17 September 1861. The town being reached by the London & North Western and Furness railways, its numerous woollen factories and tanneries provided employment for many during the volunteer period. Here, at All Saints Church, a window remembers William Wordsworth. But recruiting did not go well and after less than three years' service 1st Cumberland EVC was disbanded in 1864.

## Rifle Volunteers

All corps were included in the 1st Admin Battalion which was consolidated in 1880 to form the new 1st Cumberland RVC.

**1st (1860-1880)**—On the Eden, in north-east Cumberland, Carlisle saw the formation on 15 February 1860 of the 1st Corps with Robert Ferguson as captain, William Jackson, lieutenant and Miles MacInnes, ensign. The 2nd Corps at Whitehaven at this time comprised two companies and by June 1860 the second of these, under Captain R S Dixon, an officer formally with the 9th Light Dragoons (Lancers), was absorbed into the 1st Corps as its No 2 Company. Became 'A' to 'C' Companies of the new 1st Corps in 1880.

**1st (1880-1908)**—The 1st Admin Battalion was formed with headquarters at Carlisle in May 1860. Moved to Keswick in 1865 and in 1880 the battalion was consolidated as the new 1st Cumberland RVC, a two-battalion corps with thirteen companies: 'A', 'B' and 'C' Carlisle (late 1st Corps), 'D' Whitehaven (late 2nd Corps), 'E' Keswick (late 3rd Corps), 'F' Brampton (late 4th Corps), 'G' and 'H' Penrith (late 5th Corps), 'I' Alston (late 6th Corps), 'K' Workington (late 7th Corps), 'L' Cockermouth (late 8th Corps), 'M' Egremont (late 10th Corps). 'N' Wigton (late 11th Corps).

General Order 181 of December 1887 notified the change in designation of 1st Cumberland RVC to 1st (Cumberland) Volunteer Battalion Border Regiment. Headquarters were moved back to Carlisle in 1896 and in 1900 the companies at Whitehaven, Workington, Cockermouth, Egrement and Wigton were detached to form the 3rd (Cumberland) Volunteer Battalion. *Territorials:* Four companies of the 4th Battalion Border Regiment.

**2nd**—One company formed at the west Cumberland seaport, parish and borough of Whitehaven on 14 February 1860 with Captain Joshua Fletcher in command. A No 2 company was raised on 2 March 1860 but this, by June 1860, was taken into the 1st Corps as its No 2 Company. Became 'D' Company of the new 1st Corps in 1880.

**3rd**—Formed at Keswick on 15 February 1860 with Charles H Wade as captain and John J Spedding, lieutenant. John Teather was commissioned as ensign on 10 March. Became 'E' Company of the new 1st Corps in 1880.

**4th**—Brampton, nine miles north-east of Carlisle, was the

**Review of the Cumberland Rifle Volunteers in Rickerby Park, Carlisle, 1861.**

headquarters of the county's 4th Corps which was formed on 24 March 1860 with Captain T Charles Thompson in command. Both Lieutenant George L Carrick and Ensign William Dobson were commissioned on the following 4 April. Became 'F' Company of the new 1st Corps in 1880. The 4th Cumberland RVC was known locally as 'Belted Wills', Mr Phillip Haythornthwaite writing in *The Bulletin* of the Military Historical Society for November 1997 explaining that this name was in reference to Lord William Howard (1563-1640) who lived at Namworth Castle close to Brampton. His lordship had acquired the nickname in a piece written by Sir Walter Scott.

**5th**—Formed at Penrith on 5 March 1860 and sometimes known as the Inglewood Rangers—Inglewood Forest, the central plain of north Cumberland extending from Penrith to Carlisle. Captain William Brougham took command, Lieutenant Frederick Cowper, Jun and Ensign William Wilkinson were also appointed holding commissions dated 24 March. Became 'G' and 'H' Companies of the new 1st Corps in 1880.

**6th**—In east Cumberland, the market town of Alston formed the county's 6th Corps on 2 March 1860 with Theodore Wilson as captain. Lieutenant Joseph Dickinson and Ensign John Friend were also appointed with commissions dated 22 March. Became 'I' Company of the new 1st Corps in 1880.

**7th**—Formed at Workington on 12 April 1860 and sometimes known as the Solway Marksmen— Solway Firth, that great inlet between England and Scotland extending almost fifty miles inland, Workington almost at its most southerly point. Captain Charles Lamport, Lieutenant Michael Falcon and Ensign Antony Peat were the first officers to be commissioned. Became 'K' Company of the new 1st Corps in 1880.

**8th**—On the confluence of the rivers Derwent and Cocker, Cockermouth in western Cumberland was the headquarters of the 8th Corps. Thomas A Hoskins, Jun became captain, Thomas Drane, lieutenant and James Hartley, ensign. Formed on 24 March 1860, the 8th Cumberland RVC became 'L' Company of the new 1st Corps in 1880.

**9th**—Formed at Whitehaven on 21 May 1860 with J Spencer as captain. The corps was not seen in the Army List after June 1863.

**10th**—Formed at Egremont on the edge of the Lake District, on 3 July 1860 with Captain Henry Jefferson in command. Lieutenant John Stirling and Ensign Henry Baker received their commissions on 20 July. Became 'M' Company of the new 1st Corps in 1880.

**11th**—Formed at Wigton on 18 July 1860 with Anthony B Were as lieutenant and Thomas O Barwis, ensign. Became 'N' Company of the new 1st Corps in 1880.

**3rd (Cumberland) Volunteer Battalion Border Regiment**—Formed with headquarters at Workington in 1900 by the withdrawal of the Whitehaven, Workington, Cockermouth, Egrement and Wigton Companies of 1st (Cumberland) Volunteer Battalion Border Regiment. New personnel were also added at Workington, Frizington and Aspatria bringing the new battalion's establishment to eight companies. At St Bees south of Whitehaven, the ancient grammar school formed a cadet corps in 1903. *Territorials:* 5th Battalion Border Regiment, St Bees School becoming a contingent of the Junior Division OTC.

# Derbyshire

## Mounted Rifle Volunteers

**1st**—Formed 22 June 1860 with Captain John Brown in command after a meeting held at the Angel Inn the previous March. Headquarters were at first in Derby, but a move was made to Chesterfield by 1864. Disbanded in May 1871.

## Rifle Volunteers

Three Admin Battalions were formed by the county, the 2nd being broken up in 1869 with its corps absorbed into 3rd Admin. The 2nd Admin, which included the 2nd, 8th and 10th Corps, had been formed with headquarters at Sudbury in June 1860, moving to Ashbourne in 1864. In 1880, 1st and 3rd Admin

Battalions were consolidated to form the new 1st and 2nd Corps. Situated on the Derwent, just a few miles above where the river joins the Trent, Derby contributed five of the corps raised. The Royal Drill Hall was built for the volunteers in 1869.

**1st (1859-1880)**—Formed at Derby with Captain Charles Edmund Newton and Lieutenant William Turpie commissioned on 23 July 1859. Joined the 1st Admin Battalion and became 'A' Company of the new 1st Corps in 1880.

**1st (1880-1908)**—The 1st Admin Battalion was formed with headquarters at Derby on 10 July 1860 and consolidated as the new 1st Corps with twelve companies in 1880: 'A' Derby (late 1st Corps), 'B' Derby (late 4th Corps), 'C' and 'D' Derby (late 5th Corps), 'E' Butterley (late No 1 Company, 12th Corps), 'F' Condor Park (late No 2 Company, 12th Corps), 'G' Belper (late 13th Corps), 'H' and 'I' Derby (late 15th Corps), 'K' Derby (late (19th Corps), 'L' Long Eaton (late 20th Corps), 'M' Long Eaton (late 20th Corps and part of 13th).

A cadet corps was formed and affiliated to the 1st Admin Battalion in 1870. It disappears from the Army List in 1881, returns again in 1883, and by 1895 is shown as being formed by Derby School. Another cadet corps was formed and affiliated at Trent College in 1886, but this was disbanded towards the end of 1889. Repton School provided a company in December 1900, followed by a unit raised by the Derby General Post Office called the Postal Telegraph Messengers Cadet Corps in 1905.

The 1st Derbyshire was re-designated as 1st Volunteer Battalion Sherwood Foresters under General Order 39 of April 1887 and transferred to the Territorial Force in 1908 as 5th Battalion Sherwood Foresters. Both Derby and Repton Schools at the same time joined the OTC.

**2nd (1859-1869)**—In north Derbyshire, the 2nd Corps at Sudbury had its first officers gazetted on 6 December 1859. One company became two in February 1860, the corps joined the 2nd Admin Battalion, and was disbanded in 1869. At All Saints Church there are numerous memorials to the Vernon family, the Rt Hon George J W Lord Vernon of Sudbury Hall being made Captain Commandant of the 2nd Derbyshire RVC in February 1860.

**2nd (1880-1908)**—The 3rd Admin Battalion was formed in June 1860 with headquarters at Bakewell and absorbed the remaining two corps of the 2nd Admin Battalion in 1869. The battalion was consolidated in 1880 as the new 2nd Corps with ten companies: 'A' Chesterfield (late 3rd Corps), 'B' Chapel-en-le-Frith (late 7th Corps), 'C' Ashbourne (late 8th Corps), 'D' Bakewell (late 9th Corps). 'E' Wirksworth (late 10th Corps), 'F' Matlock (late 11th Corps), 'G' Clay Cross (late 17th Corps), 'H' Whaley Bridge (late 18th Corps), 'I' Hartington (late 21st Corps), 'K' Staveley (late 22nd Corps).

Under General Order 39 of April 1887 2nd Derbyshire RVC was re-designated as 2nd Volunteer Battalion Sherwood Foresters. Headquarters moved from Bakewell to Chesterfield in 1898 and in 1900 three new companies (two at Chesterfield, one Buxton) were formed. Transfer to the Territorial Force in 1908 was as 6th Battalion Sherwood Foresters.

**3rd**—Formed at Chesterfield with John Hallewell as captain, James B White, lieutenant and John Sanders Clarke, ensign. All three officers held commissions dated 7 January 1860. Joined the 3rd Admin Battalion and became 'A' Company of the new 2nd Corps in 1880.

**4th**—Formed at Derby with Nathaniel Charles Curzon commissioned as captain on 31 December 1859. Joined the 1st Admin Battalion and became 'B' Company of the new 1st Corps in 1880.

**5th**—Formed at Derby with William Henry Cox as captain, Alexander James Henley, lieutenant and Alexander Buchanan, ensign. All three officers held commissions dated 18 January 1860. Joined the 1st Admin Battalion and became 'C' and 'D' Companies of the new 1st Corps in 1880.

**6th**—Formed on the Wye at Buxton with Captain Francis Westby Bagshawe, Lieutenant M O Bright and Ensign William Barker commissioned on 16 February 1860. Joined the 3rd Admin Battalion but disbanded later and last seen in the Army List for December 1861.

**7th**—Formed at Chapel-en-le-Frith with Arthur Neild as captain, Norman Bennett, lieutenant and

Andrew Welsh, ensign. All three officers held commissions dated 1 February 1860. Joined the 3rd Admin Battalion and became 'B' Company of the new 2nd Corps in 1880.

**8th**—On the Henmore, Ashbourne formed the 8th Corps with Charles Okeover as captain; Andrew George Corbet, lieutenant and Edward Alfred Dyke, ensign. All three officers held commissions dated 1 February 1860. Joined the 2nd Admin Battalion, transferring to the 3rd Admin in 1869, and became 'C' Company of the new 2nd Corps in 1880.

**9th**—Formed at Bakewell with Lord George H Cavendish as captain, William Pole Thornhill, lieutenant and Robert W M Nesfield, ensign. All three officers held commissions dated 28 February 1860. Joined the 3rd Admin Battalion and became 'D' Company of the new 2nd Corps in 1880.

**10th**—Formed at Wirksworth with Albert Frederick Hurt as captain, Henry W Walthall, lieutenant and William P Huddersty, ensign. All three officers held commissions dated 10 March 1860. Joined the 2nd Admin Battalion, transferring to 3rd Admin in 1869, and became 'E' Company of the new 2nd Corps in 1880.

**11th**—Formed at Matlock with Sir Joseph Paxton as captain, Samuel Prince, lieutenant and Robert Chadwick, ensign. All three officers held commissions dated 17 March 1860. Joined the 3rd Admin Battalion and became 'F' Company of the new 2nd Corps in 1880.

**12th**—Formed as one company at Butterley with William Jessop as captain, John G N Alleyne, lieutenant and John T Featherstone, ensign. All three officers held commissions dated 3 April 1860. Joined the 1st Admin Battalion, a new company was added later at Condor Park, and become 'E' and 'F' Companies of the new 1st Corps in 1880.

**13th**—Formed at Belper with Alfred W Holmes as captain, William Statham, lieutenant and Charles W Wilkinson, ensign. All three officers held commissions dated 14 March 1860. Joined the 1st Admin Battalion and became 'G' and part of 'M' Companies, of the new 1st Corps in 1880. Belper lies on the Derwent seven miles north of Derby. Cotton yarn, hosiery and gloves have been noted as the staple industries of the town, the first cotton mill being established by the Strutt family in 1776. The Hon Arthur Strutt was commissioned as lieutenant in the 13th Corps in May 1865.

**14th**—None recorded.

**15th**—Formed at Derby with Robert E Wilmot as captain and T E Cox, ensign. Both held commissions dated 7 July 1860. Joined the 1st Admin Battalion and became 'H' and 'I' Companies of the new 1st Corps in 1880.

**16th**—Formed at Ilkeston with Meynell H M Mundy as captain, Edwin Whitehouse, lieutenant and Philip Potter, ensign. All three held commissions dated 7 September 1860. Joined the 1st Admin Battalion and disappeared from the Army List in August 1863.

**17th**—Formed at Clay Cross with Gladwin Turbutt as captain, William Milnes, lieutenant and William Clayton, ensign. All three held commissions dated 26 January 1861. Joined the 3rd Admin Battalion and became 'G' Company of the new 2nd Corps in 1880.

**18th**—Formed as one company at Whaley Bridge with Edward Hall as captain, James H Williamson, lieutenant and George W Higinbotham, ensign. All three held commissions dated 16 March 1866. Joined the 3rd Admin Battalion and became 'H' Company of the new 2nd Corps in 1880.

**19th (Elvaston)**—Headquarters of the 19th Corps were at Derby, but most of the recruiting took place in the parish of Elvaston on the River Derwent five miles to the south east. The first officers of the company were Captain Viscount C A S Peersham, Lieutenant Henry H Bemrose and Ensign Edwin Pratt. All three held commissions dated 23 April 1868. Joined the 1st Admin Battalion and became 'K' Company of the new 1st Corps in 1880.

**20th (Trent)**—Formed at Long Eaton, seven miles south-east of Derby, with James Bembridge as captain, William H Sweet, lieutenant, Robert Hogwood, ensign. All three held commissions dated 31 July 1871 and appointed at the same time were Surgeon John Ewart and Chaplain, the Rev Frederick Atkinson.

Joined the 1st Admin Battalion and became 'L' and 'M' Companies of the new 1st Corps in 1880.

**21st**—Formed at Hartington on 25 May 1872. Joined the 3rd Admin Battalion and became 'I' Company of the new 2nd Corps in 1880.

**22nd**—Formed at Staveley with Josiah Court as captain and Francis A Turner, lieutenant. Both held commissions dated 23 September 1874. Joined the 3rd Admin Battalion and became 'K' Company of the new 2nd Corps in 1880.

**23rd**—Formed at Glossop with Captain Commandant William Sidebottom commissioned on 22 January 1876. Joined the 4th Admin Battalion of the neighbouring county of Cheshire, the headquarters of which were just over nine miles away at Stockport. Became 'L' to 'N' Companies of the new 4th Cheshire RVC in 1880.

# Devonshire

## Mounted Rifle Volunteers / Light Horse Volunteers

The county raised seven corps of mounted rifle volunteers, three of which (the 4th, 5th and 7th) converted to light horse units with numbers 1st, 2nd and 3rd.

**1st**—Formed 1860 at Broadclyst with Captain Sir Thomas Dyke Acland in command. Sir Thomas was resident at Broadclyst and his commission was dated 23 February 1860. Amalgamated with the 3rd Mounted Rifles in 1872 and disbanded February 1877.

**2nd**—Formed 5 March 1860 at Exminster with Lieutenant C H Hall in command. Disbanded in July 1861.

**3rd**—Raised at Upper Ottery on 10 April 1860 with Captain Hon W W Addington in command. Amalgamated with the 1st Devonshire Mounted Rifles in 1872.

**4th**—Raised 30 April 1860 at Modbury with Captain John Bulteel in command. Became 3rd Devonshire Light Horse Volunteers in May 1865 but was not seen in the Army List after January 1875.

**5th**—Formed 24 May 1860 as 5th Mounted Rifles with headquarters at Berry and detachments at Newton Abbot and Torquay. Captain Lord Seymour commanded. Became 1st Devonshire Light Horse Volunteers in 1861, headquarters moving to Torquay in 1874. Disbanded September 1875.

**6th**—Formed in July 1860 at South Molton with Captain John L Dames in command. Disbanded October 1875.

**7th**—Formed June 1860 at Yealmpton as 7th Devonshire Mounted Rifles and became 2nd Devonshire Light Horse Volunteers in 1865. Was not seen in the Army List after January 1875.

## Artillery Volunteers

The 1st Admin Brigade of Devonshire Artillery Volunteers was formed with headquarters at Teignmouth in August 1860. In January 1861 the 6th, 10th and 13th Corps were removed and placed into the newly created 2nd Admin Brigade at Devonport. Headquarters of the 1st were removed to Torquay in 1863 and then to Exeter two years later. In January 1866 the 1st, 3rd and 4th Corps from the neighbouring county of Dorsetshire were included, these followed by the 5th and 6th

**Helmet badge, 3rd Devonshire Light Horse Volunteer Corps.**

36

upon their formation in 1868 and 1869 respectively. But in January 1873 all Dorset Corps were removed from the 1st Devonshire Brigade and placed with the 1st Hampshire. Headquarters of the 2nd Admin Brigade were moved to Dartmouth by the end of 1874, then back to Devonport in 1877. The brigade had a cadet corps attached for the period 1871 to 1879.

**Officers' waist-belt clasp, 12th Devonshire Artillery Volunteer Corps.**

**1st (1859-1880)**—Formed at Woodbury on 18 August 1859, headquarters moving to Lympstone during 1874. Became No 1 Battery of the new 1st Corps in 1880.

**1st (1880-1908)**—Formed in March 1880 by the consolidation of the 1st Admin Brigade. Headquarters remained at Exeter and the batteries were organised as follows: No 1 Lympstone (late 1st Corps), No 2 Brixham (late 11th Corps), No 3 Teignmouth (late 3rd Corps), No 4 Torquay (late 4th Corps), Nos 5 and 6 Exeter (late 5th Corps), No 7 Exmouth (late 7th Corps), No 8 Heavitree (late 8th Corps), No 9 Paignton (late 9th Corps), No 10 Ilfracombe (late 14th Corps). Under General Order 106 of September 1886 the corps was re-designated as 1st Volunteer (Devonshire) Brigade Western Division Royal Artillery, this being changed (Army Order 443) in 1889 to 1st Devonshire Artillery Volunteer Corps (Western Division Royal Artillery). *Territorials:* 4th Wessex Brigade RFA.

**2nd (1859-1871)**—Formed at Sidmouth on 4 September 1859, this corps was later disbanded and was last seen in the Army List for November 1871.

**2nd (1880-1908)**—Formed by the consolidation of the 2nd Admin Brigade in 1880. Headquarters remained at Devonport and the batteries were organised as follows: No 1 Dartmouth (late 6th Corps), No 2 Salcombe (late 10th Corps), Nos 3 to 6 Devonport Docks (late 12th Corps), Nos 7 and 8 Keyham (late 13th Corps). Re-designated as 2nd Volunteer (Devonshire) Brigade Western Division Royal Artillery by General Order 106 of September 1886, this being changed to 2nd Devonshire Artillery Volunteer Corps (Western Division Royal Artillery) in 1889 (Army Order 443). In 1900 a cadet corps was formed and affiliated by the Plymouth and Mannamead College, but this company was transferred to the 2nd Volunteer Battalion of the Devonshire Regiment in 1907. *Territorials:* Devonshire RGA.

**3rd**—Formed at Teignmouth 15 November 1859 and provided No 3 Battery of the new 1st Corps in 1880.

**4th**—Formed at Torquay 15 February 1860 and provided No 4 Battery of the new 1st Corps in 1880.

**5th**—Formed at Exeter 8 February 1860 and provided Nos 5 and 6 Batteries of the new 1st Corps in 1880.

**6th**—Formed at Dartmouth 25 January 1860 and provided No 1 Battery of the new 2nd Corps in 1880.

**7th**—Formed on 11 March 1860 and appeared in the Army List as having its headquarters at Weymouth. Exmouth was listed from July 1860, the 7th providing No 7 Battery of the new 1st Corps in 1880.

**8th**—Formed 31 March 1860, the 8th was first show as having its headquarters at Woodbury. A move was made to Topsham in 1861, then to Heavitree in 1875. No 8 Battery of the new 1st Corps was provided in 1880.

**9th**—Formed at Paignton on 2 June 1860 and provided No 9 Battery of the new 1st Corps in 1980.

**10th**—Formed at Salcombe on 7 July 1860 and provided No 2 Battery of the New 2nd Corps in 1880.

**11th**—Formed at Brixham on 20 July 1860 and provided No 2 Battery of the new 1st Corps in 1880.

**12th**—Formed with headquarters at Devonport Dockyard on 20 December 1860 and provided Nos 3 to 6 Batteries of the new 2nd Corps in 1880.

**13th**—Formed at Keyham on 7 December 1860 and provided Nos 7 and 8 Batteries of the new 2nd Corps in 1880.

**14th**—Formed at Ilfracombe on 23 June 1875 and provided No 10 Battery of the new 1st Corps in 1880.

## Engineer Volunteers

**1st**—The 1st Devonshire EVC was formed at Torquay on 28 January 1862 and in August 1869 became part of the 1st Admin Battalion of Gloucestershire Engineer Volunteers having until that date, and from April 1863, been attached to the 1st Devonshire Rifle Volunteer Corps. In 1880 the Gloucester Admin Battalion was consolidated as the 1st Gloucestershire Corps, the Devonshire personnel becoming at the same time its 'E' and 'F' Companies. But 1889 would see Devonshire once more in the Army List within the Engineer Volunteer section. The 1880 merger had also included engineer companies from Somersetshire (Nailsea and Weston-Super-Mare) and these, together with the Devonshire personnel (now recorded as being from Torquay and Exeter), were withdrawn to form a new corps designated 1st Devonshire and Somersetshire. Headquarters were placed at Exeter and the original commissions were dated 15 June 1889. *Territorials:* Wessex Divisional Engineers.

## Rifle Volunteers

A 1st Admin Battalion containing the 2nd, 3rd and 16th Corps first appeared in the Army List for June 1860. In the issue for September, however, there is no mention of a 1st Admin Battalion but instead, four are now listed and numbered as 2nd, 3rd, 4th and 5th. The corps previously shown with the 1st are now forming the 3rd Admin Battalion. By April, however, the four are now shown as 1st, 2nd, 3rd and 4th and it would be these that in 1880 provided four new corps numbered 2nd, 3rd, 4th and 5th.

**1st (Exeter and South Devon)**—The 1st Devonshire RVC is the senior volunteer unit in the United Kingdom, it being the first to be officially recognised by the Government. It was in January 1852 that Superintendant of the Exminster Lunatic Asylum, Dr John Bucknill of Exeter (through Earl Fortescue, the Lord Lieutenant of Devonshire) submitted a proposal to the Secretary of State (Sir George Grey) that a corps of volunteer riflemen be formed in South Devon for the defence of the coast. Subsequently the services of the Exeter and South Devon Rifle Corps were accepted under the Volunteer Act of 1804, the officers' commissions being signed by Queen Victoria on 4 January 1853. When the Volunteer Force got underway proper in 1859, the corps received the title 1st Devonshire (Exeter and South Devon). It absorbed the 24th Corps at Budleigh Salterton in 1860 and later comprised eleven companies after personnel were added at Exmouth, Crediton, Dawlish and Teignmouth (possibly the missing numbers 7th, 12th and 15th were intended for these locations). Exeter School formed an affiliated cadet corps in 1897. Under General Order 114 of 1885, 1st Devonshire was re-designated as 1st (Exeter and South Devon) Volunteer Battalion Devonshire Regiment and transfer to the Territorial Force in 1908 was as part of the 4th Battalion Devonshire Regiment. Exeter School Cadet Corps at the same time became part of the OTC.

In Northernhay Gardens, Exeter there is a small Renaissance pillar commemorating the formation on the 1st Devonshire RVC. The memorial, by local sculptor Harry Hems and erected in 1895, includes plaques recording the names of the first officers to receive commissions, the committee that was responsible for the formation of the corps, and a list of places from where the recruits were drawn—'Exeter, Cullompton, Tiverton, Bovey Tracey, Exmouth, Honiton, Brixham, Torquay, Totnes.'

**2nd (1859-1880)**—Formed as one company at the market town, naval base and seaport of Plymouth with Captain Charles Duperrier commissioned on 7 December 1859. No 2 Company was formed in February 1860. Joined the 2nd Admin Battalion, absorbed the 16th Corps of two companies at Stonehouse in 1874, increased by a further two companies in 1868, and became 'A' to 'F' Companies of the new 2nd Corps in 1880.

**2nd (1880-1908)**—The 2nd Admin Battalion was formed with headquarters at Plymouth in 1860 and to it were added the 2nd, 3rd, 16th and 22nd Corps. The battalion was consolidated in 1880 as the 2nd (Prince of Wales's) Corps with eleven companies: 'A' to 'F' Plymouth (late 2nd Corps), 'G' to 'I' Devonport (late 3rd Corps), 'K' and 'L' Tavistock (late 22nd Corps).

Designated 2nd (Prince of Wales's) Volunteer Battalion Devonshire Regiment under General Order 114 of 1885 and increased to twelve companies in 1900. Reduced to eight, however, in 1905. The former 3rd Corps cadet unit disappeared from the Army List in 1885, but Kelly College at Tavistock provided a company in 1894 and in 1906 the Army List indicates that the Postal Telegraph Messengers of Plymouth had been formed. This, though, disappeared in July 1907. The Plymouth and Mannamead College Cadet Corps transferred from the 2nd Devonshire RGA (Vols) in 1907. *Territorials:* Transfer to the Territorial Force in 1908 was as part of 5th (Prince of Wales's) Battalion Devonshire Regiment. The cadets at Kelly College and Plymouth and Mannamead College at the same time joined the OTC.

**3rd (1859-1880)**—Formed as one company at Devonport with Captain John Beer and Lieutenant William Clark commissioned on 7 December 1859. No 2 Company was formed on 1 March 1860. Joined the 2nd Admin Battalion. A cadet corps was formed and attached in 1874 and a third company added by 1871. Became 'G' to 'I' Companies of the new 2nd Corps in 1880.

**3rd (1880-1908)**—The 1st Admin Battalion was formed with headquarters at Exeter in 1860 and to it were added the 5th, 8th, 11th, 13th, 14th, 20th, 25th and 27th Corps. The battalion was consolidated as the new 3rd Corps in 1880 with seven companies: 'A' Cullompton (late 5th Corps), 'B' Buckerell (late 8th Corps), 'C' Bampton (late 11th Corps), 'D' Honiton (late 13th Corps), 'E' Tiverton (late 14th Corps), 'F' Ottery St Mary (late 25th Corps), 'G' Colyton (late 27th Corps).

The corps was designated 3rd Volunteer Battalion Devonshire Regiment under General Order 114 of November 1885. That same year a new company ('H') was added at Sidmouth, followed in 1900 by 'I' at Axminster. Cadet corps were formed and affiliated at All Hallows School in Honiton and at Blundell's School, Tiverton in 1900. *Territorials:* Transfer to the Territorial Force in 1908 was as part of 4th Battalion Devonshire Regiment, both All Hallows and Blundell's Schools at the same time joining the OTC.

**4th (1860-1872)**—Formed at the market town and seaport of Ilfracombe with Captain Nathan Vye, Lieutenant William Broderick and Ensign Henry Camp commissioned on 3 March 1860. Joined the 3rd Admin Battalion, disappearing from the Army List in December 1872.

**4th (1880-1908)**—The 3rd Admin Battalion was formed with headquarters at Barnstaple in 1860 and to it were added the 4th, 6th, 18th, 21st and 28th Corps. The battalion was consolidated in 1880 as the new 4th Corps with seven companies: 'A' and 'B' Barnstaple (late 6th Corps), 'C' Hatherleigh (late 18th Corps), 'D' Okehampton (late 18th Corps), 'E' Bideford (late 21st Corps), 'F' Torrington (late 21st Corps), 'G' South Molton

**1st Devonshire Rifle Volunteer Corps.**

PLAYER'S CIGARETTES

THE EXETER & SOUTH DEVON
VOLUNTEER RIFLE CORPS, 1852

(late 28th Corps).

Designated as 4th Volunteer Battalion Devonshire Regiment under General Order 114 of November 1885; an additional two companies, one each at Buckfastleigh and Torquay, were sanctioned in 1886. The United Services College Cadet Corps at Westward Ho! was formed and attached in 1900 but, having moved to Harpenden in 1904, its affiliation was transferred to the 2nd Volunteer Battalion Bedfordshire Regiment. *Territorials:* Transfer to the Territorial Force in 1908 was as 6th Battalion Devonshire Regiment.

**5th (1860-1880)**—Formed at Upper Culm Vale with Captain John W Walrond, Lieutenant R Collins and Ensign J G Sydenham commissioned on 22 March 1860. Joined the 1st Admin Battalion, headquarters moving to Cullompton twelve miles north-east of Exeter in 1862 and became 'A' Company of the new 3rd Corps in 1880.

**5th (1880-1908)**—The 4th Admin Battalion was formed with headquarters at Totnes in 1860 and to it were added the 9th, 10th, 17th, 23rd, 26th and 28th Corps. Headquarters moved to Newton Abbot in 1865. A cadet corps was formed and affiliated to the battalion in 1871, but this was not shown in the Army List after 1875. Consolidated in 1880 was as the new 5th Corps with six companies: 'A' Ashburton (late 9th Corps), 'B' Newton Abbot (late 10th Corps), 'C' Totnes (late 17th Corps), 'D' Chudleigh (late 23rd Corps), 'E' Kingsbridge (late 26th Corps), 'F' Torquay (late 26th Corps).

Designated as 5th (The Hay Tor) Volunteer Battalion Devonshire Regiment under General Order 114 of November 1885. *Territorials:* Part of 5th Battalion Devonshire Regiment.

**6th**—Formed at Barnstaple with Captain Robert Wyllie, Lieutenant Edward B Savile and Ensign John May Miller holding commissions dated 23 February 1860. Joined the 3rd Admin Battalion and became 'A' and 'B' Companies of the new 4th Corps in 1880.

**7th**—None recorded.

**8th**—Formed at Buckerell on the River Otter with Captain William Porter, Lieutenant the Hon Colin Lindsey and Ensign George Newman commissioned on 8 February 1860. Joined the 1st Admin Battalion and became 'B' Company of the new 3rd Corps in 1880.

**9th**—Formed as one company at Ashburton on the River Yeo with Captain Thomas Eales Rogers, Lieutenant Robert Coard Tucker and Ensign William Richard Coulton commissioned on 23 February 1860. Joined the 4th Admin Battalion and became 'A' Company of the new 5th Corps in 1880.

**10th**—Formed at Newton Abbot with Captain G H S Yates, Lieutenant Francis Young and Ensign Cyrus W Croft commissioned on 27 March 1860. Joined the 4th Admin Battalion and became 'B' Company of the new 5th Corps in 1880.

**11th**—Formed at Bampton with Captain Glyn Grylls and Lieutenant Charles S M Phillips holding commissions dated 28 February 1860. Joined the 1st Admin Battalion and became 'C' Company of the new 3rd Corps in 1880.

**12th**—None recorded.

**13th**—Formed at Honiton with Captain Horace V Mules, Lieutenant John H Jerrard and Ensign J R Rogers commissioned on 20 February 1860. Joined the 1st Admin Battalion and became 'D' Company of the new 3rd Corps in 1880. All Hallows School, which formed a cadet corps affiliated to the 3rd Volunteer Battalion Devonshire Regiment in 1900, moved from Honiton to Rousdon in 1938, a schoolroom (All Hallows Chapel by St Paul's Church) remains in the town as a museum.

**14th**—Formed at Tiverton with Captain John H Amory, Lieutenant F Dunsford and Ensign George Mackenzie commissioned on 1 March 1860. Joined the 1st Admin Battalion and became 'E' Company of the new 3rd Corps in 1880. The Drill Hall and Armoury, with a house next door for the Sergeant Instructor, was built in 1884.

**15th**—None recorded.

**16th**—Formed at Stonehouse close to Plymouth, with Captain Viscount Valletort, Lieutenant Richard M Dunn and Ensign Richard R Rodd commissioned on 29 February 1860. Joined the 2nd Admin Battalion and was absorbed into the 2nd Corps in 1874.

**17th**—William Ruston took command of the 17th Corps formed at Totnes on the west bank of the Dart on 3 March 1860. Joined the 4th Admin Battalion and became 'C' Company of the new 5th Corps on 1880.

**18th**—Lieutenant Lewis P Madden and Ensign Chomeley Morris, both commissioned on 1 March 1860, were the first officers gazetted to the 18th Corps which was formed at the market town of Hatherleigh in North Devon. Joined the 3rd Admin Battalion and became 'C' and 'D' Companies of the new 4th Corps in 1880.

**19th**—Formed at Okehampton but disappeared from the Army List in February 1861 having had two officers appointed—Lieutenant William Hunt Holly and Ensign Richard Hodges. Both held commissions dated 3 March 1860.

**20th**—Formed at Broadhembury, just over five miles north-west of Honiton, with Edward Drew of Hembury Grange as lieutenant, and William B Henderson, ensign. Both held commissions dated 3 March 1860. Joined the 1st Admin Battalion and was disbanded in 1875. At St Andrew's church there are several memorials to members of the Drewe family, Albert C R Drewe being gazetted lieutenant to the 20th Corps on 13 March 1865. In the village the 'Drew Arms' can be found still.

**21st**—Formed at the market town and seaport of Bideford with Captain T G Harding, Lieutenant R Reynolds and Ensign W R Keats commissioned on 6 March 1860. Joined the 3rd Admin Battalion and became 'E' and 'F' Companies of the new 4th Corps in 1880.

**22nd**—Formed at Tavistock, fifteen miles north of Plymouth, on 5 March 1860 with E B Gould appointed as captain. Joined the 2nd Admin Battalion and became 'K' and 'L' Companies of the new 2nd Corps in 1880. Kelly College, on a hill overlooking Dartmoor, was founded in 1867, a cadet corps being formed there in 1894 and affiliated to the 2nd Volunteer Battalion Devonshire Regiment. Cassel's *Gazetteer* for 1898 notes that rooms at The New Hall, built on the site of an old abbey, were then being used 'as an armoury by the Volunteers'.

**23rd**—Formed at Chudleigh, ten miles south-west of Exeter, with Lieutenant G A Ferreira and Ensign Charles Archibald Langley commissioned on 27 March 1860. Joined the 4th Admin Battalion and became 'D' Company of the new 5th Corps in 1880.

**24th**—Formed at Budleigh Salterton with Captain Frederick Blandy, Lieutenant George Peters Neave and Ensign Francis Richard Hole commissioned on 28 March 1860. Absorbed into the 1st Corps the same year.

**25th**—Formed at Ottery St Mary, Surgeon Charles William Whittry being the first officer listed with a commission dated 2 March 1860. Joined the 1st Admin Battalion and became 'F' Company of the new 3rd Corps in 1880.

**26th**—Formed at Kingsbridge with Lieutenant H Square (commission dated 5 July 1860) the first officer appointed. Joined the 4th Admin Battalion and became 'E' and 'F' Companies of the new 5th Corps in 1880.

**27th**—Formed at Colyton, just over four miles south-west of Axminster, with Lieutenant James John H Cottle commissioned on 7 December 1860. Joined the 1st Admin Battalion and became 'G' Company of the new 3rd Corps in 1880.

**28th (1861-1865)**—Formed at Lynton, east of Ilfracombe, with Robert Roe commissioned as lieutenant on 13 April 1861. Joined the 3rd Admin Battalion in 1863 and disbanded 1865.

**28th (1868-1875)**—Formed at South Brent, on the Avon seven miles west of Totnes, with Captain James Westhead commissioned on 14 October 1868. Joined the 4th Admin Battalion and disbanded 1875.

**28th (1876-1880)**—Formed at South Molton, twelve miles south-east of Barnstaple with Captain William H Brewer commissioned on 8 March 1876. Joined the 3rd Admin Battalion and became 'G' Company of the new 4th Corps in 1880.

# Dorsetshire

## Artillery Volunteers

The several corps formed during 1859 and 1860 were at first shown in the Army List as being 'united' to the 1st Hampshire Admin Brigade, but that for January 1866 shows them as part of that for Devonshire. With two new corps formed, the Dorsetshire Artillery Volunteers were in 1873 transferred back to Hampshire.

**1st (1859-1880)**—Formed at Lyme Regis on 29 December 1859 and provided No 15 Battery of the new 1st Hampshire AVC in 1880.

**1st (1886-1908)**—Formed by the removal of the Dorsetshire batteries from the 1st Hampshire AVC, the first officers being gazetted on 1 April 1886. Headquarters were first show as Portland, but Weymouth was listed by July 1886. Under General Order 106 of September 1886 the new corps was re-designated as 2nd Volunteer (Dorsetshire) Brigade Southern Division Royal Artillery then in 1889 (Army Order 443) 1st Dorsetshire AVC (Southern Division Royal Artillery). Towards the end of 1890 the personnel from around the Portland area were separated from the main corps and formed into their own. The new unit was designated as 2nd Dorsetshire AVC, but after just under four years the men were returned to the 1st. *Territorials:* The 6th Hampshire Battery and Dorsetshire Battery of the 3rd Wessex Brigade RFA and Dorsetshire RGA.

**2nd (1860-1861)**—Formed at Portland on 14 February 1860 and in November of the following year was absorbed into the 4th Corps.

**2nd (1890-1894)**—Towards the end of 1890 the 1st Corps personnel from around the Portland area were withdrawn to form a new 2nd Corps, its first officers being gazetted on 17 January 1891. Lasting for just under four years, the 2nd was disbanded, its members being absorbed back into the 1st Corps.

**3rd**—Formed at Bridport on 8 February 1860 and disbanded in 1876.

**4th**—Formed at Portland on 20 November 1860 and in the following year absorbed the 2nd Corps. Provided No 16 Battery and, with the 6th Corps, No 17 Battery of the new 1st Hampshire AVC in 1880.

**5th**—Formed at Charmouth on 31 January 1868 and provided No 18 Battery of the new 1st Hampshire AVC in 1880.

**6th**—Formed at Swanage on 28 April 1869 and, together with part of the 4th Corps, provided No 17 Battery of the new 1st Hampshire AVC in 1880.

**Officers' pouch, Dorsetshire Artillery Volunteers, c1879.**

**Officers' pouch, Dorsetshire Artillery Volunteers, c1891.**

## Rifle Volunteers

All corps joined the county's 1st Admin Battalion which formed the new 1st Corps in 1880.

**1st (1859-1880)**—Formed at Bridport, eighteen miles west of Dorchester with Lieutenant Henry Saunders Edwards commissioned on 22 August 1859. Became 'A' Company of the new 1st Corps in 1880.

**1st (1880-1908)**—The 1st Admin Battalion was formed with headquarters at

Dorchester on 9 May 1860 and consolidated as the new 1st Corps in 1880 with eleven companies: 'A' Bridport (late 1st Corps), 'B' Wareham (late 2nd Corps), 'C' Dorchester (late 3rd Corps), 'D' Poole (late 4th Corps), 'E' Weymouth (late 5th Corps), 'F' Wimborne (late 6th Corps), 'G' Sherborne (late 7th Corps), 'H' Blandford (late 8th Corps), 'I' Shaftesbury (late 9th Corps), 'K' Stalbridge (late 10th Corps), 'L' Gillingham (late 11th Corps).

Re-designated as 1st Volunteer Battalion Dorsetshire Regiment under General Order 181 of December 1887. A service company from the battalion served with the 2nd Dorsetshire Regiment in South Africa and saw action at Alleman's Nek on 11 June 1900—'I was much pleased with their action', noted General Buller in his despatch of 19 June. The general also said of Captain H L Kitson who commanded the volunteers, 'he has proved himself thoroughly capable of taking any position his rank requires.' The Sherborne School Cadet Corps was affiliated in 1888 and the County School Cadet Corps at Dorchester in 1893. The latter, however, was removed from the Army List in January 1897. *Territorials:* 4th Battalion Dorsetshire Regiment, Sherborne School joining the OTC.

**2nd**—Formed at Wareham, seventeen miles south-east of Dorchester, with Oliver William Farrer as captain, William Charles Lacey, lieutenant and Charles James Radclyfle, ensign. All three officers held commissions dated 28 January 1860. Became 'B' Company of the new 1st Corps in 1880.

**3rd**—Formed at Dorchester with Edward Leigh Kindersley as captain, Thomas Coombs, lieutenant and Robert Devenish, ensign. All three held commissions dated 14 February 1860. Became 'C' Company of the new 1st Corps in 1880.

**4th**—Formed at Poole with Captain William Parr, Lieutenant Thomas Cox and Ensign George B Aldridge commissioned on 13 February 1860. Became 'D' Company of the new 1st Corps in 1880.

**5th**—Formed at the Georgian seaside resort of Weymouth with Lieutenant George Poulter Welsford and Ensign John Thresher commissioned on 14 May 1860. Became 'E' Company of the new 1st Corps in 1880.

**6th**—Formed at Wimborne, six miles north of Poole, with Captain St John Coventry, Lieutenant Thomas Rawlings and Ensign Edward Robinson commissioned on 14 March 1860. Became 'F' Company of the new 1st Corps in 1880.

**7th**—Formed at Sherborne, six miles east of Yeovil, with Captain John Frederick Falwasser, Lieutenant John George Bergman and Ensign John Young Melmoth commissioned on 29 March 1860. Became 'G' Company of the new 1st Corps in 1880. Sherborne School formed a cadet corps in 1888. Long associated with Sherborne, the Digby family of Sherborne Castle, have numerous monuments in the town, the Rev Richard H W Digby being made chaplain to the 7th Corps in 1868.

**8th**—Formed at Blandford, sixteen miles north-east of Dorchester, with George P Mansel as captain, Robert C Farquharson, lieutenant and Francis T John, ensign. All three officers held commissions dated 29 February 1860. Became 'H' Company of the new 1st Corps in 1880.

**9th**—Formed at Shaftesbury on the Wiltshire border with Thomas B Bower, who had previously served with the 73rd Regiment of Foot, as captain, William E Barridge, lieutenant and William R H Bennett, ensign. All three officers held commissions dated 10 March 1860. Became 'I' Company of the new 1st Corps in 1880.

**10th (Blackmoor Vale)**—Formed at Sturminster Newton on the banks of the Stour with Lieutenant

**10th Dorsetshire Rifle Volunteer Corps.**

43

Montague Williams and Ensign Henry C Dashwood commissioned on 10 July 1860. Absorbed the 12th Corps at Stalbridge towards the end of 1876. Headquarters had moved to Stalbridge by April of the following year and at the same time Blackmoor Vale was added to title. Blackmoor Vale is the valley of the River Cale and is situated on the borders of Somerset and Dorset extending south-east from Wincanton. Became 'K' Company of the new 1st Corps in 1880.

**11th**—Formed at Gillingham, on the Stour where it joins the Lidden, with Lieutenant Robert S Freame commissioned on 7 July 1860. Became 'L' Company of the new 1st Corps in 1880. The Vicarage was built in 1883, home, possibly, to the Rev George Glover who became chaplain to the 11th Corps in 1877.

**12th**—Formed at Stalbridge, close to the Somerset border, with Lieutenant John R Lyon and Ensign Henry W Langton commissioned on 7 July 1860. Absorbed into the 10th Corps towards the end of 1876.

# Durham

## Artillery Volunteers

**1st (1860-1880)**—Formed at Sunderland on 14 March 1860 and in 1863 was attached for administration to the 2nd Corps until transfer to the 1st Northumberland Admin Brigade in 1873. Became Nos 13, 14 and 15 Batteries of the new 1st Northumberland AVC in 1880.

**1st (1888-1908)**—Formed in 1888 by the removal of the Durham Batteries from the 1st Northumberland AVC. The title was change in 1889 (Army Order 443) adding the sub-title Western Division Royal Artillery. By 1890 the corps consisted of eight batteries, two of which were later amalgamated as No 1 Position Battery. Headquarters of all batteries, except No 6 which was at Southwick, were in Sunderland. *Territorials:* Part of the Durham RGA.

**2nd**—Formed on 14 March 1860 at Seaham, becoming part of the 1st Northumberland Admin Brigade in 1873. Four new batteries were added from the West Rainton area 1868 (see 5th Corps) and by 1870 the 2nd Corps comprised batteries at Silksworth, West Rainton and Old Durham as well as Seaham—twelve in total. Two batteries were later merged as position artillery and that at Old Durham was moved to

Gilesgate. In 1900 a new company was formed at Gilesgate which in the following year was moved to Brandon. A cadet corps was also raised at Seaham in September 1898, but this was disbanded in 1903. Western Division Royal Artillery was added to the title in 1889 (Army Order 443). *Territorials:* 1st and 2nd Durham Batteries and Ammunition Column of the 3rd Northumbrian Brigade RFA.

**3rd**—Formed at South Shields on 14 March 1860. Absorbed the 6th Corps, also at South Shield, as No 2 Battery in 1863. Four additional batteries were later raised, the corps adding Western Division Royal Artillery to its title in 1889 (Army Order 443). *Territorials:* 4th Durham (Howitzer) Battery and Ammunition Column of the 4th Northumbrian (Howitzer) Brigade RFA.

**4th**—Formed at West Hartlepool on 14 March 1860, two of its eight batteries (Nos 4 and 5) being merged as No 1 Position Battery in 1890. The establishment was increased to one position battery and eight garrison companies in 1900, Western Division Royal Artillery being added to the title by Army Order 443 of 1889. *Territorials:* 3rd Durham Battery of the 3rd Northumbrian Brigade RFA and four companies of the Durham RGA.

**Pouch-belt badge, 3rd Durham Artillery Volunteers.**

**5th**—A 5th Corps of four batteries was shown as having been formed in the Army List for January 1869. It was recorded as having headquarters at West Rainton, but no officers were gazetted. Subsequently, by the following June, the volunteers were placed into the 2nd Corps.

**6th**—Formed at South Shields, merging with the 3rd Corps as its No 2 Battery in 1863.

## Engineer Volunteers

**1st**—The 1st Durham EVC was formed at Jarrow on 28 March 1868 and had attached to it in January of the following year the 1st Newcastle-Upon-Tyne EVC. Then, in May 1874, the two were grouped together under the title of 1st Admin Battalion of Durham Engineer Volunteers. Consolidation came in 1880, the original title being 1st Durham and Newcastle-Upon-Tyne. This, however, was amended by January 1881 to 1st Newcastle-Upon-Tyne and Durham, therefore recognising the seniority of the former. Establishment was set at thirteen companies of which 'A' to 'E' were provided by the old 1st Newcastle Corps, 'F' to 'M' by Durham. The year 1888 saw yet further reorganisation. There were seven Durham companies by now, sufficient, it was thought, to constitute a corps in their own right. Subsequently the first officers of a new 1st Durham were commissioned on 17 November of that year. *Territorials:* Durham (Fortress) Engineers.

## Rifle Volunteers

The county formed four admin battalions which were consolidated in 1880 to form four new corps numbered 1st, 2nd, 4th and 5th. All pre-1880 corps were included, save for the 3rd which was of sufficient strength to remain independent.

**1st (1860-1880)**—Formed as two companies at Stockton-on-Tees with Captains Robert Thompson and John James Wilson commissioned on 27 February 1860. Joined the 2nd Admin Battalion, transferred to 4th Admin in 1862, and became 'A' to 'C' Companies of the new 1st Corps in 1880.

**1st (1880-1908)**—The 4th Admin Battalion of Durham Rifle Volunteers was formed on 1 February 1862 with headquarters at Stockton-on-Tees and include the 1st, 15th, 16th and 19th Corps. The 21st Yorkshire (North Riding) RVC was added in 1877. The battalion was consolidated as the new 1st Corps in 1880 with eight companies: 'A' to 'C' Stockton-on-Tees (late 1st Corps), 'D' and 'E' Darlington (late 15th Corps), 'F' Castle Eden (late 16th Corps), 'G' and 'H' Middlesbrough (late 21st Yorkshire North Riding Corps).

General Order 181 of December 1887 directed a change in designation to 1st Volunteer Battalion Durham Light Infantry. Four new companies were added; 'I' Stockton, 'K' Darlington, 'L' Middlesbrough and 'M' (Cyclist) Stockton in 1900. *Territorials:* 5th Battalion Durham Light Infantry.

**2nd**—Durham's 2nd Admin Battalion was formed with headquarters at Bishop Auckland in December 1860 and to it were added the 1st, 4th, 12th, 15th, 16th, 17th, 18th, 19th, 20th and 21st Corps. In February 1862, the 1st, 15th, 16th and 19th were transferred to the 4th Admin Battalion, 2nd Admin being consolidated in 1880 as 2nd Corps with six companies: 'A' Bishop Auckland (late No 1 Company 4th Corps), 'B' Coundon (late No 2 Company 4th Corps). 'C' Darlington (late No 3 Company 4th Corps), 'D' Middleton-in-Teesdale (late 12th Corps), 'E' Stanhope (late 20th Corps), 'F' Barnard Castle (late 21st Corps).

**Pouch-belt badge, 3rh Durham Rifle Volunteers.**

In 1883 'C' Company was moved to Woodland. 'G' and 'H' Companies were added at Spennymore in 1886, then under General Order 181 of December 1887, 2nd Corps became 2nd Volunteer Battalion Durham Light Infantry. 'D' Company was disbanded in 1899 and a new 'D' formed at Crook the same year. 'I' (Cyclist) Company at Bishop Auckland, 'K' and 'L' at Consett were added in 1900, 'C' moving yet again, this time to Shildon, in 1903. *Territorials:* 6th Battalion Durham Light Infantry.

**3rd (The Sunderland)**—The 3rd Corps was formed at Sunderland on 6 March 1860 and included six companies by 1862 with Major Lord Adolphus Vane Tempest in command. The sub-title The Sunderland was authorised in 1867. The corps became 3rd (Sunderland) Volunteer Battalion Durham Light Infantry in 1887, the change being notified in General Order 181 of December. A new company was added in 1900. *Territorials:* 7th Battalion Durham Light Infantry. Cassell's *Gazetteer* for 1898 notes that the Corn Market was then held on Saturdays at the Garrison Drill Hall.

**4th (1860-1880)**—Formed as one company at Bishop Auckland with Captain William Trotter commissioned on 24 May 1860. Joined the 2nd Admin Battalion. No 2 Company was soon added at Coundon, two miles south east of Bishop Auckland, followed in 1865 by No 3 at Shildon. The latter, however, moved to Darlington in 1872. Became 'A' to 'C' Companies of the new 2nd Corps in 1880.

**4th (1880-1908)**—The 1st Admin Battalion was formed with headquarters at Durham in October 1860 and to it were added the 7th, 10th, 11th, 13th and 14th Corps. Headquarters were moved to Chester-le-Street in 1862 and the battalion was consolidated in 1880 as the new 4th Corps with ten companies: 'A' to 'C' Durham (late 7th Corps), 'D' Beamish (late 10th Corps), 'E' Chester-le-Street (late 11th Corps), 'F' Birtley (late No 1 Company, 13th Corps), 'G' Washington (late No 2 Company, 13th Corps), 'H', 'I' and 'K' Felling (late 14th Corps).

Under General Order 181 of December 1887 4th Durham RVC was re-designated as 4th Volunteer Battalion Durham Light Infantry. Headquarters moved to Durham in 1890, 'K' Company being disbanded in 1892 with a new 'K' added at Stanley. 'H' and 'I' Companies were amalgamated as 'H' in 1896, the 'I' position being taken up by a new company raised at Sacriston. 'H' Company transferred to the 5th Volunteer Battalion DLI as its 'L' Company in 1897 and at the same time a new 'H' was formed at Houghton-le-Spring. 'L' (Cyclist) Company was added at Stanley in 1900. *Territorials:* Transfer to the Territorial Force in 1908 was as 8th Battalion Durham Light Infantry. 'C' Company, however, joined the OTC as part of the Durham University contingent.

**5th**—The 3rd Admin Battalion of Durham Rifle Volunteers was formed with headquarters at Gateshead in May 1861 and to it were added the 6th, 8th and 9th Corps. The battalion was consolidated as the new 5th Corps in 1880 with eight companies: 'A' to 'C' Gateshead (late 8th Corps), 'D' to 'F' South Shields (late 6th Corps), 'G' Blaydon Burn (late No 1 Company, 9th Corps), 'H' Winlaton (late No 2 Company, 9th Corps).

The corps was designated as 5th Volunteer Battalion Durham Light Infantry by General Order 181 of December 1887. Two new companies had been added by 1887 and the battalion was subsequently reorganised as follows: 'A' to 'D' Companies at Gateshead, 'E' to 'G' Companies South Shields, 'H' Company Blaydon, 'I' and 'K' Companies Winlaton.

In 1897 'H' Company of the 4th Volunteer Battalion DLI at Felling was transferred to the 5th Volunteer Battalion as its 'L' Company. 'M' (Cyclist) Company was formed at Blaydon in 1900. *Territorials:* 9th Battalion.

**6th (1860-1863)**—Formed as one company at South Shields, on the south bank of the Tyne, with Captain John Williamson, Lieutenant Charles W Anderson and Ensign Cuthbert Young commissioned on 20 March 1860. Joined the 3rd Admin Battalion. Converted to artillery in December 1863 and was absorbed into the 3rd Durham AVC.

**6th (1867-1880)**—Formed at Tyne Docks, South Shields, under the command of Captain George Russell whose commission was dated 8 August 1867. Joined the 3rd Admin Battalion and became 'D' to 'F' Companies of the new 5th Corps in 1880.

**7th**—Formed at Durham with Captain John Fogg Elliott and Lieutenant James Monks commissioned on

24 March 1860. Joined the 1st Admin Battalion and became 'A' to 'C' Companies of the new 4th Corps in 1880.

**8th**—Formed as two companies at Gateshead with Captain George H L Hawkes and Captain Stephen W Hawkes as company commanders. Both officers held commissions dated 14 March 1860. Joined the 3rd Admin Battalion, later added a third company, and became 'A' to 'C' Companies of the new 5th Corps in 1880.

**9th**—Formed as one company at Blaydon, five miles west of Gateshead, with Captain J Cowen commissioned on 3 May 1860. Joined the 3rd Admin Battalion. Headquarters moved to Blaydon Burn suburb in 1862, No 2 Company being formed at Winlaton in 1864. Became 'G' and 'H' Companies of the new 5th Corps in 1880.

**10th**—Formed at Beamish with Captain John Joicey, Lieutenant Nathaniel Clark and Ensign George Bolton commissioned on 12 May 1860. Joined the 1st Admin Battalion and became 'D' Company of the new 4th Corps in 1880.

**11th**—Formed at Chester-le-Street with Captain Patrick S Reid, Lieutenant Thomas H Murray and Ensign Robert F Gibson commissioned on 5 June 1860. Joined the 1st Admin Battalion and became 'E' Company of the new 4th Corps in 1880. Much of the corps was recruited from the Pelton Colliery.

**12th**—Formed as one company at Middleton-in-Teesdale with Captain Robert W Bainbridge, Lieutenant John Elliott and Ensign John Sherlock commissioned on 14 July 1860. The corps was formed mainly from employees of the London Lead Company. Joined the 2nd Admin Battalion and became 'D' Company of the 2nd Corps in 1880.

**13th**—Formed as one company at Birtley with Captain Edward M Perkins, Lieutenant Augustus H Hunt and Ensign Isaac L Bell commissioned on 17 August 1860. Joined the 1st Admin Battalion. No 2 Company was later formed at Washington. Became 'F' and 'G' Companies of the new 4th Corps in 1880. Ensign Bell's family were the great iron masters of the area.

**14th**—Formed as one company at Felling with Captain William W Pattison, Lieutenant John Foster and Ensign John M Redmayne commissioned on 31 October 1860. Joined the 1st Admin Battalion, increased later to three companies, and became 'H', 'I' and 'K' Companies of the new 4th Corps in 1880.

**15th**—Formed at Darlington with Captain George J Sairfield commissioned on 6 October 1860. Joined the 2nd Admin Battalion, transferred to the 4th in 1862, and became 'D' and 'E' Companies of the new 1st Corps in 1880.

**16th**—Formed as one company at Castle Eden with Captain Robert C Bewicke, Lieutenant Robert Wilson and Ensign C H Johnstone commissioned on 14 December 1860. Joined the 2nd Admin Battalion, transferred to the 4th in 1862, and became 'F' Company of the new 1st Corps in 1880.

**17th**—Formed as one company at Wolsingham with Captain Thomas H Bates, Lieutenant John P Dolphin and Ensign William Nicholson commissioned on 24 November 1860. Joined the 2nd Admin Battalion and disbanded in 1866.

**18th**—Formed as one company at Shotley Bridge with Captain Jonathan B Richardson, Lieutenant Thomas Richardson and Ensign Charles Janson commissioned on 1 December 1860. Joined the 2nd Admin Battalion and disbanded in July 1865.

**19th**—Formed as one company at Hartlepool with Captain George William Jaffrey, Lieutenant Peter Barr and Ensign Archibald Wilson commissioned on 26 January 1861. Joined the 2nd Admin Battalion, transferred to the 4th in 1862, and was disbanded in November 1872.

**20th**—Formed as one company at Stanhope with Captain John Joseph Roddam, Lieutenant Richard Cordner and Ensign William Christopher Arnison commissioned on 19 February 1861. Joined the 2nd Admin Battalion and became 'E' Company of the new 2nd Corps in 1880.

**21st**—Formed at Startforth as the 7th Yorkshire (North Riding) RVC on 29 February 1860 and attached to the 4th Durham Admin Battalion in November 1863. In the following month, however, 7th Yorks (North Riding) moved to Barnard Castle, was placed into the 2nd Durham Admin Battalion and at the same time re-titled as 21st Durham RVC. Became 'F' Company of the 2nd Corps in 1880.

# Essex

## Artillery Volunteers

**1st (1860-1880)**—Formed at Harwich on 18 February 1860 and until September appeared in the Army List as 2nd Corps. A cadet corps was formed in December 1876. The 1st had been attached to the 1st Norfolk Admin Brigade and in 1880 provided No 5 Battery of the new 1st Norfolk AVC in 1880. But before the end of the year, and unhappy with its new position, the 1st returned to Essex as No 1 Battery of the new 1st Corps.

**1st (1880-1908)**—Formed in 1880 by the amalgamation of the 2nd and 3rd Corps. Headquarters were placed at Stafford and the new corps had an establishment of nine batteries. This was increased to ten by the end of 1880 when the former 1st Corps, then No 5 Battery of the 1st Norfolk AVC, requested to return to an Essex corps. With its seniority in mind, it came in as No 1 Battery. The new 1st Corps batteries were then reorganised as No 1 Harwich (late 1st Corps), No 2 Barking (late 2nd Corps), Nos 3 to 10 Stratford (late 3rd Corps). The Harwich Cadet Corps remained attached until its disbandment in 1884.

**Officers' waist-belt clasp, Essex Artillery Volunteers.**

Under General Order 106 of September 1886 the 1st Essex was re-designated as 2nd Volunteer (Essex) Brigade Eastern Division Royal Artillery. This, however, was change back to the former 1st Essex AVC three years later but with the additional Eastern Division Royal Artillery. By 1899 there were two batteries located at Harwich and in April these were removed to form a new corps designated as 1st Suffolk and Harwich—see under that name. *Territorials:* 2nd East Anglian Brigade RFA, five companies of the Essex and Suffolk RGA and the East Anglian (Essex) RGA.

**2nd**—Formed at Barking in April 1860 and until

**Band, 1st Essex Artillery Volunteer Corps, 1906.**

48

September appeared in the Army List as 3rd Corps. Headquarters were given as Grays after November 1860. Provided No 2 Battery of the new 1st Corps in 1880.

**3rd**—Formed at Plaistow on 26 June 1861, headquarters moving to Stratford in 1864. Provided Nos 3 to 10 Batteries of the new 1st Corps in 1880.

## Engineer Volunteers

**1st**—Formed at Weybridge on 24 December 1861, the corps was, however, disbanded in 1871 and was not shown in the Army List after June of that year.

## Mounted Rifle Volunteers

**1st**—W Y Carman records that a meeting was held at Thorpe-le-Soken on 29 December 1859 to consider the formation of a mounted corps of volunteers to be known as the East Essex Volunteer Mounted Corps. Recognition came for the corps, the title to be 1st Essex Mounted Rifle Volunteers, in January 1861. But by this time interest had waned and although the Army List showed the corps as being at Latchington with posts of a lieutenant and ensign, these were never filled and subsequently the corps was disbanded in June 1862.

## Rifle Volunteers

Essex had three admin battalions of which the 2nd, formed with headquarters at Plaistow in June 1860 with the 5th, 8th and 9th Corps, was broken up in 1866. The 1st and 3rd provided the new 2nd and 1st Corps respectively in 1880. Two sub-divisions, both numbered as 1st, appeared in the Army Lists and these can be seen under 6th and 10th Corps.

**1st (1860-1880)**—Formed at Romford with Captain Alfred Hamilton commissioned on 16 February 1860. Joined the 1st Admin Battalion, transferring to 3rd Admin Battalion in 1861, and became 'A' and 'B' Companies of the new 1st Corps in 1880.

**1st (1880-1908)**—The 3rd Admin Battalion was formed with headquarters at Ilford in July 1861 and to it were added the 1st, 2nd, 3rd, 7th, 15th, 18th, 19th, 21st and 24th Corps. Consolidation in 1880 was as the new 1st Corps with eight companies: 'A' and 'B' Romford (late 1st Corps), 'C' Ilford (late No 1 Company, 2nd Corps), 'D' Barking (late No 2 Company, 2nd Corps), 'E' Walthamstow (late No 3 Company, 2nd Corps), 'F' Brentwood (late 3rd Corps), 'G' Chipping Ongar (late 18th Corps), 'H' Hornchurch (late 15th Corps).

Re-designated as 1st Volunteer Battalion Essex Regiment by General Order 14 of February 1883. Headquarters moved to Brentwood in 1890, two new companies were added in 1896, followed by four more in 1900. Several cadet units have been associated with the battalion: Ongar Grammar School in 1865, then a company raised at Forest School, Walthamstow in May 1883. Chigwell School raised a company in 1900 and three years later a unit at Loughton and Buckhurst Hill appeared. *Territorials:* 4th Battalion Essex Regiment. The Forest and Chigwell Schools became contingents of the OTC.

**Sergeant-Major Baker, 4th Volunteer Battalion Essex Regiment.**

**2nd (1859-1880)**—Formed as one company at Ilford with Captain John Coope Davis commissioned on 12 August 1859. Joined the 1st Admin Battalion, transferring to 3rd Admin Battalion in 1861. New companies were later added at Barking and Walthamstow, the three becoming 'C' to 'E' of the new 1st Corps in 1880.

**2nd (1880-1908)**—The 1st Admin Battalion was formed with headquarters at Colchester in June 1860 and to it were added the 4th, 6th, 10th, 11th, 12th, 13th, 14th, 16th, 20th and 23rd Corps. The 1st, 2nd, 3rd and 7th also formed part of the battalion, but these corps transferred to the 3rd Admin Battalion in 1861. Headquarters moved to Chelmsford in February 1862 but transferred to Braintree upon consolidation as the new 2nd Corps in 1880. There were eight companies: 'A' and 'B' Chelmsford (late 4th Corps), 'C' and 'D' Colchester (late 6th Corps), 'E' Witham (late 10th Corps), 'F' Braintree (late 12th Corps), 'G' Maldon (late 23rd Corps), 'H' Walton-on-the-Naze (late 23rd Corps).

Designated as 2nd Volunteer Battalion Essex Regiment under General Order 14 of February 1883 and in 1895 headquarters moved yet again, this time back to Colchester. Two new companies were added in 1900. A cadet corps was formed and affiliated to the 1st Admin Battalion in 1872, but this disappeared from the Army List in October 1880. Felstead School Cadet Corps was affiliated in 1883 and in 1904 the King Edward VI School Cadet Corps was formed at Chelmsford. *Territorials:* 5th Battalion Essex Regiment.

**3rd (1859-1880)**—Formed at Brentwood with Captain Octavius Edward Coope commissioned on 12 October 1859. Joined the 1st Admin Battalion, transferring to 3rd Admin Battalion in 1861. Absorbed the 21st Corps, also at Brentwood, in 1872 and became 'F' Company of the new 1st Corps in 1880.

**3rd (1880-1908)**—Formed at Plaistow as 5th Corps comprising four companies with all officers holding commissions dated 30 January 1860. Much of the corps was recruited from the Royal Victoria Dock, its commanding officer being docks manager, Charles Cooper. Included in the 2nd Admin Battalion until 1866, renumbered as 3rd Corps in 1880, then designated 3rd Volunteer Battalion Essex Regiment in 1883. Headquarters moved to West Ham two years later. The battalion reached an establishment of thirteen companies in 1900 and a cadet corps was formed and affiliated in 1907. *Territorials:* 6th Battalion Essex Regiment.

**4th (1859-1880)**—Formed at Chelmsford with Captain William M Tufnell, Lieutenant John Henry Bringhurst and Ensign Josiah Alfred Hardcastle commissioned on 8 November 1859. Joined the 1st Admin Battalion and became 'A' and 'B' Companies of the new 2nd Corps in 1880.

**4th (1880-1908)**—Formed at Silvertown as 9th Corps on 1 February 1860 and included in the 2nd Admin Battalion until 1866. Renumbered 4th in 1880 and designated 4th Volunteer Battalion Essex Regiment in 1883. Headquarters moved to Leyton in 1900 and in that same year the battalion's establishment was increased to eleven companies. *Territorials:* 7th Battalion Essex Regiment.

**5th**—See 3rd Corps (1880-1908).

**6th**—Formed at Colchester on 8 September 1859 and known as the 1st Sub-division until December. The officers: Captain Sir Claude W C de Crespigny, Lieutenant J Fitzsimmons Bishop and Ensign Henry Egerton Green, then holding commissions dated 20 December 1859. Joined the 1st Admin Battalion and became 'C' and 'D' Companies of the new 2nd Corps in 1880.

**7th**—Formed at Rochford with Lieutenant Arthur Tawke commissioned on 8 March 1860. Joined the 1st Admin Battalion, transferring to 3rd Admin Battalion in 1861. The company disappeared from the Army List in February 1877.

**8th**—Formed as four companies at Stratford with all officers holding commissions dated 6 March 1860. The corps was recruited from staff of the Eastern Counties Railway which had reached the town in 1840. Joined the 2nd Admin Battalion in 1864 and disbanded in the following year.

**9th**—See 4th Corps (1880-1908).

**10th**—Formed at Witham on 30 December 1859 and known as 1st Sub-division until March 1860. Joined the 1st Admin Battalion and became 'E' Company of the new 2nd Corps in 1880.

**11th**—Formed at Dunmow, eleven miles north-west of Chelmsford, with Lieutenant John Mayon Wilson commissioned on 21 March 1860. Joined the 1st Admin Battalion and was disbanded on 14 August 1863.

**12th**—Formed at Braintree with Lieutenant Basil Sparrow and Ensign George Courtauld, Jun commissioned on 6 March 1860. Joined the 1st Admin Battalion and became 'F' Company of the new 2nd Corps in 1880.

**13th (Stour Valley)**—Formed at Dedham with former 42nd Royal Highland Regiment officer, Lieutenant Augustus Paterson and Ensign Edward M Alderson commissioned on 8 March 1860. Joined the 1st Admin Battalion and disappeared from the Army List in December 1870.

**14th**—Formed at Manningtree, just under nine miles from Colchester, with Lieutenant Barnard W Cocker, a former lieutenant-colonel in the 38th Regiment of Foot, and Ensign Thomas W Nunn commissioned on 17 May 1860. Joined the 1st Admin Battalion and disappeared from the Army List in June 1862.

**15th**—Formed at Hornchurch, two miles south-east of Romford, with Captain Peter E Bearblock, Lieutenant William Mashiter and Ensign Richard Denby commissioned on 11 June 1860. Joined the 3rd Admin Battalion and became 'H' Company of the new 1st Corps in 1880.

**16th**—Formed at Great Bentley, eight miles south-east of Colchester, with Lieutenant James Hardy and Ensign Joseph G Watson commissioned on 10 September 1860. Joined the 1st Admin Battalion and was disbanded in 1875.

**17th**—Formed at Saffron Walden with Captain the Hon Charles C Neville, Lieutenant Henry Byng and Ensign Douglas Lane commissioned on 23 October 1860. Included in the 2nd Admin Battalion of Cambridgeshire Rifle Volunteers from November 1863. This battalion was broken up in 1872 and its corps, including 17th Essex, were then transferred to the 1st Cambridgeshire Admin Battalion. Upon consolidation of that battalion in 1880, 17th Essex became 'I' Company of the new 1st Cambridgeshire RVC.

**18th**—Formed at Chipping Ongar with Captain Phillip J Budworth, Lieutenant Phillip H Meyer and Ensign Frederick A S Fane commissioned on 4 December 1860. Joined the 3rd Admin Battalion and became 'G' Company of the new 1st Corps in 1880. A Volunteer Drill Hall was built at Chipping Ongar in 1873.

**19th**—Formed at Epping with Lieutenant Sir William B Smyth, Bt and Ensign Loftus W Arkwright commissioned on 22 September 1860. Joined the 3rd Admin Battalion and disappeared from the Army List in November 1872.

**20th**—Formed at Haverhill with Lieutenant Ellys Anderson Stephens Walton and Ensign Henry Wyld Jackson commissioned on 27 December 1860. Joined the 1st Admin Battalion and was disbanded in 1871.

**21st**—Formed at Brentwood with Captain Sir Kingsmill G Key, Bt commissioned on 24 September 1860. Joined the 3rd Admin Battalion and was absorbed into the 3rd Corps in 1872.

**22nd**—Formed at Waltham Abbey with Captain William Leask and Lieutenant Edward S Bulmer commissioned on 27 November 1860. Placed into the 2nd Hertfordshire Admin Battalion in 1862, absorbed part of the 11th Hertfordshire RVC at Cheshunt in November 1870, and became 'H' Company of the new 1st Hertfordshire Corps in 1880. Cassell's *Gazetteer* for 1898 notes that on the banks of the Lea was a large Government establishment for refining saltpetre and for the manufacture of gunpowder, new works having been erected in 1890 about a half mile from the town for the making of cordite. Percussion caps were also made. This was the Royal Gunpowder Mills where much of the 22nd Corps was recruited.

**23rd**—Formed at Maldon with Captain James A Hamilton, late of the 41st Regiment of Foot, Lieutenant Edward H Bentall and Ensign Sampson Hanbury commissioned on 13 November 1860. Joined the 1st Admin Battalion and became 'G' and 'H' Companies of the new 2nd Corps in 1880.

**24th**—Formed as two companies at Woodford with Captain George Noble commissioned on 10 April 1861. Joined the 3rd Admin Battalion and was disbanded in 1872.

# Gloucestershire

## Artillery Volunteers

The 1st Admin Brigade of Gloucestershire Artillery Volunteers was formed with headquarters in Bristol on 28 November 1863 and to it were added the three Gloucestershire Corps together with the 1st and 2nd from Somersetshire. The brigade was consolidated in March 1880 as the new 1st Corps.

**1st (1859-1880)**—Formed at Bristol on 21 December 1859 and in 1880 provided Nos1 to 6 of the new 1st Corps.

**1st (1880-1908)**—Formed in 1880 by the consolidation of the 1st Admin Brigade. Headquarters remained in Bristol and the batteries were organised: Nos 1 to 6 Bristol (late 1st Corps), No 7 Newnham (late 2nd Corps), No 8 Gloucester (late 3rd Corps), No 9 Clevedon (late 1st Somerset Corps). A cadet corps was formed and attached at Bristol, but this disappeared from the Army List in December 1884. New batteries were later formed at Clevedon, Portishead and Weston-super-Mare. *Territorials:* 1st South Midland Brigade RFA.

**2nd**—Formed as the 2nd Sub-division at Newnham on 1 March 1860 and became 2nd Corps in the following August. Provided No 7 Battery of the new 1st Corps in 1880.

**3rd**—Formed at Gloucester on 26 Jul 1860 and provided No 8 Battery of the new 1st Corps in 1880.

## Engineer Volunteers

The 1st Admin Battalion of Gloucestershire Engineer Volunteers was formed with headquarters at Bristol in July 1867. Included were the county's two existing corps, the 1st and 2nd, the 1st Somerset EVC when formed in 1868, and the 1st Devonshire EVC from 1869. The battalion, minus the 2nd Corps, was consolidated as the 1st Gloucestershire (Gloucester, Somerset and Devon) EVC in 1880.

**1st (1861-1880)**—The 1st Corps was formed at Gloucester on 28 January 1861 and provided 'A' to 'D' Companies of the new 1st Corps in 1880.

**1st (1880-1908)**—Formed by the consolidation of the 1st Admin Battalion in 1880 with the title 1st Gloucestershire (Gloucester, Somerset and Devon) EVC and nine companies: 'A' to 'D' Gloucester (late 1st Gloucestershire), 'E' Torquay (late 1st Devonshire), 'F' Exeter (late 1st Devonshire), 'G and 'H' Nailsea (late 1st Somerset), 'I' Weston-Super-Mare (late 1st Somerset). During 1885 an additional company trained in the duties of submarine miners was formed. Headquarters were in Cardiff which resulted in the title of the corps being changed to 1st Gloucestershire (Gloucester, Somerset, Devon and Glamorgan). In addition, the Army List for January 1886 also shows 'The Western Counties Engineer Volunteer Corps' as part of the full unit designation. This, however, was shortened to 'The Western Counties' in the following March.

From 1886 the submarine mining companies of all existing engineer corps were withdrawn to form divisions of the newly created Volunteer Submarine Miners. As a result of this the submarine miners of the 1st Gloucestershire, which now numbered two companies, became the division responsible for the River Severn. As the corps once again consisted

**Sapper, 1st Gloucestershire Engineer Volunteer Corps.**

Helmet plate, 2nd
Gloucestershire Engineer
Volunteer Corps.

Helmet plate, 1st
Gloucestershire Rifle
Volunteer Corps.

Side drum,
1st Gloucestershire Engineer
Volunteer Corps.

of companies formed within Gloucestershire, Somerset and Devon, the word 'Glamorgan' was removed from the title.

Further changes took place in 1889 when in July the Somerset and Devon companies were removed to form a new corps designated as 1st Devonshire and Somersetshire. In that same month, headquarters were moved from Gloucester to Cheltenham and the sub-titles were removed from the Army List. The full title of the unit was now simply the 1st Gloucestershire Engineer Volunteer Corps. A cadet company with headquarters at Weston-Super-Mare was raised by the corps and was shown in the Army List between February 1880 and June 1888. In the following year a new company of cadets was attached. This was located at Cheltenham College and until 1889 had been affiliated to the 2nd Volunteer Battalion of the Gloucestershire Regiment. The college remained attached to the engineers until late in 1903 when it was again shown as part of the 2nd Volunteer Battalion. *Territorials:* Only 'F' Company transferred, becoming the Gloucester and Worcester Brigade Company, Army Service Corps.

**2nd**—Headquarters of the 2nd Corps were at Bristol where it had been formed on 10 April 1861 by employees of the Bristol & Eastern Railway Co. The 2nd chose not to become part of the new 1st Corps in 1880 and instead continued as an independent unit, adding 'The Bristol Engineer Volunteer Corps' to its title in 1881.

On 19 February 1876, a cadet corps had been formed and attached to the 2nd which from 1881 was shown as having its headquarters at Clifton College. *Territorials:* 1st and 2nd South Midland Field Companies and the South Midland Divisional Telegraph Company of the South Midland Divisional Engineers. The Clifton College Cadets became part if the Junior Division, OTC.

**2nd Gloucestershire
Engineer Volunteer Corps.**

## Light Horse Volunteers

**1st**—Formed May 1864 at Stroud with Captain John
Dutton Hunt in command. Captain Hunt had previously
served with the 6th Gloucestershire Rifle Volunteers, W Y
Carman stating that he died from a tragic accident in 1865.
With no replacement, the corps survived until being
disbanded in 1867.

## Rifle Volunteers

All Gloucestershire rifle corps, with the exception of the
1st, joined the 1st Admin Battalion which in 1880 formed the
new 2nd Corps. There also existed a 2nd Admin Battalion which had its headquarters at Cheltenham and
included the 7th, 10th, 13th and 14th Corps, but this disappeared from the Army List in January 1864, the
corps then being placed with the 1st Admin Battalion. A 1st Sub-division existed for a short while which
upon reaching the strength of a full company was then numbered as 8th Corps.

**1st (City of Bristol)**—Lieutenant Colonel Robert Bush, late of the 96th Foot, was commissioned as
commanding officer of the 1st Corps on 13 September 1859. The battalion comprised ten companies by
June 1860 and was permitted to include City of Bristol as part of its official title. Under General Order 63
of May 1883 1st Gloucestershire was re-designated as 1st (City of Bristol) Volunteer Battalion
Gloucestershire Regiment, the Bristol Grammar School Cadet Corps being affiliated in 1900. An eleventh
company was authorized in 1902. *Territorials:* 4th Battalion Gloucestershire Regiment. Bristol Grammar
School became a contingent of the OTC.

**2nd (1859-1880)**—Formed as one company at Gloucester Dock with Captain William Vernon Guise,
Lieutenant John Jones and Ensign Theodore Aylmer Preston, late of the 43rd Regiment of Foot. All three
held commissions dated 21 October 1859. They were later joined by John Peydell Wilson who became
surgeon to the corps. Became 'A' Company of the new 2nd Corps in 1880.

**2nd (1880-1908)**—The 1st Admin Battalion was formed with headquarters at Gloucester in 1860
and consolidated in 1880 as the new 2nd Corps with ten companies: 'A' Gloucester Dock (late 2nd Corps),
'B' Gloucester (late 3rd Corps), 'C' Stroud (late 5th Corps), 'D' Cirencester (late 9th Corps), 'E'
Cheltenham (late 10th Corps), 'F' Dursley (late 11th Corps), 'G' Coleford (late 12th Corps), 'H' Newnham
(late 12th Corps), 'I' Stow-on-the-Wold (late 15th Corps), 'K' Chipping Campden (late 16th Corps).

Re-designation as 2nd Volunteer Battalion Gloucestershire Regiment was notified in General Order
63 of 1883. A cadet corps is shown as affiliated to the 1st Admin Battalion in 1867 and in 1883 this same
unit is given as being formed by Cheltenham College. The college transferred its affiliation to the 1st
Gloucestershire Engineer Volunteers in 1889 but returned to the 2nd Volunteer Battalion in 1904.
Gloucester County School at Hempstead provided a company of cadets in 1889, as did Cirencester in 1896.
Both, however, were disbanded in 1891 and 1897 respectively. *Territorials:* 5th Battalion Gloucestershire
Regiment. Cheltenham College became a contingent of the OTC.

**3rd**—Formed as one company at Gloucester Dock with Captain Thomas De Winton, late of the Royal
Artillery, Lieutenant Henry Dowling and Ensign Richard T Smith. All three held commissions dated 21
October 1859. James P Heane was appointed surgeon to the corps in the following May. Became 'B'
Company of the new 2nd Corps in 1880.

**4th**—Formed at Stroud with Captain Henry Daniel Cholmeley, Lieutenant William Antony Freston
and Ensign John Tuppen Woodwright. All three officers held commissions dated 5 September 1859.

Disappeared from the Army List in August 1861.

**5th**—Formed at Stroud with Captain J Watts Haliwell, Lieutenant Sebastian Stewart Dickinson and Ensign Sidney Biddle. All three held commissions dated 6 September. Absorbed the 6th Corps, also at Stroud, in 1865 and became 'C' Company of the new 2nd Corps in 1880.

**6th**—Formed at Stroud, the first officers gazetted to the 6th Corps were Captain John Dutton Hunt, a local mill owner, and Ensign Arthur Twisden Playne. Both held commissions dated 7 September 1859. The Rev Edward Cornford was later appointed as chaplain to the corps and Robert Blagden, its surgeon. The establishment was completed in December when J Tuppen Wollwright joined the other officers. Interest in the corps, however, began to fall off about 1863. Captain Hunt transferred to the 1st Gloucestershire Light Horse Volunteers in May 1865 and with Ensign Playne the only officer remaining, in that same year what remained of the 6th Corps was absorbed into the 5th.

**7th**—Formed at Cheltenham, the first officer to be gazetted was Captain Robert Dwarris Gibney who was commissioned on 20 September 1859. He was joined in the following October by Lieutenant Henry Bromby and Ensign William Martin, then by William Dalton who was appointed as surgeon to the corps in February 1860. Joined the 2nd Admin Battalion, then to 1st Admin by January 1864. Disbanded in September 1864.

**8th**—Formed at Tewksbury as a half company with Lieutenant James Primatt Sargeaunt and Ensign George Howard Banaster holding commissions dated 6 December. Simon S Bowen, MD was appointed as surgeon to the corps. Known as the 1st Sub-division until March 1860, James Sargeaunt was promoted captain to a full company on 7 November. Disbanded in 1877.

**9th**—Formed at Cirencester with Captain Alex Bathurst, a former 6th Dragoon Guards officer, Lieutenant John Davis Sherston, and Ensign William Tombs Dewe holding commissions dated 13 February 1860. Edward Cripps was appointed surgeon. Became 'D' Company of the new 2nd Corps in 1880.

**10th**—Formed at Cheltenham with Captain Herbert W Wood, he had previously served as lieutenant-colonel in the 4th Madras Native Infantry, Lieutenant Shapland Swiny, late captain in the Royal Dublin City Militia, and Ensign Stanhope T Speer. All three held commissions dated 1 March 1860. Augustus Eves was appointed as surgeon. Joined the 2nd Admin Battalion, then to 1st Admin by January 1864, and became 'E' Company of the new 2nd Corps in 1880.

**11th**—Formed at Dursley with John Vizard as captain, Edward Bloxsome, lieutenant and William Cornock, ensign. All three held commissions dated 9 March 1860. William J Hill was later appointed as surgeon. Became 'F' Company of the new 2nd Corps in 1880.

**12th**—Formed with headquarters given as the Forest of Dean. The original officers of the 12th Gloucester RVC were Captain Sir Martin H C Boevey, Bt, Lieutenant John H Dighton and Ensign Sir James Campbell, Bt. All three held commissions dated 21 April 1860. Became 'G' and 'H' Companies of the new 2nd Corps in 1880.

**13th**—Formed as one company at Cheltenham with Captain Edmund P Morphy, late of the Monaghan Militia, Ensign Edward J Gregory and Robert Wollaston, MD who was appointed as surgeon. All three held commissions dated 23 March 1860. Lieutenant Thomas Swain, who was gazetted on 27 April 1860, made up the establishment. Joined the 2nd Admin Battalion, then to 1st Admin by January 1864. Disbanded in 1874.

**14th**—Formed as one company at Cheltenham, the first officer to be commissioned (3 July 1860) being Captain Sir Alex Ramsay. Lieutenant Hugh Kennedy, Ensign William Gardner and surgeon Thomas J Cottle made up the establishment on 8th August. Joined the 2nd Admin Battalion, then to 1st Admin by January 1864, and disbanded in September 1864.

**15th**—Formed as a sub-division at Stow-on-the-Wold with Lieutenant Cecil C V N Pole commissioned on 3 December 1860. Francis E B Witts joined him as ensign on 12 December. The 15th Corps remained as a sub-division until brought up to a full company in December 1868. Became 'I' Company of the new

2nd Corps in 1880.

**16th**—Formed at Moreton-in-the-Marsh, the first officer to be commissioned (23 November 1860) being Captain Sir John M Steele, Bt. He was joined by lieutenant Thomas Commeline, and Ensign William H Baker in the following December. The Rev Charles E Kennaway was appointed as chaplain to the corps and Leonard K Yelf, MD, its surgeon. Headquarters moved to Chipping Campden in 1862 and became 'K' Company of the new 2nd Corps in 1880.

**3rd Volunteer Battalion Gloucestershire Regiment**—Eight companies formed with headquarters at Bristol on 24 July 1900. *Territorials:* 6th Battalion Gloucestershire Regiment.

# Hampshire

## Artillery Volunteers

The 1st Admin Brigade was formed with headquarters at Portsmouth in January 1861. In addition to the Hampshire corps, those from Dorsetshire were also included in 1863, but were removed to the 1st Devonshire Brigade three years later. From January 1873 the several Dorsetshire AVC are once again included and would be involved in the consolidation of the 1st Hampshire as the new 1st Corps in 1880.

**1st (1860-1880)**—Formed at Bitterne on 25 April 1860, moving headquarters to Southampton in 1873. Provided Nos 1 and 2 Batteries of the new 1st Corps in 1880.

**1st (1880-1908)**—Formed in 1880 by the consolidation of the 1st Admin Brigade. Headquarters remained at Portsmouth and the batteries were organised as follows: Nos 1 to 4 Southampton (late 1st Corps), Nos 5 to 12 Portsmouth (late 2nd Corps), Nos 13 and 14 Bournemouth (late 4th Corps), No 15 Lyme Regis (late 1st Dorset Corps), No 16 Portland (late 4th Dorset Corps), No 17 Portland and Swanage (late 4th and 6th Dorset Corps). No 18 Charmouth (late 5th Dorset Corps).

Re-designated as 1st Volunteer (Hampshire) Brigade Southern Division Royal Artillery under General Order 106 of September 1886 and in the same year moved headquarters to Southsea. Also, in 1886 the Dorsetshire Batteries were removed to form their own, 1st Dorsetshire Corps. On 25 April 1888 the corps was again divided when personnel from around the Southampton area were withdrawn to form the 3rd Volunteer (Hampshire) Brigade Southern Division Royal Artillery.

Under Army Order 482 of December 1889 the 1st Volunteer Brigade was re-designated as 2nd Hampshire Artillery Volunteer Corps (Southern Division Royal Artillery) while the 3rd took on the position of 1st Hampshire AVC. As the 3rd Volunteer Hampshire Brigade contained the original 1st Corps it was this formation that became 1st Corps while the Portsmouth Batteries (the 1st Volunteer Brigade) became 2nd. *Territorials:* The 1st Corps provided the Hampshire RGA, the 2nd forming the 1st Wessex Brigade RFA and 2nd Wessex (Howitzer) Brigade RFA. One company also provided the Wessex (Hampshire) RGA.

**2nd (1860-1880)**—Formed at Southsea on 9 May 1860 and in 1871 amalgamated with the 3rd Corps. At the same time headquarters were moved to Portsmouth. Provided Nos 5 to 12 Batteries of the new 1st Corps in 1880.

**3rd**—Formed at Portsmouth on 18 August 1860, headquarters being given as Portsmouth Dockyard from March 1862. Merged with the 2nd Corps, as 2nd, in 1817.

**Hampshire Artillery Volunteers.**

**4th**—Formed at Bournemouth on 29 November 1866 and provided Nos 13 and 14 Batteries of the new 1st Corps in 1880.

## Engineer Volunteers

**1st (1862-1881)**—The county's original 1st Corps was formed at Southampton on 25 January 1862, but this would be disbanded in 1881 and its personnel absorbed by the 2nd Hampshire Rifle Volunteers.

**1st (1891-1908)**—On 1 April 1891 a new 1st Corps was raised, its headquarters this time being placed in Portsmouth. There would also, for a time, be a cadet company located at Weymouth. This, however, would later be disbanded and was not seen in the Army List after March 1902. *Territorials:* Hampshire (Fortress) Engineers.

## Mounted Rifle Volunteers/ Light Horse Volunteers

**1st Hampshire Light Horse Volunteer Corps.**

**1st**—Formed April 1860 as Mounted Rifles at Droxford with Captain J Bower in command. Captain Bower had previously served on the Staff of the 28th Madras Native Infantry and was for a time Master of the Hambledon Hounds. The corps after a few months changed to Light Horse Volunteers, but once again became Mounted Rifles in August 1863. Also known as the 'Droxford Light Cavalry'. Disbandment came in 1877.

**2nd**—Originally formed in January 1861 at Southampton as Mounted Rifles, but within a month had been renamed as Light Horse. J Brown Willis Fleming was commissioned as lieutenant on 4 January 1861 and the corps was disbanded in 1865.

## Rifle Volunteers

With the exception of the 2nd, 3rd, 10th, 14th and 19th, the several rifle corps then in existence within the county of Hampshire were, in December 1860, divided up into three admin battalions. In January 1865 a 4th Admin was formed and the Army List for that month shows it to contain the above corps. During 1868 the 3rd Admin at Fareham (formed 1860 with 7th, 8th, 12th, 17th, 20th, 21st and 22nd Corps) was broken up and its corps dispersed among the 1st and 2nd Battalions. These, together with the 4th, were consolidated in 1880 to form the new 1st, 2nd and 3rd Corps. A 4th was later formed out of the 2nd.

**1st (1859-1880)**—Formed at Winchester on 18 October 1859 with Captain Thomas Faunce, late of the 13th Regiment of Foot, and Lieutenant Charles Simeon, who had served with the 75th Foot. Joined the 1st Admin Battalion and became 'A' and 'B' Companies of the new 1st Corps in 1880.

**1st (1880-1908)**—The 1st Admin Battalion was formed with Headquarters at Winchester in December 1860 and was consolidated in 1880 as the new 1st Corps with ten companies: 'A' and 'B' Winchester (late 1st Corps), 'C' Botley (late 8th Corps), 'D' Romsey (late 11th Corps), 'E' Andover (late 13th Corps), 'F' Hartley Wintney (late 15th Corps), 'G' Alresford (late 16th Corps), 'H' Alton (late 21st Corps), 'I' Winchester (late 24th Corps), 'K' Basingstoke (late 25th Corps).

Changes made after consolidation were in 1884, when 'L' Company was added at St Mary's College,

Winchester; in 1889, when 'M' Company was raised from the Aldershot section of 'H', and in 1892, when another company was formed at Stockbridge. The latter, according to CT Atkinson's *Regimental History of the Hampshire Regiment* (Vol. 1), became an ASC (Volunteers) company in 1903. The total establishment by 1900 stood at eighteen companies. There was also a cadet corps affiliated at Winchester College since 1870. The 1st Hampshire was re-designated as 1st Volunteer Battalion Hampshire Regiment under General Order 91 of 1885. *Territorials:* 4th Battalion Hampshire Regiment. The Winchester College company, together with the cadet corps, became a contingent of the OTC.

**2nd (1859-1880)**—Formed at Southampton with Thomas Willis Fleming commissioned as captain on 24 February 1860. Joined the 4th Admin Battalion and became 'A' to 'D' Companies of the new 2nd Corps in 1880.

**2nd (1880-1908)**—The 4th Admin Battalion was formed in January 1865, moving headquarters from Lyndhurst to Southampton in 1872. Consolidated in 1880 as the new 2nd Corps with nine companies: 'A' to 'D' Southampton (late 2nd Corps), 'E' Lymington (late 3rd Corps), 'F' Christchurch (late 10th Corps), 'G' Lyndhurst (late 14th Corps), 'H' and 'I' Bournemouth (late 19th Corps).

By 1883 the establishment of the 2nd Corps had reached twelve companies, but in 1885 this was reduced to eight when part of the corps was detached to form the new 4th Hampshire RVC. According to the regimental history of the Royal Hampshire Regiment, the companies removed were those from the Bournemouth, Christchurch, Lymington and Ringwood. This would suggest that one of the Bournemouth companies ('H' or 'I') had been lost and its place taken by another at Ringwood. Also, in 1885 the corps took the title of 2nd Volunteer Battalion Hampshire Regiment. Another new company was raised in 1900. *Territorials:* 5th Battalion Hampshire Regiment.

**3rd (1859-1880)**—Formed at Lymington on 30 December 1859 under the command of former 12th Dragoons officer, Captain Richard H Smith Barry. Joined the 4th Admin Battalion and became 'E' Company of the new 2nd Corps in 1880.

**3rd (1880-1908)**—The 2nd Admin Battalion was formed with headquarters at Portsmouth in December 1860 and consolidated as the new 3rd Corps in 1880 with eleven companies: 'A' to 'E' Portsmouth (late 5th Corps), 'F' and 'G' Gosport (late 6th Corps), 'H' Havant (late 4th Corps), 'I' Petersfield (late 12th Corps), 'K' Fareham (late 7th Corps), 'L' Porchester (late 23rd Corps).

A new company was added in 1884 and in 1897 a cadet corps was formed and affiliated by Portsmouth Grammar School. In 1900 an additional six companies were raised, followed in 1905 by another cadet corps at Churcher's College near Petersfield. The 3rd Corps was re-designated as 3rd Volunteer Battalion Hampshire Regiment by General Order 91 of September 1885. In 1893 HRH the Duke of Connaught was made Hon Colonel and from that year the title of the battalion became 3rd (The Duke of Connaught's Own) Volunteer Battalion. *Territorials:* 6th Battalion Hampshire Regiment. Portsmouth Grammar School and Churcher's College became contingents of the OTC.

**4th (1859-1880)**—Formed at Havant, just under seven miles north-east of Portsmouth, on 3 February

1860 and joined the 2nd Admin Battalion. The first officer to be commissioned into the corps was Captain Edward Davison. Became 'H' Company of the new 3rd Corps in 1880.

**4th (1885-1908)**—We have seen how in April 1885 the Bournemouth, Christchurch, Lymington and Ringwood companies of the new 2nd Corps were detached so as to form a new 4th Corps of six companies. Headquarters were placed at Bournemouth and shortly after formation the title of the corps was changed to 4th Volunteer Battalion Hampshire Regiment. Bournemouth raised a new company in 1891, followed by another at Fordingbridge in 1895. Three more companies were added: Bournemouth again, and one of Mounted Infantry in 1900 which became known as the New Forest Scouts. Bournemouth School Cadet Corps was formed and affiliated in 1903 and a company at Lymington in 1905. *Territorials:* 7th Battalion Hampshire Regiment. Bournemouth School became a contingent of the OTC.

**5th (The Portsmouth Rifle Volunteer Corps)**—Formed at Portsmouth with Captain Commandant George P Vallaney, late of the Indian Army, commissioned on 16 March 1860. Joined the 2nd Admin Battalion and became 'A' to 'E' Companies of the new 3rd Corps in 1880. The Portsmouth Grammar School, which formed a cadet corps in 1897, moved into a new building in 1878.

**6th**—Formed at Gosport on 9 March 1860 and joined the 2nd Admin Battalion. The first officer to be commissioned was Captain William Yates Peel. Became 'F' and 'G' Companies of the new 3rd Corps in 1880.

**7th**—Formed at Fareham on 14 May 1860, the first officer to be commissioned being Lieutenant William Kelsall. Joined the 3rd Admin Battalion, transferred to the 2nd in 1868, and became 'K' Company of the new 3rd Corps in 1880. The corps was also recruited from the neighbouring villages of Wymering and Porchester.

**8th**—Formed as two companies at Botley with Captain Commandant Robert Richardson in command on 14 May 1860. By July, headquarters were being shown as Bitterne, on the Southampton road to the west. Joined the 3rd Admin Battalion, transferring to 1st Admin Battalion in 1868, and became 'C' Company of the new 1st Corps in 1880.

**9th**—None recorded.

**10th**—Formed at Christchurch with Captain James H H Earl of Malmesbury commissioned on 9 March 1860. Joined the 4th Admin Battalion and became 'F' Company of the new 2nd Corps in 1880.

**11th**—Formed at Romsey, seven miles south-west of Southampton, on 24 March 1860 with Captain Thomas W Henderson, Lieutenant Alexander Stead and Ensign George Allsop. Joined the 1st Admin Battalion and became 'D' Company of the new 1st Corps in 1880.

**12th**—Formed at Petersfield on 28 April 1860 with Captain Edward H Chawner, Lieutenant Sir W W Knighton and Ensign George Haw Seward. Joined the 3rd Admin Battalion, transferred to 2nd Admin in 1868, and became 'I' Company of the new 3rd Corps in 1880. At the north end of College Street, Churcher's College formed a cadet corps in 1905.

**13th**—Formed at Andover, its services accepted on 13 May 1860; the first appointed officers of the corps were: Captain W W Humphrey, Lieutenant Allan B Heath and Ensign Phillip H Poore. Joined the 1st Admin Battalion and became 'E' Company of the new 1st Corps in 1880.

**14th**—Formed at Lyndhurst on 16 June 1860 with Captain Alexander H L Popham, Lieutenant William C D Esdale and Ensign Walter Williams. Joined the 4th Admin Battalion and became 'G' Company of the new 2nd Corps in 1880.

**15th**—Formed at Yateley, five miles from Farnborough, the services of the 15th Corps were accepted on 30 May 1860 with Lieutenant George Mason, late of the 4th Foot, and Ensign Frederick G Stapleton. Joined the 1st Admin Battalion, moved headquarters to Hartley Wintney in 1870 and became 'F' Company of the new 1st Corps in 1880.

**16th**—Formed at Alresford, just under seven miles north-east of Winchester, the services of the 16th Corps were accepted on 14 June 1860. Lieutenant Francis J P Mar and Ensign William Gatty were the first officers to be commissioned. Joined the 1st Admin Battalion and became 'G' Company of the new 1st Corps in 1880.

**17th**—Formed at Titchfield, six miles north-west of Gosport, on 29 August 1860 with Lieutenant George Wingate and Ensign Frederick Bradshaw. Joined the 3rd Admin Battalion, transferred to the 2nd in 1868, and was disbanded in 1874.

**18th**—Formed at Basingstoke, the services of the 18th Corps were accepted on 31 July 1860 with Captain Thomas Harvey and Lieutenant Chaloner W Chute appointed as its first officers. Joined the 1st Admin Battalion but was disbanded in 1864.

**19th**—Formed at Bournemouth on 18 August 1860 and joined the 4th Admin Battalion. Lieutenant Charles A King and Ensign Henry Ledgard was the first officers to be commissioned. Became 'H' and 'I' Companies of the new 2nd Corps in 1880.

**20th**—Formed at Wickham, twelve miles north-west of Portsmouth, on 27 July 1860 with Lieutenant Henry Carter and Ensign Charles B Smith the first officers appointed. Joined the 3rd Admin Battalion, transferred to the 2nd in 1868, and was disbanded in 1874.

**21st**—Formed at Alton, eleven miles from Basingstoke, the services of the 21st Corps were accepted on 10 August 1860. The company's first officers were Lieutenant Cecil Rivers and Ensign James B Coulthard. Joined the 3rd Admin Battalion, transferring to 1st Admin Battalion in 1868, and became 'H' Company of the new 1st Corps in 1880.

**22nd**—Formed at Bishops Waltham, just over nine miles south-east of Winchester, on 13 September 1860 with Lieutenant Butterworth P Shearer and Ensign Walter Clark. Joined the 3rd Admin Battalion and disbanded in 1865.

**23rd**—Formed at Cosham on 29 November 1860 and joined the 2nd Admin Battalion with Lieutenant Edward Goble and Ensign Henry Monk the first officers to be commissioned. Headquarters moved to Porchester in 1869 and became 'L' Company of the new 3rd Corps in 1880.

**24th**—Formed from the senior members and staff at Winchester College on 21 December 1874 with J C Moore as lieutenant and Charles D Collier, sub-lieutenant. Joined the 1st Admin Battalion and became 'I' Company of the new 1st Corps in 1880.

**25th**—Formed at Basingstoke with Lieutenant Gerald R Fitzgerald and Surgeon Charles F Webb the first to be commissioned on 9 June 1875. Joined the 1st Admin Battalion and became 'K' Company of the new 1st Corps in 1880.

# Herefordshire

## Rifle Volunteers

All corps formed within the county joined the 1st Admin Battalion which was consolidated as the new 1st Corps in 1880.

**1st (1860-1880)**—Formed as one company at Hereford on 10 April 1860 with Robert Feildon, who had served previously as a lieutenant colonel in the 44th Regiment of Foot, taking command. Became 'A' Company of the new 1st Corps in 1880.

**1st (1880-1908)**—The 1st Admin Battalion of Herefordshire Rifle Volunteers was formed with headquarters at Hereford on 20 February 1861. From 1864 the 1st, 2nd and 3rd Radnorshire RVC were shown in the Army List as part of the battalion, which was consolidated as the new 1st Corps in 1880 with ten-and-a-half companies: 'A' Hereford (late 1st Corps), 'B' Ross-on-Wye (late No 1 Company, 2nd Corps), 'C' Ledbury (late 3rd Corps), 'D' Bromyard (late 4th Corps), 'E' Ross-on-Wye (late No 2 Company, 2nd Corps), 'F' Leominster (late 6th Corps), 'G' Kington (late 7th Corps), 'H' Hereford (late 8th Corps), 'I' Presteigne (late 1st Radnorshire Corps), 'K' Rhayader (late 2nd Radnorshire Corps). The half-company was located at Hereford

Became a Volunteer battalion (without change of title) of the King's Shropshire Light Infantry in 1881 and in the same year the two Ross companies ('B' and 'E') were merged as 'B'. A new 'E' Company was formed at Weobley in 1889. Also, in 1889 a Bearer Company was formed at Hereford to serve the Welsh Border Infantry Brigade. This company, as no authorization had been received to increase the establishment of the battalion, formed part of 'A' Company.

In 1905 several further changes in organisation took place: 'L' Company was added at Hereford from members of the Cyclist Section created there in 1888, and 'M' was formed at Ruardean. An amalgamation between 'I' and 'G' Companies took place and the Bearer Company was constituted as a separate unit designated Welsh Border Brigade Company RAMC (Vols.). In 1902 the Hereford Cathedral School applied to the War Office to form a cadet corps which was affiliated to the 1st Herefordshire RVC on 28 March 1903. *Territorials:* The Herefordshire Battalion King's (Shropshire Light Infantry); this was changed after a few months, however, to the Herefordshire Regiment. Hereford Cathedral School became a contingent of the OTC.

**2nd**—Formed as one company at Ross-on-Wye on 27 March 1860 with Captain Kingsmill M Power, who had previously served as a captain in the 16th Dragoons, Lieutenant Nathaniel K Cobins and Ensign Francis W Herbert. Became 'B' and 'E' Companies of the new 1st Corps in 1880.

**3rd**—Formed as one company at Ledbury on 27 March 1860, the Earl Somers taking command with Lieutenant Thomas Heywood, late of the 16th Dragoons, and former 79th Regiment of Foot officer, Ensign James M Aynesley as his junior officers. Became 'C' Company of the new 1st Corps in 1880.

**4th**—Formed as one company at Bromyard on 15 May 1860 with Captain Charles E Hopton, a former officer of the 23rd (Royal Welsh Fusiliers) Regiment of Foot, Lieutenant Thomas S Uphill and Ensign James P Eckley as its first officers. Became 'D' Company of the new 1st Corps in 1880.

**5th**—Formed at South Archenfield with Captain Edward O Partridge in command on 15 May 1860. Was later disbanded and disappeared from the Army List in January 1873.

**6th**—Formed as one company at Leominster with Captain the Rt Hon Robert D Rodney Lord Rodney in command on 4 May 1860. Became 'F' Company of the new 1st Corps in 1880.

**7th**—Formed as one company at Kington on 18 May 1860 with Captain John Coke, Lieutenant John G R War and Ensign Anthony Temple. Became 'G' Company of the new 1st Corps in 1880.

**8th**—Formed as one company at Hereford on 27 September 1860 with Captain Richard Arkwright, Lieutenant Richard Clarkson and Ensign James Phillips. The corps was made up entirely from members of a lodge of Oddfellows. Became 'H' Company of the new 1st Corps in 1880.

# Hertfordshire

## Light Horse Volunteers

**1st**—Formed 19 November 1862 at Bishops Stortford with Captain John Dobele Fairman in command. The first parade was held at the Railway Inn, the corps comprising two troops and a band by 1865. Disbanded and was last seen in the Army List for June 1879.

## Rifle Volunteers

The several rifle corps formed within the county were placed into one or other of two admin battalions, the 1st taking in the corps from the western half of Hertfordshire, the 2nd incorporating those in the east. In 1880 the seniority of the old 1st Corps (2nd Admin Battalion) was recognised, and the eventual reorganisation resulted in the 1st Admin Battalion numbered as the new 2nd Corps, while the 2nd Admin became 1st.

**1st (1859-1880)**—Formed as one company at Hertford on 22 November 1859 and joined the 2nd Admin Battalion. The Rt Hon Earl Cowper took command, his junior officers being Lieutenant William

Robert Baker and Ensign the Hon Henry Frederick Cowper. A second company was added on 26 October 1860, the two to form 'A' and 'B' Companies of the new 1st Corps in 1880. J D Sainsbury in his book *Hertfordshire Soldiers,* tells how the 1st Corps had came about as the result of a meeting held by members of the Hertford Rifle Club on 25 October 1859.

**1st (1880-1908)**—The 2nd Admin Battalion was formed with headquarters at Hertford in October 1860, the 22nd Essex RVC at Waltham Abbey being added to the Hertfordshire corps in 1862. The battalion was consolidated as the new 1st Corps in 1880 with eight companies: 'A' and 'B' Hertford (late 1st Corps), 'C' Bishop's Stortford (late 6th Corps), 'D' Ware (late 9th Corps), 'E' Royston (late 10th Corps), 'F' Welwyn (late No 1 Company, 14th Corps), 'G' Hitchin (late No 2 Company, 14th Corps), 'H' Waltham Abbey and Cheshunt (late 22nd Essex Corps).

Re-designated as 1st (Hertfordshire) Volunteer Battalion Bedfordshire Regiment under General Order 181 of 1887. A new company ('I') was added at Hoddesdon in 1900. Three cadet corps were affiliated to the battalion: Haileybury College in 1886, Bishop's Stortford Grammar School and Hertford Grammar School in 1906. *Territorials:* Part of the Hertfordshire Regiment, although portion of the battalion went to form a nucleus of the 1st and 2nd Hertfordshire Batteries Royal Field Artillery. All three cadet corps became contingents of the OTC.

**2nd (1860-1880)**—Formed as one company at Watford on 5 January 1860 with Lieutenant the Hon Reginald A Capel and Ensign Charles F Humbert. Joined the 1st Admin Battalion and became 'A' Company of the new 2nd Corps in 1880.

**2nd (1880-1908)**—The 1st Admin Battalion was formed with headquarters at Little Gaddesden in October 1860 and was consolidated as the new 2nd Corps in 1880 with five companies: 'A' Watford (late 2nd Corps), 'B' St Albans (late 3rd Corps), 'C' Ashridge (late 4th Corps), 'D' Hemel Hempstead and Redbourn (late 5th Corps), 'E' Great Berkhamsted and Tring (late 7th Corps).

Headquarters remained at Little Gaddesden, but later moved to Hemel Hempstead. In 1883 a new company ('F') was added at Tring, then, under General Order 181 of December 1887, the 2nd Corps was re-designated as 2nd (Hertfordshire) Volunteer Battalion Bedfordshire Regiment. 'G' Company was added at Watford in 1892 and cadet corps formed and affiliated to the battalion at Berkhamsted School and St Albans School in 1891 and 1903 respectively. Another cadet corps, the United Services College, joined the battalion in May 1904 having moved its location from Westward Ho! to Harpenden. Yet another move, this time to Windsor in 1907, saw the company transferred to the 1st London RE (Vols). *Territorials:* Part of the Hertfordshire Regiment. The cadet corps became contingents of the OTC.

**3rd**—Formed as one company at St Albans on 5 March 1860 with Lieutenant William T K Church and Ensign William H Evans. Joined the 1st Admin Battalion and became 'B' Company of the new 2nd Corps in 1880.

**4th**—Formed as one company at Ashridge on 1 March 1860 with Captain William P Cust and Lieutenant William Paxton. Joined the 1st Admin Battalion and became 'C' Company of the new 2nd Corps in 1880. Ashridge Park near Berkhamsted was the seat of the Cust family—Adelbert Wellington Browlow Cust, Earl Brownlow, later commanded the 4th Corps and after that the 2nd (Hertfordshire) Volunteer Battalion Bedfordshire Regiment.

**5th**—Formed as one company at Hemel Hempstead on 10 March 1860 with Captain Robert Eden in command, John Day as lieutenant and Henry Balderson, ensign. Joined the 1st Admin Battalion and became 'D' Company of the new 2nd Corps in 1880.

**6th**—Formed as one company at Bishop's Stortford on 20 March 1860 with Captain John A Houblon in command, Thomas H Holyn as lieutenant and Frederick W Nash, ensign. Joined the 2nd Admin Battalion and became 'C' Company of the new 1st Corps in 1880.

**7th**—Formed as one company at Great Berkhamsted on 13 March 1860 and joined the 1st Admin Battalion. A former commander in the Royal Navy, Arthur Tower, took command, his junior officers being

Lieutenant H Pearse and Ensign John H Salter. Absorbed the 8th Corps, five miles to the south-east at Tring, on 1 May 1866 and became 'E' Company of the new 2nd Corps in 1880.

**8th**—Formed as one company at Tring on 20 April 1860 with Lieutenant Richard Bright and Ensign Arthur H Jenney. Joined the 1st Admin Battalion and was absorbed into the 7th Corps on 1 May 1866.

**9th**—Formed as one company at Ware on 13 June 1860 with William Parker as captain; Charles Cass, lieutenant and James Cullyer, ensign. Joined the 2nd Admin Battalion and became 'D' Company of the new 1st Corps in 1880.

**10th**—Formed as one company at Royston and Baldock on 25 June 1860 with Joseph Simpson as captain; John Phillips, lieutenant and Henry Perkins, ensign. Joined the 2nd Admin Battalion and became 'E' Company of the new 1st Corps in 1880.

**11th**—Formed as one company at Cheshunt on 25 August 1860 with Francis G Goodliffe as captain, Livingston War, lieutenant and John M Levick, ensign. Joined the 2nd Admin Battalion and disbanded 22 November 1870 with part of the corps being absorbed into the 22nd Essex RVC.

**12th**—Formed at Hitchin, close to the border with Bedfordshire, on 15 September 1860 with Frederick P D Radcliffe as captain, George E Hughes, lieutenant and Charles Times, ensign. There was also a sub-division at Stevenage. Joined the 2nd Admin Battalion and disbanded on 27 February 1867.

**13th**—Formed at Watton-on-Stone on 8 September 1864 and joined the 2nd Admin Battalion. Disbanded on 28 July 1868, Lieutenant Russell H Barrington and Ensign Herbert B Hodges being the only officers commissioned.

**14th**—Formed as one company at Welwyn on 13 September 1876 and joined the 2nd Admin Battalion. No.2 Company formed at Hitchin in 1877 and became 'F' and 'G' Companies of the new 1st Corps in 1880.

# Huntingdon

## Mounted Rifle Volunteers / Light Horse Volunteers

**1st**—Originally formed by the Duke of Manchester as 1st Huntingdonshire Mounted Rifles in December 1859. The Duke is credited as the first man to advocate the creation of mounted volunteers within the new Volunteer Movement. Recruiting was not confined to one county, the original three troops being one in Huntingdonshire and two in Bedfordshire: 'A' at Kimbolton, 'B' Bedford and 'C' Sharnbrook. A change in name to Light Horse occurred within a few months of formation. Men from the disbanded in July 1863 2nd Cambridgeshire Mounted Rifles were absorbed, many of the university undergraduates, and in June 1868 a new 'D' (Cambridge) Troop was formed. Also known as the Duke of Manchester's Light Horse, the corps was disbanded in September 1882.

## Rifle Volunteers

**1st**—Only one numbered corps was raised within the county. Formed at Huntingdon on 18 April 1860 and from 1872 included in the 1st Admin Battalion of Cambridgeshire Rifle Volunteers. The first officers to be appointed to the corps, which became 'J' Company of the new 1st Cambridgeshire RVC in 1880, were Captain the Hon Octavius Duncombe, late of the 1st Life Guards, Lieutenant John M. Heathcote, Jun and Ensign William V Theed. From Cromwell's birthplace, the corps moved to St Neots, nine miles to the south-west on the east bank of the Ouse, in 1876.

**4th (Hunts) Volunteer Battalion, Bedfordshire Regiment**—Formed on 4 December 1900. Six companies were authorized, the recruiting for these being carried out in the main from around Huntingdon, St Ives, Fletton and St Neot's. *Territorials:* Four companies of the 5th Battalion Bedfordshire Regiment.

# Isle of Man

## Artillery Volunteers

**1st**—Formed at Douglas on 15 February 1861 and by 1869 had reached an establishment of two batteries. Included in the 1st Admin Brigade of Cheshire Artillery Volunteers until disbanded in 1875.

**2nd**—Formed at Laxey on 8 July 1864, the 2nd Corps was later disbanded and last seen in the Army List for December 1872.

## Rifle Volunteers

**1st (1860-1870)**—Formed at Castletown with Patrick T Cunningham commissioned as lieutenant on 29 September 1860. The Rev Edward Ferrier was appointed as chaplain at the same time. Headquarters moved to Ballasalla, just under three miles to the north-east of Castletown, in 1867. On 10 March 1870 the War Office issued an order directing the disbandment of the 1st Isle of Man RVC with effect from 14 July 1870.

**1st (1880-1908)**—Formed as 2nd Corps at Douglas with Captain J S G Taubman in command on 29 September 1860. Renumbered as 1st in 1880 and designated 7th (Isle of Man) Volunteer Battalion King's (Liverpool Regiment) under Army Order 81 of March 1888. The battalion was not included in the Territorial Force and instead continued service as 7th VB King's from 1908 under the volunteer system. In *A Military History of the Isle of Man* B E Sargeaunt notes that on 28 June 1873 the corps paraded 'at the Drill Shed on the Lake (Douglas)' prior to leaving by rail to form a Guard of Honour to His Excellency the Lieutenant Governor of the Isle of Man on the occasion of the first railway line being opened on the island from Douglas to Peel. Also recorded is the opening of a new rifle range at Howe Farm, Douglas Head on 10 August 1895. Prior to this the corps had, between 1884 and 1894, used a range at Langness. A new drill hall in Peel Road, Douglas was opened in June 1896.

**2nd**—See 1st Corps (1880-1908).

**3rd**—Formed at Ramsey on 29 September 1860 with George Hall as captain, Edward Yates, lieutenant and John C Goldsmith, ensign. The corps was later disbanded and appeared for the last time in the Army List for June 1869.

**4th**—Formed at Crosby to the north-west of Douglas on 24 April 1866 with Captain Thomas K Clucas in command. Disappeared from the Army List in December 1870, the War Office having directing disbandment on the previous 10 March.

# Isle of Wight

## Rifle Volunteers

All rifle corps formed were included in the 1st Admin Battalion which became the new 1st Corps in 1880. Two numbered sub-divisions appeared in the Army List which were later numbered as 4th and 5th Corps.

**1st (1860-1880)**—Formed as one company at Ryde on 25 January 1860 with Sir John Lees as captain, Charles Cavendish Clifford, lieutenant and Francis Newman, ensign. Absorbed the 3rd Corps, also at Ryde, as No 2 Company in 1864 and became 'A' and 'B' Companies of the new 1st Corps in 1880.

**1st (1880-1908)**—The 1st Admin Battalion of Isle of Wight Rifle Volunteers was formed with headquarters at Newport on 5 July 1860 and consolidated in 1880 as the new 1st Corps with eight companies: 'A' and 'B' Ryde (late 1st Corps), 'C' and 'D' Newport (late 2nd Corps), 'E' Nunwell (late 4th Corps), 'F' and 'G' Ventnor (late 5th Corps), 'H' Cowes (late 7th Corps).

**Waist-belt clasp, 1st Isle of Wight Rifle Volunteer Corps.**

Re-designated as 5th (Isle of Wight 'Princess Beatrice's') Volunteer Battalion Hampshire Regiment under General Order 91 of September 1885, Princess Beatrice being the wife of HRH Prince Henry of Battenberg, the battalion's first Hon Colonel. In 1900 a cyclist company was added at Newport. *Territorials:* 8th Battalion Hampshire Regiment.

**2nd**—Formed as one company at Newport on 14 January 1860 with Sir John Simeon as captain, Arthur H Estcourt, lieutenant and John Tooke, ensign. Increased to two companies in 1874 and became 'C' and 'D' Companies of the new 1st Corps in 1880. Cassell's *Gazetteer* for 1897 notes that the Volunteer Drill Hall was also used for 'dramatic entertainments'.

**3rd**—Formed as one company at Ryde on 25 January 1860 with John B W Fleming as captain, George Rendall, lieutenant and Ernest Edwards, ensign. Absorbed into the 1st Corps in 1864.

**4th**—Formed at Nunwell on 16 February 1860 with Sir Henry Oglander as lieutenant and Augustus F Leeds as ensign. Known as the 1st Sub-division until July when increased to a full company—the two officers being promoted to captain and lieutenant, Francis W Popham joining them as ensign. Became 'E' Company of the new 1st Corps in 1880. Nunwell Park was the seat of the Oglander family.

**5th**—Formed at Ventnor on 25 February 1860 with Albert J Hambrough as lieutenant and Charles F Fisher as ensign. Known as the 2nd Sub-division until October when increased to a full company—the officers were promoted to captain and lieutenant, William M Judd joining them as ensign. Increased to two companies sometime in 1879 and became 'F' and 'G' Companies of the new 1st Corps in 1880.

**6th**—Formed at Sandown on 31 March 1860 with Henry Farnell as captain and Sir George Lowther, late of the 69th Regiment of Foot, lieutenant. The 6th Corps was last seen in the Army List for March 1862.

**7th**—Formed as one company at Cowes on 27 April 1860 with William S Graham, late of the 2nd Bengal European Light Cavalry, as captain, John R Mann, lieutenant and James B Bird, ensign. Became 'H' Company of the new 1st Corps in 1880.

**8th**—Formed at Freshwater on 6 July 1860 with Benjamin T Cotton as lieutenant and William C Plumley as ensign. The corps disappeared from the Army List in February 1869.

# Kent

## Artillery Volunteers

The 1st Admin Brigade of Kent Artillery Volunteers was formed with headquarters at Gravesend in August 1860 and consolidated in May 1880 as the new 1st Corps.

**1st (1859-1880)**—Formed at Gravesend on 20 October 1859 and provided two batteries of the new 1st Corps in 1880.

**1st (1880-1908)**—Formed in 1880 by the consolidation of the 1st Admin Brigade. Headquarters remained at Gravesend and the corps comprised eleven batteries: Gravesend (2), Faversham (2), Blackheath (2), Sandgate (1), Gillingham (1), Sheerness (3). The 1st Corps was re-designated under General Order 77 of 1887 as the 3rd Volunteer (Kent) Brigade Cinque Ports Division Royal Artillery. This title was retained until 1889 when 1st Kent Artillery Volunteer Corps (Eastern Division Royal Artillery) appeared in the Army Lists. *Territorials:* Seven companies of the Sussex and Kent RGA and the Home Counties (Kent) RGA.

**2nd (1859-1880)**—Formed at Faversham on 15 November 1859 and in 1880 provided two batteries of the new 1st Corps.

**2nd (1880-1908)**—Formed of six batteries by the renumbering of the 9th Corps at Plumstead, moving headquarters to Lewisham in 1905. *Territorials:* 10th and 11th County of London (Howitzer) Batteries and

Ammunition Column of the 4th London (Howitzer) Brigade RFA.

**3rd (1859-1860)**—Formed at Folkestone on 7 November 1859 and was later de-designated as 1st Cinque Ports AVC. The corps appeared as such for the first time in the Army List for April 1860.

**3rd (Royal Arsenal) (1880-1908)**—Formed in 1880 of six batteries by the renumbering of the 10th Corps at Royal Arsenal, Woolwich. Increased to eight batteries and in 1889 was converted to position artillery. The Royal Naval School at Eltham formed a cadet corps attached to the 3rd in 1902. *Territorials:* 4th, 5th and 6th County of London Batteries and Ammunition Column of the 2nd London Brigade RFA. The cadet corps became part of the Junior Division OTC at the same time being re-designated as Eltham College.

**4th**—Formed at Sheerness on 9 January 1860 and was absorbed into the 13th Corps late 1866.

**5th**—Formed at Blackheath on 28 February 1860 and provided two batteries of the new 1st Corps in 1880.

**6th**—A 6th Corps appeared in the Army List for March 1860 but was removed the following month having had no location or officers allotted to it.

**7th**—A 7th Corps with headquarters at Greenwich first appeared in the Army List for March 1860. No officers were gazetted and the corps was removed in March 1862.

**8th**—None formed.

**9th**—Formed at Plumstead on 13 February 1860 and renumbered as 2nd Corps in 1880.

**10th**—Formed at the Royal Arsenal in Woolwich on 28 February 1860 and was by August permitted to include Royal Arsenal in its title. Renumbered as 3rd Corps in 1880.

**11th**—Formed at Sandgate on 25 February 1860 and provided one battery of the new 1st Corps in 1880.

**12th**—Formed at Gillingham on 6 March 1860 and provided one battery of the new 1st Corps in 1880.

**13th**—Formed at Sheerness on 1 March 1860 and absorbed the 4th Corps in 1866. Provided three batteries of the new 1st Corps in 1880.

**14th**—Formed with headquarters at Woolwich Dockyard on 29 March 1860, the sub-title Dockyard being given in the Army List from August and Royal Dockyard after April of the following year. The corps was later disbanded and last seen in the Army List for April 1870.

## Rifle Volunteers

The county formed five Admin battalions, the 1st, 2nd 4th and 5th later to provide the new 3rd, 1st, 2nd and 5th Corps respectively. The 3rd Admin Battalion, which was formed with headquarters at Maidstone in August 1860 and included the 1st, 9th, 12th, 15th, 19th, 20th, 22nd, 31st, 38th and 39th Corps, was broken up in 1874. There were two numbered sub-divisions: for 1st, see 13th Corps, 2nd, see 14th Corps.

**1st (1859-1877)**—Formed as two companies at Maidstone on 25 August 1859 with Captain Commandant Edward Scott in command. Joined the 3rd Admin Battalion, transferred to 2nd Admin in 1874, and became 'A' and 'B' Companies of the new 1st Corps in 1877. Many in Maidstone were employed in the production of paper—leading mill owners, John Hollingworth and R J Balston were members of the 1st Kent Corps.

**1st (1877-1908)**—The 2nd Admin Battalion of Kent Rifle Volunteers was formed with headquarters at Tunbridge Wells on 3 July 1860, moving to Penshurst in 1863, Sevenoaks in 1867 and Tonbridge in 1871. The battalion was consolidated in 1877 as the new 1st Corps with eight companies: 'A' and 'B' Maidstone (late 1st Corps), 'C' Tonbridge (late 14th Corps), 'D' Tunbridge Wells (late 17th Corps), 'E' Penshurst (late 23rd Corps), 'F' Leeds Castle (late 31st Corps), 'G' Sevenoaks (late 33rd Corps), 'H' Westerham (late 35th Corps).

Under General Order 14 of February 1883 the 1st Corps was re-designated as 1st Volunteer Battalion Queen's Own (Royal West Kent Regiment). The establishment was increased to eleven companies in 1900. Several cadet corps were formed and affiliated to the battalion: Skinner's School at Tunbridge Wells in 1901, a company at Westerham in 1904 and Maidstone Grammar School in 1906. *Territorials:* Parts of both the 4th and 5th Battalions Queen's Own Royal West Kent Regiment. Skinner's and Maidstone Schools joining the OTC.

**2nd (1859-1860)**—See 2nd Cinque Ports Corps.

**2nd (East Kent) (1880-1908)**—The 4th Admin Battalion of Kent Rifle Volunteers was formed with headquarters at Canterbury in August 1860 and included the 5th, 6th, 16th, 24th, 29th and 36th Corps. In April 1874 the 2nd, 7th and 8th Cinque Ports RVC joined the Kent corps of 4th Admin and together they were amalgamated as the new 5th Kent (East Kent) RVC. The 5th Kent remained as part of the 4th Admin Battalion which now also included the 4th, 5th and 10th Cinque Ports Corps. By the end of 1874, however, the Cinque Ports companies had been absorbed into the 5th Kent. This brought its establishment up to ten companies: 'A' Ramsgate, 'B' and 'C' Canterbury, 'D' Hythe, 'E' Sittinbourne, 'F' Folkestone, 'G' Margate, 'H' Ashford, 'I' Wingham, 'K' Dover and 'L' New Romney.

Charles Igglesden notes in his book *History of the East Kent Volunteers* how 'A' (Ramsgate) Company were disadvantaged in not having a drill hall or headquarters. They met for some years in Ellington Park, or St George's Hall, but at the time of writing his book (1899) he notes that drills were being carried out at the Sergeant Instructor's house in Cavendish Street, and at Chatham House. Permission had been given in 1877 to raise a detachment at Minster, but with just nine men enrolling the project was closed down within the year.

Both 'B' and 'C' Companies at Canterbury drilled under the Corn Exchange until 1887 when they got the use of the Agricultural Hall. The armoury was at first in an old disused public house in Burgate Street called The Volunteer; later, though, the weapons were kept an Northgate Street, in yet another old pub—The Old City Arms. The Hythe Company Used premises in Bank Street as headquarters until taking over an old chapel in Great Conduit Street in 1882. The Folkestone contingent was disbanded in 1878 and the 2nd Corps would be without an 'F' Company for the remainder of its existence.

In September 1880 the 5th Corps was renumbered as 2nd and in 1883, under General Order 63 of May, was designated as 1st Volunteer Battalion Buffs (East Kent Regiment). The year 1888 saw 'H' Company at Ashford moving into a new drill hall in Tufton Street, then in 1893, 'I' Company was transferred to Lydd. The headquarters of 'D' Company moved from Hythe to Folkestone in 1896, and those of the battalion from Canterbury to Dover in 1901. Additional personnel were raised at Westgate-on-Sea, Herne Bay, Birchington, Broadstairs, Canterbury and Dover during the war in South Africa which brought the establishment of the battalion up to sixteen companies—two being cyclist formations. A reduction, however, to twelve was made in 1905, these in 1907 being listed as Ramsgate, Canterbury (2), Birchington, Folkestone, Sittingbourne, Herne Bay, Margate, Ashford, Wingham, Dover and Lydd. *Territorials:* 4th Battalion Buffs.

Associated with the battalion were several cadet corps, the first of which was formed at Dane Hill School, Margate in 1889. This company was disbanded, however, in 1897. The Chatham House College Company was formed at Ramsgate in 1891 and in 1908 became part of the OTC. Also affiliated, and to join the OTC in 1908, were the South Eastern College Cadets at Ramsgate (formed in 1898 and re-designated St Lawrence College in 1907); Dover College Cadet Corps (formed 1901); St Edmund's School, Canterbury and Sir Roger Manwood's School in Sandwich (both formed 1903). Other cadet units associated with the 1st Volunteer Battalion were at Margate College (formed 1892 and disbanded 1901) and New College Schools Herne Bay (see 4th Volunteer Battalion Queen's Own Royal West Kent Regiment below).

**3rd (1859-1880)**—Formed as one company at Lee on 7 November 1859 with Henry Burrard Farneil as captain, Henry D Drury, lieutenant and William H L Barnet, ensign. Joined the 1st Admin Battalion and increased to two companies in February 1864. Became 'A' and 'B' Companies of the new 3rd Corps in 1880.

**3rd (West Kent) (1880-1908)**—The 1st Admin Battalion was formed with headquarters at Blackheath on 12 June 1860 and consolidated in 1880 as the 3rd Kent (West Kent) RVC with eleven companies: 'A' and 'B' Lee (late 3rd Corps), 'C' and 'D' Dartford (late 12th Corps), 'E' Greenwich (late 13th Corps), 'F' Bromley (late 18th Corps), 'G' and 'H' Blackheath (late 25th Corps), 'I' Deptford (late 27th Corps), 'K' Charlton (late 28th Corps), 'L' Deptford (late 34th Corps).

General Order 14 of February 1883 directed re-designation to 2nd Volunteer Battalion Queen's Own (Royal West Kent Regiment). By 1900 the strength of the battalion stood at thirteen companies and in that year the Proprietary School in Blackheath, and Quernmore School at Bromley, were affiliated. *Territorials:* Transfer to the Territorial Force in 1908 was as part of the 20th Battalion London Regiment. Quernmore School at the same time became part of the OTC. Uniform: green/black. Mr J W Reddyhoff, writing in the *Bulletin* of the Military Historical Society in November 1987, noted that the West Kent Volunteer Freemason Lodge No 2041 was formed from within the battalion on 14 March 1884.

**4th (1859-1880)**—Formed as one company at Woolwich on 21 December 1859 with George E Thorold as captain, William Henry Carter, lieutenant and John Mathew Butler, ensign. Formed part of the 1st Admin Battalion until 1870 when attached to the 26th Corps. Became part of the new 4th Corps in 1880.

**4th (Royal Arsenal) (1880-1908)**—The 26th Kent RVC with headquarters at the Royal Arsenal in Woolwich first appears in the Army List for April 1860 and is shown as a two-battalion corps—the first officers' commissions were dated 25 February; that of the commanding officer, Colonel Alex T Tulloh of the Royal Artillery, 29 February. It was at first intended to number the 2nd Battalion as 30th Corps, but this arrangement never appeared in any Army List. By August 1860 the corps comprised sixteen companies and had obtained permission to include Royal Arsenal as part of its official title. In July 1864 the corps was divided. The 1st Battalion became 21st Corps, which was to fill the gap in the county's list left by the disbandment of the Lewisham RVC in 1861, while the 2nd Battalion remained with the number 26th. Both units retained Royal Arsenal as part of their title, and from January 1865 the 26th Corps is shown as having its headquarters at the Royal Gun Factory Office, Woolwich.

The 21st and 26th were once again united when in 1870 they were merged under the title of 26th Kent (Royal Arsenal) RVC. The 4th Corps, also at Woolwich, was absorbed in 1880, the whole at the same time being renumbered as 4th Kent (Royal Arsenal) RVC with an establishment of ten companies. The new 4th Corps was designated as 3rd Volunteer Battalion Queen's Own (Royal West Kent Regiment) in 1883. *Territorials:* Part of the 20th Battalion London Regiment.

**5th (1859-1874)**—Formed as one company at Canterbury on 1 December 1859 with Edward Plummer as captain, Henry George Austin, lieutenant and H T Sankey, ensign. Soon to join them were C Holttum as surgeon, and the Dean of Canterbury, Doctor Henry Alford, who became chaplain to the corps. Canterbury was to raise two companies as it was the wish of some in the city to separate the volunteers by class. The 5th Corps was to be made up of professionals and tradesmen, the 6th from the working classes. A glance at the muster roll of the 5th Corps will show that both Captain Plumber and Ensign Sankey were solicitors, while Lieutenant Austin was the surveyor to the Dean and Chapter of Canterbury. Among the other ranks we find included victuallers, a brewer, chemists, tailors, a hotel proprietor, jeweller, boot maker, butcher, gardener, printer, schoolmaster, cabinetmaker, tobacconist, watchmaker, builders and a baker. Joined the 4th Admin Battalion and became part of the new 5th (East Kent) Corps in 1874. St Edmund's School at St Thomas's Hill, Canterbury formed a cadet corps in 1903.

**5th (1874-1880)**—See 2nd Corps (1880-1908).

**5th (The Weald of Kent) (1880-1908)**—The 5th Admin Battalion was formed with headquarters at Cranbrook in May 1861 and as well as several Kent corps also included the 3rd Cinque Ports and 17th Sussex, the latter being transferred to 1st Cinque Ports Admin Battalion by November 1861. The additional title The Weald of Kent was added in 1877. The battalion was consolidated in 1880 as the new 5th Corps with seven companies: 'A' Cranbrook (late 37th Corps), 'B' Hawkhurst (late 38th Corps), 'C' Staplehurst (late 40th Corps), 'D' Lamberhurst (late 41st Corps), 'E' Brenchley (late 42nd Corps), 'F' Rolvenden (late 43rd Corps), 'G' Tenterden (late 3rd Cinque Ports Corps).

Under General Order 63 of May 1883 the 5th Corps was re-designated as 2nd (The Weald of Kent) Volunteer Battalion the Buffs (East Kent Regiment). The Cranbrook Grammar School Cadet Corps was formed in February 1900 and until the following December, when it transferred to the 2nd Volunteer Battalion, was attached to the 1st Cadet Battalion of the Buffs. *Territorials:* Transfer to the Territorial Force in 1908 was as 5th Battalion Buffs. Cranbrook Grammar School at the same time became part of the OTC.

**6th**—Formed as one company at Canterbury with Captain George Austin, Lieutenant Allen Fielding, who was the city's Town Clark, and Ensign James Delmar, Jun. All three held commissions dated 6 December 1859. As previously mentioned in the notes referring to the 5th Corps of 1859-1874, it was the intention in Canterbury to divide the several classes in the city by placing the volunteers into two separate companies. We have seen how the 5th Corps was to include professionals and tradesmen, whereas the 6th was to be made up of the working classes. But inspection of the muster roll of the corps shows more or less similar descriptions of occupation—shoe maker, engineer, upholsterer, artist, stonemasons, jeweller, tailors, etc. Obviously these were the men working for those that saw themselves suitable for the 5th. And the nicknames given locally to each corps seem also to have been based on class distinction—the 'Fighting 5th', and the 'Drunken 6th', possibly saying it all. Joined the 4th Admin Battalion and became part of the new 5th (East Kent) Corps in 1874.

**7th**—Formed as one company at Kidbrooke on 21 December 1859 with Simon F Jackson (late captain and adjutant, East Kent Militia) as captain, Frederick Morris, lieutenant and Richard J Walmesley, ensign. Joined the 1st Admin Battalion and was disbanded in January 1869.

**8th**—Formed as one company at Sydenham on 22 December 1859 with John Scott Russell as captain, J Hiscutt Crossman, lieutenant and William Morphew, ensign. Joined the 1st Admin Battalion, disappearing from the Army List in April 1871.

**9th**—Formed as one company at Chatham on 31 December 1859 with George Robinson Brock as captain, Charles Isaacs, lieutenant and James Grover, ensign. Joined the 3rd Admin Battalion but removed from the Army List in December 1872.

**10th**—None recorded.

**11th**—Formed as one company at Farnborough on 24 January 1860 with Montague Lubbock as captain, Edward Osmond Berens, lieutenant and William Darwin, ensign. Joined the 2nd Admin Battalion and was disbanded in November 1862.

**12th**—Formed as one company at Dartford on 23 February 1860 with Thomas Hern Fleet as captain, Charles Edward Rashleigh, lieutenant and Thomas Butler, ensign. Joined the 3rd Admin Battalion, transferred to the 1st Admin in 1874, and became 'C' and 'D' Companies of the new 3rd Corps in 1880.

**13th**—Formed at Greenwich on 11 November 1859 and known as the 1st Sub-division until February 1860. John Robert Harris became captain, William Bristow, lieutenant and Thomas William Marchant, ensign. Joined the 1st Admin Battalion and formed 'E' Company of the new 3rd Corps in 1880.

**14th**—Formed at Tonbridge on 2 December 1859 and known as the 2nd Sub-division until March

1860. The Rt Hon Charles Stewart, Viscount Hardinge was appointed as lieutenant and Henry Dorlen Streatfeild as ensign. Viscount Hardinge had previously served as a major with the Kent Militia Artillery. Joined the 2nd Admin Battalion and became 'C' Company of the new 1st Corps in 1877.

**15th**—Formed as one company at Sutton Valence, six miles south-east of Maidstone, on 15 February 1860 with Sir Edmund Filner, Bt, late of the Grenadier Guards, as captain, David Arthur Monro, lieutenant and Thomas Balston, ensign. Muster rolls of the corps show that almost half of the 15th Corps were farmers and agricultural workers from, as well as Sutton Valence, East Sutton, Headcorn and Linton. Joined the 3rd Admin Battalion and disbanded in 1873.

**16th**—Headquarters of the 16th Corps were at Sittingbourne the company, however, was also recruited from among the neighbouring villages of Milton, Greenstreet, Rainham and Tynham. The first appointed officers were Captain John Dixon Dyke, who had previously served with the Madras Army, local banker, Lieutenant William Frederick Baring and Ensign William Whitehead Gascoyne who owned land in the area. All held commissions dated 15 February 1860. In the early years of the 16th Kent RVC drills took place at the Corn Exchange in Sittingbourne, at the Dover Castle Inn at Greenstreet and at a barn belonging to a Mr Paxman at Rainham. Eventually headquarters were set up at the Town Hall and a range opened in 1862 at the Motley Hill Butts, Rainham. Joined the 4th Admin Battalion and became part of the new 5th (East Kent) Corps in 1874.

**17th**—Formed as one company at Tunbridge Wells on 29 March 1860 with Cuthbert J Fisher as captain, John S Wigg, lieutenant and Charles R F Lutwidge, ensign. Joined the 2nd Admin Battalion and became 'D' Company of the new 1st Corps in 1877.

**18th**—Formed as three companies at Bromley on 26 March 1860 with Captain Commandant Clement Satterthwaite in command. Joined the 1st Admin Battalion, was later reduced in size and became 'F' Company of the new 3rd Corps in 1880.

**19th**—Formed as two companies at Rochester on 23 February 1860 with captains Henry Bowen, who had previously served with the Scots Fusiliers Guards, and Captain Henry Savage in command. Joined the 3rd Admin Battalion and was removed from the Army List in January 1874.

**20th**—Formed as a sub-division at Northfleet on 11 April 1860 with Bedford W Kenyon as lieutenant and George Turner, ensign. Joined the 3rd Admin Battalion and disbanded in 1868.

**21st (1860-1861)**—Formed as a sub-division at Lewisham on 25 February 1860 with Thomas W Parker as Lientenant and Stephen J Newman as ensign. Joined the 1st Admin Battalion and disbanded in October 1861.

**21st (1864-1870)**—See 4th (1880-1908).

**22nd**—Formed as one company at Sheerness on 30 March 1860 with Richard Conryn as captain, Robert Chapman, lieutenant and Caleb Selby, ensign. Joined the 3rd Admin Battalion and disbanded in November 1870.

**23rd**—Formed as one company at Penshurst on 28 February 1860 with Captain William Wells, who had served previously with the 1st Life Guards, Lieutenant Edward O Streathfield, late of the 47th Regiment of Foot, and Ensign Richard D Turner. Joined the 2nd Admin Battalion and became 'E' Company of the new 1st Corps in 1877.

**24th**—Formed as one company at Ash, just under three miles west of Sandwich, with Frederick M Godden as captain, William Gillow, lieutenant and Thomas T Collett, ensign. All three held commissions dated 29 February 1860. The 24th joined the 4th Admin Battalion and although it flourished for a time began to reduced in strength as interest diminished. There were just fifty-eight on the muster roll in 1865, this dwindling steadily over the coming years until disbandment was ordered in 1869.

**25th**—Formed as one company at Blackheath on 18 February 1860 with former 55th Madras Native Infantry colonel, John Blaxland as captain, William P J Rogers, lieutenant and William G Barnes, ensign. Joined the 1st Admin Battalion, increased to two companies in 1877, and became 'G' and 'H' Companies of the new 3rd Corps in 1880.

**26th**—See 4th Corps (1880-1908).

**27th**—Formed as one company at Deptford on 28 February 1860 with Edward Wilkinson as captain, William Benjamin Pembroke, lieutenant and Charles Stubbins, ensign. The corps was recruited mainly from the dockyards. Joined the 1st Admin Battalion and became 'I' Company of the new 3rd Corps in 1880.

**28th**—Formed as one company at Charlton on 18 February 1860 with ex Royal Marines colonel, George W Congden, in command. His junior officers were Lieutenant George H Graham and Ensign William Carlyl. Joined the 1st Admin Battalion and became 'K' Company of the new 3rd Corps in 1880.

**29th**—Formed as one company at Ashford with Stephen P Groves, late of the 1st Dragoon Guards, as captain, William Pomfret Burra, lieutenant; John Furley, a local solicitor, as ensign, and Henry Maund who was appointed as surgeon. All four held commissions dated 15 March 1860. The first enrolment of the 29th Kent RVC took place on 15 March and shown on the muster roll are a number of varied trades and professions. The list includes a gas manager, paperhanger, several tailors, carpenters, bank clerks and mechanics, an inn keeper, footman, Sergeant J H Bailey who was an auctioneer, and Private James Harris who ran a sweet shop.

The first drills of the corps were held in the yard of the railway station. The armoury was originally in the basement of the Assembly Rooms, later moving to premises in Elwick Road opposite the entrance to the cattle market. The volunteers even had their own social club in rooms behind the offices of the *Kentish Express* in Park Street. In 1860 attempts were made to set up a sub-division at the nearby village of Wye, but this was short-lived. Wye in fact provided a number of recruits to the main company—students enrolling when the South Eastern Agricultural College was opened there. A glance at a Kent local paper around about October 1861 would reveal the sad event on 12 October which saw the accidental death of Sergeant Instructor Whorley from a rifle bullet to the head at the Warren range. Joined the 4th Admin Battalion and became 'H' Company of the new 5th (East Kent) Corps in 1874.

**30th**—This number was intended for No 2 Company of the 26th Corps but was never used.

**31st**—Formed as one company at Leeds Castle on 23 March 1860 with Charles Wykeham Martin as captain, Baldwin Francis Duppa, lieutenant and George Blackett, ensign. Joined the 3rd Admin Battalion, transferring to 2nd Admin Battalion in 1874, and became 'F' Company of the new 1st Corps in 1877.

**32nd**—Formed as one company at Eltham on 22 March 1860 with Frederick George Saunders as captain, Robert Courage, lieutenant and Thomas Jackson, ensign. Joined the 1st Admin Battalion and disbanded in 1876.

**33rd**—Formed as one company at Sevenoaks on 23 March 1860 with Multon Lambarde as captain, Nelson Bycroft, lieutenant and the Earl of Brecknock, ensign. Joined the 2nd Admin Battalion and became 'G' Company of the new 1st Corps in 1877. At the west end of the north aisle of St Nicholas's Church can be seen monuments to Captain Multon and his family.

**34th**—Formed as one company at Deptford on 23 March 1860 with former member of the Canadian Volunteers, H E Montgomerie as captain, James Batten, lieutenant and Edward Callow, ensign. Joined the 1st Admin Battalion and became 'L' Company of the new 3rd Corps in 1880.

**35th**—Formed as a sub-division at Westerham on 7 March 1860 with John Board as lieutenant and Charles R Thomson, ensign. Joined the 2nd Admin Battalion and was made up to a full company on 5 March 1861. Became 'H' Company of the new 1st Corps in 1877.

**36th**—Formed as one company with headquarters at Wingham, six miles east of Canterbury. The first officers appointed were: Captain N H D'Aeth, Lieutenant J Bridges Plumtre, who was from Goodstone, and Ensign Charles John Plumtre who came from Fredville. All three held commissions dated 18 May 1860. Joining them later were the Rev William Hales as chaplain and Doctor Frederick H Sankey who was appointed as surgeon.

A glance at the first muster roll taken by the 36th Corps shows that as well as Wingham, recruits joined from the neighbouring villages of Littleborne, Nonnington, Goodnestone and Inkham. Also shown are the numerous trades and professions followed by the volunteers—an innkeeper, several bakers, builders and shoemakers; Private George Reakes who was a veterinary surgeon at Littleborne; painters, a saddler, Private George Holloway who laid bricks at Nonnington; a groom, a gamekeeper and two related engine drivers, Thomas and George Pegden, who lived at Wingham. Joined the 4th Admin Battalion and became 'I' Company of the new 5th (East Kent) Corps in 1874.

**37th**—Formed at Cranbrook on 6 June 1860 and soon comprised six companies with Major John Bell in command. In the *London Gazette* dated 5 April 1861 it was noted that the 37th was to divide and its companies formed into separate and independent corps, these to be grouped together as an administrative battalion. The battalion, which was numbered as 5th, was formed in the following month and the corps created from the 37th were: 37th, 38th, 40th, 41st, 42nd, 43rd and 44th. The 37th, which remained at Cranbrook, became 'A' Company of the new 5th Corps in 1880.

**38th (1860)**—Formed at Sheerness on 30 May 1860 and joined the 3rd Admin Battalion. Disbanded in October of the same year.

**38th (1861-1880)**—Formed with headquarters at Hawkhurst as part of the 37th Corps. Detached in April 1861 as 38th Corps and at the same time placed into the 5th Admin Battalion. Disbanded in 1872 but reformed again in May 1877. Became 'B' Company of the new 5th Corps in 1880.

**39th**—Formed as one company at West Malling on 26 June 1860 with Maximilian H Dalison as captain, Frederick Devon, lieutenant and Henry D Wildes as ensign. Joined the 2nd Admin Battalion, transferring to 3rd Admin Battalion in May 1861. Was later disbanded and disappeared from the Army List in August 1874.

**40th**—Formed at Staplehurst as part of the 37th Corps. Detached in April 1861 as 40th Corps and at the same time placed into the 5th Admin Battalion. The officers were Captain Thomas S Usborne, Lieutenant Henry Hoar, Jun and Ensign Thomas H Cole.

**1st Volunteer Battalion Buffs (East Kent Regiment).**

Became 'C' Company of the new 5th Corps in 1880.

**41st**—Formed at Goudhurst, four miles north-west of Cranbrook, as part of the 37th Corps. Detached in April 1861 as 41st Corps and at the same time placed into the 5th Admin Battalion. The officers were Captain Samuel T Newington, Lieutenant H F S Marriott and Ensign George Hinds. Headquarters moved to Lamberhurst, just to the south-east, in 1874 and became 'D' Company of the new 5th Corps in 1880.

**42nd**—Formed at Brenchley, seven miles north-east of Tunbridge Wells, as part of the 37th Corps. Detached in April 1861 as 42nd Corps, with Captain John M Hooker in command, and at the same time placed into the 5th Admin Battalion. Absorbed the 44th Corps at Lamberhurst in May 1863 and became 'E' Company of the new 5th Corps in 1880.

**43rd**—Formed at Rolvenden as part of the 37th Corps. Detached in April 1861 as 43rd Corps, with Lieutenant Thomas Ayerst in command, and at the same time placed into the 5th Admin Battalion. Became 'F' Company of the new 5th Corps in 1880.

**44th**—Formed at Lamberhurst as part of the 37th Corps. Detached in April 1861 as 44th Corps, with Lieutenant Arthur C Ramsden in command, and at the same time placed into the 5th Admin Battalion. Absorbed into the 42nd Corps in May 1863.

**45th**—Formed as one company at Rochester on 4 July 1861 with Jesse Thomas as captain, Charles Ross Ford, lieutenant and John William D'eath, ensign. Joined the 3rd Admin Battalion, transferring to 2nd Admin in 1874. Disbanded in 1876.

**4th Volunteer Battalion Queen's Own (Royal West Kent Regiment)**—Formed with headquarters at Chatham on 27 April 1900 with nine companies and disbanded in 1908. Borden School Cadet Corps was attached in 1903 but removed from Army List in November 1906—the officers, however, now appear under New College Schools (affiliated to 1st VB Buffs) at Herne Bay.

**1st Cadet Battalion the Buffs (East Kent Regiment)**—Formed on 24 October 1894 with four companies at St George's Hall, Ramsgate. Headquarters moved to Margate in 1903. Disbanded in June 1907.

# Lancashire

## Artillery Volunteers

To cater for its smaller corps, Lancashire raised four administrative brigades. The 1st was formed with headquarters in Liverpool and included the 1st, 2nd, 6th, 7th, 8th, 13th, 14th and 20th Corps, the 2nd, also in Liverpool had the 9th, 12th and 17th. The 3rd was found at Blackburn with the 5th, 18th, 22nd, 23rd and 26th Corps, Preston being the headquarters of the 4th which had allotted to it the 10th, 21st, 24th, 25th and 27th. The 1st, 2nd and 3rd Brigades were all in existence before the end of 1860. The 4th found its way into the Army List in 1863. Due to disbandment, by 1869 the 1st Admin Brigade was down to one corps and was subsequently removed from the Army List.

**1st**—Formed of two batteries in Liverpool on 16 November 1859 and joined the 1st Admin Brigade upon its formation in February 1860. Absorbed the 14th Corps as No 3 Battery in July 1860. *Territorials:* Nos 1 to 5 Companies of the Lancashire and Cheshire RGA.

**2nd (1859-1864)**—Formed at Crosby on 3 December 1859. Joined the 1st Admin Brigade and in September 1864 disappeared from the Army List (see also 9th Corps).

**2nd (1880-1908)**—Formed in 1880 by the consolidation of the 2nd Admin Brigade. Headquarters remined at Edge Hill and the batteries were organised: Nos 1 to 12 (late 12th Corps), Nos 13, 14, 15 (late 17th Corps). Headquarters are given as Windsor Barracks from 1881, by 1890 the corps being made up entirely of position batteries. *Territorials:* 1st West Lancashire Brigade RFA.

**3rd (1860)**—No pre-1880 3rd Corps seems to have been formed. However, the 9th appeared in the Army List as such for one month only (February 1860).

**3rd (1880-1908)**—Formed in 1880 by the consolidation of the 3rd Admin Brigade with headquarters in Blackburn and the batteries located as follows: Nos 1 to 4 Blackburn (late 5th Corps), No 6 Church (late 5th Corps), Nos 7, 8 and 9 Bolton (late 18th Corps), Nos 10, 11 and 12 Chorley (late 23rd Corps), Nos 13 and 14 Southport (late 26th Corps). In 1889 the personnel from the Bolton area were withdrawn to form a new corps numbered as 9th and by 1891 the 3rd Corps was made up entirely of position batteries. *Territorials:* 1st East Lancashire Brigade RFA

**4th**—Formed in Liverpool on 5 December 1859, in the main recruited from the clerks and other personnel of Liverpool firms. Headquarters were at first shown as being located at the offices of the Liverpool and London Insurance Company. By 1893 the 4th was made up entirely of position batteries. *Territorials:* 4th West Lancashire (Howitzer) Brigade RFA.

**5th (1860-1880)**—Formed at Blackburn on 9 January 1860, joining the 3rd Admin Brigade in October 1861. Absorbed the 22nd Corps at Church in 1869.

**5th (1880-1908)**—Formed in 1880 by the consolidation of the 4th Admin Brigade. Headquarters were at Preston and the nine batteries were provided by the formed 10th Corps (1), 21st Corps (5), 24th Corps (2) and 25th Corps (1). The new 5th was made up entirely of position batteries by 1891. *Territorials:* 2nd West Lancashire Brigade RFA.

**6th (1859-1863)**—Formed at Liverpool on 20 December 1859. Joined the 1st Admin Brigade and absorbed the 20th Corps in 1861. The 6th Corps was last seen in the Army List for December 1863.

**6th (1880-1908)**—The reorganisations of 1880 saw the 15th Corps in Liverpool renumbered as 6th and by 1893 consisted entirely of position artillery. *Territorials:* 3rd West Lancashire Brigade RFA.

**7th (1859-1869)**—Formed in Liverpool at the Windsor Iron Works on 21 December 1859 and was shown in the Army List for March 1860 as having been absorbed into the 1st. In that for the following June, however, the 7th is once again listed, this time as part of the 1st Admin Brigade. Disbanded and last seen in the Army List for August 1869.

**7th (1880-1908)**—The reorganisations of 1880 saw the 19th Corps at Manchester renumbered as 7th (The Manchester Artillery) and by 1890 consisted entirely of position artillery. *Territorials:* 2nd East Lancashire Brigade RFA.

**8th**—Formed in Liverpool on 9 January 1860 and in the Army List for March 1860 is shown as having been absorbed into the 1st Corps. The 8th appears once again as such in the following June, this time as part of the 1st Admin Brigade. However, the corps was removed from the brigade by the end of 1860. Headquarters were at first shown as being at the Mersey Steel and Iron Company, but

**Officers' sabretache, 7th Lancashire Artillery Volunteers.**

74

**2nd Volunteer Battalion South Lancashire Regiment.**

from 1870 Toxteth Park is given. The 8th absorbed the 25th Lancashire Rifle Volunteer Corps in April 1864. *Territorials:* East and West Lancashire RGA.

**9th (1859-1863)**—Some confusion seems to have arisen concerning the precedence of the corps formed in the Crosby and Kirkdale areas. The Army List for December 1859 shows a 2nd Corps with headquarters at Kirkdale, three officers appearing with the corps all bearing commissions dated 3 December 1859. In the List for February 1860 two of the three officers are now shown as being part of the 1st Corps. The remaining officer and the 2nd Corps are now listed as having their headquarters at Great Crosby. Also in the February List a 9th Corps appears for the first time and has its headquarters recorded as Kirkdale. In the same List another Kirkdale corps appears and is numbered as 3rd with officers holding commissions dated 5 December 1859. The March edition indicates that the 3rd (Kirkdale) had been renumbered as 2nd and the corps previously holding the 9th position had been removed. In June the numbering of the two corps seems to have been resolved as we now see Kirkdale as 9th, and Crosby as 2nd. The 9th joined the 2nd Admin Brigade in November 1860 and in late 1863 was absorbed into the 12th Corps.

**9th (1889-1908)**—As previously mentioned the 9th Corps, made up entirely of position artillery, was formed by the Bolton members of the 3rd Corps in 1889. *Territorials:* 3rd East Lancashire Brigade RFA.

**10th**—Formed at Kirkham on 15 March 1860 and joined the 4th Admin Brigade in 1863.

**11th**—Formed in Liverpool on 19 February 1860 and disappeared from the Army List in August 1867.

**12th**—Formed in Liverpool on 19 February 1860 and joined the 2nd Admin Brigade in the following December. Absorbed the 9th Corps in 1863, headquarters being shown as Edge Hill from 1869.

**13th**—Formed at Everton on 28 February 1860 and placed with the 1st Admin Brigade. Removed from the Army List in November 1863.

**14th**—Formed at Liverpool on 28 February 1860 and included in the 1st Admin Brigade. Absorbed into the 1st Corps as its No 3 Battery in July 1861.

**15th**—Formed at Garston on 2 April 1860, headquarters moving to Lark Lane (later Admiral Street), Liverpool from October 1877. Renumbered as 6th in 1880.

**16th**—None raised.

**17th**—Formed at Liverpool on 3 August 1860 and included in the 2nd Admin Brigade the following year.

**18th**—Formed at Great Leven on 29 May 1860 and included in the 3rd Admin Brigade during the following year. Moved to Bolton in 1863.

**19th**—Formed in Manchester on 17 August 1860 and renumbered as 7th Corps in 1880.

**20th**—Formed at Liverpool on 8 August 1860 and included in the 1st Admin Brigade. Absorbed into the 6th Corps in 1861.

**21st**—Formed at Preston on 27 September 1860 and joined the 4th Admin Brigade in 1863.

**22nd**—Formed at Church on 23 October 1860 and included in the 3rd Admin Brigade the following year. Absorbed into the 5th Corps on 1869.

**23rd**—Formed at Chorley on 20 November 1860 and included in the 3rd Admin Brigade the following year.

**24th (1863)**—A 34th Corps at Burnley appears in the Army List for May 1863. It was removed from the Army List in September 1863 having had no officers gazetted to it.

**24th (1865)**—Formed at Lancaster on 10 August 1865 and placed into the 4th Admin Brigade.

**25th**—Formed at Blackpool on 6 July 1865 and placed into the 4th Admin Brigade.

**26th**—Formed at Birkdale on 2 December 1865 and placed into the 3rd Admin Brigade. Headquarters moved to Southport in 1866.

**27th**—Formed 3 June 1868 as the 90th Lancashire Rifle Volunteer Corps. Headquarters were at Fleetwood and the corps first appeared as the 27th AVC in the Army List for May 1870. It disappeared, however, in 1875 having been part of the 4th Admin Brigade.

## Engineer Volunteers

**1st**—Formed at Liverpool 1 October 1860 and absorbed the 2nd Corps, also in Liverpool, in 1864. In October 1884 a submarine mining company ('K' Company) was added which in 1888 provided the Mersey Division Submarine Miners. A cadet corps at Rossall School was attached to the corps in 1890. *Territorials:* Western Wireless, Air-Line and Cable Telegraph Companies, the Rossall School Cadet Corps to the OTC.

**2nd (1860-1864)**—Formed at Liverpool 29 December 1860 and absorbed into the 1st Corps during the early part of 1864.

**2nd (1864-1908)**—Formed at St Helens as 3rd Corps 13 February 1864 being renumbered as 2nd by the following April. The additional tile of The St Helens also appeared in the Army List. *Territorials:* 1st and 2nd West Lancashire Field Companies and West Lancashire Divisional Telegraph Company.

**3rd (1862)**—A 3rd Corps was formed in July 1862 and appeared as being attached to the 19th Lancashire Artillery Volunteers. No officers were ever gazetted and the 3rd made its last appearance in the Army List for October 1862. Headquarters were given as Manchester.

**3rd ((1864)**—See 2nd Corps (1864-1908).

**3rd (1901-1908)**—Formed in Manchester 28 February 1901. *Territorial:* 1st and 2nd East Lancashire Field Companies and East Lancashire Divisional Engineers.

**Mersey Division Submarine Miners/Electrical Engineers**—Formed as 'K' Company of the 1st Lancashire EVC in October 1884. Removed as the Mersey Division in 1888 and designated 'Electrical Engineers' in 1907. *Territorials:* Lancashire Fortress Engineers.

## Mounted Rifle Volunteers/Light Horse Volunteers

**1st**—Originally raised as the 1st Lancashire Mounted Rifle Volunteers in December 1859 at Manchester and became Light Horse in February 1861. In 1872 the corps is shown as having its headquarters at Leamington Place, Old Garratt Street in Manchester. Disbanded August 1873. Scarlet tunics with dark blue facings were worn, the badges featuring the three lions and label of three ends from the arms of the County Palatinate of

**4th Volunteer Battalion Manchester Regiment.**

**Arms of Manchester, a feature of many of the badges worn by volunteers associated with the Manchester Regiment.**

Lancashire. The corps was commanded by Captain Henry Anthony Bennett of 47 Dale Street, Manchester.

**2nd**—The 2nd Lancashire Light Horse Volunteers was raised in 1860 with headquarters at The Albany, Oldall Street, Liverpool. In command, Captain Nicholas Blundell. Headquarters moved to No 2 Croxfield Road, Edge Hill, Liverpool in 1865, then again in 1872 to Baines Place also in Liverpool. The corps was disbanded in February 1875.

## Rifle Volunteers

The last rifle corps to be raised and numbered in Lancashire was that formed at Flixton in 1872. This company received the title of 91st Corps and as such held the second highest number allotted to any volunteer unit in the land. The county was to provide the usual administrative battalions for its smaller corps. Of the nine created, three were to be consolidated before the general reorganisations of 1880. The remaining six, together with the larger corps, were in that year to form twenty-one. A 22nd followed in 1882. Sub-divisions numbered 1st, 2nd and 3rd existed and these can be seen under 13th and 38th Corps (1st), 14th Corps of 1859-1861 (2nd) and 14th Corps of 1880-1908 (3rd).

**1st (1859-1861)**—Formed as three companies at Liverpool with Captain Commandant Nathanial G P Bousfield in command. A Liverpool cotton merchant, Bousfield's commission was dated 11 June 1859 and as such was the first in the land to be issued under the new volunteer system. His company commanders were J Burnside Taylor and George Hunter Robertson. Joined the 1st Admin Battalion and became part of the new 1st Corps in December 1861.

**1st (1861-1908)**—The 1st Admin Battalion was formed with headquarters in Liverpool in May 1860 and to it were added the 1st, 22nd, 38th, 45th, 66th and 69th Corps. When the battalion was consolidated as the new 1st Corps of eight companies in December 1861, also included in the merger was the 14th Corps at Edge Hill. The 74th Corps in Liverpool was absorbed in 1862. Re-designation as 1st Volunteer Battalion King's (Liverpool Regiment) was notified in Army Order 81 of March 1888, the establishment of the corps being ten companies. Two more were sanctioned in 1883, another in 1900 and a cadet corps formed in April 1865 was disbanded in 1884. *Territorials:* 5th Battalion King's.

**2nd (1859-1880)**—Formed at Blackburn on 4 October 1859. Absorbed the 3rd Corps, also at Blackburn, in February 1860, this bringing the establishment of the corps up to four companies under Captains Thomas Lund, John Gerald Potter, William Harrison and Arthur Ingram Robinson. Joined the 8th Admin Battalion and became 'A' to 'H' Companies of the new 2nd Corps in 1880.

**2nd (1880-1908)**—The 8th Admin Battalion was formed with headquarters at Blackburn in March 1864 and included the 2nd, 62nd and 81st Corps. The new 2nd Corps was formed upon consolidation in 1880 with ten companies: 'A' to 'F' Blackburn (late 2nd Corps), 'G' and 'H' Over Darwen (late 2nd Corps), 'J' and 'K' Clitheroe (late 62nd Corps).

Re-designated as 1st Volunteer Battalion East Lancashire Regiment was in June 1889. *Territorials:* 4th Battalion East Lancashire Regiment. Stonyhurst College Cadet Corps, which was formed and affiliated in January 1901, joined the OTC.

**3rd (1859-1860)**—Formed at Blackburn on 4 October 1859 and absorbed into the 2nd Corps in February 1860.

**3rd (1880-1908)**—Burnley was the headquarters of the 3rd Admin Battalion which was formed in September 1860 and included the 4th, 7th, 17th, 29th, 36th, 57th, 84th, 87th, 88th and 90th Corps. Headquarters were transferred to Rossendale in 1862, to Accrington in 1865, and back to Burnley in 1874. The battalion was consolidated in 1880 as the new 3rd Corps with twelve companies: 'A' to 'D' Burnley (late 17th Corps), 'E' Padiham (late 84th Corps), 'F' to 'H' Accrington (late 7th Corps), 'J' Haslingden (late 88th Corps), 'K' Ramsbottom (late 57th Corps), 'L' Stacksteads (late 4th Corps), 'M' Lytham (late 29th Corps).

**Pouch-belt plate, 16th (3rd Manchester) Lancashire Rifle Volunteer Corps.**

Re-designation as 2nd Volunteer Battalion East Lancashire Regiment was notified by Army Order 263 of June 1889. Volunteers from the battalion served with the Regulars of the East Lancashire Regiment in South Africa during the Boer War. Lieutenant Percy S Parker, who had joined the battalion in January 1898, died of enteric fever at Heilbron on 1 February 1902. *Territorials:* 5th Battalion East Lancashire Regiment.

**4th (1859-1880)**—The 4th Corps was formed as one company, the Army List giving its location as Rossendale which is a parish and borough incorporation the towns of Bacup, Haslington and Rawtenstall. The first to receive a commission was James Munn as captain on 4 July 1859, he being followed by Servetus Aitken as lieutenant (22 August 1859), and Samuel Hal, a solicitor from Bacup, who was promoted ensign from sergeant major on 12 April 1860. James Munn, who resided at Fern Hill, Stacksteads, was the eldest son of cotton manufacturer Robert Munn and was drowned when his yacht overturned at Lytham Regatta in July 1871. There is a memorial to him in Trinity Churchyard, Tunstead, Stacksteads. The 4th Corps joined the 3rd Admin Battalion and became 'L' Company of the new 3rd Corps in 1880.

**4th (1880-1908)**—The 4th Admin Battalion was formed with headquarters at Eccles in October 1860 and included the 21st, 46th, 55th, 60th, 67th, 76th and 91st Corps. Headquarters moved to Manchester in 1862, Wigan by the beginning of 1877, and back to Manchester in 1879. The battalion was consolidated in 1880 as the new 4th Corps with thirteen companies: 'A' to 'E' Wigan (late 21st Corps), 'F' Swinton (late No.1 Company, 46th Corps), 'G' Eccles (late No.2 Company, 46th Corps), 'H' Leigh (late 55th Corps), 'J' Atherton (late 60th Corps), 'K' Worsley (late 67th Corps), 'L' and 'M' Farnworth (late 76th Corps), 'N' Flixton (late 91st Corps).

The Farnworth Companies ('L' and 'M') were transferred to the 14th Corps in 1883. Re-designated as 1st Volunteer Battalion Manchester Regiment in 1888. Volunteers from the battalion went to South Africa, the first draft going out under Lieutenant H C Darlington and seeing service in Natal and the Transvaal. Action was seen at Reint Vlei and Belfast, in which two men were killed. Two further drafts followed the first. An additional company was sanctioned in 1900. *Territorials:* 5th Battalion Manchester Regiment.

**Pouch-belt plate and pouch badge, 1st Volunteer Battalion Manchester Regiment.**

**5th (1859-1862)**—Formed as two companies at Liverpool on 19 August 1859 with Adam Stuart Gladstone and Robert John Tinley as captains, Charles Edward Crosbie and Jacob Willink, lieutenants, Samuel Sandbach Parker and Richard George Bushby, ensigns. It would seem that not all were satisfied with how recruiting for the 5th Corps was being carried out. On record is a meeting held by Adam Gladstone at the Liverpool Sessions House on 20 May 1859 in which one R J Tilney (and others) smashed the ballot-boxes. Joined the 2nd Admin Battalion and became part of the new 5th Corps in 1862.

**5th (Liverpool Rifle Volunteer Brigade) (1862-1908)**—The 2nd Admin Battalion was formed with headquarters at Liverpool in May 1860 and to it were added the 5th, 14th, 19th, 39th, 63rd, 64th, 68th, 71st and 86th. The 81st was included for a few months in 1861 but was then transferred to 8th Admin Battalion. In March 1862 the battalion was consolidated as the new 5th Corps with the additional title of The Liverpool Rifle Volunteer Brigade, at the same time adding additional companies by absorbing the 32nd and 79th Corps. With an establishment of ten companies the 5th Corps was re-designated as 2nd Volunteer Battalion King's (Liverpool Regiment) in 1888. The battalion sent three drafts out to South Africa, the first seeing action at Laing's Nek and Belfast. Among the casualties was Lieutenant William Henry Kenyon who died of enteric fever at No 4 Stationary Hospital, Newcastle. Back home, a memorial in his memory was placed in Sefton Park Presbyterian Church by all ranks of the 2nd Volunteer Battalion. *Territorials:* 6th Battalion King's (Liverpool Regiment).

**6th (1st Manchester)**—Formed as twelve companies in Manchester on 25 August 1859, the Viscount Grey de Wilton being appointed as Lieutenant Colonel Commandant on 19 February 1860. A number of large Manchester firms such as Messrs J P and E Westhead, and Messrs J and N Phillips provided whole companies. No 12 Company (headquarters in Eccles) was absorbed into the 46th Corps at Swinton in October 1860, the 43rd at Fallowfield being absorbed in 1861. The 6th Corps for many years occupied headquarters at Wolstenholm's Court, Market Street, Manchester and afterwards at 3 Stretford Road, Hulme. Designation as 2nd Volunteer Battalion Manchester Regiment was notified in Army Order 409 of 1888. A new company was sanctioned in 1890, followed by two more in 1900. *Territorials:* Transfer to the Territorial Force in 1908 was as 6th Battalion Manchester Regiment, 'N' Company, however, which had been formed at Manchester University, became part of the Senior Division OTC.

**7th (1859-1880)**—Formed as one company at Accrington on 20 September 1859 with John Hargreaves Jun as captain, William Halstead Dewhirst, lieutenant and William Bullough, ensign. Joined the 3rd Admin Battalion and absorbed the 36th Corps, also at Accrington, in 1861. Increased to two companies in 1867, three in 1874, and became 'F' to 'H' Companies of the new 3rd Corps in 1880.

**7th (1880-1908)**—The 7th Admin Battalion was formed with headquarters at Ashton-under-Lyne in November 1863 and included the 23rd and 31st Corps. Consolidated as the new 7th Corps in 1880 with twelve companies: 'A' to 'F' at Ashton-under-Lyne (late 23rd Corps) and 'G' to 'M' which were formed by the 31st at Oldham. The letter 'I' was not used. In 1882 the establishment was reduced when the Oldham companies were withdrawn to form a new corps numbered as 22nd, the remainder being designated as 3rd Volunteer Battalion Manchester Regiment in 1888. Three additional companies were sanctioned in 1900. *Territorials:* 9th Battalion Manchester Regiment.

**8th**—Acceptance of the services of a corps of riflemen at Bury was received on 8 August 1859, the commissions of Captain John Hutchinson, Lieutenant William Hardman and Ensign Oliver Ormerod Walker being signed on 22 August. T H Hathurst wrote in *A History and Some Records of the Volunteer Movement in Bury* how the 8th Corps embraced members of every branch of local society: '…there were gentry and the manufacturers, men of large families and men with no family at all, skilled workmen of high standing in their calling, clerks and labourers.' In February 1860 a second company was raised and in July a third and fourth, both at Heywood, and another at Radcliffe in December 1863. T H Hathurst records that within a few days of the Radcliffe men being drafted into the battalion the corps was formed into six companies—he later notes these as being located as Nos 1 and 2 (Bury), Nos 3 and 4 (Heywood) and Nos 5 and 6 (Bury). A corps of very high standard, a Liverpool paper wrote of the 8th Lancashire in 1869 that it was 'amongst

the best drilled men in the county'. The corps was re-designated as 1st Volunteer Battalion Lancashire Fusiliers under General Order 14 of 1883 and in the same year two more companies were added. The Bury Grammar School Cadet Corps was formed and affiliated in 1892. *Territorials:* Transfer to the Territorial Force in 1908 was as 5th Battalion Lancashire Fusiliers. Bury Grammar School at the same time joined the OTC.

**9th (1859-1880)**—Formed as one company at Warrington on 16 September 1859 with J Fenton Greenland as captain, John Richard Pickmere, Jun, lieutenant and Sylvanus Reynolds, ensign. Joined the 9th Admin Battalion in 1865 and by 1880 comprised six companies which provided 'A' to 'F' Companies of the new 9th Corps.

**9th (1880-1908)**—The 9th Admin Battalion was formed with headquarters at Warrington on 16 September 1865 and included the 9th and 49th Corps. These were merged as 9th Corps in 1880, the combined strength of seven companies being located: 'A' to 'F' at Warrington (late 9th Corps) and 'G' at Newton-le-Willows (late 49th). The new 9th Corps was designated 1st Volunteer Battalion South Lancashire Regiment in 1886. During 1900-1903 additional personnel were sanctioned, bringing the establishment of the battalion up to eleven companies. *Territorials:* 4th Battalion South Lancashire Regiment.

**10th (1859-1876)**—Formed at Lancaster on 20 September 1859. Joined the 5th Admin Battalion in 1862 and became 'A' and 'B' Companies of the new 10th Corps in 1876.

**10th (1876-1908)**—The 5th Admin Battalion was formed with headquarters at Ulverston in April 1861 and to it were added the 10th, 37A, 37B, 37C, 52nd, 53rd, 65th and 75th Corps. Consolidated as the new 10th Corps in 1876 with nine companies: 'A' and 'B' Lancaster (late 10th Corps), 'C' and 'D' Ulverston (late 37A Corps), 'E' and 'F' Barrow (late 37B Corps), 'G' Hawkshead (late 37C Corps), 'H' Rossall (late 65th Corps), 'J' Grange (newly formed).

The newly formed 'J' Company also included a detachment at Cartmel which had been formed by former members of the old 53rd Corps. The 10th Corps was re-designated as 1st Volunteer Battalion King's Own (Royal Lancaster Regiment) in 1883. 'K' and 'L' Companies were added at Dalton in 1887, 'L' moving to Millom in 1889. The Rossall Company was disbanded in 1890, its cadet corps at the same time being transferred to 1st Lancashire Engineer Volunteers. In 1900, the battalion was divided so as to form a new 2nd Volunteer Battalion, the 1st remaining at Ulverston with 'A' and 'B' Companies at Ulverston; 'C' and 'D' at Barrow; 'E', Hawkshead; 'F', Barrow; 'G' Dalton and 'H' Millom. *Territorials:* 4th Battalion King's Own.

**11th (Preston) (1859-1880)**—Formed at Preston on 4 October 1859 and in February 1860 absorbed two other Preston corps, the 12th and 30th, bringing the establishment to three companies—the Hon Newsham Pedder, late of the 3rd Royal Lancashire Militia; William Henry Goodair and George Eastham were captains. Joined the 6th Admin Battalion and in 1865 Preston was authorised to be included in the title. In 1866 the 44th Corps at Longton was also absorbed into the 11th, as was the 61st at Chorley in November 1868. Now of eight companies, in 1880 the 11th Corps became 'A' to 'E' and 'G', 'H' and 'J' Companies of the new 11th Corps.

**11th (1880-1908)**—The 6th Admin Battalion was formed with headquarters at Preston in September 1861 and included the 11th, 44th, 59th and 61st Corps. Consolidated in 1880 as the new 11th Corps with nine companies: 'A' to 'E' Preston (late 11th Corps), 'F' Leyland (late 59th Corps), 'G', 'H' and 'J' Chorley (late 11th Corps).

The corps was re-designated as 1st Volunteer Battalion Loyal North Lancashire Regiment under General Order 14 of February 1883. Two new companies were sanctioned in 1900. *Territorials:* 4th Battalion Loyal North Lancashire Regiment.

**12th (1859-1860)**—Formed at Preston on 7 October 1859 and absorbed into the 11th Corps in February 1860.

**12th (1880-1908)**—Formed at Rochdale on 24 February 1860 as 24th Corps, its first officers being Captain Joseph Fenton, Lieutenant Henry Fishwick and Ensign Theodore R Phillippi. Three new companies were added in 1861, a fifth in 1868, sixth in 1869 and a seventh in 1875. Renumbered 12th in 1880 and designated as 2nd Volunteer Battalion Lancashire Fusiliers under General Order 14 of February 1883. *Territorials:* 6th Battalion Lancashire Fusiliers.

**13th**—The 13th at Southport first appeared in the Army List for October 1859 as the 1st Sub-division. In that for the following December the corps is shown as a full company, its officers, Captain William McInroy, Lieutenant George Bretherton and Ensign John A Robinson, holding commissions dated 6 December. Now of two companies, was amalgamated with 54th Corps at Ormskirk in 1880. Later increased to six (four at Southport, two, Ormskirk), and designated 3rd Volunteer Battalion King's (Liverpool Regiment) in 1888. Two more companies were sanctioned in 1899, the personnel being found out of the Mounted Infantry and Cyclist sections. The battalion was disbanded in 1908.

**14th (1859-1861)**—Formed at Edge Hill on 10 November 1859 and known as the 2nd Sub-division until December. Soon comprised two companies, both company commanders, Tyndal Bright and John Brady, holding commissions dated 16 February 1860. Joined the 2nd Admin Battalion and became part of the new 1st Corps in December 1861.

**14th (1880-1908)**—Formed at Bolton on 2nd December 1859 and known as the 3rd Sub-division until numbered as 27th in February 1860—by now four companies with Major William Gray in command. Increased to six companies in 1861, eight in 1863. Amalgamated with the 82nd Corps at Hindley in 1876, renumbered as 14th in 1880, and designated 2nd Volunteer Battalion Loyal North Lancashire Regiment in 1883. In the same year 'L' and 'M' (Farnworth) Companies of the 4th Corps were transferred to the battalion. Two new companies were sanctioned in 1900. *Territorials:* 5th Battalion Loyal North Lancashire Regiment.

**15th**—Formed as four companies at Liverpool on 10 January 1860, a 5th being added in the following November. An interesting article by Mr Dennis Reeves regarding the origins of No 5 Company appeared in the *Bulletin* of the Military Historical Society for May 2003. In the early days of the Volunteer Movement it was found that members of the press and allied trades, because of their anti-social working hours, were restricted from joining the Volunteers. The answer was to raise a corps composed entirely of such workers, the first steps towards this end being in the form of an advertisement which appeared in the *Liverpool Daily Post* for 28 September 1860 headed 'Liverpool Press Corps of Volunteers'. The item had called for men interested to come forward and enrol at a meeting to be held on the following day. At that meeting, records Dennis Reeves, Mr William Henry Peat, Proprietor of the *Liverpool Daily Times* was elected as chairman with his editor, Mr William Maitland, as one of his Honorary Secretaries. Subsequently a 'No 1 Press Company' was enrolled consisting of those employed in newspaper management, printing shop owners and booksellers—there were in this company, 'no working class newspaper printers' (Reeves). The company was sworn in at the Lyceum drill hall at Bold Street on 6 October 1860 and carried out drills at the Seel Street Police Station. The 15th Corps was re-designated 4th Volunteer Battalion King's (Liverpool Regiment) by General Order 81 of March 1888. *Territorials:* 7th Battalion King's (Liverpool Regiment).

**16th (3rd Manchester)**—Eight companies under the command of Major John Snowdon Henry formed in Manchester as the 40th Lancashire (3rd Manchester) RVC on 29 February 1860. Renumbered as 16th in 1880 and designated 4th Volunteer Battalion Manchester Regiment in 1888, the headquarters at this time being in Burlington Street, Manchester and the strength twelve companies. *Territorials:* 7th Battalion

Manchester Regiment.

**17th (1860-1880)**—Formed as two companies at Burnley on 16 January 1860 with Captains John Dugdale and Henry Moore the first company commanders. Joined the 3rd Admin Battalion, increased to three companies in 1866, four in 1868, and became 'A' to 'D' Companies of the new 3rd Corps in 1880.

**17th (1880-1908)**—Formed as the 56th Corps of four companies at Salford on 5 March 1860 with Major George A Hill taking command as of 20 July 1860. Renumbered 17th in 1880 (by now eight companies) and joined the Manchester Regiment as one of its Volunteer battalions (without change in title) in 1881. Transferred to the Lancashire Fusiliers as 3rd Volunteer Battalion in March 1886. The Salford Cadet Corps was formed and affiliated to the battalion in 1888 but disbanded in 1891. Some 117 Volunteers served in South Africa, Private A Brown being awarded the Royal Humane Society's First Class Bronze Medal for saving Private A Rogers of the King's Own from drowning in the Buffalo River. *Territorials:* 7th and 8th Battalions Lancashire Fusiliers.

**18th (Liverpool Irish)**—Formed as the 64th Corps at Liverpool on 25 April 1860 with Captain James G Plunket in command. Joined the 2nd Admin Battalion, increased to two companies in June 1860, later four, then, six in September 1863. Liverpool Irish was included in the title from 1864. Headquarters about this time are shown in the Army List as 9 Everton Crescent, Liverpool, moving later to 206 Netherfield Road North. Renumbered as 18th Corps in 1880 and designated 5th (Irish) Volunteer Battalion King's (Liverpool Regiment) in 1888. In 1900 the battalion was increased to eight companies, but in 1905 one of these was disbanded and replaced by a cyclist company. *Territorials:* 8th Battalion King's.

**19th (1860-1862)**—Much can be understood regarding the two-year existence of this corps thanks to an article by Mr Dennis Reeves published in the *Bulletin* of the Military Historical Society for February 1972. As a result of a meeting held at the George Hotel, Liverpool by some influential Scots then resident in the city, a resolution was passed that a Scottish corps should be raised, the suggested title being the Black Watch Scottish Volunteer Rifles. Sufficient numbers came forward to form a No 1 (Lowland) Company, followed quickly by No 2 (Highland). Temporary headquarters were found in the Liverpool and London Chambers in Dale Street, but soon a house was rented in Great George Square which served as a combined headquarters and storehouse. Acceptance by the Government came on 10 January 1860, the title allowed in no way reflecting the Scottish origins and simply shown in the Army List as 19th Lancashire RVC. A strong corps now of three companies, the company commanders Captains James Maxwell, G A Mackenzie and James M Dowie were all sworn in at Seel Street police station within a few days. The 19th Corps was placed into the 2nd Admin and as such were included in the consolidation of that battalion as 5th Corps in 1862, Denis Reeves noting that the old 19th had now become its 'B' (Scottish) Company.

**19th (Liverpool Press Guard) (1880-1908)**—Formed in Liverpool in January 1861 as the 80th Corps from employees of the newspaper and printing trades—the 2 March edition of the *Illustrated London News* included a full-page engraving showing the corps being sworn in at St George's Hall. The additional title Liverpool Press Guard was added in 1862. For details of the events that led up to the formation of the 80th Corps we must turn to an article published in the *Bulletin* of the Military Historical Society in May 2003 in which Dennis Reeves records how a number of pressmen met in the library of St George's Hall to discuss the formation of a corps. At this time there was already a 'Press' Company in Liverpool but, as the cost of uniform and equipment was in the main beyond the reach of the average print worker, this was confined to the management and press owners. The meeting included Mr George McCorquodale, a printer of 38 Castle Street, who was subsequently to become the Lieutenant Colonel of the 80th Corps. The 80th, its services accepted on 10 January 1861, at first comprised five companies; three more were approved on 19 January. Lieutenant-Colonel McCorquodale was a resident of Newton-le-Willows where men from his printing works had enrolled into the 73rd Lancashire RVC. On 31 March 1863, this corps was incorporated into the 80th as its No 9 Company. McCorquodale's eldest son Hugh took command. Renumbered 19th in 1880 and designated 6th Volunteer Battalion King's (Liverpool Regiment) in 1888. A cyclist company was added in 1902, but by 1907 one company had been disbanded. *Territorials:* 9th Battalion King's (Liverpool Regiment).

As a follow up to Dennis Reeves's article both Garry Gibbs and W Y Carman provided illustrations showing how the Liverpool Press Guard took the latter part of their title seriously. In both we see Grenadier Guard-style scarlet jackets and bearskin headdress, grenade badges, and even the buttons on the tunic are arranged as in the senior guards regiment. One item, however, is possible unique: a early button showing an old printing press.

**20th (2nd Manchester)**—The 33rd Lancashire RVC of four companies formed at Ardwick 28 January 1860. A fifth was soon added and in 1863 the 78th Corps, another Ardwick corps, was absorbed. In 1864 the 28th Corps, known as 2nd Manchester and with a large number of Irish within its ranks, was also absorbed—the sub-title now taken into use by the 33rd. The overall strength of the corps now stood at fourteen companies. Renumbered 20th in 1880 and designated 5th (Ardwick) Volunteer Battalion, Manchester Regiment in 1888. A cadet corps was formed and affiliated in the same year. An additional company was sanctioned in 1900. *Territorials:* 8th Battalion Manchester Regiment. Mr J W Reddyhoff writing in the *Bulletin* of the Military Historical Society in November 1997 notes that the East Lancashire Centurion Freemason Lodge No.2322 was formed from within the battalion on 23 July 1889.

**21st (1860-1880)**—Formed as two companies at Wigan on 20 January 1860, its company commanders being Captains Nathaniel Eckersley and Egerton Leigh Wright. Joined the 4th Admin Battalion in 1869, the establishment was increased to five companies during the 1870s, and in 1880 became 'A' to 'E' Companies of the new 4th Corps. The Volunteer Drill Hall was opened in 1884.

**21st (1880-1908)**—Formed in 1880 by the amalgamation of the 47th Corps, raised as five companies at St Helens on 29 February 1860 (Major Commandant David Gambler in command), and the 48th, which was formed as one company at Prescot under Captain Walter Wren Driffield on 15 March 1860. The combined establishment of six companies was later increased to eight. Designated 2nd Volunteer Battalion South Lancashire Regiment in 1886. *Territorials:* 5th Battalion South Lancashire Regiment.

**22nd (1860-1863)**—Formed as two companies in Liverpool on 30 January 1860 with Captain Commandant Edward Brailsford Bright in command. The corps was included in the 1st Admin Battalion until December 1861, disappearing from the Army List in 1863.

**22nd (1882-1908)**—Formed at Oldham on 29 July 1882 by the withdrawal of the Oldham companies from the 7th Corps, the establishment by the end of the year rising to eight companies. Designated 6th Volunteer Battalion Manchester Regiment in 1888, two additional companies were sanctioned in 1900. *Territorials:* 10th Battalion Manchester Regiment.

**23rd**—Formed as two companies at Ashton-under-Lyne on 7 February 1860 with Captains John Lees and Ely Andrew in command. Joined the 7th Admin Battalion, the establishment steadily rising to six companies, and became 'A' to 'F' Companies of the new 7th Corps in 1880.

**24th**—See 12th Corps (1880-1908).

**25th**—Formed in Liverpool on 9 January 1860 with Alexander McNeil as captain; Charles Lee Campbell, lieutenant and Robert Horsfall, ensign. Absorbed into the 8th Lancashire Artillery Volunteers in April 1864. The corps was recruited in the main from the Mersey Ironworks.

**26th**—Formed as three companies at Haigh on 9 February 1860 with John Thompson as Captain Commandant. Disbanded in April 1864.

**27th**—See 14th Corps (1880-1908).

**28th (2nd Manchester)**—Formed at Manchester on 21 February 1860, much of the corps was made up of Irishmen living in the area. Absorbed the 70th Corps at Droylesden in 1862, and in 1864 was itself absorbed into the 33rd Corps.

**29th**—Formed as one company at Lytham on 28 January 1860 with George J Lennock as captain, Thomas Fair, lieutenant and William Elsworth Stevenson, ensign. Joined the 3rd Admin Battalion in 1864 and became 'M' Company of the new 3rd Corps in 1880.

**30th**—Formed at the Preston suburb of Fishwick on 16 January 1860 and absorbed into 11th Corps by the following month.

**31st**—Formed as one company at Oldham on 1 February 1860 with John George Blackburne as captain, Hilton Greaves, lieutenant and William Blackburne, ensign. Joined the 7th Admin Battalion, the establishment steadily rising to six companies, and became 'G', 'H', 'J' and 'K', 'L' and 'M' Companies of the new 7th Corps in 1880.

**32nd (Victoria Rifles)**—Formed as one company at Liverpool on 28 January 1860 with William Walker as captain, George Henry Garratt, lieutenant and Frederick Allender, ensign. Absorbed into the new 5th Corps in March 1862.

**33rd (2nd Manchester)**—See 20th Corps (1880-1908).

**34th**—None recorded.

**35th**—None recorded.

**36th**—Formed as one company at Accrington on 7 January 1860 with Robert Ellis Green as captain; Walter Watson, lieutenant and John Bullough, ensign. Joined the 3rd Admin Battalion and was absorbed into the 7th Corps in 1861.

**37th (North Lonsdale)**—The 37th Lancashire RVC was formed with the additional title North Lonsdale as a direct result, notes Mr Howard Ripley in an article published in *The Bulletin of the Military Historical Society* in November 1994, of a meeting held at the Assembly Room in Ulverston on 1 December 1859. Here, William Gale, the senior Deputy Lieutenant for Lonsdale North, proposed the formation of a corps drawn from the Ulverston, Dalton, Hawkshead, Broughton, Cartmel and Barrow areas. Official acceptance received, the first commissions were dated 29 February 1860. Although the early Army Lists suggest that the towns previously mentioned were to be organised as separate corps, the eventual outcome was to be a single battalion of four companies and two sub-divisions numbered as 37th and with C C Spencer, the Marquis of Hartington as major-in-command as of 12 July. In April 1861, however, the *London Gazette* announced that the 37th Lancashire was to divide as five individual corps, the 37A, 37B, 37C, 52nd and 53rd. See under those numbers for further information.

**37A**—Formed at Ulverston on 28 February 1860 as a company of the 37th Corps with Captain William George Ainslie in command. Separated as 37A in April 1861 and placed into the 5th Admin Battalion. Became 'C' and 'D' Companies of the new 10th Corps in 1876.

**37B**—Formed at Barrow-in-Furness on 28 February 1860 as a company of the 37th Corps with Captain James Ramsden in command. Separated as 37B in April 1861 and placed into the 5th Admin Battalion. Absorbed the 52nd Corps at Dalton in 1870 and became 'E' and 'F' Companies of the new 10th Corps in 1876. There is a statue to Sir James Ramsden in the town.

**37C**—Formed at Hawkshead on 28 February 1860 as a company of the 37th Corps with Captain William Alcock Beck in command. Separated as 37C in April 1861 and placed into the 5th Admin Battalion. Became 'G' Company of the new 10th Corps in 1876.

**38th**—Formed in the Fairfield area of Liverpool on 20 January 1860 and known as the 1st Sub-division until March. Lieutenant George Frederick Martin was the first officer commissioned. Joined the 1st Admin Battalion and became part of the new 1st Corps in December 1861.

**39th**—An article by Mr D Reeves published in *The Bulletin of the Military Historical Society* in February 1974 records how on 16 November 1859 a meeting was held at the Liverpool Institute to discuss the possibilities of forming a corps of Welsh Riflemen in the town. At a second meeting held at the Common Hall on 25 November and a committee was formed to take care of recruitment and fund raising. A uniform of grey with red facings was proposed. The services of the corps as the 39th Lancashire RVC of one company were eventually accepted by the War Office, its appointed officers Captain William James Griffith, Lieutenant William Henry Lloyd and Ensign Benjamin Gibson being gazetted on 9 February 1860. Drills soon began at the Welsh School in Russell Street and an additional sub-division was later formed at Everton. The corps maintained its own storehouse at 37 Russell Street and undertook musketry at the Hightown (Altcar) range. Joined the 2nd Admin Battalion and in March 1862 became No 5 (Welsh) Company of the new 5th Corps.

**40th (3rd Manchester)**—See 16th Corps (1880-1908).

**41st**—Formed as one company at Liverpool on 16 February 1860 with Richard Patchett as captain, John Tyson, lieutenant and Hugh McMonagle, ensign. Disappeared from the Army List in February 1864.

**42nd**—Formed as one company at Childwall on 3 March 1860 with Samuel R Graves as captain, Harold Cunningham, lieutenant and Henry C Lucy, ensign. Disbanded in 1870.

**43rd**—Formed at Fallowfield on 11 February 1860 and absorbed into 6th Corps the following year.

**44th**—Formed as one company at Longton on 2 March 1860 with William Naylor as captain, John McKean, lieutenant and Henry Hunt, ensign. Joined the 6th Admin Battalion and absorbed into the 11th Corps in 1866.

**45th**—Formed in Liverpool on 27 February 1860 with Percy C Dove as captain and Thomas H Bowen, ensign. Joined the 1st Admin Battalion and became part of the new 1st Corps in December 1861.

**46th**—Formed as one company at Swinton on 24 February 1860 with J Bowers as captain, Jonathan Dorking, lieutenant and Thomas Beckton, ensign. Joined the 4th Admin Battalion and at the same time absorbed No 12 (Eccles) Company of the 6th Corps. Became 'F' and 'G' Companies of the new 4th Corps in 1880.

**47th**—See 21st Corps (1880-1908).

**48th**—See 21st Corps (1880-1908).

**49th**—Formed at Newton-le-Willows on 3 March 1860 with J Hornby Burley as captain, Julius Caesar J Bailey, lieutenant, and Robert Stephenson, ensign. Joined the 9th Admin Battalion in 1865 and became 'G' Company of the new 9th Corps in 1880.

**50th**—None recorded.

**51st**—Formed as one company at Liverpool on 3 March 1860 with Captain George M Corryde Bentley in command. Absorbed the 72nd Corps at Old Swan in 1862 and disappeared from the Army List in August 1866.

**52nd**—Formed at Dalton on 28 February 1860 as part of the 37th Corps. Separated as 52nd in April 1861 and placed into the 5th Admin Battalion. Absorbed into 37B Lancashire RVC in 1870.

**53rd**—Formed at Cartmel on 28 February 1860 as part of the 37th Corps. Separated as 53rd in April 1861 and placed into the 5th Admin Battalion. Disbanded in 1875.

**54th**—Formed as one company at Ormskirk on 15 March 1860 with Richard Welsby as captain, J H Pye, lieutenant and Henry Barton Wareing, ensign. Now of two companies, was absorbed into the 13th Corps in 1880.

**55th**—Formed as a sub-division at Leigh on 3 March 1860 with George Edward Jee as lieutenant and Henry Kirkpatrick, ensign. Increased to a full company in June, joined the 4th Admin Battalion in October 1861, and became 'H' Company of the new 4th Corps in 1880.

**56th**—See 17th Corps (1880-1908).

**57th**—Formed as one company at Ramsbottom on 26 March 1860 with Thomas Greig Stork as captain, James Wild, lieutenant and William Grant McLean, ensign. Joined the 3rd Admin Battalion late in 1861 and became 'K' Company of the new 3rd Corps in 1880.

**58th**—None recoded.

**59th**—Formed as a sub-division at Leyland on 29 February 1860 with J C Morrell as lieutenant and Thomas H Morrell, ensign. Increased to a full company in September 1861, joined the 6th Admin Battalion, and became 'F' Company of the new 11th Corps in 1880.

**60th**—Formed as one company at Atherton on 6 March 1860 with J P Fletcher as captain, John D Selby, lieutenant and Ralph Fletcher, Jun, ensign. Joined the 4th Admin Battalion in October 1861 and became 'J' Company of the new 4th Corps in 1880.

**61st**—Formed as two companies at Chorley on 6 March 1860 with Richard Smethurst and George H Lightoller as captains. Joined the 6th Admin Battalion and was absorbed into the 11th Corps in November 1868.

**62nd**—Formed as one company at Clitheroe on 27 March 1860 with William Garnet as captain, Frederick S Leach, lieutenant and Felix W Grimshaw, ensign. Joined the 8th Admin Battalion, a second company was added in December 1873, and became 'J' and 'K' Companies of the new 2nd Corps in 1880.

**63rd**—Formed at Toxteth Park on 9 April 1860 with Isaac Simm as Captain and James Nuttall, lieutenant. Joined the 2nd Admin Battalion and became part of the new 5th Corps in 1862.

**64th**—See 18th Corps (1880-1908).

**65th**—Formed at Rossall School, Fleetwood, on 27 April 1860 with John H Croad as captain, Arthur D Gill, lieutenant and Edward V Forshall, ensign. An entry in *The Times* dated 16 June 1860 reports the swearing in of the first members of the 65th. The corps was formed by masters and senior boys of Rossall School and the paper noted that this was the first instance of a large public school enrolling under the provisions of the Volunteer Act. The 65th joined the 5th Admin Battalion in 1863 and in 1873 a cadet corps was formed by the junior boys. Became 'H' Company of the new 10th Corps in 1876.

**66th**—Formed in Liverpool on 25 April 1860 with Captain Joseph Mayer in command. Joined the 1st Admin Battalion and became part of the new 1st Corps in December 1861.

**67th**—Formed as one company at Worsley on 7 May 1860 with Nathaniel Topp as captain, John N K Grover, lieutenant and Peter Rasbotham, Jun, ensign. Joined the 4th Admin Battalion and became 'K' Company of the new 4th Corps in 1880.

**68th**—Formed at Liverpool on 31 May 1860 with Captain William G Bradley in command. Joined the 2nd Admin Battalion and became part of the new 5th Corps in 1862.

**69th**—Formed in Liverpool on 31 May 1860 with Henry Tristian as captain, Charles V Macarthy, lieutenant and John Archer, ensign. Joined the 1st Admin Battalion and became part of the new 1st Corps in December 1861.

**70th**—Formed at Droylesden on 5 May 1860 and absorbed into the 28th Corps in 1862.

**71st (Liverpool Highland)**—Dennis Reeves in an article published by the Military Historical Society in February 1972 notes that the 71st Corps was formed in Liverpool mainly from ex-members of No 2 Company of the 19th (Liverpool Scottish Rifles), the first officer's commission (Captain John Scott) being dated 24 May 1860. This one company corps, which was also known as the Liverpool Highland, joined the 2nd Admin Battalion and in January 1862 was increased to two companies when the Scottish element of the 79th Corps was absorbed. The 71st was not included when the 2nd Admin Battalion was consolidated as 5th Corps in March 1862, choosing instead to remain independent. Declining numbers, however, saw the corps disbanded in June 1863.

**72nd**—Formed as one company at Old Swan, Liverpool on 8 June 1860 with Charles A J McBride as captain, Richard S Harding, lieutenant and Thomas Varty, ensign. Absorbed into the 51st Corps in 1862.

**73rd**—Formed at Newton on 8 June 1860 from workers at McCorquodale's Print Works. Absorbed into the 80th Corps as its No 9 Company on 31st March 1863. A number of the McCorquodale family were officers in the corps.

**74th**—Formed in Liverpool on 2 July 1860 and absorbed into the new 1st Corps in 1862.

**75th**—Formed at Broughton-in-Furness on 28 August 1860 but was removed from the Army List in February of the following year. The corps returns in April 1861, however, and is now shown as part of the 5th Admin Battalion. The 75th was eventually disbanded in 1875.

**76th**—Formed as one company at Farnworth on 3 July 1860 with Alfred Barnes as captain, Alfred Topp, lieutenant and Thomas Kershaw, ensign. Joined the 4th Admin Battalion, increased to two companies in 1877, and became 'L' and 'M' Companies of the new 4th Corps in 1880.

**77th**—Formed as one company at Widnes on 1 October 1860 with John Knight as captain,

**L D Greenhalgh, 4th Volunteer Battalion Manchester Regiment.**

James Hallows, lieutenant and Reginald Young, ensign. Disappeared from the Army List in August 1863.

**78th (4th Manchester)**—Dennis Reeves in an article published by the Military Historical Society in February 1977 records how on 15 October 1859 a letter appeared in the *Manchester Guardian* suggesting the formation of a local Scottish Volunteer Rifle Corps. In consequence, the first members to enrol met for their first drill at the large hall above 37 Corporation Street on Saturday 10 December 1859. Known unofficially as the Manchester Scottish, this corps, by now comprising two companies, subsequently joined a new unit at Alnwick titled 78th Lancashire (4th Manchester) RVC. Acceptance of its services were notified in the *Manchester Guardian* on 25 September 1860 and headquarters of the 78th were placed at 4 Kennedy Street. With a strength of six companies the corps was incorporated into the 33rd Corps in 1863.

**79th**—Formed as three companies in Liverpool on 16 February 1861, the company commanders being James Cuthbert, John Rogers and Robert Lamont. Absorbed into the new 5th Corps in March 1862.

**80th**—See 19th Corps (1880-1908)

**81st**—Formed as a sub-division at Withnell on 20 February 1861 with John A Parke as lieutenant and George Hoult, ensign. Included in 2nd Admin Battalion for a short time but attached to the 2nd Corps by the end of 1861. Increased to a full company in March 1863 and joined the 8th Admin Battalion in July 1864. Headquarters were transferred to Wheelton in the same year, and in 1876 the corps was disbanded.

**82nd**—Formed as one company at Hindley, just under three miles from Wigan, on 14 June 1861 with John Johnson as captain, J B Latham, lieutenant and Thomas Southwark, ensign. Amalgamated with the 27th Corps as 27th in 1876.

**83rd**—Formed as one company at Knowsley on 11 February 1861 with Captain H R Whistler in command. Disappeared from the Army List in December 1872.

**84th**—Formed as one company at Padiham on 18 February 1861 with James Dugdale, Jun as captain, Edward Sutcliffe, lieutenant and J Bury Haworth, ensign. Joined the 3rd Admin Battalion and became 'E' Company of the new 3rd Corps in 1880.

**85th**—None recorded.

**86th**—In was at a meeting held at Liverpool's Custom House on 23 November 1860 that a decision was taken to form a corps of riflemen from within the Civil Service. Known at first as the Civil Service Rifle Corps, but by most as the Customs Corps, the two companies sanctioned by the War Office were given the title of 86th Lancashire RVC. Captain Commandant Jeremiah C Johnstone received a commission dated 18 May 1861. Joined the 2nd Admin Battalion and became part of the new 5th Corps in 1862.

**87th**—Formed at Nelson on 7 February 1862. Joined the 3rd Admin Battalion but disappeared from the Army List in June 1865.

**88th**—Formed as one company at Haslingden on 27 February 1863 with George William L Schofield as captain, Abraham Haworth, lieutenant and J T Stott, ensign. Joined the 3rd Admin Battalion and became 'J' Company of the new 3rd Corps in 1880.

**89th**—None recorded.

**90th**—Formed at Fleetwood on 3 June 1868. Joined the 3rd Admin Battalion and was disbanded in 1870.

**91st**—Formed as one company at Flixton on 14 August 1872 with Adam Stott as captain. Joined the 4th Admin Battalion and became 'N' Company of the new 4th Corps in 1880. Flixton is seven miles from Manchester; Cassel's *Gazetteer* for 1895 notes that 'in the town is a Volunteer Drill Hall, which is also used for public assembles, and is capable of accommodating 500 persons.'

**2nd Volunteer Battalion King's Own (Royal Lancaster Regiment)**—Formed from the 1st Volunteer Battalion in 1900. Headquarters were placed at Lancaster and there were six companies located: 'A' to 'D' in Lancaster; 'E' Morecambe and 'F' Grange. *Territorials:* 5th Battalion King's Own.

**8th (Scottish) Volunteer Battalion King's (Liverpool Regiment)**—Mr David A Rutter writing in the *Bulletin* of the Military Historical Society in May 1978, noted that the idea of a Scottish Volunteer Corps in Liverpool was suggested in a letter signed 'G Forbes Milne' which appeared in the press on 27 January 1900. Lord Balfour subsequently headed the committee formed to see this through—permission to raise the proposed unit coming from the War Office on 30 April 1900. Enrolment in the 8th (Scottish) Volunteer Battalion King's (Liverpool Regiment) began in the following November; Major C Forbes-Bell becoming commanding officer (commission dated 10 October), Captain J C Robertson, late of the West India Regiment, his Adjutant. Eight companies were sanctioned, but it would seem that just four were in existence by the end of the year. In 1902 Lieutenant John Watson and twenty-one other ranks sailed for South Africa where they were to serve alongside of the 1st Battalion Gordon Highlanders. Also, from the battalion, but serving with the Imperial Yeomanry, was Lieutenant John Anderson Bingham who died from wounds received at De Hook on 11 February 1902. At home, the strength of the battalion had grown to the required eight companies and a new drill hall had been opened at 7 Fraser Street. *Territorials:* 10th (Scottish) Battalion, King's (Liverpool Regiment).

**1st Cadet Battalion King's (Liverpool Regiment)**—Formed in January 1890 with headquarters at the Gordon Institute in Stanley Road, Liverpool. Amalgamated with 2nd Cadet Battalion King's in 1904.

**2nd Cadet Battalion King's (Liverpool Regiment)**—Formed in 1902 and amalgamated with the 1st Cadet Battalion King's in 1904.

**1st Cadet Battalion Manchester Regiment**—Formed in February 1889 with A P Ledward as Hon Major. Headquarters were at Tongue Street Manchester.

# Leicestershire

## Rifle Volunteers

All corps formed within the county joined the 1st Admin Battalion which in 1880 provided the new 1st Corps.

**1st (1859-1880)**—Formed as one company at Leicester with Captain Mansfield Turner commissioned on 31 August 1859. Ensign Samuel Harris was gazetted on the following 5 September, then Lieutenant Alfred Donisthorpe on 1 March 1860. Became 'A' Company of the new 1st Corps in 1880.

**1st (1880-1908)**—The 1st Admin Battalion of Leicestershire Rifle Volunteers was formed with headquarters at Leicester in July 1860 and consolidated as the new 1st Corps with eleven companies in 1880: 'A' Leicester (late 1st Corps), 'B' Belvoir (late 2nd Corps), 'C' Melton Mowbray (late 3rd Corps), 'D' and 'E' Leicester (late 4th Corps), 'F' and 'G' Leicester (late 5th Corps), 'H' Loughborough (late 6th Corps), 'J' Ashby-de-la-Zouch (late 8th Corps), 'K' Leicester (late 9th Corps), 'L' Hinckley (late 10th Corps).

A new company was raised at Market Harborough in 1882 and in the following year General Order 14 of February directed that the 1st Corps was to be re-designated as 1st Volunteer Battalion Leicestershire Regiment. Further increases in establishment saw new companies added, two at Leicester and one each at

Wigston and Mountsorrel in 1900. Volunteers from the battalion served in South Africa alongside the Regulars of the Leicestershire Regiment and saw action at Laing's Nek, Belfont and in the operations around Lydenberg. General Buller noted in his despatches the effective handling by the volunteers of the Boers in the Crocodile Valley on 4 September 1900. Casualties numbered four killed and four wounded. *Territorials:* 4th Battalion (formed by the Leicester and Wigston personnel) and 5th Battalion (formed by the remainder less the Belvoir Company which was disbanded) of the Leicestershire Regiment.

**2nd**—Formed as one company at Belvoir with William Earle Welby as captain, George Gordon, lieutenant and George Gillett, ensign. All three held commissions dated 13 February 1860. Became 'B' Company of the new 1st Corps in 1880.

**3rd**—Formed as one company at Melton Mowbray on 2 March 1860 with Edward H M Clarke as captain, George Marriott, lieutenant, Frederick J Oldham, ensign and Nathanial Whitchurch who was appointed as surgeon. Became C' Company of the new 1st Corps in 1880.

**4th**—Formed as one company at Leicester with George Henry Hodges commissioned as captain on 4 March 1860. He was later joined by Lieutenant George Bankart and Ensign Thomas Wood Cox who were both gazetted on 9th April. Increased to two companies in November 1863 and became 'D' and 'E' Companies of the new 1st Corps in 1880.

**5th**—Formed as one company at Leicester with Robert Brewin as captain, Joshua T Wordsworth, lieutenant and Charles S Smith, ensign. All three officers held commissions dated 3 March 1860. Increased to two companies in 1879 and became 'F' and 'G' Companies of the new 1st Corps in 1880.

**6th**—Formed as one company at Loughborough with Edward Warner commissioned as captain on 7 July 1860. He was later joined by Lieutenant John H Eddowes, Ensign Isaac B Dobell and Surgeon William G Palmer, all three being gazetted on 1st August 1860. Became 'H' Company of the new 1st Corps in 1880.

**Button, 1st Volunteer Battalion Leicestershire Regiment.**

**Other ranks' helmet plate, 1st Volunteer Battalion Leicestershire Regiment.**

**7th**—Formed as a sub-division at Lutterworth with Theophilus J Levett commissioned as lieutenant on 6 October 1860. He was later joined by Ensign Arthur W Arkwright (gazetted 18 October) and Charles Bond, MD who was appointed surgeon to the corps in November 1860. During the next five years sufficient recruits had enrolled and in consequence 7th Leicestershire became a full company in 1866. Interest later diminished, however, and the corps was disbanded in 1873.

**8th**—Formed as one company at Ashby-de-la-Zouch with Alexander Hadden as captain, Henry E Smith, lieutenant and Thomas Fisher, ensign. All three were commissioned on 16 September 1860. The Rev John Denton looked after the men's spiritual welfare as chaplain, while Surgeon Percy Dicken saw to their medical needs. Became 'J' Company of the new 1st Corps in 1880.

**9th**—Formed as one company at Leicester with George Clarke Bellairs as captain, Edgar Franklin Cooper, lieutenant and Thomas Edmund Paget, ensign. All three held commissions dated 24 December

1860. Became 'K' Company of the new 1st Corps in 1880.

**10th**—Formed as one company at Hinckley with William Brookes as captain, James H Ward, lieutenant and John C D D Cotman, ensign. All three held commissions dated 27 November 1860. Became 'L' Company of the new 1st Corps in 1880.

# Lincolnshire

## Artillery Volunteers

The 1st Admin Brigade was formed with headquarters at Grimsby in July 1861. It included all three corps raised and in 1880 was consolidated as the new 1st Corps.

**1st (1860-1880)**—Formed at Boston on 12 January 1860 and provided Nos 1 and 2 Batteries of the new 1st Corps in 1880.

**1st (1880-1908)**—Formed in 1880 by the consolidation of the 1st Admin Brigade with an establishment of six and a half batteries. Headquarters remained at Grimsby and the batteries were organised as follows: Nos 1 and 2 Boston (late 1st Corps), Nos 3, 4 and 5 Grimsby (late 2nd Corps), No 6 and the half battery Louth (late 3rd Corps). From 1890 the 1st Lincolnshire consisted of four position, later heavy, batteries. *Territorials:* 1st North Midland Brigade RFA.

**2nd**—Formed at Grimsby on 27 January 1860 and provided Nos 3, 4 and 5 Batteries of the new 1st Corps in 1880.

**3rd**—Formed at Louth on 12 November 1860 and provided No 6 and the half battery of the new 1st Corps in 1880.

## Engineer Volunteers

**Humber Division Submarine Miners/Electrical Engineers**—Formed in 1886, its first officers being commissioned 11 September. Disbanded 1891, the submarine mining defences on the Humber having been placed with the Militia.

## Mounted Rifle Volunteers/Light Horse Volunteers

**1st**—Mention of a Mounted Rifle Volunteers corps with headquarters at Spalding was made in the Army List for May 1860, but no officers were ever gazetted, and recruits were few. Removed by February 1861. In 1867, however, the 1st Lincolnshire Light Horse was raised at Great Limber by the Earl of Yarborough. Disbanded in 1887.

## Rifle Volunteers

The county formed three admin battalions of which the 3rd was later broken up. It had been formed at Boston on 6 July 1860 and included the 4th, 13th, 14th, 16th and 17th Corps. The 1st and 2nd were to provide the new 1st and 2nd Corps in 1880. There also existed a 1st Sub-division, see 2nd Corps (1859-1880) and 12th Corps.

**1st (1859-1880)**—Formed at Lincoln on 26 October 1859 with Weston C Amcotts in command and joined the 1st Admin Battalion. A report in the 18 January 1861 issue of the *Illustrated London News* refers to an event that took place on the previous 29 December which saw 'three companies' of the 1st Lincolnshire RVC form up on the iced-over River Witham wearing skates and, in perfect order, skated off several miles downriver. Became 'A', 'B' and 'C' Companies of the new 1st Corps in 1880. Ian Becket in *Riflemen Form* notes that three of Lincoln's largest employers—Clayton, Shuttleworth & Co at Stamp End Iron Works; Ruston, Proctor & Co, of the Sheaf Iron Works and Robey & Co of the Perseverance Iron Works—encourage their employees to join by offering to supply uniforms at a repayment of 1s 6d weekly. Both Joseph Shuttleworth and Nathaniel Clayton became officers. Looking for all the world like a castle, the Rifle Drill Hall was presented by Joseph Ruston and opened in the 1890.

**1st (1880-1908)**—Formed with headquarters at Lincoln on 15 May 1860, the 1st Admin Battalion included the 1st, 2nd, 6th, 7th, 9th, 11th, 12th, 19th and 20th Corps. The battalion was consolidated as the new 1st Corps in 1880 with eleven companies: 'A', 'B', 'C' Lincoln (late 1st Corps), 'D' Louth (late 2nd Corps), 'E' Great Grimsby (late 6th Corps), 'F' Spilsby (late 7th Corps), 'G' Horncastle (late 9th Corps), 'H' Alford (late 11th Corps), 'I' Barton (late 12th Corps), 'J' Gainsborough (late 19th Corps), 'K' Market Rasen (late 20th Corps).

**Cap badge, 1st Volunteer Battalion Lincolnshire Regiment.**

The headquarters of 'K' Company had moved to Frodingham by 1881. General Order 63 of May 1882 directed a change in designation to 1st Volunteer Battalion Lincolnshire Regiment. In June 1900 the establishment of the battalion was reduced to seven companies: 'A' to 'D' at Lincoln; 'E' and 'F' Gainsborough, 'G' Horncastle, the remainder of the strength going to form the 3rd Volunteer Battalion Lincolnshire Regiment. Lincoln Grammar School Cadet Corps was formed and affiliated in 1903. *Territorials:* Transfer to the Territorial Force in 1908 saw the Lincoln and Horncastle Companies as part of the 4th Battalion Lincolnshire Regiment while the Gainsborough personnel joined the 5th.

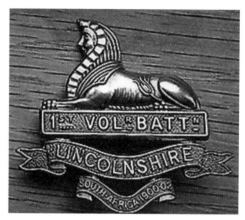

**Cap badge, 1st Volunteer Battalion Lincolnshire Regiment.**

**2nd (1859-1880)**—Formed at Louth on 21 November 1859 with William Henry Smyth as captain, William Chaplain, lieutenant and William Thomas Kime, ensign. Known as the 1st Sub-division until January 1860, joined the 1st Admin Battalion, and became 'D' Company of the new 1st Corps in 1880.

**2nd (1880-1908)**—Formed with headquarters at Grantham on 21 May 1860, the 2nd Admin Battalion included the 3rd, 5th, 8th, 15th and 18th Corps; the 4th, 13th, 16th and 17th being added upon the breakup of 3rd Admin in 1862. The battalion was consolidated as the new 2nd Corps in 1880 with eight companies: 'A', 'B' Grantham (late 3rd Corps), 'C' Boston (late 4th Corps), 'D' Stamford late 5th Corps), 'E' Sleaford (late 8th Corps), 'F' Spalding (late 13th Corps), 'G' Gosberton (late 17th Corps), 'H' Billingborough (late 18th Corps).

Re-designation as 2nd Volunteer Battalion Lincolnshire Regiment was notified in General Order 63 of 1883. King's School, Grantham Cadet Corps was formed and affiliated in 1904. *Territorials:* Transfer to the Territorial Force in 1908 was as part of 4th Battalion Lincolnshire Regiment. King's School at the same time became part of the OTC.

**3rd**—Formed as two companies at Grantham on 28 February 1860 with William Earle Welby and Charles J B Parker as company commanders. Joined the 2nd Admin Battalion and became 'A' and 'B' Companies of the new 2nd Corps in 1880.

**4th**—Formed as one company at Boston on 9 February 1860 with Frederick L Hopkins as captain, Thomas Wright, lieutenant and William Gee, ensign. Joined the 3rd Admin Battalion, transferring to 2nd in 1862, and became 'C' Company of the new 2nd Corps in 1880.

**5th**—Formed as one company at Stamford on 14 February 1860 with Richard Cautley, late of the Bengal Army, as captain, Robert N Newcomb, lieutenant and J Phillips, Jun, ensign. Joined the 2nd Admin Battalion and became 'D' Company of the new 2nd Corps in 1880.

**6th**—Formed as one company at Great Grimsby on 20 March 1860 with William H Daubney as captain, Peter K Seddon, lieutenant and Richard J Nainby, ensign. Joined the 1st Admin Battalion and became 'E' Company of the new 1st Corps in 1880.

**7th**—Formed as one company at Spilsby on 17 March 1860 with Henry Hollway as captain, Harwood Makinder, lieutenant and John W Preston, ensign. Joined the 1st Admin Battalion and became 'F' Company of the new 1st Corps in 1880.

**8th**—Formed as one company at Sleaford on 23 February 1860 with A Wilson as captain, Henry Peacock, lieutenant and Bruce Tomlinson, ensign. Joined the 2nd Admin Battalion and became 'E' Company of the new 2nd Corps in 1880.

**9th**—Formed as one company at Horncastle on 22 March 1860 with Henry F Conington as captain, Richard Clitherow, lieutenant and Robert Jalland, ensign. Joined the 1st Admin Battalion and became 'G' Company of the new 1st Corps in 1880.

**10th**—None recorded.

**11th**—Formed as one company at Alford on 23 February 1860 with John Samuel Lister as captain, Augustus Laurent, lieutenant and John Higgins, Jun, ensign. Joined the 1st Admin Battalion and became 'H' Company of the new 1st Corps in 1880.

**12th**—Formed at Barton-on-Humber on 12 January 1860, with George Charles Uppleby as lieutenant and John Stephenson, ensign, and known as the 1st Sub-division until March. Joined the 1st Admin Battalion and became 'I' Company of the new 1st Corps in 1880.

**13th**—Formed as one company at Spalding on 28 February 1860 with T Hilliam as captain, FT Selby, lieutenant and Ashley Maples, ensign. Joined the 3rd Admin Battalion, transferring to the 2nd in 1862, and became 'F' Company of the new 2nd Corps in 1880.

**14th**—Formed at Swineshead, seven miles south-west of Boston, on 6 March 1860 with John Cooper, Jun, as lieutenant and Frederick H Bate, ensign. Joined the 3rd Admin Battalion and disbanded in 1861.

**15th**—Formed as one company at Bourne on 23 April 1860 with J Compton Lawrence as captain, Edward Hardwicke, lieutenant and John Thomas Pawlett, ensign. Joined the 2nd Admin Battalion and disbanded in 1873.

**16th**—Formed at Holbeach on 20 March 1860 with William S Clark as lieutenant. Joined the 3rd Admin Battalion, transferring to the 2nd in 1862. Disbanded later and last seen in the Army List for November 1871.

**17th**—Formed as one company at Donington on 17 March 1860 with Richard G Calthrop as captain, John Holland, lieutenant and George Casswell, ensign. Joined the 3rd Admin Battalion, transferring to the 2nd Admin in 1862. Moved to Gosberton, just to the south-east, in 1876 and became 'G' Company of the new 2nd Corps in 1880.

**18th**—Formed as one company at Folkingham on 13 March 1860 with Henry Smith as captain, William Emerson Chapman, lieutenant and William Cragg, ensign. Joined the 2nd Admin Battalion, moved three miles to the east at Billingborough in 1872, and became 'H' Company of the new 2nd Corps in 1880.

**19th**—Formed as one company at Gainsborough on 10 July 1860 with John E Saunders as captain, Francis Gamble, Jun, lieutenant and Thomas H Oldman, ensign. Joined the 1st Admin Battalion and became 'J' Company of the new 1st Corps in 1880.

**20th**—Formed at Market Rasen on 16 July 1860 with John Brown as lieutenant and William Goodson, ensign. Joined the 1st Admin Battalion and became 'K' Company of the new 1st Corps in 1880.

**3rd Volunteer Battalion Lincolnshire Regiment**—Formed with headquarters at Grimsby in June 1900 by the withdrawal from 1st Volunteer Battalion of its Louth, Grimsby, Spilsby, Alford, Barton and Frodingham companies. The King Edward VI Grammar School Cadet Corps at Louth was formed and affiliated in 1905, followed by Grimsby Municipal College Cadet Corps in 1906. *Territorials:* Part of 5th Battalion Lincolnshire Regiment. In 1908 both the King Edward VI and Grimsby Schools joined the OTC.

# London

## Artillery Volunteers

**1st**—Formed on 15 April 1863 the 1st London (City) AVC occupied several headquarters within the City of London, the first being at No 5 Farringdon Street. Originally six batteries, the establishment was increased to sixteen when at the beginning of 1883 an amalgamation took place between the 1st London and 1st Surrey AVC. The ten Surrey batteries were situated over a large area but in the main were recruited around Brixton, Loughborough, Shepherd's Bush and Camberwell. *Territorials:* 1st (City of London), 6th London and 7th London Brigades RFA.

## Engineer Volunteers

**1st**—Formed on 19 March 1862, the 1st London EVC had its first headquarters at Old Jewry, a move to 27 Barbican being made in 1868, then to Islington in 1877. Two cadet corps have been associated with the 1st London Engineers: the Reading School Company, which was formed in 1900, and the United Services College at St Marks, Windsor. The latter unit had originated in 1900 and at that time was located at Westward Ho and affiliated to the 4th Volunteer Battalion Devonshire Regiment. In 1905 the college moved to Harpenden and its cadet corps made part of the 2nd (Hertfordshire) Volunteer Battalion Bedfordshire Regiment. The move to Windsor and the link to the 1st London Engineer occurred in 1907. Both units in 1908 became contingents of the Junior Division Officer Training Corps. *Territorials:* Transfer to the Territorial Force in 1908 saw the engineers converted to artillery, the units formed being the 1st and 2nd London Royal Garrison Artillery.

**1ᴿˢᵀ LONDON ENGINEER VOLUNTEERS**
OFFICER, MARCHING ORDER.

**1st London Engineer Volunteer Corps.**

## Rifle Volunteers

**1st (City of London Rifle Volunteer Brigade)**—Formed as a result of an inaugural meeting convened by the Lord Mayor held on 23 July 1859; Richards in *His Majesty's Territorial Army* noting that within a week some 1,200 had enrolled. The first officers' commissions were dated 14 December 1859, by which time recruiting had reached in excess of 1,800—the men forming two battalions each of eight companies. HRH Field Marshall the Duke of Cambridge became honorary colonel, George Montagu Hicks, a former officer on the 41st Regiment of Foot and Governor of Whitecross Street Prison, commanding officer. The corps occupied several headquarters: 17 Finsbury Place South, EC2; later 48 Finsbury Pavement, EC2, and after that, 130 Bunhill Row, EC1. Absorbed the 12th Tower Hamlets RVC at Stoke Newington in 1870 and became a Volunteer battalion (without change of title) of the King's Royal Rifle Corps in 1881. After the Boer War the strength of the brigade fell off resulting in a reduction in establishment, first to ten, then to eight companies—in the last year of the Volunteer Force (1907) a strength of just 489 out of an establishment of 928 was returned. *Territorials:* 5th Battalion London Regiment.

The first mention of a cadet corps having been formed within the brigade was in the Army List for May 1877. There was, however, a unit formed as early as 1860 which according to one source had a strength of 400 boys. Included in the c1860 cadet unit were boys from the Merchant Taylors, City of London, University College and King's College School, and in 1900 these school corps are shown in the Army List by name for the first time. By 1902 the schools, together with the 1877 unit, appear under the heading of 1st City of London Cadet Corps with a total establishment of five companies. Became part of the OTC in 1908.

**2nd**—Formed 16 May 1860 from employees of the newspaper and printing trade—much of the corps was made up of workers at the *Daily Mail* and the printing firms of Messrs Eyre and Spottiswoode and Messrs Harmsworth—George A Spottiswoode and William Spottiswoode being among the first officers to be commissioned. With headquarters at Little New Street, the 2nd London was known unofficially as The Printers' Battalion. Absorbed the 48th Middlesex RVC in 1872, making an overall strength of nine companies, and joined the King's Royal Rifle Corps (without change in title) as one of its Volunteer battalions in 1881. In 1887 the memorial stone to a new headquarters at 57a Farringdon Road was laid. At headquarters, the memorial bearing the names of the six to lose their lives in South Africa is surrounded by that commemorating the sacrifice made in 1914-1918. The City of London School Cadet Corps became affiliated in 1905. *Territorials:* 6th Battalion London Regiment. The City of London School in 1908 became part of the OTC.

**3rd (City of)**—Recruiting began late in 1860—a number coming forward from the ranks of the old Temple Bar and St Paul's Association Volunteers which had been formed in 1798—and the first officers' commissions were dated 8 March 1861. Sir William de Bathe was appointed as commanding officer. Twelve companies were soon established, the majority of the men being of the 'Artisan' class which led to the unofficial title of the Working Men's Brigade. Headquarters were at 26 Great Tower Street, moving later to 38 New Broad Street, then to 79 Farringdon Street, EC4 and finally to 24 Sun Street, Finsbury. Became a

Volunteer Battalion of the King's Royal Rifle Corps (without change in title) in 1881, the additional title of (City of) being shown in the Army List by 1904. *Territorials:* 7th Battalion London Regiment.

**4th (1861-1865)**—Formed as eight companies on 2 October 1861 with Lieutenant Colonel William Henry Sykes in command. Headquarters were at 8 Union Court, Broad Street, EC. Later reduced to six companies and disappeared from the Army List in April 1865.

**4th (1900-1905)**—Two companies formed on 18 May 1900 from ex-members of the Grocers' Company Schools in Clapton, North East London. With the 1st London RVC provided a volunteer battalion of the King's Royal Rifle Corps. The 4th Corps was disbanded in 1905, Major General Sir Frederick Maurice noting in his *History of the London Rifle Brigade* that 'the numbers having fell off, what remained of the 4th London was absorbed into 'E' company of 1st London'.

**5th**—In February 1973 Bryn Owen, writing in *The Bulletin of the Military Historical Society*, recalled

**1st London Rifle Volunteer Corps.**

**3rd London Rifle Volunteer Corps.**

how he had found in the *Swansea Herald* for 21 November 1860 a report giving details of a meeting held at the Freemasons Tavern by influential Welshmen in the City of London. Its purpose: to discuss the possibility of raising a Welsh Corps in the capital. Mr Owen later found a second reference to the corps in the form of a brief entry dated 2 February 1861 published in *The Star of Gwent* which told how the London Welsh Rifles had attended their first drill in the Floral Hall adjoining the Covent Garden Theatre. The corps apparently numbered 150 at this time and additional parades were also being held at the London residence of Sir Watkyn Williams Wynn. There is no doubt that at this point the London Welsh Corps was uniformed and badged,

**Officers' helmet plate,**
**3rd London Rifle Volunteer Corps.**

**1st London Rifle**
**Volunteer Corps.**

**3rd London Rifle**
**Volunteer Corps.**

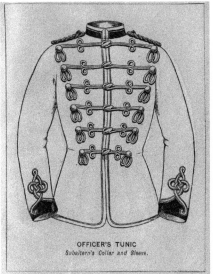
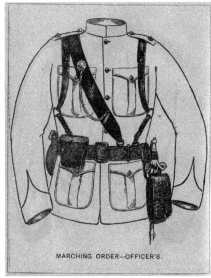

**Pages from the 1891 Dress Regulations for the 1st London Rifle Volunteer Corps.**

Mr Owen illustrating with his article a splendid silver device bearing the title London Welsh Rifle Corps with a rampant dragon centrepiece.

Later, in May 1996, Mr Howard Ripley placed an item in *The Bulletin of the Military Historical Society* which more or less tidied up the mystery of the London Welsh. The *Volunteer Service Gazette* in May 1861, he states, reported that drills were being held at the Ward School in Aldersgate by a 'London Welsh Rifle Corps'. Nothing, however, appeared in the Army List regarding this formation, but in January 1862 (the *Gazette* again) notice was given that the services of the '5th (Welsh) London Rifle Volunteers' had been accepted.

In the following month the 5th did indeed appear in the Army List (the heading made no mention of the word Welsh, however) indicating that the corps was to be of two companies. Headquarters were given as 160 Aldersgate Street, but the expected six officers were not listed. This to be the case right up until 1863 when in May, all reference to a 5th London RVC disappeared.

# Middlesex

## Artillery Volunteers

The 1st Admin Brigade of Middlesex Artillery Volunteers was formed on 21 June 1864. Headquarters were at No 28 Leicester Square and the corps included were the 1st Middlesex and 1st Tower Hamlets. In 1873 the Tower Hamlets Corps was disbanded, as was the 1st Middlesex three years later. The brigade thereafter ceased to exist.

**1st**—Formed on 16 July 1860, its first headquarters being recorded as No 70 Quadrant, Regent Street. A series of moves later followed with the corps ending up at Leicester Square by 1863. Disbanded in 1876.

**2nd**—Formed on 26 April 1861, headquarters moving from Custom House to the Artillery Barracks in Leonard Street in 1890. *Territorials:* 3rd London Brigade RFA.

**3rd**—The first headquarters of the 3rd Corps were recorded as Islington where it was formed on 12 September 1861. Several other premises were occupied, the last on record being in Lower Kennington Lane. The 3rd enjoyed the distinction of having the Prince of Wales as its Honorary Colonel whose uniform can be seen on display at the Royal Artillery Museum, Woolwich.

From the outset Lord Truro, who raised the 3rd, was determined to make it one of the leading artillery volunteers corps in the country and it would not be long before it became recognised as something of a 'Corps d'Elite'. Living up to its regimental motto 'Together Heave' the 3rd would take many prizes over the years at the National Artillery Association's annual competition, including the Queen's Prize three times. Demand to join was so high that it was able to insist on a minimum height requirement of 5 feet eleven inches.

A special feature of the 3rd was that it was organised into three divisions each with four batteries and its own headquarters. The 1st Division was at Armoury House in Farringdon Road, the 2nd at Lower Kennington Lane and the 3rd was at Porteous Road in Paddington. The latter was popularly known as The Paddington Light Horse. In addition to the three divisions the 3rd also had its own Ambulance Detachment and a Cyclist Section for orderly work. There was also an active and well organised Carbine Club, an Athletic Club and at one time a Regimental Newspaper. Each recruit upon joining, which in 1890 had to be for a minimum of four years, had to pay two guineas towards the cost of his complete uniform. The 3rd Middlesex did not adopt the blue helmet and preferred instead to retain its unique brown racoon skin busby. Unique too were the officers' busbies which were made from the racoon's brown and white ringed-tail fur. This produced a mottled look which was likened to that of a tiger and gave rise to the nickname 'Truro's Tigers'. *Territorials:* 5th London Brigade RFA.

**4th**—The 4th Corps, which also held the sub-title Authors, was formed on 4 December 1865 with headquarters at the West Brompton Cricket Ground. As the name implies, the corps consisted of writers and members of literary circles. Interest fell off, however, and, low in numbers, the authors were absorbed into the 3rd Corps in January 1870.

## Engineer Volunteers

**1st**—The senior Engineer Volunteer Corps was the 1st Middlesex which was formed 6 January 1860 by the staff of the South Kensington Museum (name changed to Victoria and Albert in 1899). South Kensington formed part of the corps title, but this disappeared from the Army List in August 1862. Headquarters were moved from the museum to College Street, Fulham in 1866, and the corps comprised nine companies, one of which was located at the Royal Indian Engineering College at Coopers Hill. *Territorials:* The units formed upon transfer to the Territorial Force in 1908 were the 3rd and 4th London Field Companies and Telegraph Company, all of the 2nd London Divisional Engineers. The Tonbridge School Cadet Corps, which had been affiliated to the 1st Middlesex in 1893, in 1908 became part of the Junior Division Officer Training Corps.

**London Electrical Engineers**—Formed with headquarters in Victoria Street, Westminster in 1897. The corps comprised four companies and was made up from men of science, leading members of the electrical profession, electricians and students of electrical engineering recruited from as far away as the Midlands. Headquarters moved to Regency Street, also in Westminster, in 1900. *Territorials:* London Division Electrical Engineers.

**Engineer and Railway Volunteer Staff Corps**—This organisation first appeared in 1865 and had its first commissions dated 21 January. The corps, which was also known as The Engineer and Railway Transport Volunteers was made up entirely of officers, most of whom held principle jobs in the country's railway companies. The corps occupied several premises as headquarters: 24 Great George Street (1865 to 1880), 9 Victoria Chambers (1880 to 1885), Great George Street again (1885 to 1900), 21 Dalahay Street (1900 to 1902), 8 The Sanctuary (1902 to 1905) and then to Dean's Yard. All these addresses were within the City of Westminster.

**1st Middlesex Engineer Volunteers.**

## Light Horse Volunteers

**1st**—Formed at Tattersall's Horse Sale Yard at Hyde Park Corner in January 1861 and within a few months the 2nd Middlesex Light Horse at St James's Place was absorbed. Unofficially the corps was known as the 1st Metropolitan Light Horse. Disbanded 1866.

**2nd**—Formed with headquarters at 1 St James's Place in February 1861 by the Hon Charles Robert Claude Baron Truro. Amalgamated with the 1st Middlesex Light Horse in July 1861.

## Rifle Volunteers

Like the counties of Kent, Essex and Surrey, Middlesex also recruited its volunteer corps throughout the Greater London area. Previous to 1880 fifty numbered corps were raised and to administer those of insufficient strength, seven admin battalions were formed. Of the seven, only two, the 2nd and 7th, survived up to 1880 and the reorganisations of that year. The 6th was absorbed into the 2nd and the remaining four were broken up, their corps being made independent. The 1st Admin Battalion was formed in August 1860 and had its headquarters at Tyndale Place, Islington. The corps included were the 4th and 7th, the battalion being removed from the Army List in March 1861 upon their amalgamation. The 3rd Battalion, its headquarters never recorded, was formed in August 1860 with the 39th and 40th Corps and was broken up in April 1861. Also to disappear in that month was the 4th Battalion, headquarters at Cardington Street in Euston, formed August 1860 with 20th, 29th and 37th Corps. The 5th Battalion, which was also formed in August 1860, had its headquarters at Custom House and included the 26th and 42nd Middlesex RVC. In 1880 the remaining two battalions and the surviving independent corps were organised into twenty-five new corps, the 2nd and 7th Admin Battalion providing the 3rd and 8th. Afterwards, a 26th and 27th Corps were formed.

**1st (Victoria)**—Upon the general disbandment of volunteers in 1814 the Duke of Cumberland's Sharpshooter, which had been formed in 1803, was permitted to continue service—although not formally recognised as a military body, but as a rifle club. In 1835 permission was granted to style the club as the Royal Victoria Rifle Club and in 1853 sanction to form a volunteer corps was given. As the Victoria Volunteer Rifle Corps, whose first officers' commissions were dated 4 January 1853, the club subsequently, in 1859,

Helmet plate.
1st Middlesex Rifle
Volunteer Corps.

Pouch-belt plate,
38th Middlesex Rifle
Volunteer Corps.

Pouch-belt plate,
24th Middlesex
Rifle Volunteer Corps.

became the 1st Middlesex RVC. The additional title Victoria was added by March 1860.

Headquarters were in Kilburn, but a move was made to Marlborough Place, off Hamilton Terrace, St John's Wood in 1867. Became a Volunteer battalion of the King's Royal Rifle Corps (without change in title) in 1881. Headquarters moved to 56 Davies Street, Westminster in 1892, and in the same year an amalgamation took place on 1 June with the 6th Middlesex (St George's) RVC. The new title adopted was 1st Middlesex (Victoria and St George's). *Territorials:* Transfer to the Territorial Force in 1908 saw the 1st Middlesex amalgamated with the 19th Middlesex to form the 9th Battalion London Regiment. A cadet corps with headquarters in Marlborough Place was formed towards the end of 1866, but this was later disbanded and was last seen in the Army List for January 1898. Mr J W Reddyhoff writing in the *Bulletin* of the Military Historical Society in November 1997 notes that the Victoria Rifles Freemason Lodge No 1124 (later No 822) was formed from within the corps on 4 June 1860.

**1st Cadet Battalion Royal Fusiliers.**

**2nd (South Middlesex)**—Formed with headquarters at Beaufort House, Waltham Green on 14 October 1859. Raised by Viscount Ranelagh, the 2nd Corps included among its first officers: Evan Macpherson, late major in the 68th Regiment of Foot, the Hon W E Fitzmaurice, major, 2nd Life Guards, F H Atherely, of the Rifle Brigade and long time MP for the Isle of Wight, John Walrond Clark of the 10th Dragoons, and Charles Smyth Vereker who had served as lieutenant-colonel in the Limerick Artillery Militia. Among the junior officers were: Lord Ashley and the Hon Robert Bourke, afterwards Earl of Mayo and Governor General of India. Recruitment went well and within a few months the strength of the corps, one of the largest in the country, stood at sixteen companies. By the end of March 1860 some 1,261 members had subscribed twenty-one shillings each on being enrolled. In addition every man paid the cost of his uniform and equipment, besides an annual regimental subscription of twenty-one shillings.

As founder of the 2nd Middlesex Viscount Ranelagh's crest of a dexter arm embowed in armour and grasping a dart was used on the later uniforms as a collar badge. His Lordship was to command the corps until his death in November 1885. Became a volunteer battalion (without change in title) of the King's Royal Rifle Corps in 1881 and

**1st Middlesex Light Horse. Watercolour by G Laporte.**

**1st Middlesex Light Horse. Print published by Groom, Wilkinson & Co, 1860.**

in 1902, the tenancy at Beaufort House having come to an end, moved to new headquarters at Fulham House, 7 High Street, Fulham. This historic property had once been owned by Sir Ralph Warren, Lord Mayor of London in 1536 and 1543, and later the Cromwell family. A fine gateway was purported to have been built by Inigo Jones, and the Officers' Mess possessed a number of carvings by Grinling Gibbons.

The strength of the 2nd Middlesex eventually fell to twelve companies, the headquarters of these, in addition to Fulham, being found at Chelsea, Chiswick, Hammersmith, Kensington, Brompton, Knightsbridge and Acton. The headquarters of 'K' Company were at the War Office. A cadet corps was formed in 1865, but this was removed from the Army List in 1880. St Paul's School at West Kensington formed a cadet corps in 1890—B L Montgomery, the future field marshal, becoming a pupil of the Army Class in 1902. *Territorials:* In 1908 some 300 officers and other ranks of the 2nd Middlesex provided a nucleus for the 10th Battalion Middlesex Regiment. However, the 10th was regarded as a new unit and no connection with any previous volunteer corps was permitted. Consequently, the battle honour 'South Africa 1900-02' gained by the volunteers from the 2nd Middlesex while serving as part of the City Imperial Volunteers was not carried forward. St Paul's School, in 1908, became part of the OTC.

In the *Bulletin* of the Military Historical Society for August 1993, a button was offered for identification

**7TH MIDDLESEX RIFLE VOLUNTEERS**
**(LONDON SCOTTISH)**
**PRIVATE, MARCHING ORDER**

**MOUNTED INFANTRY**
OF THE QUEEN'S WESTMINSTERS
13TH MIDDLESEX VOLUNTEERS.
**CORPORAL, MARCHING ORDER**

which bore the inscription 'Volunteer Corps of Old Blues'. In the centre was a representation of the head and shoulders of King Edward VI. Subsequent research by Mr Howard Ripley (MHS May 1996) discovered an item published in the *Volunteer Service Gazette* for 30 June 1860 indicating that a volunteer corps had been raised from former pupils of Christ's Hospital School in the City of London. In a latter edition, however, it was announced that as insufficient numbers had come forward from the 'Old Blues' those already enrolled should be merged into Viscount Ranelagh's 2nd Middlesex. Another item published in the *Bulletin* (November 1997) deals with Freemasonry in the Volunteer Force and in this Mr J W Reddyhoff notes that South Middlesex Lodge No 1160 (later No.858) was formed from within the 2nd Corps on 12 February 1861.

**3rd (Hampstead) (1859-1880)**—E T Evans, in his book *Records of the Third Middlesex Rifle Volunteers* records how in about June 1859 three residents of Hampstead

**7th Middlesex Rifle Volunteer Corps.**

**13th Middlesex Rifle Volunteer Corps.**

**Left: Captain Henry H Williams, 19th Middlesex Rifle Volunteer Corps.**

**Right: 20th Middlesex Rifle Volunteer Corps.**

(Messrs Jay, Bennett and another) met a number of Highgate residents at the Spaniards Inn to consider the formation of a volunteer corps; through lack of interest, however, nothing more was done until Monday 4 July when another meeting took place at the residence of J Gurney Hoare, Esq of The Hill, Hampstead Heath. Subsequently the 3rd Middlesex RVC was formed with a strength of sixty, the first drills taking place at the Holly Bush Assembly Rooms and the Infant School in Well Road. The first officers, John R MacInnes, Basil Field and George Holford, were gazetted on 6 December 1859. In May 1860 rifle practice began at Child's Hill. During 1860 the corps used the Christ Church School for drill, Evans mentioning a 'Kilburn' contingent that used the St Mary's School in that area for a short time. Permission was obtained to increase the establishment to two companies in September 1860.

The corps joined the 2nd Admin Battalion of Middlesex Rifle Volunteers on 28 November 1860 and in 1862 permission was received to include Hampstead in the title. New headquarters in Well Walk were taken over on Tuesday 16 December 1862. The building was a former chapel and before that, the old Hampstead pump-room. These premises, and the house next door, were used until notice to quite was received at the end of 1881. Not having the required enrolled strength, the corps was reduced to one company and a sub-division in July 1864. A room was taken for drill purposes at Hendon for volunteers recruited there in July 1866, but lack of interest in the area saw the detachment soon disbanded. The Hampstead Athletic Club, which met at Well Walk, was formed from within the corps in 1878. In March 1880 the 2nd Admin Battalion was consolidated as 3rd Middlesex RVC, the 3rd Corps becoming its 'A' and 'B' Companies.

**3rd (1880-1908)**—The 2nd Admin Battalion of Middlesex Rifle Volunteers was formed on 28 November 1860 and consisted then of the 3rd, 13th and 14th Corps. Battalion headquarters were at Southwood Lane, Highgate. Drills took place at Albany Street Barracks. Absorbed the 6th Admin Battalion containing the 12th, 33rd and 41st Corps on 17 January 1862. An Orderly Room was established at 96 Farringdon Street, London, EC at the end of March 1864. Battalion headquarters moved to Crouch End, Hornsey in October 1870 and in 1880 consolidation took place as 3rd Corps with nine companies: 'A', 'B' Hampstead (late 3rd Corps), 'C' Barnet (late 12th Corps), 'D' Hornsey (late 13th Corps), 'E', F' Highgate (late 14th Corps), 'G' Tottenham (late 33rd Corps), 'H', 'I' Enfield Lock (late 41st Corps).

A new company ('K') was added at Enfield Town in September 1881. Sanction to form a drill station attached to 'A' and 'B' (Hampstead) Companies at Hendon was obtained from the War Office in 1884, the first drill taking place at the Assembly Rooms, the Burroughs in the beginning of February 1885. In the same year, 'D' (Hornsey) Company began recruiting in Southgate, Wood Green and Finsbury Park. The new Southgate detachment carried out drills in the Village Hall. 'E' and 'F' (Highgate) Companies also recruited at North Finchley. The corps was designated 1st Volunteer Battalion Middlesex Regiment in 1898. Highgate

School Cadet Corps was affiliated in 1883 but, with no officers appointed, this was removed from the Army List by the end of 1884. The school appears again, however, in 1892.

As a result of the war in South Africa permission was received to increase the battalion's establishment by three companies, the total establishment by the end of 1900 being now: Hampstead and Barnet, one company each; Hornsey four, Highgate two, Tottenham three and Enfield two. *Territorials:* 7th Battalion Middlesex Regiment. Highgate School in 1908 became part of the Junior Division, OTC.

**4th (West London)**—Formed as one company at Islington with Alfred Alexander as captain, Edward Russell Cummins, lieutenant and John William Docwra, ensign. All three held commissions dated 15 October 1859. Joined the 1st Admin Battalion and absorbed the 5th and 6th Corps in June 1860, the 8th in August 1860. This brought the establishment up to four companies with Major Charles R C Baron Truro in command. Amalgamated with the 7th Corps in 1861, West London being added to the title in 1864. Headquarters moved from 1 Tyndale Place to Swallow Street, Piccadilly and became a volunteer battalion (without change in title) of King's Royal Rifle Corps in 1881. Headquarters were moved to Adam and Eve Mews off Kensington High Street in 1885 having been situated in the West End of London since 1864. Designated 4th (Kensington) in 1905. *Territorials:* 13th Battalion London Regiment.

Members of the corps served with the City Imperial Volunteers in South Africa. A memorial to all those from Islington who died in that conflict was erected by the people of the borough at Highbury Fields opposite Highbury Station in July 1905.

**5th (1859-1860)**—Formed as one company at Islington with James Childs commissioned as captain on 27 December 1859. Absorbed into the 4th Corps in June 1860.

**5th (West Middlesex) (1880-1908)**—Formed as 9th Corps with headquarters at Lord's Cricket Ground, St John's Wood on 14 October 1859. There were six companies at first, raising to eight in April 1860—the Rt Hon Granville Augustus William, Baron Radstock taking command as lieutenant-colonel commandant. Renumbered as 5th in 1880. Became a volunteer battalion (without change in title) of the Royal Fusiliers in the following year but transferred in 1883 to the King's Royal Rifle Corps. Headquarters moved to 29 Park Road, Regents Park. Absorbed the 9th Corps at Harrow in 1899, bringing with it the Harrow School Cadet Corps. The latter to become the 27th Corps on 1 April 1902 and serving as such until disbandment in January 1906. The personnel then returned to the 5th Corps as a cadet company. *Territorials:* 9th Battalion Middlesex Regiment, the cadet corps in 1908 joining the OTC.

**6th (1859-1860)**—Formed as one company at Islington in November 1859 and absorbed into the 4th Corps in June 1860.

**6th (St George's) (1880-1892)**—Formed in the Parish of St George's, Westminster—headquarters have included 2 Boyle Street, Old Burlington Street and 8 Mill Street off Regent Street—as the 11th Middlesex (St George's) RVC on 14 January 1860. With four companies the Hon Charles Hugh Lindsay of the Grenadier Guards was appointed as major commandant, his company commanders being G M Ives (Coldstream Guards), Sir J E Harrington, Bt, J C Knox and George H Elliott. The last two both former officers with the 2nd Dragoon Guards. The companies were recruited from the Bond Street, Grosvenor Square, Hanover Square and Belgravia areas. The corps was renumbered as 6th in 1880 and became a volunteer battalion (without change in title) of the King's Royal Rifle Corps in the following year. Amalgamated with 1st Middlesex RVC on 1 June 1892.

**7th (1859-1861)**—Formed as one company at Islington with Alfred J Ebsworth commissioned as captain on 26 November 1859. John Reynolds, Jun became his lieutenant, J Poole Wagstaff, his ensign. Joined the 1st Admin Battalion and amalgamated with the 4th Corps in 1861.

**7th (London Scottish) (1880-1908)**—The services of a rifle corps composed of Scotsmen living in the London area were accepted by the War Office on 2 November 1859. The corps consisted of six companies and was designated as the 15th Middlesex (London Scottish) RVC, Lord Elcho (afterwards Earl of Wemyss) being appointed as lieutenant colonel in command. Headquarters were established at 8 Adelphi Terrace, Westminster and the six companies were located: No 1 (Highland) 10 Pall Mall, East, No 2 (City) The Oriental Bank, No 3 (Northern) Rosemary Hall Islington, No 4 (Central) Scottish Corporation House Crane Court, No 5 (Southern) 68 Jermyn Street, No 6 (Western) Chesterfield House West London.

Members of the corps paid an entrance fee of £1 (abolished in 1862) and were required to provide their own uniforms and equipment. General Grierson in *Records of the Scottish Volunteer Force* notes that of the 600 men originally enrolled, 340 were artisans who paid no entrance fee and only a five shillings per year subscription, and of these only fifty provided their own uniforms, the rest being equipped from a central fund.

In 1861 No 2 Company became No 7 and a new No 2, together with a No 8, were raised. No 3 Company was absorbed into the rest in 1865 and the following year company numbers were replaced by letters. This required the following reorganisation: 'A' Company (formed by No 1), 'B' Company (newly formed), 'C' Company (from No 4), 'D' Company (from No 5), 'E' Company (from No 2 and No 6), 'F' Company (from No 7), 'G' Company (left vacant), 'H' Company (from No 8).

The 15th was renumbered as 7th in September 1880 and in the following year a new 'G' Company was formed. At the same time the corps became a volunteer battalion (without change in title) of the Rifle Brigade. Additions in 1884 were 'I' and 'K' Companies. Some 218 Volunteers from the corps saw active service in South Africa, the first contingent under Lieutenant B C Green joining the City Imperial Volunteers in December 1899. Four men were mentioned in despatches, two receiving the Distinguished Conduct Medal. Another detachment served with the 2nd Battalion Gordon Highlanders, one man, Sergeant W F Budgett, and ten men were wounded when a shell burst immediately above the Volunteers on 8 September 1901 near Lydenburgh. *Territorials:* 14th Battalion London Regiment, headquarters having moved to Adam

**36th Middlesex
Rifle Volunteer Corps.**

**16th Middlesex
Rifle Volunteer Corps.**

**15th Middlesex
Rifle Volunteer Corps.**

Street in 1873, then 1 Adam Street, Adelphi, then James Street, Buckingham Gate in 1886. Mr J W Reddyhoff, writing in the *Bulletin* of the Military Historical Society in November 1997, noted that the London Scottish Freemason Lodge No 2310 was formed from within the corps on 18 April 1889.

**8th (1859-1860)**—Formed as one company at Islington in November 1859 and absorbed into the 4th Corps in August 1860.

**8th (South West Middlesex) (1880-1908)**—The 7th Admin Battalion was formed with headquarters at Whitton Park, Hounslow in April 1861 and included the 16th, 24th, 30th, 43rd, 44th and 45th Corps. Included South West Middlesex in its title and was consolidated in 1880 as the new 8th Corps with eight companies: 'A', 'B', 'C', 'D' Hounslow (late 16th Corps), 'E' Uxbridge (late 24th Corps), 'F' Ealing (late 30th Corps), 'G' Sunbury (late 43rd Corps), 'H' Stains (late 44th Corps).

Re-designated as 2nd Volunteer Battalion Middlesex Regiment in 1887. The Ealing Schools Cadet Corps was formed and affiliated in 1901. An increase in establishment to ten companies was authorised in 1900, but this was reduced back to eight four years later. *Territorials:* 8th Battalion Middlesex Regiment. Mr J W Reddyhoff writing in *The Bulletin of the Military Historical Society* in November 1997 noted that the Gostling Murray Freemason Lodge No 1871 was formed from within the battalion on 3 August 1880.

**9th (1859-1880)**—See 5th Corps (1880-1908).

**9th (1880-1908)**—The first officers of the 18th Corps, formed at Harrow as one company, were John Charles Templer, captain, Edward Francis Elliott, lieutenant and Duncan Mackenzie, ensign. All three held commissions dated 30 December 1859. Also appointed were Thomas Bridgewater, MD as surgeon, and the Rev F W Farrar who became chaplain. Much of the corps was recruited from the staff and senior boys of Harrow School which, in 1870, provided a cadet corps. Renumbered as 9th Corps in 1880 and became a volunteer battalion (without change of title) of the Royal Fusiliers the following year. Transferred to King's Royal Rifle Corps under General Order 99 of July 1883. Now four companies, the 9th amalgamated with the 5th Corps (as 5th) in 1899.

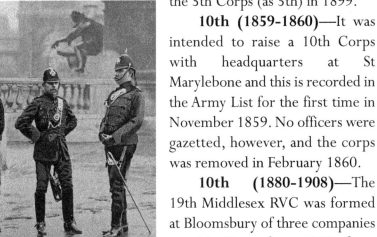

**10th (1859-1860)**—It was intended to raise a 10th Corps with headquarters at St Marylebone and this is recorded in the Army List for the first time in November 1859. No officers were gazetted, however, and the corps was removed in February 1860.

**10th (1880-1908)**—The 19th Middlesex RVC was formed at Bloomsbury of three companies on 13 December 1859 from members of the Working Men's College in Great Ormond Street, Holborn. The commanding officer was Thomas Hughes, the author of *Tom Brown's Schooldays*, which led to

**Top: 16th Middlesex Rifle Volunteer Corps.**

**Left: 46th Middlesex Rifle Volunteer Corps 1875. Watercolour by R Simkin.**

the corps often being referred to as 'Tom Brown's Corps'. The 19th later comprised ten companies of which three were supplied by the college, others by the St John's Institute in Cleveland Street, the Price Belmont Works at Battersea, the Working Men's College in Paddington Green and the Westminster parishes of St Luke and St. Anne's. Headquarters later moved to 33 Fitzroy Square.

Renumbered 10th in 1880 and became a volunteer battalion (without change in title) of the King's Royal Rifle Corps in 1881. General Order 99 of July 1883, however, directed a transfer to the Royal Fusiliers and re-designation as 1st Volunteer Battalion. An eleventh company was added in 1900. *Territorials:* 1st Battalion London Regiment.

**11th (St George's) (1860-1880)**—See 6th Corps (1880-1892).

**11th (Railway) (1880-1908)**—On 13 December 1859 the 20th Corps of three companies was formed with headquarters at Euston Square mainly from men employed by the London and North Western Railway Company. Thomas Edward Bigge, who had previously served with the 23rd Royal Welsh Fusiliers, was appointed captain commandant in command. The corps was included in the 4th Admin Battalion until May 1861 and in 1880 renumbered as 11th. Joined the King's Royal Rifle Corps (without change in title) as one of its volunteer battalions in 1881, transferring to the Middlesex Regiment in 1882 and then the Royal Fusiliers as its 3rd Volunteer Battalion in 1890. Additional personnel were sanctioned in 1900/01 bringing the establishment from eight to thirteen companies. After the war in South Africa, however, a reduction was made to eleven. The battalion occupied several headquarters in the Euston area, was at 5 Albany Street, Regent's Park, then from Edward Street, off Hampstead Road. *Territorials:* 3rd Battalion London Regiment.

**12th (1859-1880)**—E T Evans in his book *Records of the Third Middlesex Rifle Volunteers* notes that the 12th Middlesex RVC was brought into existence through the exertions of Mr Wilbraham Taylor of Hadley Hurst—a gentleman usher to the Queen who had organised a meeting at the Town Hall, Barnet to consider the question of raising a volunteer corps in the Barnet and Hadley areas on 6 July 1859. Pending the official acceptance of the services of the corps, a number of men were enrolled at Hadley Hurst and drills commenced at the Militia Barracks, Barnet. Notification of the Queen's acceptance was read on parade on 15 October 1859, the first commissions being granted on 20 October 1859—Captain Wilbraham Taylor, Lieutenant Charles Addington Hanbury.

The headdress worn by the

**Top: 1st Volunteer Battalion Royal Fusiliers.**

**Right: 46th Middlesex Rifle Volunteer Corps 1876. Watercolour by R Simkin.**

12th Middlesex was of a style called Garibaldi, this leading to the corps's nickname 'the Garibaldians'. A rifle range was taken into use at Moat Mount, Highwood Hill in 1860 and the 12th joined the 6th Admin Battalion of Middlesex Rifle Volunteers in 1860. With other corps of 6th Admin, the 12th joined the county's 2nd Admin Battalion on 17th January 1862. A cadet corps was formed at Brunswick House School, but this was disbanded after two years. A new range on ground owned by Mr Henry Hyde of the Manor House, Monken Hadley was opened on 21 March 1863. In the same year a house in High Street, Barnet was taken into use as an armoury and a combined armoury, drill-shed and headquarters was set up in High Street, Barnet in 1871. Became 'C' Company of the new 3rd Middlesex in 1880.

**12th (Civil Service) (1880-1908)**—From the very beginning of the Volunteer Movement it had been intended to merge all units raised by government departments into one corps. In the early months there had been formed the 21st, 27th, 31st and 34th Corps, all of which were manned by civil servants, and it would be these that in June 1860 were merged as the 21st Middlesex (Civil Service) RVC with former Scots Guards officer Lieutenant Colonel William C Viscount Bury in command.

Headquarters were placed at Somerset House and the several companies, eight in all, were organised: 'A' (Audit Office), late No.1 Company, 21st Corps, 'B' (Post Office), late No.2 Company, 21st Corps, 'C' (Post Office), late No.3 Company, 21st Corps, 'D' (Inland Revenue), late No.1 Company, 27th Corps), 'E' (Inland Revenue), late No.2 Company, 27th Corps, 'F' (Whitehall), late No.1 Company, 31st Corps, 'G' (Whitehall), late No.2 Company, 31st Corps, 'H' (Admiralty) late 34th Corps.

It should be noted that the two Post Office companies, made up as they were from senior staff, were in no way connected with the 49th Middlesex RVC—later to become the Post Office Rifles—which comprised the lower grades of postal workers.

In July 1866 an additional company ('K') was raised by the clerks and senior members of the Bank of England and at the same time 'F' (Whitehall) and 'G' (Whitehall) Companies were amalgamated as 'G'. The 21st Corps was renumbered as 12th in 1880 and became a volunteer battalion (without change in title) of the King's Royal Rifle Corps in the following year. A change in designation did occur, however, in May 1898 when the corps became styled as The Prince of Wales's Own 12th Middlesex (Civil Service) RVC—HRH having been honorary colonel since its formation. Two new companies, 'F' and 'I' (Cyclist) were raised from employees of the London County Council in 1900 and a cadet corps was formed and affiliated in 1903. *Territorials:* 15th Battalion London Regiment.

There exists the *Blue Book* which was first published in 1899 with the purpose of providing 'useful information' to members—the battalion's 'Standing Orders' in fact. Details included are of the annual nine-

**15th Middlesex Rifle Volunteer Corps.**

**Officer, 2nd Administrative Battalion Middlesex Rifle Volunteers.**

**Other ranks helmet plate, 20th Middlesex Rifle Volunteer Corps.**

day camp at Old Deer Park, Richmond, notes on the rifle range at Runnymede in Surrey, and the regimental tailor, who was Hobson and Son of 1/2 Great Lexington Street, London

**13th (1859-1880)**—Formed as a result of a meeting held at Crouch Hall, Crouch End on the evening of Friday 10 June 1859. Application to form a corps was subsequently submitted, notification that its services had been accepted as 13th Middlesex RVC being received on 2 November 1859—Joseph H Warner was appointed as captain; J Bird, lieutenant and John Martineau Fletcher, ensign. Establishment was fixed at one company. Headquarters were in Hornsey. Joined the 2nd Admin Battalion on 22 November 1860. The corps used a range belonging to the 12th Middlesex RVC at Highwood Hill and another at Hornsey Wood House. A range at Tottenham was taken in 1862. E T Evans notes the death from small-pox in 1865 of Sergeant Henry St John Walton, a window in his memory being erected in Hornsey Church. Thirty recruits were enrolled at Southgate in 1866 but plans to set up a company or sub-division at Wood Green were dropped in 1869. At a general meeting of the corps held on 26 April 1870 it was announced that a lease had been taken out on premises in Crouch End for use as headquarters. Evans records a general fall off in numbers, the year 1872 seeing a reduction from seventy to sixty-four of which the majority were resident in Southgate. Upon the consolidation of 2nd Admin Battalion in 1880, the 13th became 'D' Company of the new 3rd Corps.

**13th (Queen's) (1880-1908)**—The post 1880 13th Corps was originally numbered as the 22nd Middlesex (Queen's) at Pimlico having been formed in January 1860 from several companies raised earlier, a standing order of the time stating that 'On 13 January 1860, the Queen's Rifle Volunteers amalgamated with the several companies raised in the parishes of St. John's, St. Margaret's, St Mary's Strand, St Paul's Covent Garden, St James, St Martin's in the Fields, St Anne's John Street, St Clement Danes and with the King's College.' Also included in the corps was a number of men that had enrolled into a corps formed at Messrs J Broadwood & Sons Ltd of Horseferry Road, Westminster. The first officers' commissions were dated 25 February 1860. The corps comprised fifteen companies, divided into two battalions, under the command of Lieutenant Colonel Commandant the Earl Grosvenor. Headquarters were given as Westminster from March 1860. The corps was renumbered as 13th in 1880 and became a volunteer battalion (without change in title) of the King's Royal Rifle Corps in 1881. By 1900 the establishment had reached sixteen companies which were organised and named as follows: 'A', 'B', 'C', 'D' Pimlico Division, 'E', 'F' St John's Division, 'G' St Margaret's Division, 'H' St James's Division, 'I', 'K' St Martin's Division, 'L' Schoolbread's Company, 'M' St Clement Dane's Division, 'O' Royal Welsh, 'R' Greater Westminster, 'S' Mounted Infantry, 'T' Cyclists.

A cadet corps was formed in 1900. Headquarters are noted as 106 Buckingham Palace Road and after that, James Street, Westminster. *Territorials:* 16th Battalion London Regiment. Mr J W Reddyhoff writing in *The Bulletin of the Military Historical Society* in November 1997 noted that the Queen's Westminster Freemason Lodge No 2021 was formed from within the battalion on 14 November 1883.

**14th (1860-1880)**—E T Evans records in his book *Records of the Third Middlesex Rifle Volunteers* that the origins of the 14th Corps lay in a private meeting held to discuss the possibilities of forming a Volunteer Rifle Corps in Highgate and is vicinity at the home of William H Bodkin (afterwards Sir William Bodkin) on 24 May 1859. A subsequent meeting was held at the Swain's Lane cricket field on 21 June 1859. First drills later took place at Swain's Lane. The services of the Highgate Volunteers were accepted in the autumn of 1859, the War Office allotting the title 14th Middlesex RVC with an establishment of one company. Officers' commissions were dated 2 November 1859. Headquarters were established at Southwood Lane, Highgate in a building belonging to the governors of Highgate School. An additional company was authorised on 16 February 1860—Captain Commandant Josiah Wilkinson in command—and a third in June 1860. Although the latter was never formed. Rifle practice was now taking place at Hornsey Wood House and drills, not only in Highgate, but in Gray's Inn Hall or Gardens, and frequently at Albany Street Barracks. The corps became part of 2nd Admin Battalion on 28 November 1860. Evans notes how in 1860 efforts

were made to form companies at Kentish Town and Finchley without success. There were, however, always many members of the 14th that were resident in those areas. A cadet corps was formed and affiliated to the corps at Christ College, Finchley in 1864, its commanding officer being appointed on 5 December—but this was disbanded towards the end of 1867. Headquarters, at the end of 1870 were moved to Hornsey, but were back again at Highgate in 1879. The new location, Northfield Hall, being taken over on 6 January. Establishment was reduced to one company on 23 September 1874, but a new second company was authorised before the end of 1876, its first officer not, however, being commissioned until 10 January 1878. Became 'E' and 'F' Companies of the new 3rd Corps in 1880.

**14th (Inns of Court) (1880-1908)**—Formed as 23rd Corps at Lincoln's Inn, London from members of the legal profession on 15 February 1860 with six companies under the command of Lieutenant Colonel Commandant William B Brewster, late of the Rifle Brigade. Renumbered as 14th in 1880 and became a volunteer battalion (without change in title) of the Rifle Brigade in 1881. The St Peter's College Cadet Corps, Westminster was affiliated in 1902 and shown as Westminster School from May 1904. *Territorials:* It was the intention to transfer the 14th to the Territorial Force in 1908 as the 27th Battalion of the London Regiment, but the members were not happy with this decision and chose to continue service as the Inns of Court OTC instead.

**15th (London Scottish) (1859-1880)**—See 7th Corps (1880-1908).

PLAYER'S CIGARETTES

THE LONDON SCOTTISH RIFLE VOLUNTEER CORPS, 1859.

**15th (The Customs and Docks) (1880-1908)**—Formed as the 26th Corps with headquarters at Custom House, London on 9 February 1860 and recruited from Customs Officers in the London Docks—four companies under the command of Major Commandant Ralph William Grey. Joined the 5th Admin Battalion and amalgamated with 9th Tower Hamlets RVC in 1864 under the title 26th (The Customs and Docks). Absorbed the 42nd Corps, also a dockland formation, in 1866, and the 8th Tower Hamlets in 1868. Now with thirteen companies, was renumbered 15th in 1880 and became a volunteer battalion (without change of title) of the Rifle Brigade in 1881. By 1891 the establishment had been reduced to eight companies. *Territorials:* Part of 17th Battalion London Regiment.

**16th (1860-1880)**—Formed as two companies at Hounslow on 6 January 1860 with Charles Edward Murray as captain commandant. Joined the 7th Admin Battalion, increased to four companies by 1863, and became 'A' to 'D' Companies of the new 8th Corps in 1880.

**15th Middlesex Rifle Volunteer Corps.**

**16th (London Irish) (1880-1908)**—The 28th Corps of eight companies was raised as a result of a meeting arranged by Mr G T Dempsey, an Irishman resident in London, at his rooms in Essex Street, Strand in the latter weeks of 1859. Headquarters were placed at Burlington House and the first officers' commissions were dated 28 February 1860. It is of interest to note that out of the nineteen officers recorded in the Army List for December 1860, no less than five held tiles: the Marquis of Donegal (lieutenant colonel), Lord Otho A Fitzgerald (captain), Lord Ashley (captain), Lord Francis N Conynhham (lieutenant) and the Earl of Belmore (ensign). Headquarters were transferred to York Buildings, Adelphi in 1866, Leicester Square in 1869, King William Street in 1873 and Duke Street, Charring Cross in 1897. The 28th was renumbered as 16th in 1880 and became a volunteer battalion (without change of title) of the Rifle Brigade in 1881. *Territorials:* 18th Battalion London Regiment. Mr J W Reddyhoff writing in *The Bulletin of the Military Historical Society* in November 1997 notes that the London Irish Rifles Freemason Lodge No 2312 was formed from within the battalion on 24 May 1899.

**17th (North Middlesex)**—Formed as the 29th Corps of five companies at St Pancras on 1 March 1860, Lieutenant Colonel Viscount Enfield taking command. A good number of recruits for this corps were provided by men from Lord Elcho's proposed corps, the 'Euston Road Rifles'. Included in the 4th Admin Battalion for period August-December 1860 and in 1861 moved headquarters to Regent's Park. Included 'North Middlesex' in the title from 1864 and moved once again, this time to High Street Camden Town, during the same year. Renumbered 17th in 1880 and became a volunteer battalion (without change in title) of the Middlesex Regiment in 1881. *Territorials:* 19th Battalion London Regiment.

**18th (1859-1880)**—See 9th Corps (1880-1908).

**18th (1880-1908)**—A little over five years after the first railway passengers had boarded their trains below the iron work of Matthew Digby Wyatt's roof at Paddington Station, a short distance to the north in the Vestry Hall, the committee set up to establish a corps of riflemen in Paddington had agreed to present the plans gathered so far to the War Office.

January 10 1860, and another meeting on record indicates that as of that date, no sanction had yet been received from the War Office; but nonetheless, recruiting had gone well and within a few days sufficient numbers had come forward to man a full company. By 29 February, the date of the first officer's commission, a second had been raised and in March a captain commandant had been appointed in the form of Major General David Downing (late of the Indian Army) who, on the 7th, attended a levee of Volunteer Officers given by Queen Victoria at St James's Palace. By this time the Paddington Volunteers, their motto 'arm for peace', had been ranked as 36th in the County of Middlesex.

A third company well underway, the 36th Middlesex held its first parade and march around the borough on 8 May, 1860. A band made up of Metropolitan Railway workers and musicians from the Working Men's College at Paddington Green led the way. Weeks later, at the first Volunteer Review held in Hyde Park, Nos. 1 and 2 Companies took the field and earned much praise for their smartness and soldierly appearance from those present.

Well on the way to four companies now a cadet corps had also been formed, along with a drum and bugle band. Situated in the grounds of St Mary's Church next to Paddington Green, the Vestry Hall provided headquarters, while across the Harrow Road at the Hermitage Street Fire Station, drills were carried out and weapons stored. The corps also had the use of two riding schools—Pearce's in Westbourne Grove and Gapp's in Gloucester Terrace.

In 1865 the 36th Middlesex provided the Guard of Honour when HRH the Prince of Wales laid the foundation stone of the Paddington Infirmary (later Paddington General Hospital) adjacent to the Workhouse in the Harrow Road near Lock Bridge. Four years later, as the Vestry Hall began to grow into the Town Hall, temporary headquarters had to be found in rooms above the King and Queen public house in Harrow Road. This was a location within view of the next move which took the 36th across Paddington Green to Greville House, once the premises of the Working Men's College, and before that the home of Emma Hart, the

**13th Middlesex Rifle Volunteer Corps.**

future Lady Hamilton and friend of Lord Nelson.

A gradual increase in establishment seems to have taken place over the first ten years of the corps's existence. Mention of a No. 7 Company at Kensal Green made up mainly from employees of the Metropolitan Railway is noted in 1870 and in 1872, 'H' Company (presumably letters have replace numbers by now) is on record as having held a dinner on 10 September. The 36th was renumbered as 18th in 1880 and in the following year became a volunteer battalion (without change in title) of the Rifle Brigade.

The premises at Paddington Green becoming more and more crowded as the battalion grew—transport and ambulance sections had been added to the still growing number of companies, and the band was restricted to practising in the hallways—so in 1895 property was acquired at 207-209 Harrow Road which occupied enough land to permit the building of a drill hall and rifle range. On the evening of 31 March 1896, the 18th were marched out of Paddington Green for the last time. Making their way past St Mary's Church, Sarah Siddons in her white Carrara not yet looking on, and into the Harrow Road where the parade took the battalion past the old Vestry Hall (now Town Hall), Paddington Green Police Station (later made famous in the film *The Blue Lamp*), Porteus Road, where the local artillery volunteers met and drilled, over the bridge that crossed the Grand Junction Canal and took the road down to where it skirted the Great Western, past the Red Lion public house to headquarters. The journey today is in the most part within the shadow of the great Westway Flyover. *Territorials:* 10th Battalion London Regiment.

Mr J W Reddyhoff, writing in *The Bulletin of the Military Historical Society* in November 1997, notes that the Paddington Rifles Freemason Lodge No 2807 was formed from within the battalion in 1900.

**19th (1859-1880)**—See 10th Corps (1880-1908).

**19th (St Giles and St George's Bloomsbury) (1880-1908)**—Four companies formed as 37th Corps with headquarters at the Local Board of Works, Holborn on 31 March 1860 with Major John W Jeakes in command. Joined the 4th Admin Battalion in August 1860 but was made independent in May of the following year. Headquarters moved in 1861 to the Foundling Hospital in Guildford Street, WC1. Comprised eight companies by 1866. The additional title St Giles and St George's, Bloomsbury was added in 1869 and in 1880 the corps was renumbered as 19th. Became a volunteer battalion (without change in title) of the Rifle Brigade in 1881. Headquarters moved to Chenies Street, Bedford Square, WC1 in 1887. *Territorials:* The 19th Middlesex was amalgamated with 1st Middlesex to form the 9th Battalion London Regiment. Mr J W Reddyhoff writing in *The Bulletin of the Military Historical Society* in November 1997 noted that the Bloomsbury Rifles Freemason Lodge No 2362 was formed from within the battalion on 1 May 1890.

**20th (1859-1880)**—See 11th Corps (1880-1908).

**20th (Artists) (1880-1908)**—Formed as three companies with headquarters at Burlington House, London on 25 May 1860 with the painter, Henry W Phillips as captain commandant. Numbered as 38th, the corps was recruited from painters, sculptors, musicians, architects, actors and other members of artistic occupations. A private in the corps was Queen's Medallist and Engraver to the Signet J W Wyon who was responsible for designing the Artists Rifles badge. An apt device, it included the heads of Mars, the god of war, and Minerva, the goddess of the arts. Later increased to four, then six companies. Headquarters moved to the Arts Club, Hanover Square in 1869, the word Artists being included in the title from 1877. Renumbered 20th in 1880 and as eight companies with headquarters at in Fitzroy Square became a volunteer battalion (without change in title) of the Rifle Brigade in 1881. A move was later made to Duke's Road. The University College School Cadet Corps was affiliated in 1904. *Territorials:* 28th Battalion London Regiment. The University College School in 1908 became a contingent of the OTC.

**21st (1860)**—Three companies formed with headquarters at Somerset House, London on 2 January 1860 from staff of the Audit Office and Post Office. The three company commanders were Captains Francis Alfred Hawker, Nicholas H Harrington and John L de Plat Taylor. Became 'A', 'B' and 'C' Companies of the new 21st Corps in June 1860.

**21st (Civil Service) (1860-1880)**—See 12th Corps (1880-1908).

**21st (The Finsbury Rifle Volunteer Corps) (1880-1908)**—Formed as the 39th Corps of eight companies at Clerkenwell on 6 March 1860, Thomas H Colvill, late of the 74th Regiment of Foot, and at the time Governor of Coldbathfields Prison, being appointed as lieutenant colonel in command. Included in the 3rd Admin Battalion until 1861 and 'The Finsbury RVC' was added to the title in 1862. Increased to ten companies in the 1870s, renumbered 21st in 1880. Became a volunteer battalion (without change in title) of the Rifle Brigade in 1881, transferring to the King's Royal Rifle Corps in 1883. Two new companies were authorized in 1900. *Territorials:* From headquarters in Penton Street, Pentonville, the 21st transferred to the Territorial Force in 1908 as the 11th Battalion London Regiment.

**22nd (Queen's) (1860-1880)**—See 13th Corps (1880-1908).

**22nd (Central London Rifle Rangers) (1880-1908)**—From members of the legal profession, formed as the 40th Corps of eight companies at Gray's Inn, London on 30 April 1860 and included in the 3rd Admin Battalion until 1861 when made independent. In that year Lieutenant Colonel Alfred P F C Somerset, late of the 13th Regiment of Foot, took command, Central London Rifle Rangers was added to title and the 35th Corps at Enfield was absorbed. Renumbered 22nd in 1880, became a volunteer battalion (without change in title) of the Royal Fusiliers in 1881, and transferred to the King's Royal Rifle Corps in the following year. Mayall College Cadet Corps at Herne Hill was affiliated in 1891 but removed from the Army List in 1899.

Volunteers from the corps saw active service in South Africa during the Boer War. Lieutenant W Brian L Alt, who had been first commissioned into the 22nd on 2 June 1894—his father, W J Alt, had commanded the corps since1881—was killed

**32nd Middlesex Rifle Volunteer Corps.**

at Diamond Hill on 12 June 1900 while serving with the City Imperial Volunteers. He would be the only officer of the CIV to lose his life. Also, from the 22nd Middlesex RVC was Charles Gwyn Trivet Bromfield who died from wounds received in action near Boshof on 16 February 1902. From the ranks, he had risen to captain in the 87th Company, Imperial Yeomanry. *Territorials:* 12th Battalion London Regiment.

**23rd (Inns of Court) (1860-1880)**—See 14th Corps (1880-1908).

**23rd (1880-1908)**—It was in January 1861 that the War Office accepted the services of a corps of volunteer riflemen raised within the City and Westminster areas of London. Number 5 Victoria Street, just a short walk down from Westminster Abbey, was its first headquarters, Sir John Villiers Shelley (MP for Westminster) its first Commanding Officer and 46 its allotted number within the fast growing order of battle of Middlesex RVC. Such was the enthusiasm that when the corps, in June 1861, moved just around the corner to new headquarters at 31 Great Smith Street—across the road from the building was the first free public library in London which had been opened four years earlier—eight companies (four in the City, four in Westminster) had been formed. The rank and file, according to one source, was drawn almost entirely from 'the respectable working classes', while the officers were men 'of good social position'. VC hero of the Crimea Lieutenant Colonel Sir Charles Russell was appointed as first honorary colonel in 1877 and he was succeeded six years later by Lord Wolsely.

During the next three years the 46th Middlesex RVC was to be subject to two changes in designation: firstly as 23rd Middlesex (this to comply with the general 1880 renumbering of Volunteer Corps throughout the country), then in 1883 as 2nd Volunteer Battalion Royal Fusiliers. The corps had been allotted as one of that regiment's four volunteer battalions two years previous. In 1899 a new headquarters was built just around the corner from Great Smith Street at 9 Tufton Street. The move to Tufton Street coincided of course with the commencement of the war in South Africa, the battalion sending out a total of four officers and more than 150 other ranks to serve alongside the 2nd Royal Fusiliers. Nine of that number were either killed or died while on active service. *Territorials:* 2nd Battalion London Regiment.

**24th (1860-1880)**—Formed as two companies at Uxbridge on 22 February 1860 with Lieutenant William Edward Hilliard and Ensign John F W de Salis the first officers to receive commissions. Joined the 7th Admin Battalion, reduced to one company in 1873, and became 'E' Company of the new 8th Corps in 1880.

**24th (1880-1908)**—The formation of a Rifle Corps at the General Post Office in London was sanctioned by the War Office on 13 February 1868. Designated as 49th Middlesex, it was to consist of seven companies each recruited from the minor staff of the several London postal districts and departments—the senior members had enrolled separately and had, since 1860, formed part of the 21st Corps at Somerset House. With headquarters at the General Post Office, London, the seven companies were recruited: 'A', from EC District, 'B', Inland Office, 'C', Newspaper and Money-Order Offices, 'D', WC District, 'E', E, SW and S Districts, 'F', N and NW Districts, 'G', E and SE Districts.

In June 1869 a new 'H' Company provided by SW District was formed, this being followed in July 1870 by 'I' Company from the Telegraph Branch. By the end of 1876 sufficient numbers had been enrolled by the E and SE Districts to increase the establishment by one company and subsequently, from January 1877, 'G' Company was recruited from E District only while the SE men provided the new 'K'. The 49th was renumbered as 24th in 1880 and in the following year became a volunteer battalion (without change of title) of the Rifle Brigade.

On 18th July 1882 the War Office approved a scheme for the formation by the 24th Middlesex RVC of an Army Post Office Corps (APOC). The idea being that this would undertake all postal duties connected with an army on active service overseas. The APOC would be placed on the Army Reserve and consist of two officers and 100 men, all recruited from the 24th. It followed that on 8 August 1882, London postal workers embarked to join the expeditionary force then in Egypt.

In 1883 the telegraph company 'I' was recruited up to 200 and subsequently divided as two divisions,

'A' and 'B', and shown in the Army List as 'Field Telegraph Companies' (FTC). The formation of the FTC had been authorised to run along the same lines as the APOC, the FTC to consist of fifty rank and file. In 1889 both the APOC and FTC were constituted as companies of the 24th, the former becoming 'M' Company, while the telegraph personnel formed 'L'. Additional companies were raised by the 24th during the Boer War, the battalion supplying regular drafts for the front line. At the General Post Office in Aldersgate Street, opposite Gresham Street, a bronze tablet was erected to commemorate those who lost their lives. *Territorials:* 8th Battalion London Regiment. Unique among the Volunteer and later Territorial Forces was the battle honour 'Egypt 1882' which had been gained by the work of the 24th Corps during that campaign. Although 'South Africa 1899-1902' was soon to appear below the name of the regiment in the Army List, it would not be until 1908 that the honour gained in Egypt was recognised.

**25th (1860)**—The February 1860 *Army List* indicates that a 25th Corps was to be formed at St Martin's-in-the-Fields, London. No officers were gazetted, however, and the corps was removed in March 1860.

**25th (Bank of England) (1875-1907)**—In July 1866 the clerks and senior staff of the Bank of England formed a company of Rifle Volunteers which became part of the 21st Middlesex (Civil Service) RVC. On 1 December 1875 a new company was formed, this time by the porters and messengers of the bank. The new company with Captain Samuel O Gray, Lieutenant Walter J Coe and Ensign John H Green, was designated as 50th (Bank of England), being renumbered 25th in 1880. The corps was disbanded in 1907.

**26th (1860-1864)**—See 15th Corps (1880-1908).

**26th (Cyclist) (1888-1908)**—Notification of the acceptance of a corps of Cyclist in Middlesex was received on 11 February 1888. The new formation to rank after the 25th (Bank of England) Corps and to be made up of three troops lettered: 'A', 'B' and 'C—this would be the first battalion in the history of the British Army to be completely dedicated to a cyclist role. The cyclists functioned as scouts, signallers, pulled Colt machine guns into action attached to specially designed carriages and even, according to one source writing in the *Volunteer Gazette,* practised laying their machines down in the road so as to hinder oncoming enemy cavalry. The battalion's first headquarters was at Ashley Place where, seven years after formation of the corps, the first red bricks of John Francis Bentley's Westminster Cathedral would be set in place. By the end of 1888, however, a move had been made to Hare Court, this time in the City and within a few yards of the Temple Church and Fleet Street. Further moves would be made: first to 2 Queen's Road, West Chelsea (1890); 69 Lillie Road, West Brompton (1899) and Horseferry Road, Westminster (1904). Upon formation, the 26th Corps was allotted to the King's Royal Rifle Corps as one of its volunteer battalions. It transferred to the Rifle Brigade in 1889. *Territorials:* 25th London Regiment.

**27th (1860)**—Two companies formed with headquarters at Somerset House, London on 10 February 1860 from the staff of the Inland Revenue office. William Ennis, who had previously served with the 11th Dragoons, was made captain commandant in command. Became 'D' and 'E' Companies of the new 21st Corps in June 1860.

**27th (Harrow School) (1902-1906)**—On 1 April 1902 the cadet corps formed at Harrow School and hitherto attached to the 5th Middlesex RVC became a corps in its own right. Designated as 27th Middlesex, the new corps was allotted to the King's Royal Rifle Corps as one of its volunteer battalions. The 27th appeared as such for the last time in the Army List for April 1906, being disbanded officially with effect from the previous 31 January—the personnel returning to the 5th Corps as a cadet company.

**28th (London Irish)**—See 16th Corps (1880-1908).

**29th**—See 17th Corps.

**30th**—Formed as one company at Ealing on 29 February 1860 with Captain John Fitz Maurice, KH, late colonel in the Rifle Brigade, in command. Joined the 7th Admin Battalion and became 'F' Company of the new 8th Corps in 1880.

**31st**—Two companies formed with headquarters at Whitehall, London on 25 February 1860 from the management and staff of various Government offices. The first officers to be commissioned were Captain Thomas Taylor, Lieutenant Richard Mills and Ensign Frederick William Kirby. Became 'F' and 'G' Companies of the new 21st Corps in June 1860.

**32nd**—Two companies formed with headquarters in Seymour Place, St Marylebone with Captain Commandant the Hon Thomas Charles Bruce being commissioned on 14 February 1860. On 27 October 1860 the *Illustrated London News* published a short item regarding the 32nd: 'The 32nd Middlesex Rifle Corps, known to the public as the "Six-foot Volunteer Guards", was established last February, with a view to meet the requirements of men whose stature ... rendered their appearance in the ranks of ordinary-sized corps somewhat awkward. More than one hundred and fifty gentlemen of the required standard, including several military officers and six-footers from other corps, have been enrolled.'

The corps carried on their drills at either St George's Barracks or Hungerford Hall. The military artist Lady Butler (1864-1933) mentions in her autobiography how 'I stuffed my sketch books with British Volunteers ... there was a very short-lived corps called the Six-foot Guards!' The 32nd Middlesex was disbanded in 1868.

**33rd**—A meeting for the purpose of forming a corps of rifle volunteers in the Tottenham area was held by the churchwardens of the parish at the Lecture Hall, Tottenham on Wednesday 28 December 1859. E T Evans, in his history of the 3rd Middlesex RVC, notes that during the meeting 'a gentleman of the Quaker persuasion, who spoke against the movement, occasioning some uproar, but the meeting refused to hear him.' Some sixty enrolled and these were soon drilling at the National Schoolroom, Marsh Lane, Tottenham. On 16 February, the services of the Tottenham Volunteers were accepted, the War Office allotting the title 33rd Middlesex RVC and an establishment of one company—George Goss to be captain; Edward B L Hill, lieutenant and William A Hall, ensign. Recruits were also found in neighbouring Edmonton. An armoury was set up at Northumberland Park and rifle practice took place at Tottenham Marches and Enfield Lock. A cadet corps of one company was formed in September 1860 consisting of fifty-eight pupils from Bruce Castle School and twenty-two others. Joined the 6th Admin Battalion in 1860, transferring to 2nd Admin in January 1862. Evans records that the novelist Anthony Trollope delivered a lecture at the Lecture Hall on 8 April 1864 in aid of funds for the corps. One of the officers, Captain William A Hall, died in October 1867, a tablet in his honour being erected in the parish church. Became 'G' Company of the new 3rd Corps RVC in 1880.

**34th**—Formed as one company at the Admiralty, London on 22 February 1860 with William Willis as captain, Charles John Cox, lieutenant and Thomas Bell Gripper, ensign. Became 'H' Company of the new 21st Corps in June 1860.

**35th**—Formed as one company at Enfield with captain A P F C Somerset commissioned on 20 April 1860. Joined the 6th Admin Battalion and was absorbed into the 40th Corps in April 1861.

**36th**—See 18th Corps (1880-1908).

**37th (St Giles and St George's)**—See 19th Corps (1880-1908).

**38th (Artists)**—See 20th Corps (1880-1908).

**39th (The Finsbury Rifle Volunteer Corps)**—See 21st Corps (1880-1908).

**40th (Central London Rifle Rangers)**—See 22nd Corps (1880-1908).

**41st**—Three companies formed at Enfield Lock, their services being accepted on 11 June 1860—Gordon S Munro, Charles Sendey and William C Barnes being appointed as captains. Members were principally employees in the Royal Small Arms Factory. Joined the 6th Admin Battalion, transferring to the 2nd Admin Battalion in January 1862. E T Evans in his history of the 3rd Middlesex RVC notes that 'as a special favour the officers were permitted to carry gilt-mounted swords, presumably because the corps was raised at the Royal Small Arms Factory, and for the like reason the royal arms were borne upon the officers' pouches'. Evans also notes that a member of the corps, Bugle Major Kennedy, had served in the 17th Lancers as trumpeter, and had taken part in the Light Brigade charge at Balaclava. Establishment reached six companies in 1868, reducing to four in July 1872, three on 17 June 1873, two in 1874. Evans remarks that the fall off in numbers was due to the introduction of machinery in the factory to replace hand labour. Became 'H' and 'I' Companies of the new 3rd Corps in 1880.

**42nd**—Formed as one company at St Catherine's Docks, London with Thomas W Collet as captain, Thomas Crundwell, lieutenant and Rupert Flindt, ensign. All three held commissions dated 19 June 1860. Joined the 5th Admin Battalion and was absorbed into the 26th Corps by 1866.

**43rd**—Formed as one company at Hampton on 25 September 1860 with Captain Clement R Archer, late of the 4th Dragoon Guards, in command. Joined the 7th Admin Battalion, absorbed the 45th Corps at Sunbury in 1863 and moved headquarters to Sunbury in 1870. Became 'G' Company of the new 8th Corps in 1880.

**44th**—Formed as one company at Staines with James Paine as captain; Edmund G Phillips, lieutenant and Christopher C Horne, ensign. All three held commissions dated 7 December 1860. Joined the 7th Admin Battalion and became 'H' Company of the new 8th Corps in 1880. 'H' Company headquarters were in Thames Street.

**45th**—Formed as a sub-division at Sunbury on 20 December 1860 with Lieutenant William Anthony Mitchison in command. Joined the 7th Admin Battalion and was absorbed into the 43rd Corps in 1863.

**46th**—See 23rd (1880-1908).

**47th**—Formed as one company at Stanmore on 13 January 1862 with John H Hulbert as captain, Charles D E Fortnum, lieutenant and Charles E Blackwell, ensign. Also appointed was the Rev L J Bernays as chaplain. Disbanded in 1865.

**48th (or 'Havelock's)**—Formed on 27 February 1862, the corps had been raised by cartoonist George Cruikshank who had previously been involved with the 24th Surrey RVC across the Thames at Southwark. Like the 24th, the 48th Middlesex consisted entirely of members of the Temperance League. It also held the title 'or Havelock's' in memory of hero of India and noted member of the Temperance Movement, General Sir Henry Havelock (1795-1857). A strong Corps, it soon numbered eight companies, Cruikshank was appointed lieutenant-colonel in command. Headquarters were at 48 Mornington Place, St Pancras, then later at 6 Cook's Court, Serle Street, Lincoln's Inn Fields. Cruikshank's biographer (professor William Bates) recalls how the great age of the artist became a concern of his officers who in 1868 made their feeling known to the War Office. The Government, however, supported the seventy-six-year-old commander and subsequently issued an order cashiering the fourteen officers that had signed the document. But great damage had been done and Cruikshank's resignation soon followed. 'Havelock's' was removed from the title about November 1870. Interest in the corps steadily waned and the 48th made its last appearance in the Army List for January 1872. The corps having merged with the 2nd London.

**49th**—See 24th Corps (1880-1908).

**50th**—See 25th Corps (1875-1907).

**1st Cadet Battalion Royal Fusiliers**—Formed with headquarters at St Pancras on 8 May 1901. Moved to Pond Street, Hampstead in 1904.

# Newcastle-upon-Tyne

## Artillery Volunteers

**1st**—Formed on 2 June 1860 and comprising eight batteries by 1889. The eight were reorganised into four position batteries that year and by Army Order 443 Western Division Royal Artillery was added to the title. *Territorials:* 5th Durham (Howitzer) Battery of the 4th Northumbrian (Howitzer) Brigade RFA.

**2nd**—The 2nd Corps appeared in the Army List for the first time in January 1865, having been formed from one battery of the 1st Northumberland AVC. Attached to the 1st Northumberland Admin Brigade,

the corps disappeared from the Army List in February 1868 after being absorbed into the 3rd Northumberland AVC.

## Engineer Volunteers

**1st (1860-1880)**—Formed 11 September 1860, joining the 1st Admin Battalion of Durham Engineer Volunteers in 1874. The battalion was consolidated at 1st Durham (Durham and Newcastle-upon-Tyne) in 1880, Newcastle providing 'A' to 'E' Companies.

**1st (1880-1908)**—When the 1st Durham Admin Battalion was consolidated in 1880, it at first took on the title of 1st Durham, Newcastle only appearing as half of a bracketed title. This was changed to 1st Newcastle-upon-Tyne and Durham before the end of the year, thus recognising the seniority of Newcastle. The new corps consisted of thirteen companies, 'A' to 'E' (late 1st Newcastle), 'F' to 'M' (late 1st Durham). Two submarine mining companies were formed, these becoming the Tyne Division Submarine Miners in 1888. In that same year the Durham companies were removed to form a separated corps designated as 1st Durham. *Territorials:* 1st and 2nd Northumbrian Field Companies and Northumbrian Divisional Telegraph Company.

**Tyne Division Submarine Miners/Electrical Engineers**—Raised as two companies of the 1st Newcastle-upon-Tyne and Durham Engineer Volunteers in 1884. These were removed in 1888 to form the Tyne Division with headquarters at North Shields. Designated as 'Electrical Engineers' in 1907. *Territorials:* Durham Fortress Engineers.

## Rifle Volunteers

**1st**—Formation of the 1st Newcastle-upon-Tyne RVC began in 1859 when the Newcastle Rifle Club decided to form a corps. By the end of the year sufficient members had been enrolled to form a battalion of nine companies. The first officers were gazetted on 22 February 1860, Sir John Fife becoming commanding officer, Robert Robey Redmayne his second-in-command. The nine companies were made up from all sections of the Newcastle community, each being given names indicating the origins of their members, e.g. Quaysiders, Oddfellows or Temperance. There was even a kilted company recruited from Scotsmen resident in the city and one known as Guards which required its members to be not less than six foot in height. Others came from the Hampton factory, two from Robert Stephenson's locomotive works, another was found at the Elswick Ordnance factory. The battalion had increased to thirteen companies by 1861, but this establishment was later reduced to eight. Designation as 3rd Volunteer Battalion Northumberland Fusiliers was notified in General Order 14 of February 1883 and two new companies were added (one from Durham University) in 1900. *Territorials:* Transfer to the Territorial Force in 1908 was as 6th Battalion Northumberland Fusiliers. The University company at the same time became a contingent of the Senior Division, OTC.

# Norfolk

## Artillery Volunteers

In the Army List for November 1864 a 1st Admin Brigade of Norfolk Artillery Volunteers is shown as having been formed at Great Yarmouth. Included in the brigade were the 1st Norfolk AVC, 1st, 2nd and 3rd Suffolk and the 1st Essex corps. A 2nd Norfolk joined when formed in 1869, as did the 4th Suffolk the year before. Became the new 1st Corps in 1880.

**1st (1859-1880)**—Formed with headquarters at Great Yarmouth on 29 September 1859. Much of the corps was recruited in Norwich and in 1869 the volunteers from that area were withdrawn to form a 2nd Corps.

**1st (1880-1908)**—Formed by the consolidation of the 1st Admin Brigade in 1880. Headquarters remained at Great Yarmouth and the batteries were organised as follows: Nos 1 and 2 Great Yarmouth (late 1st Corps), Nos 3 and 4 Norwich (late 2nd Corps), No 5 Harwich (late 1st Essex), No 6 Lowestoft (late 1st Suffolk), No 7 Aldborough (late 3rd Suffolk), No 8 Beccles (Late 4th Suffolk). Within a few months No 5 Battery at Harwich had made it clear to the War Office that it was not satisfied with its new position and subsequently, by the end of 1880, the battery was removed and placed with the 1st Essex. The reorganisation saw Nos 6 to 8 Batteries renumbered as 5 to 7. Under General Order 106 of September 1886 the corps became the 1st Volunteer (Norfolk) Brigade Eastern Division Royal Artillery. This was changed, however, to 1st Norfolk AVC (Eastern Division Royal Artillery) in 1889. A cadet corps was formed and affiliated at Beccles in October 1906.

**Officers' sabretache, Norfolk Artillery Volunteers.**

*Territorials:* 1st East Anglian Brigade RFA and 3rd East Anglian (Howitzer) Brigade RFA with the Beccles Cadet Corps attached.

**2nd**—Two batteries formed at Norwich from part of the 1st Corps in 1869, the first officers being commissioned 25 March. Became Nos 3 and 4 Batteries of the new 1st Corps in 1880.

## Mounted Rifle Volunteers/Light Horse Volunteers

**1st**—Raised in March 1861 at Norwich as the 1st Norfolk Mounted Rifle Volunteers. Formation had came about as a result of a public meeting held in November 1860 at the Royal Hotel in Norwich. Lieutenant (later captain) Francis Hay Gurney, previously of the 3rd Norfolk Rifle Volunteers, took command. The change to Light Horse Volunteers was in October 1862, disbandment in November 1867. The *Norfolk Chronicle* for April 1861 reported that the corps was wearing scarlet jackets with blue facings, white breeches and a busby headdress that had a blue bag.

## Rifle Volunteers

Three admin battalions were formed (two numbered as 1st) which later provided the new 2nd, 3rd and 4th Corps. Six numbered sub-divisions appeared in the early Army Lists: for 1st see 6th Corps, 2nd see 7th Corps, 3rd, see 8th Corps, 4th see 9th Corps, 5th see 10th Corps and 6th see 11th Corps.

**1st (1859-1860)**—Formed at Norwich on 31 August 1859 and became part of the new 1st Corps by February 1860.

**1st (City of Norwich) (1860-1908)**—In the Army List for February 1860 the 1st, 2nd and 3rd

Norfolk RVC are shown as having been amalgamated under the title of 1st (City of Norwich) RVC. The new formation comprised six companies under the command of Major Commandant John Davy Brett who had previously served with the 7th Dragoons. Designated 1st Volunteer Battalion Norfolk Regiment in 1883. A cadet corps was formed in 1893, but this was absorbed into the 1st Cadet Battalion Norfolk Regiment in 1895. *Territorials:* Transfer to the Territorial Force in 1908 was as part of the 4th Battalion Norfolk Regiment.

**2nd (1859-1860)**—Formed at Norwich on 15 September 1859 and became part of the new 1st Corps by February 1860.

**2nd (Great Yarmouth) (1860-1880)**—Formed as the 4th Corps at Great Yarmouth on 3 September 1859 and soon comprised four companies under the command of Major J H Orde. Renumbered as 2nd by September 1860. Towards the end of 1877 joined the 1st Admin Battalion and became 'A', 'B', 'C' and 'D' Companies of the new 2nd Corps in March 1880.

**2nd (1880-1908)**—The 1st Admin Battalion was formed with headquarters at Great Yarmouth towards the end of 1876 and included the 2nd Norfolk RVC with the 4th, 14th and 17th Suffolk—this was the second admin battalion to hold this number, the original having been consolidated as 3rd Corps in 1872. The new 1st Admin was consolidated as the new 2nd Corps in March 1880 with nine companies: 'A', 'B', 'C', 'D' Great Yarmouth (late 2nd Norfolk Corps), 'E' Gorleston (newly formed), 'F' Bungay (late 4th Suffolk), 'G' Beccles (late 14th Suffolk), 'H', 'I' Lowestoft (late 17th Suffolk).

Re-designated as 2nd Volunteer Battalion Norfolk Regiment under General Orde 79 of June 1883, a tenth company being added in 1885. *Territorials:* Part of 5th Battalion Norfolk Regiment.

**3rd (1859-1860)**—Formed at Norwich on 2 September 1859 and became part of the new 1st Corps by February 1860.

**3rd (1872-1908)**—On 4 April 1861 the original 1st Admin Battalion was formed with headquarters at Fakenham and to it were added the 5th, 6th, 10th, 11th, 12th, 13th, 15th, 16th, 17th, 19th, 23rd and 24th Corps. Headquarters transferred to Norwich in 1862, then to East Dereham in 1866. On 3rd July 1872 the battalion was consolidated as the new 3rd Corps of ten companies. General Order 79 of June 1883 notified re-designation as 3rd Volunteer Battalions Norfolk Regiment. A cadet corps was formed by the 5th Corps at King's Lynn in 1867 and this appears with headquarters at East Dereham from 1883 but is shown once again at King's Lynn from 1885. The company finally disappeared from the Army List in February 1888. Another cadet corps was formed at the Norfolk County School at North Elmham in 1888, but this too was disbanded and last seen in 1893. Next came Gresham's School at Holt in 1902. *Territorials:* Transfer to the Territorial Force in 1908 was as part of 5th Battalion Norfolk Regiment. Gresham's at the same time joined the OTC.

**4th (1859-1860)**—See 2nd Corps (1860-1880).

**4th (1872-1908)**—The 2nd Admin Battalion was formed with headquarters at Norwich on 25 March 1861 and to it were added the 7th, 8th, 9th, 14th, 18th, 20th, 21st and 22nd Corps. The 16th and 23rd joined in 1863, but these were transferred to 1st Admin in 1864. Consolidated in 1872 as the new 4th with six companies and designated 4th Volunteer Battalion Norfolk Regiment in 1883. Harleston, Diss, Loddon, Stalham, Blofield and Attleborough were the company locations in 1899, four more being added in 1900. *Territorials:* Transfer to the Territorial Force in 1908 was as part of 4th Battalion Norfolk Regiment.

**5th**—Formed as one company at King's Lynn on 5 September 1859 with William Swatman Bt as captain, Francis Joseph Cresswell, lieutenant and Somerville Arthur Gurney, ensign. Joined the 1st Admin Battalion in 1863, a cadet corps being formed and affiliated in 1867. Became part of the new 3rd Corps in 1872.

**6th**—Formed at Aylsham on 23 September 1859 and known as 1st Sub-division until March. 1860. The first officers to receive commissions were Lientenant Henry Scott and Ensign Harold Augustus Ernuin. Joined the 1st Admin Battalion and became part of the new 3rd Corps in 1872.

**7th**—Formed at Harleston on 30 September 1859 and known as the 2nd Sub-division until March 1860. The first officers to be commissioned were Captain Charles Mortlock, Lieutenant William T W Wood and Benjamin Charles Chaston. Joined the 2nd Admin Battalion and became part of the new 4th Corps in 1872.

**8th**—Formed at Diss on 7 October 1859 and known as the 3rd Sub-division until March 1860. The first officers to receive commissions were Lieutenant George Edward Frere and Ensign Thomas William Salmon. Joined the 2nd Admin Battalion and became part of the new 4th Corps in 1872.

**9th**—Formed at Loddon on 8 October 1859 and known as the 4th Sub-division until March 1860. The first officers to be commissioned were Lieutenant Thomas William B Proctor Beauchamp and Ensign Richard Henry Gilbert. Joined the 2nd Admin Battalion and became part of the new 4th Corps in 1872.

**10th**—Formed at Fakenham on 20 October 1859 and known as the 5th Sub-division until March 1860. The first officers to be commissioned were Lieutenant Sir Willoughby Jones, Bt and Ensign Robert Nicholas Hammond. Joined the 1st Admin Battalion and disbanded in 1866.

**11th**—Formed at Holkham on 21 October 1859 and known as the 6th Sub-division until March 1860. The first to be commissioned were Lieutenant James Holloway and Ensign Charles Horatio Day Blyth. Joined the 1st Admin Battalion and became part of the new 3rd Corps in 1872.

**12th**—Formed with headquarters given in the Army List as Eynesford, on 26 April 1860, but shown as Reepham, twelve miles north-west of Norwich, by the end of 1860. The first to be commissioned were John McMahon Wilder as lieutenant and Francis S Bircham as ensign. Joined the 1st Admin Battalion and became part of the new 3rd Corps in 1872.

**13th**—Formed at Cromer on 16 April 1860 with the Rt Hon Edward Vernon Lord Suffield as lieutenant and Thomas Cremer, ensign. Joined the 1st Admin Battalion and was disbanded in 1866.

**14th**—Formed at Stalham on 18 April 1860 with Henry A Cubitt, late of the 63rd Regiment of Foot, as lieutenant and Randall Burroughs as ensign. Joined the 2nd Admin Battalion and became part of the new 4th Corps in 1872.

**15th**—Formed at East Dereham on 27 April 1860 with William R Freeman as lieutenant and Simpson Backhouse, ensign. Joined the 1st Admin Battalion and became part of the new 3rd Corps in 1872.

Extracts from the diary of the Rev Benjamin J Armstrong, who was vicar of East Dereham from 1850 to 1888, were published by Harrap in 1949. Rev Armstrong mentions how, on 6 June 1859, he attended a public meeting at the Corn Hall in which he spoke urging people to form a Dereham Rifle Corps. The proposed corps having formed, drills were being held at the Corn Hall by 7 May when Rev Armstrong noted some thirty Volunteers wearing grey uniform, the ranks containing a 'fat old banker of seventy, and next to him, perhaps, a slim youth of seventeen.'

Benjamin Armstrong was appointed Chaplain to the 15th Corps on 19 July 1868, his diary going on to reveal a number of interesting incidents. On the way to camp at Hunstanton Park in June 1868, 'Near Wells the van took fire, and, as it contained the ammunition, considerable excitement was felt till it was extinguished.' Gradually the several corps belonging to the 1st Admin Battalion changed their uniforms from grey to scarlet, Rev Armstrong noting that on 25 July 1877 although 'two-thirds' of the battalion had done so, the 15th had yet to comply. On 8 September 1878, however: 'In the afternoon I preached to the local Company of Volunteers, who appeared in their scarlet uniform and black helmets ....'

**16th**—Formed at Swaffham on 12 June 1860 with William A T Amhurst as captain; Antony Hammond, lieutenant and Andrew Margam, ensign. Joined the 2nd Admin Battalion in 1863, transferring to the 1st in the following year, and became part of the new 3rd Corps in 1872.

**17th**—Formed at Snettisham, on the coast road to Hunstanton, on 4 September 1860 with William C T Campbell as captain, John de C Hamilton, lieutenant and Charles W Preedy, ensign. Joined the 1st Admin Battalion in 1863, moving headquarters to Heacham, just to the north along the old Lynn & Hunstanton line, in 1867. Became part of the new 3rd Corps in 1872.

**18th**—Formed at Blofield on 16 August 1860 with William H Jary as lieutenant and Edward Gilbert, ensign. Joined the 2nd Admin Battalion and became part of the new 4th Corps in 1872.

**19th**—Formed at Holt on 1 March 1861 with George Barker as lieutenant and George Wilkinson, ensign. Joined the 1st Admin Battalion and became part of the new 3rd Corps in 1872.

**20th**—Formed at Attleborough on 6 October 1860 with Sir R T Buxton Bt as captain, Thomas Beevor, lieutenant and A J E B Smyth, ensign. Joined the 2nd Admin Battalion and became part of the new 4th Corps in 1872.

**21st**—Formed at Wymondham on 11 October 1860 with Edmund H W Bellairs as captain, George Forrester, lieutenant and Edmund Larke, ensign. Joined the 2nd Admin Battalion and became part of the new 4th Corps in 1872.

**22nd**—Formed at Thetford on 13 December 1860 with Thomas Thornhill Jun as lieutenant and Alexander H Baring, ensign. Joined the 2nd Admin Battalion and became part of the new 4th Corps in 1872.

**23rd**—Formed at Downham Market on 23 February 1861 with William Bagge as lieutenant and Thomas Lancelot Reed, ensign. Joined the 2nd Admin Battalion, transferring to the 1st in 1864, and became part of the new 3rd Corps in 1872.

**24th**—Formed at North Walsham on 13 November 1862 with J Duff, late of the 23rd Royal Welsh Fusiliers as captain, Martin J Shepheard, Lientenant and John Shepheard, ensign. Joined the 1st Admin Battalion and became part of the new 3rd Corps in 1872.

**1st Cadet Battalion Norfolk Regiment**—Formed with headquarters at the Drill Hall, Theatre Street, Norwich as four companies on 23 January 1895. Location is given later as St Peter's Hall, Norwich, and by 1898 as Britannia Barracks. The battalion was last seen in the Army List for March 1900.

# Northamptonshire

## Engineer Volunteers

**1st**—Headquarters of the 1st Northamptonshire EVC were at Peterborough where it was formed on 11 November 1867. The corps did not transfer to the Territorial Force and was disbanded with effect from 31 March 1908.

## Mounted Rifle Volunteers

**1st**—Formed in March 1860 at Overstone and Moulton by Lieutenant-Colonel Robert Lloyd Lindsay who had won the Victoria Cross during the Crimean War. The corps was raised mainly from local farmers and members of the Pytchley Hunt. With just forty volunteers on the strength, the colonel's commission was only as a lieutenant. As Lord Wantage, he noted in his memoir that the corps was drilled in his park at Overstone in 'their scarlet Norfolk jackets and grey breeches'. Disbanded in November 1869.

## Rifle Volunteers

All rifle corps formed within the county joined the 1st Admin Battalion which became the new 1st Corps in 1880. A 1st Sub-division was shown in Army List for March 1860 with headquarters at Overstone, but this was removed the following month.

**1st (1859-1880)**—Formed at Althorp on 29 August 1859 from tenants of Earl Spencer's estate. The earl took command, John Beasley, Jun, his lieutenant. Became 'A' Company of the new 1st Corps in 1880.

**1st (1880-1908)**—The 1st Admin Battalion was formed with headquarters at Northampton on 8 August 1860 and consolidated in 1880 as the new 1st Corps with thirteen companies: 'A' Althorp (late 1st

## 1st Northamptonshire Rifle Volunteer Corps.

Corps), 'B' Towcester (late 2nd Corps), 'C' to 'G' Northampton (late 3rd Corps), 'H' and 'I' Peterborough (late 6th Corps), 'K' and 'L' Wellingborough (late 7th Corps), 'M' Daventry (late 8th Corps), 'N' Kettering (late 9th Corps).

Re-designated as 1st Volunteer Battalion Northamptonshire Regiment under General Order 181 of December 1887. Three new companies were added in 1900. Wellingborough Grammar School Cadet Corps was formed and affiliated in 1900, Oundle School Cadet Corps in 1902. *Territorials:* Transfer to the Territorial Force in 1908 was as 4th Battalion Northamptonshire Regiment. Two of the Peterborough companies, however, were converted to artillery, under the title of Northamptonshire Battery RFA, and as supply and transport troops, the East Midland Brigade Company ASC. Wellingborough and Oundle Schools became contingents of the Junior Division, OTC.

**2nd**—Formed at Towcester on 19 October 1859 with the Rt Hon George William Fermor, Earl of Pomfret, in command; his lieutenant being John Wardlaw who had previously served with the King's Own Militia. Became 'B' Company of the new 1st Corps in 1880.

**3rd**—A 3rd Corps appeared in the Army List for March 1860, but this disappeared in the following April having had no officers or location allotted to it. This position in the county list was to remain vacant until 1872 when, upon the amalgamation of the two Northampton corps (4th and 5th) as 3rd of five companies, the space was filled. The new 3rd Corps became 'C' to 'G' Companies of the new 1st Corps in 1880.

**4th**—Formed as one company at Northampton, its members were described as 'professional men and tradesmen', on 15 February 1860 with William Alexander Barr as captain, William Griffiths Hollis, lieutenant, and George Norman Welton, ensign. Increased to two companies in December 1861, then to three in March 1865. Amalgamated with the 5th Corps in 1872 and renumbered as 3rd.

**5th**—Formed as one company by the Northampton firm of Messrs Isaac, Campbell & Co on 3 March 1860 with Samuel Isaac as captain, Saul Isaac, lieutenant and Michael L Levey, ensign. Increased to three companies by the end of 1861, amalgamated with the 4th Corps in 1872, and renumbered as 3rd Corps.

**6th**—Formed at Peterborough on 3 March 1860 with the Hon George W Fitzwilliam as captain, Leonard Deacon, lieutenant, and John Beecroft, ensign. Became 'H' and 'I' Companies of the new 1st Corps in 1880.

**7th**—Formed at Wellingborough on 20 September 1860 with Henry M Stockdale as captain, local solicitor George H Burnham, lieutenant, and William C Trotman, ensign. Became 'K' and 'L' Companies of the new 1st Corps in 1880.

**8th**—Formed at Daventry on 23 November 1860 with Rainald Knightley as captain, Edmund C Borton, lieutenant and Thomas Willoughby, ensign. Became 'M' Company of the new 1st Corps in 1880.

**9th**—Formed at Kettering on 22 April 1867 with Frederick M Eden as captain, John G Willows, lieutenant and J W Dryland, ensign. Became 'N' Company of the new 1st Corps in 1880.

# Northumberland

## Artillery Volunteers

The 1st Admin Brigade was formed with headquarters at Tynemouth early in 1865 and, in addition to the Northumberland corps, also included the 2nd Newcastle. The 1st Durham was added in 1873 and in that same year brigade headquarters were moved to Newcastle. The 1st Northumberland and Durham AVC was formed upon consolidation in 1880.

**1st (1859-1880)**—Formed at Tynemouth on 16 August 1859 and in the following May absorbed the 2nd Corps as No 2 Battery. New batteries were later raised at Willington Quay, North Shields and Newcastle but in September 1864 personnel of the latter were removed to form their own unit, the 2nd Newcastle. The Willington Quay members were the next to go when in January 1865 they became the 3rd Northumberland Corps. Became Nos 1 to 6 Batteries of the new 1st Corps in 1880.

**1st (1880-1908)**—Formed by the consolidation of the 1st Admin Brigade in 1880 with the title 1st Northumberland and Durham. Headquarters were placed at Newcastle and the fifteen batteries were organised as follows: Nos 1 to 6 Tynemouth (late 1st Northumberland), Nos 7 to 12 Newcastle (late 3rd Northumberland), Nos 13 to 15 Sunderland (late 1st Durham). In April 1881 the 1st to 6th Batteries were removed to form their own corps, the 3rd Northumberland following in 1888 by the Durham portion of the corps which formed a new 1st Durham AVC. Under General Order 443 of 1889 Western Division Royal Artillery was added to the title of the corps which now comprised four position batteries. Of these, No 4 was formed by the Elswick Ordnance Company. In 1900 the corps formed a complete battery for service in South Africa, its guns being provided by the Elswick Works. *Territorials:* 1st Northumbrian Brigade RFA.

**2nd (January-May 1860)**—Formed at Tynemouth on 12 January 1860 and was absorbed into the 1st Corps as its No 2 Battery in the following May.

**2nd (1860-1908)**—The services of a 3rd Corps at Alnwick were accepted on 20 February 1860, this corps taking on the position as 2nd Corps in the following May. In 1862 permission was granted on 3 March to form a 2nd Battery and in 1864 four additional batteries were raised. Now with six batteries, the 2nd Corps was recruited from around the Alnwick, Longhoughton, Felton, Shilbottle, Rennington and Warkworth areas. In 1866 permission was received on 11 April to include the words The Percy in the title. From the early days of the corps attempts had been made to include this reference to the fact that the Dukes of Northumberland had been associated with, not only the present corps, but the artillery volunteers that had been raised at Alnwick back in 1805.

During 1866 a detachment of horse artillery was formed and attached to headquarters at Alnwick. In the following year sanction was given to increase the establishment to seven batteries and the officers and men of the horse artillery were formed into a separate battery designated a 'A'. But in 1872, and in consequence of the Government's withdrawal of its field guns, 'A' Battery was disbanded,

**Northumberland Artillery Volunteers, 1870.**

and the horse gunners distributed between Nos 1 and 2 Batteries. An 8th Battery was formed on 10 March 1868 at Rothbury. By the end of 1872 detachments of the corps were located at Alnmouth, Alnwick, Boulmer, Broomhill, Chatton, Felton, Glanton, Longhoughton, Rennington, Shilbottle, Warkworth and Wooler. The following year new stations were formed at Acklington, Eglingham, Amble, Widdrington and Lucker, but the one at Broomhill was abolished.

In 1874 a half battery was established at North Sunderland, but the same year the Elingham detachment was disbanded. New stations were later formed at Bamburgh, Holy Island, Embleton and Craster in 1877, 1878 and 1881 respectively. But in 1877 Widdrington, and in 1879 Amble, Acklington and Lucker were abolished. Eglingham, however, was re-established in 1881, as was Broomhill three years later. Eglingham was again given up in 1885 and in 1888 Nos 1 and 2 Batteries were amalgamated as the 1st Position Battery. The Embleton Station was abolished in 1891, but reformed again in 1896, as was Widdrington in 1892. In 1896 a new station was formed at Ashington but by the end of that year both Rothbury and Wooler had closed down. In 1889 and under Army Order 443 Western Division Royal Artillery was added to the title.

Between 1888 and 1908 many artillery corps were to include both position and garrison units and did so without too much complication. It was, however, considered by the 2nd (Percy) that their mixed armament was unsatisfactory and the complication of it and difficulty of working two distinct units was not suitable. Several attempts were made by the corps to convert to all position batteries but the War Office refused permission on the grounds that in its view the northern parts of the County of Northumberland were unsuited for this type of armament. It was also proposed that the gunners should amalgamate with the 1st Berwick-on-Tweed AVC, but this was ignored. Instead a counter-proposal to turn the corps into an infantry battalion was put forward by the Government. This too was not accepted by the 2nd (Percy) whose commanding officer immediately sent in his resignation. Subsequently disbandment of the corps was ordered by the War Office with effect from 31 October 1902.

**3rd (1860)**—See 2nd Corps (1860-1908).

**3rd (1860-1864)**—Formed at Blythe on 23 November 1860 but disappeared from the Army List in January 1864.

**3rd (1865-1880)**—Formed by the withdrawal of the Willington Quay personnel from the 1st Corps in January 1865. The 2nd Newcastle-upon-Tyne AVC was absorbed in 1867, headquarters at the same time moving to Newcastle. Became Nos 7 to 12 Batteries of the new 1st Corps in 1880.

**3rd (1881)**—Formed by the withdrawal of Nos 1 to 6 Batteries of the new 1st Corps in April 1881. But these batteries had at one time been the senior in the county and it followed that the new position of 3rd was not acceptable. Unable to claim the 1st position, the Tynemouth gunners took on the title of the Tynemouth Artillery Volunteer Corps. *Territorials:* Tynemouth RGA.

## The Tynemouth Artillery Volunteers—See 3rd Corps (1881) above.

## Rifle Volunteers

Two admin battalions were formed of which the 2nd was broken up in 1865. The 1st went on to provide the new 1st Corps in 1880. The 2nd had been formed with headquarters at Tynemouth in August 1861 and included the 1st, 8th and 9th Corps. Headquarters moved to Walker in 1863.

**1st (1859-1862)**—Formed at Tynemouth on 16 August 1859 and absorbed the 2nd Corps, also at Tynemouth, in February 1860. The corps, which included companies at Walker and Cramlington, was raised by coal owner Edward Potter and divided as 1st, 8th and 9th Northumberland RVC in August 1861 and at the same time placed into the newly formed 2nd Admin Battalion. Of the three, the 1st Corps was disbanded in October 1862.

**1st (1880-1908)**—The 1st Admin Battalion was formed with headquarters at Alnwick in November

1860 and into it were placed the 2nd, 3rd, 4th, 5th, 6th, 7th, 10th, 11th and 12th Corps. The 1st Berwick-upon-Tweed was also included. Consolidated as the 1st Northumberland and Berwick-upon-Tweed RVC with ten companies in 1880: 'A' Hexham (late 2nd Corps), 'B' Morpeth (late 3rd Corps), 'C' Belford (late 4th Corps), 'D' Alnwick (late 5th Corps), 'E' Bellingham (late 6th Corps), 'F' Allendale (late 7th Corps), 'G' Berwick-upon-Tweed (late 1st Berwick-upon-Tweed), 'H' Lowick (late 10th Corps), 'I' Corbridge (late (11th Corps), 'K' Haltwhistle (late 12th Corps).

Under General Order 14 of February 1883 the 1st Corps was re-designated as 1st Volunteer Battalion Northumberland Fusiliers. In 1885 the Lowick Company was disbanded and in its place a new 'K' was formed at Newburn. Nine years later the personnel of this company were transferred to the 2nd Volunteer Battalion and at the same time replaced by a new 'H' at Prudhoe. Headquarters moved to Hexham in 1891 and two new companies were added in 1900. By this time certain reorganisations had taken place within the battalion resulting in the company locations being arranged as: Hexham (2), Belford, Alnwick, Bellingham, Haydon Bridge, Prudhoe, Corbridge, Haltwhistle and Morpeth (2). The two Hexham companies ('A' and 'B') were merged as 'A' in 1903, a replacement 'B' being found by the transfer of No 7 Company of the 2nd Northumberland Royal Garrison Artillery Volunteers at Ashington. *Territorials:* Transfer to the Territorial Force in 1908 was as 4th Battalion Northumberland Fusiliers, the Alnwick personnel providing the nucleus of the 7th Battalion.

**2nd (1860)**—Formed at Tynemouth on 4 January 1860 and absorbed into the 1st Corps in the following month.

**2nd (1860-1880)**—Formed at Hexham on 10 March 1860 with John M Ridley as captain, Richard J Gibson, lieutenant and William B Ridley, ensign. Joined the 1st Admin Battalion and became 'A' Company of the new 1st Corps in 1880.

**2nd (1880-1908)**—Formed at Walker as three companies of the 1st Corps and made independent as 8th Corps in August 1861. Placed into the newly formed 2nd Admin Battalion and renumbered as 2nd Corps in 1880. Designated 2nd Volunteer Battalion Northumberland Fusiliers in 1883, the corps by then consisted of six companies, all at Walker, lettered 'A' to 'F'. In 1894 the Newburn Company of the 1st Volunteer Battalion was transferred to the 2nd as 'G'. The following year 'H' was formed at Wallsend and in 1900 additional personnel raised saw the battalion's companies rearranged as follows: Walker (4), Newburn (2), Wallsend (2) and Gosforth (2). *Territorials:* 5th Battalion Northumberland Fusiliers.

**3rd**—Formed at Morpeth on 12 March 1860 with George Brummell as captain, Charles Septimus Swan, lieutenant and William Jobling, ensign. Joined the 1st Admin Battalion and became 'B' Company of the new 1st Corps in 1880.

**4th**—Formed at Wooler on 23 April 1860 with the Earl of Tankerville as captain in command. Joined the 1st Admin Battalion,

**1st RST VOLUNTEER BATTN. NORTHUMBERLAND FUSILIERS, PRIVATE, ON "SENTRY GO".**

**1st Volunteer Battalion Northumberland Fusiliers.**

moved to Belford in 1861, and became 'C' Company of the new 1st Corps in 1880.

**5th**—Formed at Alnwick on 27 March 1860 with Walter J Browne, a former major general of the Bombay Army, as captain and John Atkinson Wilson, lieutenant. Joined the 1st Admin Battalion and became 'D' Company of the new 1st Corps in 1880.

**6th**—Formed at Tynedale on 23 April 1860 with William H Charlton as captain, Edward C Charlton, lieutenant and Francis Charlton, ensign. Joined the 1st Admin Battalion and became 'E' Company of the new 1st Corps in 1880. Although the 6th Corps headquarters location is given in the Army List through to 1880, the records accompanying the overall reorganisations of that year show 'E' Company as being at Bellingham.

**7th**—Formed at Allendale on 11 September 1860 with Thomas Sopwith as captain, Joseph Coats, lieutenant and George Armison, ensign. Joined the 1st Admin Battalion and became 'F' Company of the new 1st Corps in 1880.

**8th**—See 2nd Corps (1880-1908).

**9th**—Formed at Cramlington from one company of the 1st Corps in August 1861. Joined the 2nd Admin Battalion and disbanded in December 1864.

**10th**—Formed at Lowick on 20 December 1861 with the Earl of Durham as captain, Henry Gregson, lieutenant and Thomas Hunt, ensign. Joined the 1st Admin Battalion and became 'H' Company of the new 1st Corps in 1880.

**11th**—Formed at Lee St John on 25 April 1868 with Richard Gibson as captain, John P Walton, lieutenant and James Mewburn, ensign. Joined the 1st Admin Battalion and moved to Corbridge in 1876. Became 'I' Company of the new 1st Corps in 1880.

**12th**—Formed at Haltwhistle on 3 July 1878. Joined the 1st Admin Battalion and became 'K' Company of the new 1st Corps in 1880.

# Nottinghamshire

## Rifle Volunteers

All rifle corps formed within the county, other than the 1st, joined the 1st Admin Battalion which provided the new 2nd Corps in 1880.

**1st (Robin Hood)**—In the Army List for October 1859, five separate companies of unnumbered rifle volunteers are shown as having been formed at Nottingham. In that for December the five now appear as having been amalgamated under the title of The Robin Hood RVC, the officers' commissions being dated 15 November 1859. By March 1860 the corps had been designated as the 1st Nottinghamshire (Robin Hood) RVC and comprised nine companies, a formed Rifle Brigade officer, Robert Crawford, being appointed as lieutenant-colonel commandant. Became a volunteer battalion (without change in title) of the Sherwood Foresters in 1881 and as such contributed volunteers for the war in South Africa—the first contingent under Captain Turner sailing in February 1900. Richards, in *His Majesty's Territorial Army*, notes that 'during their presence at the seat of war they were in three pitched battles and no less than twenty-five engagements, and under fire on twenty-eight occasions.' Sergeant Hickinbottom was mentioned in despatches and awarded the Distinguished Conduct Medal.

By 1881 the Robin Hoods comprised ten companies, an eleventh was added in 1895, a twelfth, a year later, and in 1900/01 a further six brought the establishment up to eighteen companies. These were then divided equally into two battalions. A cadet corps was also formed at this time by Nottingham High School. *Territorials:* Transfer to the Territorial Force in 1908 was as 7th Battalion Sherwood Foresters, Nottingham High School Cadet Corps at the same time became part of the OTC.

**2nd (1860-1880)**—Formed as one company at East Retford on 3 March 1860 with Charles S Burnaby as captain, T Wagstaff, lieutenant and John Smith, ensign. Became 'A' Company of the new 2nd Corps in

1880.

**2nd (1880-1908)**—The 1st Admin Battalion was formed at Newark in May 1861, headquarters being transferred to East Retford in 1865. The battalion was consolidated in 1880 as the new 2nd Corps with eight companies: 'A' East Retford (late 2nd Corps), 'B', 'C' Newark (late 3rd Corps), 'D' Mansfield (late 4th Corps), 'E' Thorney Wood Chase (late 5th Corps), 'F' Collingham (late 6th Corps), 'G' Worksop (late 7th Corps), 'H' Southwell (late 8th Corps).

In 1887, under General Order 39 of April, the 2nd Corps was re-designated as 4th (Nottinghamshire) Volunteer Battalion Sherwood Foresters, headquarters transferring to Newark in 1890. Two cadet corps were associated with the battalion: Worksop College in 1900 and the Queen Elizabeth School at Mansfield in 1906. *Territorials:* Transfer to the Territorial Force in 1908 was as 8th Battalion Sherwood Foresters, both Worksop College and Queen Elizabeth School at the same time joining the OTC.

**3rd**—Formed as one company at Newark on 3 March 1860 with Sir Henry Bromley, Bt as captain, William Newton, lieutenant and James H Betts, ensign. Increased to two companies in March 1863 and became 'B' and 'C' Companies of the new 2nd Corps in 1880.

**4th**—Formed as one company at Mansfield on 9 March 1860 with James Salmond as captain, J Paget as lieutenant and Charles Seely, Jun, ensign. Became 'D' Company of the new 2nd Corps in 1880.

**5th**—Formed as one company on 9 March 1860 with Mansfield Parkyns as captain, Charles Storer, lieutenant and William L Hoskinson, ensign. Headquarters are given as Thorney Wood Chase, the southern division of Sherwood Forest. Became 'E' Company of the new 2nd Corps in 1880.

**6th**—Formed as one company at Collingham on 9 March 1860 with Thomas S Wooley as captain, William L Dominichetti, lieutenant and John Broadbent, ensign. Became 'F' Company of the new 2nd Corps in 1880. Probably among the finest records of service within the Volunteer Force is that of the Wooleys, a member of that family commanding the 6th Corps (and later 'F' Company) for just two years short of a half century.

**7th**—Formed as one company at Worksop on 28 April 1860 with James Mason, late of the 94th Regiment of Foot as captain, Henry S Hodding, lieutenant and Frederick M Buy, ensign. Became 'G' Company of the new 2nd Corps in 1880.

**8th**—Formed as one company at Southwell on 7 July 1860 with John H Becher as captain, Thomas Elliott, lieutenant and Harrington O'Shore, ensign. Became 'H' Company of the new 2nd Corps in 1880.

# Oxfordshire

## Light Horse Volunteers

**1st**—Formed January 1864 at Banbury with Captain the Hon W H J North in command. Disbanded in 1870.

## Rifle Volunteers

All corps, other than the 1st, joined the 1st Admin Battalion which became the new 2nd Corps in 1875.

**1st (Oxford University)**—On 8 August 1859 three companies of rifle volunteers were formed within Oxford

**1st Volunteer Battalion
Oxfordshire Light Infantry.**

University. A fourth followed on 16 December. In the Army List for February 1860 all four companies are shown as having been amalgamated under the title of 1st University of Oxford RVC. Fifth and sixth Companies were added in March 1860 with, in command, the Hon Robert C H Spencer, late of the Royal Artillery. In 1887, under General Order 181 of December, the corps was re-designated as 1st (Oxford University) Volunteer Battalion Oxfordshire Light Infantry. Magdalen College School Cadet Corps was formed and affiliated in May 1873, but this disbanded late in 1884. Another unit known as the Oxford Military College Cadet Corps was formed in July 1885, but again, this was to be removed from the Army List in January 1898. In 1908 the corps became the Oxford University Contingent Senior Division OTC.

**2nd (1860-1875)**—Formed at Oxford on 4 February 1860 with Henry Atkins Bowyer, late of the 14th Dragoons, as captain, John Parsons, Jun, lieutenant and Thomas Mallam, ensign. Became part of the new 2nd Corps in July 1875.

**2nd (1875-1908)**—The 1st Admin Battalion was formed with headquarters at Oxford in May 1860 and consolidated as the new 2nd Corps of six companies on 8 July 1875—a seventh being added at Chipping Norton in 1876. The title of 2nd Volunteer Battalion Oxfordshire Light Infantry was assumed under General Order 181 of December 1887. Two new companies were formed in 1900. *Territorials:* 4th Battalion Oxfordshire Light Infantry.

**3rd**—Formed as one company at Banbury on 13 February 1860 with John Edmund Severne, late of the 16th Dragoons, as captain, Timothy Edward Cobb, lieutenant and John Potts, ensign. A second company was raised from workers at the Britannia Works (where agricultural implements were manufactured) in May 1860. Became part of the new 2nd Corps in July 1875.

**4th**—Formed at Henley-on-Thames on 13 March 1860 with Thomas F Maitland as lieutenant and Arthur D'O Brooks, ensign. Became part of the new 2nd Corps in July 1875.

**5th**—Formed at Woodstock on 26 May 1860 with Charles E Thornhill as captain, William E Taunton, lieutenant and James Clinch, ensign. Part of the company was detached to form the 9th Corps in October 1861, headquarters of 5th Corps then changing to Witney. Disbanded in December 1864.

**6th**—Formed at Deddington on 25 April 1860 with Samuel Field as lieutenant and C D Faulkner, ensign. Became part of the new 2nd Corps in July 1875.

**7th**—Formed at Bicester on 12 May 1860 with William W M Dewar as lieutenant and C J Bullock Marsham, ensign. Disbanded in 1870.

**8th**—Formed at Thame on 27 November 1860 with Phillip T H Wykenham as lieutenant and Duncan G Robinson, ensign. Became part of the new 2nd Corps in July 1875.

**9th**—Formed from part of the 5th Corps in October 1861 with headquarters at Woodstock with Captain Charles E Thornhill in command. Became part of the new 2nd Corps in July 1875.

# Shropshire

## Artillery Volunteers

**1st**—The first and only artillery volunteer corps to be formed within the county was originally raised as the 9th Shropshire Rifle Volunteers on 2 March 1860. Headquarters were at Shrewsbury and the re-designation as artillery took effect from 23 July 1860. As the 1st Shropshire AVC the corps was placed with the Cheshire Admin Brigade in 1863. This also included the 1st Staffordshire AVC which with the Shropshire gunners and the 1st Worcestershire AVC were then grouped together as a new brigade designated as 1st Staffordshire. But this was short lived and by the October 1867 Army List all three corps were shown as being once again with the Cheshire Brigade. In 1869 the corps were again removed, this time so as to form the 1st Shropshire Admin Brigade whose commanding officer was gazetted on 15 May. By April 1874, however, the 1st Worcestershire AVC had been removed and placed with the recently formed Monmouthshire Brigade. On 25 May 1880 the brigade was consolidated as the 1st Shropshire and Staffordshire AVC. Headquarters were placed at Etruria and the eight battery establishment was organised as follows: Nos 1 to 4 Shrewsbury (late 1st Shropshire), Nos 5 to 8 Etruria (late 1st Staffordshire). Headquarters moved to Shelton in 1889 and in the following year the corps was reorganised into four position batteries. *Territorials:* The Staffordshire portion of the corps formed the 1st Staffordshire Battery RFA while the Shropshire gunners provided the Shropshire Battery RHA and the Welsh Border Mounted Brigade Ammunition Column.

## Rifle Volunteers

Two admin battalions were formed which in 1880 provided the new 1st and 2nd Corps. There was also a 1st Sub-division which became the 7th Corps.

**1st (1859-1880)**—Formed as one company at Shrewsbury on 14 December 1859 with Thomas Cholmon Deley as captain, William Harley Bailey, lieutenant and Charles Chandler, ensign. Joined the 1st Admin Battalion and became 'A' Company of the new 1st Corps in 1880.

*Below, Bob Marrion's illustration of 2nd Shropshire Rifle Volunteer Corps c.1896. Officer (left) and other rank.*

**1st (1880-1908)**—The 1st Admin Battalion was formed with headquarters at Shrewsbury in July 1860 and to it were added the 1st, 4th, 5th, 6th, 10th, 11th, 14th, 16th and 17th Corps. The 2nd and 4th Montgomeryshire RVC were also included between 1873 and 1876. The battalion was consolidated in 1880 as the new 1st Corps with eight companies: 'A' Shrewsbury (late 1st Corps), 'B' Shrewsbury (late 17th Corps), 'C' Condover (late 5th Corps), 'D' Ironbridge (late 6th Corps), 'E' Shifnal (late 14th Corps), 'F' Bridgnorth (late 4th Corps), 'G' Ludlow (late 10th Corps), 'H' Cleobury Mortimer (late 11th Corps).

Re-designated as 1st Volunteer Battalion King's (Shropshire Light Infantry) by General Order 181 of December 1887. The Shrewsbury School Cadet Corps and the Bridgnorth Cadet Corps were formed and affiliated in 1900, the Shrewsbury Town Cadet Corps in 1906. *Territorials:* Transfer to the Territorial Force in 1908 was as part of 4th Battalion King's (Shropshire Light Infantry), the Shrewsbury School Cadets at the same time joining the OTC.

**2nd Shropshire Rifle Volunteer Corps.
Watercolour by R J Marrion.**

**2nd (1860-1880)**—Formed as one company at Market Drayton on 15 February 1860 with Alfred Hill, late of the 68th Regiment of Foot, as captain, William Manly Wilkinson, lieutenant and George Gordon Warren, ensign. The latter had once served with the Royal Flint Militia. Joined the 2nd Admin Battalion and became 'A' Company of the new 2nd Corps in 1880.

**2nd (1880-1908)**—The 2nd Admin Battalion was formed with headquarters at Shrewsbury in July 1860 and to it were added the 2nd, 3rd, 7th, 8th, 12th, 13th, 15th and 18th Corps. The battalion was consolidated in 1880 as the new 2nd Corps with seven companies: 'A' Market Drayton (late 2nd Corps), 'B' Whitchurch (late 3rd Corps), 'C' Wellington (late 7th Corps), 'D' Hodnet (late 8th Corps), 'E' Wem (late 12th Corps), 'F' Oswestry (late 15th Corps), 'G' Newport (late 18th Corps).

Corps headquarters were transferred to Newport shortly after consolidation. 'H' Company was added at Ellesmere in 1885 and in 1887, under General Order 181 of December, 2nd Shropshire RVC became 2nd Volunteer Battalion King's (Shropshire Light Infantry). Ellesmere College Cadet Corps was formed and affiliated in 1900. *Territorials:* Part of 4th Battalion King's (Shropshire Light Infantry), Ellesmere College joining the OTC.

**3rd**—Formed as one company at Whitchurch on 13 February 1860 with Clement Delves Hill as captain, William Lee Brookes, lieutenant and Charles Clay, ensign. Joined the 2nd Admin Battalion and became 'B' Company of the new 2nd Corps in 1880.

**4th**—Formed as one company at Bridgnorth on 13 February 1860 with John Charles Lloyd as captain, Hubert Smith, lieutenant and William Bache, ensign. Joined the 1st Admin Battalion and became 'F' Company of the new 1st Corps in 1880.

**5th**—Formed as one company at Condover on 5 March 1860 with William J Hope Edwards as captain, George Downward, lieutenant and William James Hughes, ensign. Joined the 1st Admin Battalion and became 'C' Company of the new 1st Corps in 1880.

**6th**—Formed as one company at Much Wenlock on 29 February 1860 with William Layton Lowndes as captain, Roger Charles Blackeway, lieutenant and William R Anstice, ensign. Joined the 1st Admin Battalion, moving headquarters to Ironbridge in 1863, and became 'D' Company of the new 1st Corps in 1880.

**7th**—Formed at Wellington on 17 September 1859 and known as the 1st Sub-division until February 1860, its appointed officers being: Captain Thomas Campbell Eyton, the Hon Robert Charles Herbert, lieutenant and William Anslow, ensign. Joined the 2nd Admin Battalion and became 'C' Company of the new 2nd Corps in 1880. The 7th Corps Drill Hall was in King Street.

**8th**—Formed as one company at Hodnet on 2 March 1860 with Algernon C H Percy of Hodnet Hall as captain, Walter Minor, lieutenant and William Powell, ensign. Joined the 2nd Admin Battalion and became 'D' Company of the new 2nd Corps in 1880.

**9th**—Formed as one company at Shrewsbury on 2 March 1860 with William

**1st Volunteer Battalion South Staffordshire Regiment.**

Field as captain, William Patchett, lieutenant and Arthur J Peece, ensign. Converted to artillery and re-designated as 1st Shropshire AVC in July 1860.

**10th**—Formed as one company at Ludlow on 2 March 1860 with Sir C H R Broughton as captain, Rodney Anderson, lieutenant and John Kilvert, ensign. Joined the 1st Admin Battalion and became 'G' Company of the new 1st Corps in 1880.

**11th**—Formed as one company at Cleobury Mortimer on 4 May 1860 with Charles W Wicksted as captain, Adam P Trow, lieutenant and Charles C Purton, ensign. Joined the 1st Admin Battalion and became 'H' Company of the new 1st Corps in 1880.

**12th**—Formed at Wem on 3 May 1860 with John N C Vaughan as lieutenant and John E Eversall, ensign. Joined the 2nd Admin Battalion and became 'E' Company of the new 2nd Corps in 1880.

**13th**—Formed as one company at Ellesmere on 2 June 1860 with Richard G Jebb as captain, the Hon Abelbert Cust, lieutenant and Salisbury Mainwaring, ensign. Joined the 2nd Admin Battalion and was disbanded in 1879.

**14th**—Formed as on company at Shifnal on 21 April 1860 with Henry Corbett, late of the Shropshire Militia, as captain, Daniel Jones, lieutenant and John Meire, ensign. Joined the 1st Admin Battalion and became 'E' Company of the new 1st Corps in 1880.

**15th**—Formed at Oswestry on 28 April 1860 with John Hamer as lieutenant and George H Williams, ensign. Joined the 2nd Admin Battalion and became 'F' Company of the new 2nd Corps in 1880.

**16th**—Formed at Munslow, ten miles north of Ludlow, on 24 May 1860 with C O C Pemberton as lieutenant and T Wetherhead, ensign. Joined the 1st Admin Battalion and was disbanded in 1863.

**17th**—Formed as one company at Shrewsbury on 8 January 1861 with William Salt as captain, William Patchett, lieutenant and Thomas C Townshend, ensign. Joined the 1st Admin Battalion and became 'B' Company of the new 1st Corps in 1880.

**18th**—Formed as one company at Newport on 17 January 1862 with Thomas F Boughey as captain, Edward Hodges, lieutenant and John Holland, Jun, ensign. Joined the 2nd Admin Battalion and became 'G' Company of the new 2nd Corps in 1880.

# Somersetshire

## Artillery Volunteers

**1st**—Formed at Clevedon on 18 June 1860 and in November 1863 was included in the 1st Admin Brigade of Gloucestershire Artillery Volunteers. Provided No 9 Battery of the new 1st Gloucestershire AVC in 1880.

**2nd**—Formed at Weston-Super-Mare on 30 July 1860 and also included in the Gloucestershire Admin Brigade. Disbanded in 1867.

## Engineer Volunteers

**1st**—The 1st Somersetshire EVC was formed with headquarters at Nailsea on 5 September 1868. Popular in the area, establishment was quickly raised to three companies: Nailsea (2), Weston-Super-Mare (1) and in 1873 headquarters were moved to Weston-Super-Mare. From formation, the 1st Somersetshire was included in the 1st Admin Battalion of Gloucestershire EVs and in 1880, upon consolidation, would provide "G", "H" and "I" Companies of the newly created 1st Gloucestershire.

## Rifle Volunteers

Three Admin Battalions were formed which provided the new 1st, 2nd and 3rd Corps in 1880. There was also a 1st Sub-division which became the 7th Corps.

**1st (1859-1880)**—Formed as one company at Bath on 20 October 1859 with John Randle Ford, late of the 95th Regiment of Foot, as captain, Thomas Frederick Inman, lieutenant and Henry Batchelor Inman, ensign. Joined the 1st Admin Battalion and became 'A' Company of the new 1st Corps in 1880.

**1st (1880-1908)**—The 1st Admin Battalion was formed with headquarters at Bath in August 1860 and to it were added the 1st, 2nd, 7th, 14th, 17th, 18th and 22nd Corps. Consolidated in 1880 as the new 1st Corps with seven companies: 'A' Bath (late 1st Corps), 'B' Bathwick (late 2nd Corps), 'C' Keynsham (late 7th Corps), 'D' Warleigh Manor (late 14th Corps), 'E' Lyncombe (late 17th Corps), 'F' Walcot (late 18th Corps), 'G' Kilmersdon (late 22nd Corps).

Under General Order 261 of October 1882 the 1st Corps became 1st Volunteer Battalion Somerset Light Infantry making it the first in the land to take on the title of its parent regiment. A new company was added in 1885, followed by two more in 1900. Three school cadet corps were associated with the battalion: Bath College, becoming affiliated in March 1900; King Edward's School in Bath, in the same year; Monkton Combe School joining in 1904. *Territorials:* Transfer to the Territorial Force in 1908 was as parts of both the 4th and 5th Battalions Somerset Light Infantry. Bath College, King Edward's and Monkton Combe at the same time joined the OTC.

**2nd (1859-1880)**—Formed as one company at Bathwick on 21 October 1859 with Edmund Francis Ansley as captain, Henry Holland Burne, lieutenant and William Attfield, ensign. Joined the 1st Admin Battalion and became 'B' Company of the new 1st Corps in 1880.

**2nd (1880-1908)**—The 2nd Admin Battalion was formed with headquarters at Taunton in August 1860 and included the 3rd, 5th, 8th, 9th, 11th, 12th, 16th, 20th, 21st, 26th and 28th Corps. Consolidated in 1880 as the new 2nd Corps with twelve companies: 'A' and 'B' Taunton (late 3rd Corps), 'C' Wellington (late 8th Corps), 'D' Williton (late 9th Corps), 'E' Wiveliscombe (late 12th Corps), 'F' Yeovil (late 16th Corps), 'G' Crewkerne (late 20th Corps), 'H' Langport (late 21st Corps), 'I' Bridgewater (late 5th Corps), 'K' and 'L' Bridgewater (late 26th Corps), 'M' South Petherton (late 28th Corps).

Re-designated as 2nd Volunteer Battalion Somerset Light Infantry under General Order 261 of October 1882. A new company was added in 1900 and in 1901 and 1903 respectively both the County School at Wellington and King's College in Taunton provided affiliated cadet corps. *Territorials:* Transfer to the Territorial Force in 1908 was as parts of both 4th and 5th Battalions Somerset Light Infantry. County School and King's College at the same time joined the OTC.

**3rd (1859-1880)**—Formed as one company at Taunton on 22 October 1859 with William Ayshford Sanford as captain, Arthur Allen, lieutenant and Richard Easton, ensign. Joined the 2nd Admin Battalion and became 'A' and 'B' Companies of the new 2nd Corps in 1880.

**3rd (1880-1908)**—The 3rd Admin Battalion was formed with headquarters at Wells in August 1860 and included the 4th, 6th, 10th, 13th, 15th, 19th, 23rd, 24th, 25th and 27th Corps. Consolidated in 1880 as the new 3rd Corps with nine companies: 'A' Burnham (late 4th Corps), 'B' Weston-super-Mare (late 6th Corps), 'C' Wells (late 10th Corps), 'D' Frome (late 13th Corps), 'E' Shepton Mallet (late 15th Corps), 'F' Glastonbury (late 19th Corps), 'G' Castle Cary (late 23rd Corps), 'H' Keinton (late 25th Corps), 'I' Langford (late 27th Corps).

Headquarters moved to Weston-Super-Mare in 1882 and by General Order 261 of October 1882 re-designation took place as 3rd Volunteer Battalion Somerset Light Infantry. *Territorials:* Transfer to the Territorial Force in 1908 was as parts of both 4th and 5th Battalions Somerset Light Infantry.

**4th**—Formed as one company at Burnham on 12 January 1860 with Benjamin Tuthill Allen as captain, Joshua Allen, lieutenant and Charles James Brody Mais, ensign. Joined the 3rd Admin Battalion and became 'A' Company of the new 3rd Corps in 1880.

**5th**—Formed as one company at Bridgewater on 14 January 1860 with Gabriel Stone Poole as captain, Charles Robert Bate, lieutenant and William John Ford, ensign. Joined the 2nd Admin Battalion and became

'I' Company of the new 2nd Corps in 1880.

**6th**—Formed as one company at Weston-Super-Mare on 11 February 1860 with James Adeane Law as captain, Samuel Edward Baker, lieutenant and Charles Whitting, ensign. Joined the 3rd Admin Battalion and became 'B' Company of the new 3rd Corps in 1880.

**7th**—Formed at Keynsham on 25 February 1860 and known as the 1st Sub-division until April, the first appointed officers of the 7th Somerset RVC were: Captain James Ireland C Ireland, Lieutenant Charles John Simmons and Ensign Harford Lyne. The corps was recruited mainly from farmers and farm workers. Joined the 1st Admin Battalion and became 'C' Company of the new 1st Corps in 1880.

**8th**—Formed as one company at Wellington, seven miles south-west of Taunton, on 28 February 1860 with William Burridge as captain, William Thomas, lieutenant and F S Bridget, ensign. Joined the 2nd Admin Battalion and became 'C' Company of the new 2nd Corps in 1880. Company headquarters were in South Street.

**9th**—Formed at Williton, on the road from Taunton to Minehead, on 22 February 1860 with John Halliday as lieutenant and John Blommart, ensign. Joined the 2nd Admin Battalion and became 'D' Company of the new 2nd Corps in 1880.

**10th**—Formed as one company at Wells on 14 February 1860 with Edwin Lovell as captain, William J Slade Foster, lieutenant and William Chester Berrymen, ensign. Joined the 3rd Admin Battalion and became 'C' Company of the new 3rd Corps in 1880.

**11th**—Formed at Stogursey on 21 February 1860 with George Fownes Luttrell as lieutenant and Robert Guy Evered, ensign. Joined the 2nd Admin Battalion, moved headquarters just to the south at Nether Stowey on the Bridgewater road in 1868, and was disbanded in 1873.

**12th**—Formed as one company at Wiveliscombe, eleven miles west of Taunton, on 29 February 1860 with Henry George Moysey as captain, Richard Bere, lieutenant and Benjamin Boucher, ensign. Joined the 2nd Admin Battalion and became 'E' Company of the new 2nd Corps in 1880.

**13th**—Formed as one company at Frome on 9 March 1860 with James W D T Wickham as captain, Francis P Devenish, lieutenant and John Sinkins, ensign. Joined the 3rd Admin Battalion and became 'D' Company of the new 3rd Corps in 1880. Frome is twelve miles south of Bath; recruits were also drawn from the neighbouring villages of Nunney and Berkley.

**14th**—Formed as one company at Warleigh Manor, three miles east of Bath, on 5 March 1860 with Edward Sawyer as captain, William Sanderson, lieutenant and Henry Mills Skrine, ensign. Joined the 1st Admin Battalion and became 'D' Company of the new 1st Corps in 1880.

**15th**—Formed as one company at Shepton Mallet on 24 March 1860 with Henry Ernst as captain, Henry T Wickham, lieutenant and Samuel Craddock, ensign. Joined the 3rd Admin Battalion and became 'E' Company of the new 3rd Corps in 1880.

**16th**—Formed as one company at Yeovil on 4 April 1860 with Thomas Messiter as captain, Robert Donne, lieutenant and Henry S Watts, ensign. Joined the 2nd Admin Battalion and became 'F' Company of the new 2nd Corps in 1880.

**17th**—Formed as one company at Lyncombe on 2 March 1860 with William V Hewitt as captain, George J Robertson, lieutenant and John S Falkner, ensign. Joined the 1st Admin Battalion and became 'E' Company of the new 1st Corps in 1880.

**18th**—Formed as one company at Walcot, close to Bath, on 3 March 1860 with B H Holme, late of the 88th Regiment of Foot, as captain, Arthur W Weston, lieutenant and Robert Allen Cook, ensign. Joined the 1st Admin Battalion and became 'F' Company of the new 1st Corps in 1880.

**19th**—Formed as one company at Glastonbury on 17 March 1860 with Arthur W A Hood, a former captain in the Royal Navy, as captain, William G L Lovell, lieutenant and Walter T Swayne, ensign. Joined the 3rd Admin Battalion and became 'F' Company of the new 3rd Corps in 1880.

**20th**—Formed as one company at Crewkerne on 25 April 1860 with William Mathews as captain,

John J Tidcombe, lieutenant and James H Jolliffe, ensign. Joined the 2nd Admin Battalion and became 'G' Company of the new 2nd Corps in 1880.

**21st**—Formed as one company at Langport on 12 April 1860 with Richard T Combe as captain, John Louch, lieutenant and Walter Bagshot, ensign. Joined the 2nd Admin Battalion and became 'H' Company of the new 2nd Corps in 1880.

**22nd**—Formed as one company at Temple Cloud, ten miles south of Bristol, on 10 September 1860 with William B Nash as captain, Wallington Coates, lieutenant and Jacob F Y Mogg, ensign. Joined the 1st Admin Battalion, moving headquarters to Kilmersdon in 1869, and became 'G' Company of the new 1st Corps in 1880.

**23rd**—Formed as one company at Wincanton on 30 June 1860 with William S W Sandford as captain, Thomas E Rogers, lieutenant and Herbert Messiter, ensign. Joined the 3rd Admin Battalion, moving headquarters to Castle Cary in 1863, and became 'G' Company of the new 3rd Corps in 1880.

**24th**—Formed as one company at Somerton on 20 July 1860 with Francis H Dickinson as captain, George Tuson, lieutenant and William Fraser, ensign. The corps also recruited from the neighbouring villages of Kingweston, Kingdon and Long Sutton. Joined the 3rd Admin Battalion and was disbanded in 1871.

**25th**—Formed as one company at Baltonsborough on 14 January 1861 with Ebenezer Chaffey as captain, Reginald Dickinson, lieutenant and Robert Culling, ensign. Joined the 3rd Admin Battalion, moving headquarters just to the south-east at Keinton in 1870, and became 'H' Company of the new 3rd Corps in 1880.

**26th**—Formed as one company at Bridgewater on 5 February 1861 with Henry Bridge as captain, John Woodland, lieutenant and Joseph B Clarke, ensign. Joined the 2nd Admin Battalion and became 'K' and 'L Companies of the new 2nd Corps in 1880.

**27th**—Formed as one company at Wrington on 23 July 1861 with Nathaniel John Newnham, Jun, late of the Bombay Army, as captain, Charles Edwards, lieutenant and Oliver Coathupe, ensign. Joined the 3rd Admin Battalion, moving headquarters to Langford, just to the south-east, in 1866, and became 'I' Company of the new 3rd Corps in 1880.

**28th**—Formed as one company at South Petherton, five miles north of Crewkerne, on 4 November 1876 with Malachi L Blake as captain, Henry W Tuller, lieutenant and Robert McMillan, sub-lieutenant. Joined the 2nd Admin Battalion and became 'M' Company of the new 2nd Corps in 1880.

# Staffordshire

## Artillery Volunteers

**1st**—On 18 December 1860 one battery of artillery volunteers was formed at Etruria which three years later was included in the 1st Cheshire Brigade. But in 1866 the corps, together with those from Shropshire and Worcestershire and also with the 1st Cheshire, joined the newly formed 1st Staffordshire Admin Brigade at Etruria. This formation was, however, short lived and by October 1867 had been broken up. The several corps were once again placed with the Cheshire Brigade. In 1869 it was the turn of Shropshire to form an admin brigade, the corps as before coming from Staffordshire, Shropshire and Worcestershire. The latter, however, was transferred to Monmouthshire in 1874, the remaining two now consisting of four batteries each. In May 1880 the 1st Shropshire Brigade was consolidated as the 1st Shropshire and Staffordshire AVC of eight batteries, the Staffordshire gunners providing Nos 5 to 8.

## Rifle Volunteers

Five Admin Battalions were formed which became the 1st to 5th new Corps in 1880. There was also a 1st Sub-division which became the 14th Corps.

**1st (1859-1880)**—Formed at Handsworth on 15 August 1859 with Henry Elwell as captain, Sir Francis Edward Scott, Bt, lieutenant and Richard L H Mile, ensign. Joined the 3rd Admin Battalion and became 'A' and 'B' Companies of the new 1st Corps in 1880.

**1st (1880-1908)**—Handsworth was the headquarters of the 3rd Admin Battalion, formed in July 1860 and containing the 1st, 15th, 17th, 18th, 20th, 27th, 31st and 35th Corps. The battalion was consolidated in 1880 as the new 1st Corps with eight companies: 'A' and 'B' Handsworth (late 1st Corps), 'C' Brierley Hill (late 15th Corps), 'D' Kingswinford (late 18th Corps), 'E' West Bromwich (late 20th Corps), 'F' Seisdon (late No 2 Company, 27th Corps), 'G' Patshull (late No 1 Company, 27th Corps), 'H' Smethwick (late 31st Corps).

Under General Order 63 of May 1883 the 1st Corps was re-designated as 1st Volunteer Battalion South Staffordshire Regiment, the headquarters of 'D' Company later transferring to Wordsley. 'I' Company was formed at Smethwick and 'K' at West Bromwich in 1900, followed by 'L' (Cyclist) at Handsworth in 1901. 'G' was later disbanded and at the same time a battalion reorganisation resulted in the following company locations: Handsworth (3), Brierley Hill (2), West Bromwich (2), Sutton Coldfield and Smethwick (2). *Territorials:* Transfer to the Territorial Force in 1908 saw the bulk of the battalion converted to engineers and formed into the 1st North Midland Field Company RE. Some of the Handsworth personnel, however, remained as infantry and became part of the 5th Battalion South Staffordshire Regiment. The Handsworth Grammar School Cadets, which had been affiliated since 1907, at the same time joined the OTC.

**2nd (1859-1880)**—Formed at Longton on 30 September 1859 with William Kenwright Harvey as captain, Edward Clarke, lieutenant and William Goddard, ensign. Joined the 1st Admin Battalion and became 'A' Company of the new 2nd Corps in 1880.

**2nd (The Staffordshire Rangers) (1880-1908)**—Stoke-upon-Trent was the headquarters of the 1st Admin Battalion, formed in May 1860 and including the 2nd, 3rd, 6th, 9th, 10th, 13th, 16th, 28th, 36th, 37th, 38th and 40th Corps. The battalion was consolidated in 1880 as the new 1st Corps, The Staffordshire Rangers being soon permitted as part of the official title. There were eleven companies: 'A' Longton (late 2nd Corps), 'B' Hanley (late 3rd Corps), 'C' Burslem (late 6th Corps), 'D' Tunstall (late 9th Corps), 'E' Stoke-upon-Trent (late 10th Corps), 'F' Kidsgrove (late 13th Corps), 'G' and 'H' Newcastle-under-Lyne (late 16th Corps), 'J' Leek (late 28th Corps), 'K' Hanley (late 36th Corps), 'L' Stone (late 40th Corps).

Re-designation as 1st Volunteer Battalion North Staffordshire Regiment was notified in General Order 14 of February 1883. The cadet corps at Stoke-upon-Trent (see 10th Corps) was removed from the Army List in 1884 and battalion establishment reached fourteen companies by 1900 but was later reduced to thirteen. *Territorials:* 5th Battalion North Staffordshire Regiment.

**3rd (1859-1880)**—Formed at Hanley on 27 September 1859 with Thomas C Brown Westhead as captain, Septimius Bourne, lieutenant and John Dimmock, ensign. Joined the 1st Admin Battalion and became 'B' Company of the new 2nd Corps in 1880.

**3rd (1880-1908)**—Walsall was the headquarters of the 5th Admin Battalion, formed in November 1860 and including the 4th, 14th, 22nd, 33rd and 34th Corps. The battalion was consolidated in 1880 as the new 3rd Corps with six companies: 'A' and 'B' Walsall (late 4th Corps), 'C' Bloxwich (late 14th

**J Newman, 4th Staffordshire Rifle Volunteer Corps.**

Corps), 'D' Brownhills (late 22nd Corps), 'E' Cannock (late 33rd Corps). 'F' Wednesbury (late 34th Corps).

Re-designated as 2nd Volunteer Battalion South Staffordshire Regiment under General Order 63 of May 1883. A new company was later added at Walsall, but this was soon disbanded. In 1884 another company was formed at Walsall, together with one at Wednesbury, 'E' Company at the same time moving to Brownhills. 'D' Company at Brownhills was disbanded before 1901 but reformed later at Walsall. 'I' was added at Walsall in 1901. Also in 1901, Queen Mary's School at Walsall provided a cadet corps. *Territorials:* Transfer to the Territorial Force in 1908 was as part of 5th Battalion South Staffordshire Regiment. Queen Mary's School at the same time joined the OTC.

**4th (1859-1880)**—Formed at Walsall on 4 November 1859 with Charles Frederick Darwall as captain, John W Newman, lieutenant and Frederick Furhman Clarke, ensign. Joined 5th Admin Battalion and became 'A' and 'B' Companies of the new 3rd Corps in 1880.

**4th (1880-1908)**—Included in the 4th Admin Battalion, formed with headquarters at Wolverhampton in May 1860, was the 5th, 11th, 12th, 23rd, 26th, 29th, 30th and 32nd Corps. The battalion was consolidated in 1880 as the new 4th Corps with twelve companies: 'A', 'B' and 'C' Wolverhampton (late Nos.1, 2 and 3 Companies, 5th Corps), 'D' Willenhall (late No.4 Company, 5th Corps), 'E' Tipton (late 11th Corps), 'F' Sedgley (late 29th Corps), 'G' and 'H' Bilston (late 12th Corps), 'I' Wolverhampton (late 23rd Corps), 'K' and 'L' Wolverhampton (late 32nd Corps), 'M' Tettenhall (late 30th Corps).

Re-designation as 3rd Volunteer Battalion South Staffordshire Regiment was notified By General Order 63 of May 1883. 'N' (Cyclist) Company was added at Wolverhampton in 1900, 'H' Company moved to Darlaston in the same year. *Territorials:* 6th Battalion South Staffordshire Regiment. Mr J W Reddyhoff writing in *The Bulletin of the Military Historical Society* in November 1997 noted that the Freemason's Tudor Lodge of Rifle Volunteers No 1838 was formed from within the battalion on 16 July 1879.

**5th (1859-1880)**—Formed at Wolverhampton on 26 December 1859 with former Coldstream Guards officer, George Augustus Vernol as captain, Frederick Walton, lieutenant and Henry Underhill, ensign. Joined the 4th Admin Battalion and absorbed the 26th Corps at Willenhall as No.4 Company in 1874. Became 'A' to 'D' Companies of the new 4th Corps in 1880.

**5th (1880-1908)**—The corps included in the 2nd Admin Battalion, formed with headquarters at Lichfield in July 1860, were the 7th, 8th, 19th, 21st, 24th, 25th and 39th. The battalion was consolidated in 1880 as the new 5th Corps with eight companies: 'A' Burton-upon-Trent (late 7th Corps), 'B' Burton-upon-Trent (late 8th Corps), 'C' Tamworth (late 19th Corps), 'D' Rugeley (late 21st Corps), 'E' Lichfield (late 24th Corps), 'F' and 'G' Stafford (late 25th Corps), 'H' Burton-upon-Trent (late 39th Corps).

Re-designation as 2nd Volunteer Battalion North Staffordshire Regiment was notified in General Order 14 of February 1883, headquarters transferring to Burton-upon-Trent in 1884. A new company was added at Uttoxeter in 1900, Denstone College Cadet Corps affiliated in the same year. In the north aisle of Lichfield Cathedral on 1st August 1903, a window was dedicated by the Bishop of Lichfield to those Staffordshire Volunteers that fell in South Africa. *Territorials:* 6th Battalion North Staffordshire Regiment.

**1st Volunteer Battalion
South Staffordshire Regiment.**

Denstone College joined the OTC.

**6th**—Formed at Burslem, twenty miles north-east of Stafford, on 28 December 1859 with Richard Edwards as captain, Gilbert Elliott, lieutenant and William Baker, ensign. Joined the 1st Admin Battalion and became 'C' Company of the new 2nd Corps in 1880.

**7th**—Formed at Burton-upon-Trent on 10 February 1860 with George Tenant, one of the brewery family, as captain, Henry Warde, lieutenant and Richard Radcliff, ensign. Joined the 2nd Admin Battalion and became 'A' Company of the new 5th Corps in 1880. At Burton, in the 1890s, it is said that the breweries employed more than 7,000 people, many of them joining the 7th.

**8th**—Formed at Burton-upon-Trent on 10 February 1860 with Abram Bass, of the brewing family, as captain, John Gretton, Jun, lieutenant and John Anderson, ensign. Joined the 2nd Admin Battalion and became 'B' Company of the new 5th Corps in 1880.

**9th**—Formed at Tunstall on 4 January 1860 with William Adam, Jun, as captain, John Nash Peake, lieutenant and William Simms Ball, ensign. Joined the 1st Admin Battalion and became 'D' Company of the new 2nd Corps in 1880.

**10th**—Formed at Stoke-upon-Trent on 19 January 1860 with M Daintry Hollins as captain, Edward Copland, lieutenant and Edward Adams, ensign. Joined the 1st Admin Battalion and became 'E' Company of the new 2nd Corps in 1880. A cadet corps was formed in 1875.

**11th**—Formed at Tipton, just to the north of Dudley, on 11 January 1860 with William Barrows, Jun, as captain, William Hall, lieutenant and George Homfray, ensign. Joined the 4th Admin Battalion and became 'E' Company of the new 4th Corps in 1880.

**12th**—Formed at Bilston on 26 January 1860 with John Nock Bagnall as captain, Benjamin Whitehouse, lieutenant and T Waterhouse, ensign. Joined the 4th Admin Battalion and became 'G' and 'H' Companies of the new 4th Corps in 1880.

**13th**—Formed at Kidsgrove on 26 February 1860 with William S Williamson as captain, Edward Williamson, lieutenant and Thomas Brindley, ensign. Joined the 1st Admin Battalion and became 'F' Company of the new 2nd Corps in 1880.

**14th**—Formed at Bloxwich, three miles north-west of Walsall, on 10 December 1859 and known as the 1st Sub-division until March 1860. The first two officers were Lieutenant George Strongitarm and Ensign Edward Jenks Stanley. Joined the 5th Admin Battalion and became 'C' Company of the new 3rd Corps in 1880.

**15th**—Formed at Brierley Hill on 1 August 1860 with Frederick Smith as captain, Henry O Firmstond, lieutenant and Joseph B Cochrane, ensign. Joined the 3rd Admin Battalion and became 'C' Company of the new 1st Corps in 1880.

**16th**—Formed at Newcastle-under-Lyme on 24 February 1860 with J Knight as captain, William Henry Dutton, lieutenant and John Smith Mayer, ensign. Joined the 1st Admin Battalion and became 'G' and 'H' Companies of the new 2nd Corps in 1880. The old barracks, which was taken over by the volunteers, has been described as a quadrangular imposing building in modern Italian style. Clothing for the army was made at the Enderley Mills.

**17th**—Formed at Seisdon on 21 February 1860 with George Pudsey Aston as captain, Frederick Turton Sparrow, lieutenant and William Aston, ensign. Joined the 3rd Admin Battalion and was absorbed into the 27th Corps as its No 2 Company in 1873.

**18th**—Formed at Kingswinford on 21 February 1860 with Benjamin St John Mathews as captain, John Barrows, lieutenant and J Pearson, ensign. Joined the 3rd Admin Battalion and became 'D' Company of the new 1st Corps in 1880.

**19th**—Formed at Tamworth on 21 February 1860 with Francis Willington as captain, Robert Whately Nevil, lieutenant and John Webster Mayou, ensign. Joined the 2nd Admin Battalion and became 'C' Company of the new 5th Corps in 1880.

**20th**—Formed at West Bromwich on 25 February 1860 with Thomas Bagnall, Jun as captain, Henry Williams, lieutenant and Edwin Hooper, ensign. Joined the 3rd Admin Battalion and became 'E' Company of the new 1st Corps in 1880.

**21st**—Mr P G Smith, in an item published in the *Bulletin* of the Military Historical Society in February 1981, tells how the proposed tile of the eventual 21st Corps was the Rugeley Rangers—'come join the Rugeley Rangers', so said a verse written by a local draper that appeared in the press. An alternative name, but not one the Rugeley Volunteers delighted in, was The Poisoners. That then notorious poisoner, William Palmer, having been a doctor in Rugeley. Sanction to form the corps came on 18 February 1860, Captain Newton John Lane's commission being dated 23 February, those for Lieutenant Josiah Spode and Ensign Robert Landor being signed on the day after. The headmaster of Rugeley Grammar School, the Rev. Edward R Pitman, was made acting chaplain. The Rugeley company joined the 2nd Admin Battalion and in 1880 became 'D' Company of the new 5th Corps.

**22nd**—Formed at Brownhills on 24 February 1860 with John Harrison as captain, William Bealy Harrison, lieutenant and Robert Nelson Boyd, ensign. Joined the 5th Admin Battalion and became 'D' Company of the new 3rd Corps in 1880.

**23rd**—Formed at Wolverhampton on 1 March 1860 with A Clement Foster Gough as captain, George Singleton Tudor, lieutenant and Thomas Ironmonger, ensign. Joined the 4th Admin Battalion and became 'I' Company of the new 4th Corps in 1880.

**24th**—Formed at Lichfield on 6 March 1860 with William Biddulph Parke, late of the 60th King's Royal Rifle Corps, as captain, Charles J Mott, lieutenant and John St V Jervis, ensign. Joined the 2nd Admin Battalion and became 'E' Company of the new 5th Corps in 1880. A contingent from 'E' Company, under Captain W R Coleridge Roberts, formed a Guard of Honour at the laying up of the old Colours of the 38th Regiment at Lichfield Cathedral on 1st August 1903.

**25th**—Formed at Stafford on 6 March 1860 with Viscount Sandon of Sandon Hall, Stafford as captain, Robert William Hand, lieutenant and John Lea, ensign. Joined the 2nd Admin Battalion and became 'F' and 'G' Companies of the new 5th Corps in 1880.

**26th**—Formed at Willenhall on 27 February 1860 with Ralph Dickenson Gouch as captain and William Deakin, lieutenant. Joined the 4th Admin Battalion and was absorbed into the 5th Corps as its No 4 Company in 1874.

**27th**—Formed as one company at Patshull on 7 March 1860 with William Walter Earl of Dartmouth taking command. Joined the 3rd Admin Battalion and absorbed the 17th Corps at Seisdon as No 2 Company in 1873. Became 'F' and 'G' Companies of the new 1st Corps in 1880.

**28th**—Formed at Leek on 26 April 1860 with William B Badnall as captain, John Russell, lieutenant and Charles H Halcombe, ensign. Joined the 1st Admin Battalion in May 1861 and became 'J' Company of the new 2nd Corps in 1880.

**29th**—Formed at Sedgley on 9 April 1860 with Henry B Whitehouse as captain, Edward J Gibbs, lieutenant and Daniel G Ward, ensign. Joined the 4th Admin Battalion and became 'F' Company of the new 4th Corps in 1880.

**30th**—Formed at Tettenhall on 30 March 1860 with Edward P Stubbs as captain, James Prior, lieutenant and Thomas Evans, ensign. Joined the 4th Admin Battalion and became 'M' Company of the new 4th Corps in 1880.

**31st**—Formed at Smethwick on 19 April 1860 with Sampson Hanbury as captain, Ralph Docker, lieutenant and George Stevens, ensign. Joined the 3rd Admin Battalion and became 'H' Company of the new 1st Corps in 1880.

**32nd**—Formed at Wolverhampton on 19 April 1860 with Henry Loveridge as captain, William H Tudor, lieutenant and Alfred Young, ensign. Joined the 4th Admin Battalion and became 'K' and 'L' Companies of the new 4th Corps in 1880.

**33rd**—Formed at Cannock on 14 July 1860 with Joseph S Mosely as captain, Bernard Gilpin, lieutenant and George Lee, ensign. Joined the 5th Admin Battalion and became 'E' Company of the new 3rd Corps in 1880.

**34th**—Formed at Wednesbury on 11 May 1860 with Thomas Russell as captain, John Hunt Thursfield, lieutenant and George Gaddick Whitehouse, ensign. Joined the 5th Admin Battalion and became 'F' Company of the new 3rd Corps in 1880.

**35th**—Formed at Kinver, four miles from Stourbridge, on 3 July 1860 with Offley F D Wakeman as captain, Robert Woodward, Jun, lieutenant and Joseph L Stenson, ensign. Joined the 3rd Admin Battalion and was disbanded in 1864.

**36th**—at Hanley on 18 June 1860 with Edward J Ridgway as captain and Clement Wedgwood, lieutenant. Joined the 1st Admin Battalion and became 'K' Company of the new 2nd Corps in 1880.

**37th**—Formed at Cheadle on 30 August 1860 with John W Phillips as captain, John Adamthwaite, lieutenant and Charles J Biagg, ensign. Joined the 1st Admin Battalion, disappearing from the Army List in November 1872.

**38th**—Formed at Eccleshall on 17 September 1860 with Robert Hargreaves as captain, Basil Fitzherbert, lieutenant and Thomas Robinson, ensign. Joined the 1st Admin Battalion and disbanded in 1869.

**39th**—Formed at Burton-upon-Trent on 27 September 1860 with member of the brewing family, William H Worthington as captain, Josiah T Poyser, lieutenant and William Drewery, ensign. Joined the 2nd Admin Battalion and became 'H' Company of the new 5th Corps in 1880.

**40th**—Formed at Stone on 1 December 1860 with Basil T Fitzherbert as captain. Joined the 1st Admin Battalion and became 'L' Company of the new 2nd Corps in 1880.

# Suffolk

## Artillery Volunteers

**1st**—Formed at Lowestoft on 10 July 1860 and later attached to the 1st Norfolk Admin Brigade. Provided No 6 Battery of the new 1st Norfolk AVC in 1880.

**2nd**—Formed at Walton on 15 October 1860 and later attached to the 1st Norfolk Admin Brigade. Disbanded in 1871.

**3rd**—Formed at Aldborough as the 9th Suffolk Rifle Volunteer Corps on 9 March 1860. Much of the corps was recruited in the Leiston area and in the early part of 1861 the 9th was divided to form the 9th at Leiston and 21st at Aldborough. In 1863 it was decided to convert the 21st to an artillery unit, April of the following year seeing the 3rd Suffolk AVC entering the Army List. The new gunners joined the 1st Norfolk Admin Brigade and in 1880 provided No 7 Battery of the new 1st Norfolk AVC in 1880.

**4th**—Formed at Beccles on 14 July 1868 and joined the Norfolk Admin Brigade. Provided No 8 Battery of the new 1st Norfolk AVC in 1880.

## Rifle Volunteers

Three admin battalions were formed of which the 3rd was broken up in 1877. The 1st and 2nd were, in 1880, consolidated as the new 6th and 1st Corps. Formed in November 1860 with headquarters at Halesworth, the 3rd Admin Battalion included the 4th, 7th, 9th, 14th, 15th and 17th Corps. Its headquarters were transferred to Lowestoft in 1865. There was also a 1st Sub-division which became the 1st Corps in 1860.

**1st (1859-1880)**—Formed at Ipswich on 11 October 1859 and known as the 1st Sub-division until January 1860. Its first officers were: Captain Robert Ramsey, Lieutenant Henry Haward and Ensign Sterling

## 2nd Volunteer Battalion Suffolk Regiment.

Westhorp. Joined the 2nd Admin Battalion and became 'A', 'B' and 'C' Companies of the new 1st Corps in 1880.

**1st (1880-1908)**—Woodbridge was the headquarters of the 2nd Admin Battalion, formed on 24 October 1860 and including the 1st, 2nd, 3rd, 5th, 8th, 12th and 21st Corps. The 7th and 9th were added in 1877. The battalion was consolidated in 1880 as the new 1st Corps with eight companies: 'A', 'B' and 'C' Ipswich (late 1st Corps), 'D' Framlingham (late 2nd Corps), 'E' Woodbridge (late 3rd Corps), 'F' Halesworth (late 7th Corps), 'G' Saxmundham (late 8th Corps), 'H' Leiston (late 9th Corps).

Under General Order 181 of December 1887 the 1st Corps became 1st Volunteer Battalion Suffolk Regiment, a new company being added in 1900. The Queen Elizabeth's School, Ipswich, Cadet Corps was formed and affiliated in 1889, disappearing from the Army List by the end of 1891, but reappearing again in 1900. Framlingham College also formed a cadet corps in 1901. *Territorials:* Transfer to the Territorial Force in 1908 was as 4th Battalion Suffolk Regiment, both Queen Elizabeth's School and Framlingham College at the same time joining the OTC.

**2nd**—Formed at Framlingham on 1 March 1860 with Edwin Blomfield as captain, John Pierson, lieutenant and Nathaniel G Barthropp, ensign. Joined the 2nd Admin Battalion and became 'D' Company of the new 1st Corps in 1880.

**3rd**—Formed at Woodbridge on 26 January 1860 with Francis Capper Brooke, late of the Grenadier Guards, as captain, F W B Lord Rendlesham, lieutenant and Arthur George Brooke, ensign. Joined the 2nd Admin Battalion and became 'E' Company of the new 1st Corps in 1880.

**4th**—Formed at Bungay on 1 February 1860 with John Margitson as captain, William Mann, lieutenant and Phillip Salter Millard, ensign. Joined the 3rd Admin Battalion, transferring to the 1st Norfolk Admin Battalion in 1877, and became 'F' Company of the new 2nd Norfolk RVC in 1880.

**5th**—Formed at Wickham Market on 16 February 1860 with Andrew Arcdeckne as lieutenant and William George Murial, ensign. Joined the 2nd Admin Battalion and was disbanded in 1875.

**6th (1860-1880)**—Formed at Stowmarket on 13 February 1860 with Walter Robert Tyrell, late of the Royal Horse Guards, as captain, H Aston Oakes, lieutenant and Thomas Mingaye Golding, ensign. Joined the 1st Admin Battalion and became 'A' Company of the new 6th Corps in 1880.

**6th (1880-1908)**—The 1st Admin Battalion was formed on 30 July 1860 and is first shown with headquarters at Stowmarket. From August 1961 the Army List give the battalion's location as being at Bury St Edmunds, and from April 1864 as Sudbury. Included in the battalion were the 6th, 10th, 11th, 12th, 13th, 16th, 18th, 19th and 20th Suffolk Corps, the 9th Cambridgeshire being added in July 1862. When consolidation came in 1880, 1st Admin would be the only battalion in the land to retain the number of its senior company, the new 6th Suffolk RVC following on directly after the new 1st. The 6th had eight companies: 'A' Stowmarket (late 6th Corps), 'B' and 'C' Eye (late 10th Corps), 'D' Sudbury (late 11th Corps), 'E' and 'F' Bury St Edmunds (late 13th Corps), 'G' Hadleigh (late 16th Corps), 'H' Newmarket (late 20th Corps).

Re-designated as 2nd Volunteer Battalion Suffolk Regiment under General Order 181 of December 1887, headquarters transferring to Bury St Edmunds in 1899. There was a reduction in establishment to seven companies in 1889, but this was brought back to eight in 1900. A cadet corps at King Edward's School, Bury St Edmunds was raised and affiliated in 1900. *Territorials:* 5th Battalion Suffolk Regiment, the King Edward School Cadets joined the OTC.

**7th**—Formed at Halesworth on 28 February 1860 with Thomas Rank as captain, Edward Deck, lieutenant and Fairly B Strathern, ensign. Joined the 3rd Admin Battalion, transferring to the 2nd in 1877, and became 'F' Company of the new 1st Corps in 1880.

**8th** —Formed at Saxmundham on 29 February 1860 with William B Long as captain, George Waller Bates, lieutenant and Ellis Wade, ensign. Joined the 2nd Admin Battalion and became 'G' Company of the new 1st Corps in 1880.

**9th**—Formed as two companies with headquarters at Aldeburgh on 9 March 1860 with Captain Arthur Thelluson in command. Joined the 2nd Admin Battalion. Much of the corps was recruited just to the south-east in the Leiston area and in the early part of 1861 the 9th was divided: the Aldborough portion being made independent as 21st Corps, while the Leiston personnel remained as 9th. At the same time, the new arrangement saw the corps placed into 3rd Admin Battalion, but a return was made to the 2nd in 1877. Became 'H' Company of the new 1st Corps in 1880. The Volunteer Drill Hall at Leiston was built in 1862.

**10th**—Formed at Eye on 6th March 1860 with Phillip H Michell, late of the 47th Regiment of Foot, as captain, Sir Edward C Kerrison, lieutenant and the Hon John Major H Major, ensign. Joined the 1st Admin Battalion and became 'B' and 'C' Companies of the new 6th Corps in 1880.

**11th**—Formed at Sudbury on 14th April 1860 with W J W Poley as lieutenant and Robert F Stedman, ensign. Joined the 1st Admin Battalion and became 'D' Company of the new 6th Corps in 1880.

**12th**—Formed at Bosmere, one mile south-east of Needham Market, on 1 June 1860 with John Hayward as lieutenant and John K Sedgwick, ensign. Joined the 1st Admin Battalion, transferring to 2nd in June 1861. Moved to Needham Market in the same year and disbanded in 1866.

**13th**—Formed as two companies at Bury St Edmunds on 11 May 1860 with Fuller M Wilson and John S Phillips as company commanders. Joined the 1st Admin Battalion and became 'E' and 'F' Companies of the new 6th Corps in 1880. In the town was the Depot of the 12th (later Suffolk) Regiment.

**14th**—Formed at Beccles on 1 May 1860 with George Wilson as captain, William M Crowfoot, lieutenant and James Read, ensign. Joined the 3rd Admin Battalion, transferring to the 1st Norfolk Admin Battalion in 1877, and became 'G' Company of the new 2nd Norfolk RVC in 1880.

**15th**—Formed at Wrentham on 9 June 1860 with John F Vincent as lieutenant and Samuel A Goodwin, ensign. Joined the 3rd Admin Battalion and was disbanded in 1865. Wrentham (actually in Norfolk) lies six miles north-east of Thetford.

**16th**—Formed at Hadleigh, ten miles west of Ipswich, on 2 July 1860 with John F Robinson as lieutenant and George Freeman, ensign. Joined the 1st Admin Battalion and became 'G' Company of the new 6th Corps in 1880.

**17th**—Formed at Lowestoft on 11 September 1860 with Edward Leathes as captain, Thomas Lucas, lieutenant and Robert Johnson, ensign. Joined the 3rd Admin Battalion, transferring to the 1st Norfolk Admin Battalion in 1877, and became 'H' and 'I' Companies of the new 2nd Norfolk RVC in 1880.

**18th**—Formed at Wickhambrook on 22 October 1860 with William G Strutter as lieutenant and Joseph R Bromley, ensign. Joined the 1st Admin Battalion and was disbanded in 1870.

**19th**—Formed at Brandon on 23 April 1861 with Charles A D Tyssen as captain, John Gates, lieutenant and John Wood, ensign. Joined the 1st Admin Battalion and was disbanded in 1863.

**20th**—Formed at Mildenhall on 23 May 1861 with William Payne as captain, James Read, Jun, lieutenant and Frederick H Harris, ensign. Joined the 1st Admin Battalion, absorbing the 9th Cambridgeshire RVC in 1862, and moved to Newmarket in 1871. Became 'H' Company of the new 6th Corps in 1880.

**21st**—Formed at Aldeburgh from part of the 9th Corps, the 21st was first seen in the Army List for June 1861—Lieutenant Newson Garrett in command. Joined the 2nd Admin Battalion and became the 3rd Suffolk Artillery Volunteer Corps in 1864.

# Surrey

## Artillery Volunteers

**1st (1860-1864)**—Headquarters of this corps, formed 12 October 1860, are given in the Army List as No 12 Union Place, Lambeth Road. Recruiting went well at first—a strength of three batteries was soon reached—but by 1864 interest had fallen off, resulting in the disbandment of the corps that year.

**1st (1880-1908)**—Formed as 2nd Corps at Brixton on 10 November 1860 and by 1877 held an establishment of ten batteries recruited in the main from the Brixton, Loughborough, Camberwell and Shepherd's Bush areas. Renumbered as 1st Corps in 1880, headquarters moving to Camberwell in the following year. Amalgamated with the 1st London AVC to form the 1st London (City of London) AVC, Surrey providing No 7 to 16 Batteries.

**2nd**—See 1st Corps (1880-1908).

## Engineer Volunteers

**1st**—The 1st Surrey EVC was formed 4 April 1862, its headquarters given in the Army List as 60 Blackman Street. No mention of the unit was made after November 1863. (Note: the part of Borough High Street in Southwark south of St George's Church was known as Blackman Street until 1880.)

## Mounted Rifle Volunteers/Light Horse Volunteers

**1st**—A special issue of the *Illustrated London News* dated 27 October 1860 included a colour plate showing representatives of the several Metropolitan corps at a recent review held in Hyde Park. Among them is a representative of the 1st Surrey Mounted Rifles wearing a dark green uniform with red collar and cuffs. The corps had been formed at Clapham in April 1860, Captain Walter Mellor being commissioned 2 April, and by March 1862 had been converted to Light Horse. Disbanded in June 1868.

## Rifle Volunteers

Four admin battalions were formed which, in 1880, provided the new 3rd, 4th, 5th and 6th Corps. There were also three numbered sub-divisions, 1st, 2nd and 3rd, and these became the 9th, 14th and 15th Corps.

**1st (South London)**—Formed as the South London RVC at Camberwell on 14 June 1859. Subsequent headquarters were listed as Camberwell Green, then Peckham (Hanover Park), Flodden Road from 1865—a good number of early recruits to the corps were drawn from the Sports Club, Hanover Park. Absorbed the 3rd Corps, also at Camberwell, as No 2 Company by February 1860—title from then on appearing in the Army List as 1st Surrey (South London) RVC.

The establishment soon rose to eight companies, the men recruited in the main throughout Camberwell, Clapham and Peckham, with Lieutenant Colonel

**1st Surrey Rifle Volunteer Corps.**

Commandant John Boucher, late of the 5th Dragoon Guards, in command. A cadet corps was formed at Dulwich College in 1878. Became a volunteer battalion of the East Surrey Regiment in 1881, but although ranked as 1st, there was no change in title. *Territorials:* Transfer to the Territorial Force in 1908 was as 21st Battalion London Regiment, Dulwich College at the same time joining the OTC.

According to Mr J W Reddyhoff, writing in *The Bulletin of the Military Historical Society* in November 1997, the Macdonald Freemason Lodge No 1216 was formed from within the battalion on 13 March 1868.

**2nd**—Formed as one company at Croydon on 16 June 1859, followed by a second in March 1860. James Hunter Campbell, formerly of the Bengal Artillery, and Adam Stewart were the company commanders. Headquarters were in the old Croydon Barracks. Included in the 1st Admin Battalion from September 1860 but in March 1867, after new personnel had been recruited from around the Crystal Palace, Norwood and Caterham areas, the establishment was brought up to six companies and the 2nd Corps was made independent. The Whitgift School Cadet Corps was formed and affiliated in 1874. Re-designated as 1st Volunteer Battalion Queen's (Royal West Surrey Regiment) in March 1883, there would be ten companies in 1900, reducing to nine in 1903—seven at Croydon, one each at Crystal Palace and Caterham. *Territorials:* Transfer to the Territorial Force in 1908 was as 4th Battalion Queen's, the Whitgift School cadets at the same time joining the OTC.

**3rd (1859-1860)**—Formed at Camberwell on 26 August 1859 and absorbed into the 1st Corps as its No 2 Company by February 1860.

**3rd (1880-1908)**—Headquarters of the 1st Admin Battalion, formed in September 1860, were at Croydon and to it were added the 2nd, 4th, 8th, 11th, 20th, 21st, 25th and 26th Corps. Headquarters transferred to Wimbledon in 1862, Southwark in 1868 and Thornton Road, Clapham Park in 1869. The battalion was consolidated in 1880 as the new 3rd Corps with seven companies: 'A', 'B' and 'C' Brixton (late 4th Corps), 'D' Carshalton (late 8th Corps), 'E' and 'F' Wimbledon (late 11th Corps), 'G' Epsom (late 25th Corps).

There was also a half-company at Brixton. Headquarters were moved back to Wimbledon in 1884, this time to St George's Road. Two new companies were added in 1886 and in December of the following year 3rd Surrey was re-designated as 2nd Volunteer Battalion East Surrey Regiment. Another two companies joined in 1900 and by 1904, after several reorganisations, company locations stood at: 'A' and 'B' Streatham; 'C' and 'D' Sutton; 'E', 'F' and 'G' Wimbledon; 'H' Epsom; 'I' Wimbledon and 'K' Epsom. A cadet corps at Epsom College was formed and affiliated in 1890. *Territorials:* Transfer to the Territorial Force in 1908 was as 5th Battalion East Surrey Regiment, Epsom College at the same time joining the OTC.

**4th (1859-1880)**—Formed as one company at Brixton on 10 September 1859, increasing to two in February 1860 with Captain Commandant Thomas Eman, late of the 2nd Regiment of Foot, in command. Joined the 1st Admin Battalion and became 'A' to 'C' Companies of the new 3rd Corps in 1880.

**4th (1880-1908)**—The 3rd Admin Battalion was formed with headquarters at Dorking in September 1860 and included the 5th, 13th, 14th, 17th, 18th, 22nd and 24th Corps. In 1880 the battalion was consolidated as the new 4th Corps with six companies: 'A' and 'B' Reigate (late 5th Corps), 'C' and 'D' Guildford (late 13th Corps), 'E' Farnham (late 18th Corps), 'F' Guildford (late 24th Corps).

There was also a half-company at Godstone provided by the 17th Corps. Headquarters transferred to Reigate in 1881 and in 1883, under General Order 37 of March, 4th Surrey RVC became 2nd Volunteer Battalion Queen's (Royal West Surrey Regiment). Headquarters moved again, this time to Guildford, in 1891. Three cadet companies were associated with the battalion: Charterhouse School Cadet Corps, formed in 1873; Cranleigh School, 1900, and Reigate Grammar School in 1907. *Territorials:* Transfer to the Territorial Force in 1908 was as 5th Battalion Queen's, Charterhouse, Cranleigh and Reigate Schools at the same time joining the OTC.

**5th (1859-1880)**—Formed at Reigate on 12 September 1859 with the Hon William J Monson as captain, Francis Henry Beaumont, lieutenant and Henry Lainson, ensign. Joined the 3rd Admin Battalion and became 'A' and 'B' Companies of the new 4th Corps in 1880.

**5th (1880-1908)**—Headquarters of the 2nd Admin Battalion, formed in September 1860, were at Walton-on-Thames and to it were attached the 6th, 9th, 11th, 12th, 15th and 16th Corps. The battalion moved to Kingston-upon-Thames in 1864 and in 1880 was consolidated as the new 5th Corps with eight companies: 'A' Esher (late 6th Corps), 'B' and 'C' Richmond (late 9th Corps), 'D', 'E', 'F' and 'G' Kingston-upon-Thames (late 12th Corps), 'H' Chertsey (late 15th Corps).

Re-designated as 3rd Volunteer Battalion East Surrey Regiment in December 1887. Two new companies, one at Egham, one at Richmond, were added in 1900. Also in that year Richmond County School Cadet Corps was formed and affiliated, as was Beaumont College at Old Windsor in 1906. In South Africa during the Boer War, Lieutenant S F Brooks died from enteric fever at Newcastle on 9 June 1900. Brooks was educated at Harrow School and commissioned in March 1897. *Territorials:* Transfer to the Territorial Force in 1908 was as 6th Battalion East Surrey Regiment, Beaumont College at the same time joining the OTC.

**6th (1859-1880)**—Formed at Esher on 29 October 1859 with Sir Henry Fletcher, late of the Grenadier Guards, as captain, John N Higginbotham, lieutenant and Robert H Few, ensign. Joined the 2nd Admin Battalion and became 'A' Company of the new 5th Corps in 1880.

**6th (1880-1908)**—The 4th Admin Battalion was formed with headquarters at Bermondsey in October 1868 and into it were placed the 10th and 23rd Corps. Headquarters transferred to Rotherhithe in 1869 and consolidation as the new 6th Corps took place in 1880. There were eight companies: 'A' and 'B' at Bermondsey, formed from the 10th Corps; 'C' to 'H' at Rotherhithe, from the 23rd. The corps was re-designated as 3rd Volunteer Battalion Queen's (Royal West Surrey Regiment) in March 1883 and headquarters moved to Bermondsey in 1884. A cadet corps was formed in Bermondsey in 1885, but this disappeared from the Army List after ten years. Another was raised, this time at Streatham Grammar School, in 1899. *Territorials:* 22nd Battalion London Regiment. The Streatham Grammar School Cadets, although the Army Council did approve its transfer to the OTC, was, however, disbanded.

**4th Volunteer Battalion Queen's (Royal West Surrey Regiment).**

**7th**—The first company of the 7th Corps was raised at Southwark on 30 November 1859; five others following by February 1860, Major Commandant Francis Marus Beresford taking command. In 1880 the 26th Corps of four companies at Lavender Hill, Clapham was amalgamated with the 7th to form a new battalion of ten companies with headquarters at Upper Kennington Lane, Southwark. The corps was designated as 4th Volunteer Battalion East Surrey Regiment in December 1887, headquarters transferring to Clapham Junction in 1902. A cyclist company was added there in 1900. *Territorials:* 23rd Battalion London Regiment.

**8th (1859-1880)**—Formed as one company at Epsom on 21 December 1859 with James Hastie as captain, John Holman Hay, lieutenant and Edward James Rickards, ensign. Joined the 1st Admin Battalion, moving headquarters to Carshalton in 1862. Became 'D' Company of the new 3rd Corps in 1880.

**8th (1880-1908)**—Formed as the 19th Corps at Lambeth on 13 March 1860 and soon comprised eight companies with Major Commandant William Roupell in command. Headquarters are given as 71 New Street, Kennington Park from 1869. Renumbered as 8th in 1880 and designated 4th Volunteer Battalion Queen's (Royal West Surrey Regiment) in March 1883. The establishment was increased to ten companies in 1890 and a cyclist company was added in 1901. The Mayall College Herne Hill Cadet Corps was formed and affiliated in 1888, but this transferred to the 22nd Middlesex RVC in 1891. Another cadet corps with headquarters at Red Cross Hill in Southwark was added in 1889 and this became the 1st Cadet Battalion Queen's in 1890. *Territorials:* 24th Battalion London Regiment.

**9th**—Formed at Richmond on 2 September 1859 and known as the 1st Sub-division until December. Comprised two companies by February 1860, Captains Morgan Yeatman and Octavius Ommanney being appointed as company commanders. Joined the 2nd Admin Battalion and became 'B' and 'C' Companies of the new 5th Corps in 1880.

**10th**—Formed as two companies at Bermondsey on 7 February 1860 with Marcus Sharpe and Benjamin Glover as company commanders. Joined the 4th Admin Battalion in October 1868 and became 'A' and 'B' Companies of the new 6th Corps in 1880. At the south end of Tower Bridge there is a bronze statue to Colonel Samuel Bourne Bevington who was commissioned ensign in the 10th Corps on 9 March 1861. He went on to command the 3rd Volunteer Battalion Queen's Royal West Surrey Regiment (1884-1899) and would become Bermondsey's first Mayor in 1900.

**11th**—Formed at Wimbledon on 11 February 1860 with James Oliphant as captain, Timothy Richards, lieutenant and John S Oliphant, ensign. Joined the 2nd Admin Battalion, transferring to the 1st in July 1862, and became 'E' and 'F' Companies of the new 3rd Corps in 1880.

**12th**—Formed at Kingston-upon-Thames on 16 February 1860 with William Marshall Cochrane as captain, Frederick M Arnold, lieutenant and Edward William Browne, ensign. Comprised four companies by the end of 1861. Joined the 2nd Admin Battalion and became 'D' to 'G' Companies of the new 5th Corps in 1880. Headquarters were in Orchard Road.

**13th**—Formed at Guildford on 18 February 1860 with William Henry Gill, late of the Rifle Brigade, as captain and William M Molyneux, ensign. The lieutenant of the original company was Ross Lewis Mangles who had won the Victoria Cross on 30 July 1857 during the Indian Mutiny. He was later Member of Parliament for Guildford. Joined the 3rd Admin Battalion and became 'C' and 'D' Companies of the new 4th Corps in 1880.

**14th**—Formed at Dorking on 9 September 1859 with Henry Walker Kerrich as lieutenant and Robert Barclay, ensign. Known as the 2nd Sub-division until March 1860. Joined the 3rd Admin Battalion and was disbanded in 1877.

**15th**—Formed at Chertsey on 25 February 1860 with Robert Hay Murray as lieutenant and Francis L Dowling, ensign. Known as the 3rd Sub-division until March. Joined the 2nd Admin Battalion and became 'H' Company of the new 5th Corps in 1880.

**16th**—Formed at Egham on 2 March 1860 with W Edgell as lieutenant and Lionel Booth, ensign. Joined the 2nd Admin Battalion and was disbanded in 1868.

**17th**—Formed at Godstone on 23 February 1860 with Charles Hampden Turner as lieutenant and Granville Levison Gower, ensign. Joined the 3rd Admin Battalion and provided a half-company of the new 4th Corps in 1880.

**18th**—Formed at Farnham on 6 March 1860 with Owen F L Ward, late of the 11th Regiment of Foot, as captain, William J Hollest, lieutenant and George Trimmer, ensign. Joined the 3rd Admin Battalion and became 'E' Company of the new 4th Corps in 1880.

**19th**—See 8th Corps (1880-1908).

**20th**—Formed at Lower Norwood on 27 April 1860 with former captain in the Royal Madras Engineers, John Ouchteriony, as commanding officer, William E Franks, lieutenant and William Ruston, ensign. Joined the 1st Admin Battalion and was disbanded in 1863.

**21st**—Formed at Battersea on 3 May 1860 with John B Burnley as captain, Alexander Webster, lieutenant and George Finch, ensign. Joined the 1st Admin Battalion in 1863 and was disbanded in 1866.

**22nd**—Formed at Albury on 16 January 1861 with William John Evelyn as captain, Thomas Lyon Thurlow, lieutenant and Edward Jekyll, ensign. Joined the 3rd Admin Battalion and was disbanded in 1875.

**23rd**—Formed at Rotherhithe on 1 February 1861 with James Payne as captain, Frederick Wood, lieutenant and James John Stoke, ensign. Increased to six companies from two in 1868, joined the 4th Admin Battalion and became 'C' to 'H' Companies of the new 6th Corp in 1880.

**24th (1861-1862)**—Formed by cartoonist George Cruikshank in Southwark on 9 March 1861, the membership being made up entirely from total abstainers. Cruikshank, who became captain commandant, called his corps Havelock's Own after hero of the Indian Mutiny and noted leader in the Temperance Movement, General Sir Henry Havelock (1795-1857). Headquarters were at St George's Road, Southwark, but were moved to 39 Bridge House, Newington Causeway by October 1861. According to one source relations, both internal and with the authorities—there were unwelcome moves afoot to merge the 24th with the 7th Surrey— were not entirely harmonious and subsequently the corps was disbanded in March 1862.

**24th (1862-1880)**—Formed at Guildford as the 25th Corps on 31 January 1862 and renumbered 24th by April of the same year. Captain Frederick George Thynne took command. Joined the 3rd Admin Battalion and became 'F' Company of the new 4th Corps in 1880.

**25th**—Formed at Epsom on 1 March 1862. Joined the 1st Admin Battalion and became 'G' Company of the new 3rd Corps in 1880.

**26th**—Formed at Shaftesbury Park, Lavender Hill, Clapham, on 28 April 1875. Joined the 1st Admin Battalion and, with an establishment of four companies, was amalgamated with the 7th Corps in 1880.

**1st Cadet Battalion Queen's (Royal West Surrey Regiment)**—Raised at the Red Cross Hall, Southwark in January 1889 as a cadet corps affiliated to the 4th Volunteer Battalion Queen's in June 1889. The idea for this corps was first put forward in January 1889—Captain Salmond of the 3rd Battalion Derbyshire Regiment being asked to take charge of formation. On the following 30 May, at Red Cross Hall, Lord Wolseley made a memorable speech which did much to encourage sufficient boys to come forward to make up two companies. A third followed in 1890, then a fourth, which subsequently led the War Office to grant permission to form the cadets into a battalion. This, the 1st Cadet Battalion, Queen's (Royal West Surrey Regiment), was to be the first independent battalion of its kind in London. There would be six companies by 1891—this was to make the battalion the strongest in England—and by 1904 the establishment stood at eight: 'A' and 'B' at Southwark; 'C' at the Passmore Edward's Settlement, St Pancras, and the Marlborough Road Board School in Chelsea; 'D' at the Haileybury Club, Stepney; 'E', St Andrew's Institute, Westminster; 'F', St Peter's Institute, Pimlico; 'G, Bethnal Green and 'H' at the Eton Mission in Hackney. In 1904 battalion headquarters transferred to Union Street, Southwark.

**2nd Cadet Battalion Queen's (Royal West Surrey Regiment) (1890-1894)**—See 1st Cadet Battalion King's Royal Rifle Corps below.

**2nd Cadet Battalion Queen's (Royal West Surrey Regiment) (1901-1908)**—Raised at Peckham in October 1901 from boys of 1st Peckham Lads' Brigade which had been formed in 1894. Headquarters were at 53 Copeland Road, Peckham and the establishment six companies.

**1st Cadet Battalion East Surrey Regiment**—Formed with headquarters at 71 Upper Kennington Lane, London in 1890 with four companies. Disbanded in 1896

**1st Cadet Battalion King's Royal Rifle Corps**—Formed as 2nd Cadet Battalion Queen's (Royal West Surry Regiment) of four companies in November 1890. Headquarters were originally at the Lambeth Polytechnic, moving later to Kirkdale in Clapham, then to Brockwell Hall, Herne Hill. Increased to six companies in 1891 and in 1894 was re-designated as 1st Cadet Battalion KRRC. Headquarters at the same time moving to Finsbury Square EC London.

# Sussex

## Artillery Volunteers

The 1st Admin Brigade of was formed with headquarters in Brighton in June 1860 and included the several corps formed within the county. It was consolidated as the new 1st Corps in 1880.

**1st (1859-1880)**—Formed at Brighton on 19 November 1859. In the Army List for September 1864 the 4th Corps at Shoreham is shown as having been absorbed into the 1st. On the 14th July 1875, however, the Shoreham Battery was removed and once again appeared as 4th corps. The 1st soon reached a strength of eight batteries of which No 6 was formed entirely from railway workers. It was this battery which in 1894 manned the armoured train constructed for the corps by the London, Brighton and South Coast Railway Company that year. The train, which was the first of its kind, consisted of a railway truck armed with ½-inch steel plates upon which was mounted a 40-pdr breech loading Armstrong gun. Provided Nos 1 to 8 Batteries of the new 1st Corps in 1880.

**1st (1880-1908)**—Formed in 1880 by the consolidation of the 1st Admin Brigade. Headquarters remained at Brighton and the twelve batteries were organised as follows: Nos 1 to 8 Brighton (late 1st Corps), No 9 Fairlight (late 2nd Corps), Nos 10 and 11 Eastbourne (late 3rd Corps), No 12 Shoreham (late 4th Corps). In 1886 the corps was divided, and a new unit designated as 2nd Sussex AVC was formed with headquarters at Eastbourne. *Territorials:* 1st Home Counties Brigade RFA.

**2nd (1860-1880)**—Formed at Fairlight on 13 March 1860 and provided No 9 Battery of the new 1st Corps in 1880.

**2nd (1886-1908)**—Formed out of the 1st Corps in 1886 with headquarters at Eastbourne. The 2nd converted its six garrison companies to three position batteries in 1900. *Territorials:* 4th and 6th Sussex Batteries of the 2nd Home Counties Brigade RFA.

**3rd**—Formed at Hailsham on 15 May 1860, headquarters moving to Eastbourne in 1878. Provided Nos 10 and 11 Batteries of the new 1st Corps in 1880.

**4th**—Formed at Shoreham on 28 December 1860 and in September 1864 was absorbed into the 1st Corps. The Shoreham volunteers were withdrawn from the 1st in 1875 and from 14 July once again constituted the 4th Corps. Provided No 12 Battery of the new 1st Corps in 1880.

**Top: Waist-belt clasp, 1st Sussex Artillery Volunteers.**

**Left: Note paper crest, Sussex Artillery Volunteers.**

**Below: Armoured train, Sussex Artillery Volunteers.**

## Engineer Volunteers

**1st**—The 1st Sussex EVC was formed at Eastbourne on 24 May 1890, forming a cadet corps at Seaford in 1891, another at the University School Hastings in 1906 and a third at St Leonards Collegiate School in the following year. *Territorials:* 1st and 2nd Home Counties Field Companies and Home Counties Divisional Telegraph Company, all part of the Home Counties Divisional Engineers. Personnel were also provided for the Kent and Sussex Fortress Engineers. All three cadet units were eventually recognised by the Territorial Force and affiliated to the Home Counties Divisional Engineers.

## Light Horse Volunteers

**1st**—Formed at Brighton in August 1871 with Captain F Smith Shenstone in command. Disbanded in 1875.

**Cap badge, 1st Volunteer Battalion Royal Sussex Regiment.**

## Rifle Volunteers

Not all Sussex RVC were included in the county's admin battalions, some being placed with Cinque Ports. Of the three Sussex battalions that were formed, only the 1st would survive to produce a consolidated corps (the new 2nd) in 1880. The 2nd Admin Battalion, which was formed with headquarters at Petworth in April 1860, included at various times the 2nd, 5th, 6th, 7th, 8th, 13th 14th and 18th Corps. Headquarters were transferred to Horsham in 1869 and the battalion was merged with 1st Admin in 1874. Brighton was the headquarters of the 3rd Battalion, formed in April 1860 with 1st, 2nd, 4th, 5th, 16th and 19th Corps and broken up in 1863. There was also a 1st Sub-division which became the 7th Corps.

**1st**—Formed as two companies at Brighton on 23 November 1859 with R Moorsom, late of the Scots Fusilier Guards, and John Stuart Roupell as company commanders. Joined the 3rd Admin Battalion but,

having reached a strength of six companies, was withdrawn in 1863. Two new companies were added in 1886 and in the following year 1st Sussex RVC became 1st Volunteer Battalion Royal Sussex Regiment. A ninth company was added in 1900, the Brighton College Cadet Corps being affiliated in the same year. Christ's Hospital Cadet Corps joined in 1904, Cottesmore School (re-designated Brighton and Preparatory Schools in 1907) in 1905. *Territorials:* Transfer to the Territorial Force was to see the 1st Volunteer Battalion convert to artillery, but this was unpopular and the officers, having refused to comply, were then placed onto the unattached list. Brighton College and Christ's Hospital joined the OTC. The 1st VB eventually, in 1912, became 6th (Cyclist) Battalion Royal Sussex Regiment.

**1st Volunteer Battalion Royal Sussex Regiment.**

**2nd (1859-1880)**—Formed as two companies at Cuckfield on 2 December 1859 with George Meek and Warden Sergisen as company commanders. Joined the 3rd Admin Battalion, transferring to the 1st Cinque Ports Admin in 1863, 2nd Sussex Admin in 1870 and finally, 1st Admin Battalion in 1874. Became 'A' and 'B' Companies of the new 2nd Corps in 1880.

**2nd (1880-1908)**—The 1st Admin Battalion was formed with headquarters at Chichester in April 1860 and included the 8th, 9th, 10th, 11th, 12th and 15th Corps. Headquarters were transferred to Worthing in 1866 and the 2nd, 5th, 6th, 7th, 13th and 18th Corps were added from 2nd Admin Battalion in 1874. The battalion was consolidated in 1880 as the new 2nd Corps with eleven companies: 'A' and 'B' Cuckfield (late 2nd Corps), 'C' East Grinstead (late 5th Corps), 'D' Petworth (late 6th Corps), 'E' Horsham (late 7th Corps), 'F' Arundel (late 9th Corps), 'G' Chichester (late 10th Corps), 'H' Worthing (late 11th Corps), 'I' Westbourne (late 12th Corps), 'K' Hurstpierpoint (late 13th Corps), 'L' Henfield (late 18th Corps).

The 2nd Sussex RVC was designated 2nd Volunteer Battalion Royal Sussex Regiment in 1887 and increased to twelve companies in 1900. The St John's College, Hurstpierpoint Cadet Corps was affiliated in 1887; Lancing College at Shoreham in 1900; Ardingly College, Hayward's Heath in 1902. Volunteers served in South Africa during the Boer War, some eighty or more going out under Major, the Duke of Norfolk, Captain Sir Walter George Barttelot, lieutenants S W P Beale and B I D'Olier. Action was seen at Welkom Farm, the Zand River, Doornkop, Johannesburg, Pretoria and Diamond Hill. Sir Walter Barttelot was killed while leading his men at Retief's Nek on 23 July 1900 and one other man, a private, lost his life during the same action. *Territorials:* 4th Battalion Royal Sussex Regiment. All three schools at the same time joined the OTC.

**3rd**—None recorded.

**4th**—Formed as one company at Lewes on 25 January 1860 with Bernard Hussey-Hunt as captain, Inigo Gell, lieutenant and William Beard, ensign. The corps was with the 3rd Admin Battalion until 1863 when transferred to 1st Cinque Ports Admin. Became 'D' Company of the new 1st Cinque Ports Corps in 1880.

**5th**—Formed as one company at East Grinstead on 9 February 1860 with Alfred Robert Margary, late of the 54th Regiment, as captain, Arthur Charles Ramsden, lieutenant and William Alston Head, ensign. Joined the 3rd Admin Battalion, transferring to 2nd Admin, then to 1st Admin Battalion in 1874. Became 'C' Company of the new 2nd Corps in 1880.

**6th**—Formed as one company at Petworth on 8 February 1860 with Walter B Barttelot, late of the 1st Dragoons, as captain, the Hon Percy S Wynham, lieutenant and Viscount Turnour, ensign. Joined the 2nd Admin Battalion, transferring to 1st Admin in 1874, and became 'D' Company of the new 2nd Corps in 1880.

**7th**—Formed at Horsham on 29 November 1859 and known as 1st Sub-division until February 1860. The officers were Captain Manton Pipon, Lieutenant Sir John H Pelly and Ensign Henry Padwick, Jun. Joined the 2nd Admin Battalion, transferring to 1st Admin in 1874, and became 'E' Company of the new 2nd Corps in 1880.

**8th**—Formed as one company at Storrington on 16 February 1860 with Sir Charles Goring as captain, Brian Barttelot, lieutenant and George Curling Joad, ensign. Joined the 1st Admin Battalion, transferring to 2nd Admin by the beginning of 1861, then back with 1st Admin Battalion in 1874. Disbanded in 1876.

**9th**—Formed as one company at Arundel on 28 February 1860 with Henry Granville, Duke of Norfolk, as Captain, Thomas Evans, lieutenant and Reginald A Warren, ensign. Joined the 1st Admin Battalion and became 'F' Company of the new 2nd Corps in 1880.

**10th**—Formed as one company at Chichester on 1 March 1860 with George G Nicholls, formerly a lieutenant-colonel in the 90th Regiment of Foot, as captain, William L Reid, lieutenant and James Powell, Jun, ensign. Joined the 1st Admin Battalion and became 'G' Company of the new 2nd Corps in 1880.

**11th**—Formed as one company at Worthing on 10 March 1860 with Thomas Galsford as captain, Henry P Crofts, lieutenant and Edward Martin, ensign. Joined the 1st Admin Battalion and became 'H' Company of the new 2nd Corps in 1880.

**12th**—Formed at Westbourne on with Lieutenant J H Osmond commissioned on 23 April 1860. Joined the 1st Admin Battalion and became 'I' Company of the new 2nd Corps in 1880.

**13th**—Formed as one company at Hurstpierpoint on 14 March 1860 with William John Campion as captain, Henry Lane, lieutenant and Charles Gordon, ensign. Joined the 2nd Admin Battalion, transferring to 1st Admin in 1874. Became 'K' Company of the new 2nd Corps in 1880. Headquarters was in High Street, Hurstpierpoint, the premises still in use by the Army Cadet Force.

**14th**—Formed at Crawley on 14 March 1860 with John J Broadwood as lieutenant and John Lemon, Jun, ensign. Joined the 2nd Admin Battalion and was disbanded in 1863.

**15th**—Formed at Bognor on 9 April 1860 with Augustine Fitzgerald as lieutenant and O'Bryen Lomax, ensign. Joined the 1st Admin Battalion and was disbanded in 1865.

**16th**—Formed at Battle on 19 May 1860 with Boyce H Combe as captain, William E M Watts, lieutenant and Julian A Worge, ensign. Joined the 3rd Admin Battalion, transferring to 1st Cinque Ports Admin Battalion in 1861. Absorbed into the 1st Cinque Ports RVC in 1876.

**17th**—Formed at Etchingham on 4 June 1860 with Francis Reeves as lieutenant and James Brooker, ensign. Formed part of 5th Kent Admin Battalion for period May to November 1861, then to 1st Cinque Ports Admin. Absorbed into 1st Cinque Ports RVC in 1876.

**18th**—Formed at Henfield on 14 June 1860 with Percy Burrell as lieutenant and Walter W Burrell, ensign. Joined the 2nd Admin Battalion, transferring to 1st Admin in 1874, and became 'L' Company of the new 2nd Corps in 1880.

**19th**—Formed at Eastbourne on 6 October 1860 with Freeman F Thomas as lieutenant and John Francis Gottwaltz, ensign. Joined the 3rd Admin Battalion, transferring to 1st Cinque Ports Admin in 1861. Disbanded 1868.

**20th (1861)**—A 20th Corps is shown in the *Army List* with headquarters at Billingshurst for January 1861 but was removed in December 1861 having had no officers appointed.

**20th (1870-1876)**—Formed at Uckfield on 27 October 1870. Joined the 1st Cinque Ports Admin Battalion and was absorbed into the 1st Cinque Ports RVC in 1876.

# Tower Hamlets

## Artillery Volunteers

**1st**—Formed at Poplar on 26 September 1860, headquarters moving to Postern Row, Tower Hill in 1869. In August 1872 the 1st Tower Hamlets AVC attended its annual inspection and as a result of the report later submitted by the inspecting officer, Lieutenant-Colonel Woolsey, RA, was ordered to disband. Colonel Woolsey in his report told how men were turning up two hours late for the parade, guns and personnel were missing when required and out of an enrolled strength of 350, only 170 bothered to turn up at all. This was, however, an improvement on the year before when just 109 were on parade. Before dismissing the parade Colonel Woolsey addressed the men who took a full five minutes to come to order and silence. He told those present that on his

*Waist-belt clasp, Tower Hamlets Artillery Volunteers.*

time he had inspected many volunteer corps but had never before seen one so inefficient. 'For what purpose' he went on to say, 'the officers held commissions and the sergeants stripes I cannot conceive'. The men before him, he said, 'represented a mere mob.' Although many corps had been disbanded in the past due to a lack of efficiency and discipline, until now all had done so on their own accord. In the case of the 1st Tower Hamlets AVC, this was the first time that the War Office had ordered disbandment.

## Engineer Volunteers

**1st**—Formed 20 June 1861, this corps is shown in the Army List as having its headquarters at the Christ Church School Rooms in Cannon Street Road. A move was made, however, to Gretton Place, Victoria Park in 1865. Disbandment of the 1st Tower Hamlets EVC was announced in the *London Gazette* for 9 October 1868. That same year the 2nd Tower Hamlets EVC was formed, personnel from the 1st being absorbed into it by November.

**2nd**—The formation of a 2nd Tower Hamlets EVC was notified in the *London Gazette* dated 9 October 1868, personnel from the disbanded 1st Corps being absorbed before the end of the year. Officers' commissions were dated 3 October, the name of the corps being 2nd Tower Hamlets (East London) Engineer Volunteers. A cadet corps formed at Bedford Grammar School in 1888 was attached, but affiliation was transferred to the 1st Bedfordshire EVC in 1900. The 2nd Corps was redesigned as the East London (Tower Hamlets) Royal Engineers (Volunteers) in September 1900. *Territorials:* 1st and 2nd London Field Companies and 1st London Divisional Telegraph Company.

## Rifle Volunteers

Tower Hamlets, London's 'East End', comprised the several areas known as 'hamlets' about and within the Tower of London. Twenty-one in all, these were recorded in 1720 as: Hackney, Norton Folgate, Shoreditch, Spitalfields, Whitechapel, Trinity Minories, East Smithfield, Tower Liberty Within, Tower Liberty Without, St Katharine's, Wapping, Ratcliffe, Shadwell, Limehouse, Poplar, Blackwall, Bromley, Bow, Old Ford, Mile End and Bethnal Green. There was one admin battalion formed which, in 1880, provided the new 2nd Corps.

**Tower Hamlets Rifle Volunteer Corps.**

**1st Tower Hamlets Rifle Volunteer Corps.**

**1st (1860)**—A 1st Corps appeared in the Army List for April 1860. Dalston was given as its headquarters and provisions were made for four companies. No officers appear to have been gazetted and the corps disappeared before the end of the year.

**1st (Tower Hamlets Rifle Volunteer Brigade) (1868-1908)**—Formed as the 2nd Corps and soon comprised seven companies located: No 1 Hackney, No 2 Dalston, No 3 Bow, No 4, 5 and 6 at Poplar and Limehouse, No 7 Clapton. James Scott Walker, who was appointed as lieutenant-colonel in command, held a commission dated 6 April 1860. The original headquarters were at Arnold House, Richmond Road, Dalston, but were transferred by the end of 1860 to Pembroke Hall, Lamb Lane in South Hackney. One of the original officers was Captain Joseph D'Aguilar Samuda, the Jewish Thames shipbuilder. The 2nd Corps was amalgamated with the 4th Corps in 1868 under the title of 1st Tower Hamlets, The Tower Hamlets Rifle Volunteer Brigade. Headquarters were placed at Robert Street, Hoxton and the establishment of the new brigade was set at fifteen companies—seven from the 2nd Corps, eight from the 4th. With effect from 1 January 1874 the 1st Corps was amalgamated with the 6th of twelve companies at Dalston. Now with a combined strength of twenty-seven companies, it was ordered by the War Office that a reduction should be made to sixteen. The reorganisation went as follows: 'A' Company from 'A', 'L', 'M' and 'N' Companies of the 1st Corps, 'B' Company from 'A' and 'L' of 6th Corps, 'C' Company from 'B' of 1st Corps, 'D' Company from 'B' of 6th Corps, 'E' Company from 'C' and 'D' of 1st Corps, 'F' Company from 'C' and 'H' 6th Corps, 'G' Company from 'E' of 1st Corps, 'H' Company from 'D' of 6th Corps, 'J' Company from 'F', 'I' and 'K' of 1st Corps, 'K' Company from 'E' of 6th Corps, 'L' Company from 'G' of 1st Corps, 'M' Company from 'F' and 'G' of 6th Corps, 'N' Company from 'H' and 'J' of 1st Corps, 'O' Company from 'J' of 6th Corps, 'P' Company from 'O' of 1st Corps, 'Q' Company from 'K' of 6th Corps.

Headquarters of the new and enlarged 1st Corps were transferred to those of the 6th Corps at Shaftesbury Street, Dalston. There would be further reorganisations when in 1874 the War Office directed this time that the brigade should reduced its companies from sixteen to twelve. Regimental Orders of 28 November 1874 showed how this was achieved: 'A' Company to be formed by 'A' and 'P', 'B' Company to be formed by 'B', 'C' Company to be formed by 'O' and 'Q', 'D' Company to be formed by 'E' and 'C', 'E' Company to be formed by 'J', 'F' Company to be formed by 'F', 'G' Company to be formed by 'G', 'H' Company to be formed by 'H', 'J' Company to be formed by 'N', 'K' Company to be formed by 'K' and 'D', 'L' Company to be formed by 'L', 'M' Company to be formed by 'M'.

The corps appeared in the Army List as one of the volunteer battalions allotted to the Rifle Brigade from 1881. There would be no change in title until May 1904 when, having been transferred, 1st Tower Hamlets became 4th Volunteer Battalion Royal Fusiliers. A cadet corps was formed in 1885, but this disappeared from the Army List during 1891. The Tower Hamlets Brigade had formed a Machine Gun Battery in 1886 and it was this, under the command of Captain E V Welby, that formed the nucleus of the machine gun section of the City Imperial Volunteers in South Africa. Welby was mentioned in despatches and his sergeant, W J Park, received the Distinguished Conduct Medal. *Territorials:* 4th Battalion London Regiment.

**2nd (1860-1868)**—See 1st Corps (1868-1908).

**2nd (1880-1908)**—The 1st Admin Battalion was formed in May 1861 and to it were added the 3rd, 7th, 9th, 10th, 11th and 12th Corps. The battalion's first headquarters were those of the 3rd Corps at Truman's Brewery in Spitalfields, but after consolidation as the new 2nd Corps in 1880, a transfer was made to Whitechapel Road. The new 2nd Corps comprised eleven companies: 'A', 'B', 'C' and 'D' Stepney (late 3rd Corps), 'E', 'F', 'G' and 'H' Mile End (late 7th Corps), 'I', 'K' and 'L' Finsbury (late 10th Corps).

From 1881 the 2nd Tower Hamlets RVC is shown as being one of the volunteer battalions allotted to the Rifle Brigade, but there would be no change in title. Headquarters moved to Bow in 1894. *Territorials:* Part of 17th Battalion London Regiment.

**3rd**—Formed at Truman's Brewery, Spitalfields with Sir T F Buxton, Bt as captain, Charles Buxton, lieutenant and Thomas King, ensign. All three held commissions dated 4 May 1860. There would be three companies by June 1861 and four by 1863. Joined the 1st Admin Battalion. Subsequent headquarters were shown in the Army List as Great Garden Street, Whitechapel, from 1865, Granby Street in Bethnal Green, from 1870, and Quaker Street, Stepney from 1873. As part of the 1st Admin Battalion, 3rd Tower Hamlets RVC became 'A' to 'D' Companies of the new 2nd Corps in 1880.

**4th**—Formed at St Leonard's, Shoreditch with five companies, increasing to eight by 1868. Captain Henry A Bale was the first commanding officer, his commission being dated 14 June 1860. Headquarters were transferred to Robert Street, Hoxton in 1864, the corps being amalgamated with 2nd Tower Hamlets RVC in 1868. St Leonard's parish included Hoxton and Haggerston; the Church, from which it takes its name, is in Shoreditch High Street.

**5th**—Formed at Dalston with James McClissock as captain, Alexander Beath, lieutenant and James T Morland, ensign. All three held commissions dated August 1860. Headquarters were transferred to Kingsland in 1861 and the corps was disbanded in 1862. Dalston and Kingsland are twin localities located on the western side of Hackney, the area expanding rapidly after Dalston Junction station was opened in 1865.

**6th (North East London Rifles)**—Formed at Dalston and comprised eight companies by the beginning of 1861, Lieutenant-Colonel George Henry Money was appointed as commanding officer his, and all other original officers holding commissions dated 25 September 1860. No doubt much of this corps was found by those volunteers intended for the original 1st Corps. During 1861 headquarters transferred from Rosemary Street to Shaftesbury Street in Hoxton and in 1865 the corps became known as the North East London Rifles. Increased to ten companies, then to twelve in February 1866, and when amalgamated with the 1st Corps in January 1874 provided its 'B', 'D', 'F', 'H', 'K', 'M', 'O' and 'Q' Companies. A cadet corps was formed during the early years of the 6th Corps and was present at the Cadet Review held at the Crystal Palace on 11 September 1862. No mention of the unit, however, was made in the Army List.

**7th**—Formed at Mile End with George E Ludbrook as captain, John B Jenkins, lieutenant and Thomas J Ludbrook, ensign. All three held commissions dated 13 September 1860. Joined the 1st Admin Battalion and became 'E' to 'H' Companies of the new 2nd Corps in 1880.

**8th**—Formed with headquarters at the West India Dock, Poplar with Charles H Wigram as captain, Thomas H Sheppy, lieutenant and James G Clark, ensign commissioned on 7 November 1860. Robert G Tatham was appointed surgeon to the corps at the same time. Absorbed into the 26th Middlesex RVC in 1868.

**9th**—Formed with headquarters at London Dock House with Thomas Chandler as captain, John B Fisher, lieutenant and Samuel J Ball, ensign. All three held commissions dated 23 November 1860. Joined the 1st Admin Battalion and was absorbed into the 26th Middlesex RVC in 1864.

**10th**—Formed as two companies at Goodman's Fields with Captain George S Davies and Captain Joseph Hobbs commissioned as company commanders on 13 December 1860. Joined the 1st Admin Battalion, moving to Mile End Gate in 1861; Great Garden Street, Whitechapel in 1865; Chapel Street, Shoreditch in 1872 and Finsbury in 1874. Later increased to three companies and in 1880 became 'I', 'K' and 'L' Companies of the new 2nd Corps.

**11th**—An item in *The Times* for 5 December 1860 reported that at a meeting held at Zetland Hall in Mansell Street, Goodman's Fields the previous evening, it was decided to form a corps of rifle volunteers from London's Jewish population. Two companies were formed quite quickly, one commanded by Captain Barnett Lazurus, the other by Captain David Barnett. Both held commissions dated 21 February 1861.

Headquarters are given in the Army List as Goodman's Fields and by June 1861 the 11th Tower Hamlets RVC is shown as being part of the 1st Admin Battalion. Regarding the disbandment of the corps in 1864, Mr Harold Pollins writes in *The Bulletin of the Military Historical Society* for February 1998 that although the 11th had got off to a good start (it numbered 180 within three months of its formation) little interest had been shown from the Jewish community as a whole—their financial support was essential in as much as at the time funds were not provided by the government. More important, noted Mr Pollins, was talk of lax discipline and a general dissatisfaction among all ranks. Subsequently, all but one of the original officers resigned and, although others took their place, the 11th Tower Hamlets RVC was disbanded and removed from the Army List in August 1864.

**12th**—Formed as two companies at Stoke Newington with Captain Alfred Heales and Captain Richard W Merington as company commanders. All six officers held commissions dated 24 April 1861 and they were joined by Samuel Elwin Brand who was appointed as surgeon in May. Joined the 1st Admin Battalion in 1863 and was absorbed into the 1st London RVC in 1870.

**1st (Duke of Norfolk's Own) Cadet Battalion, The Rifle Brigade**—Formed in the Tower Hamlets area on 28 May 1904 with headquarters at Mile End. There were four companies, all being disbanded in 1906.

# Warwickshire

## Artillery Volunteers

**1st**—Warwickshire were without artillery volunteers, or at least its own corps, until 1900. In 1890 the 1st Worcestershire AVC, which included personnel from Monmouthshire, lost its Welsh batteries. To make up for the loss it would seem that the required new recruits were found from the Warwickshire area, as from 1892 the title of the corps appeared as the 1st Worcestershire and Warwickshire AVC. By 1900 the Warwickshire portion of the corps was sufficient in size to form a separate unit designated as 1st Warwickshire. The corps, which had an establishment of four position batteries with headquarters in Birmingham appeared for the first time in the Army List for June. *Territorials:* 3rd South Midland Brigade RFA.

## Rifle Volunteers

All corps outside Birmingham joined the 1st Admin Battalion which provided the new 2nd Corps in 1880.

**1st (Birmingham)**—Formed in Birmingham on 4 November 1859 and amalgamated with the 3rd and 6th Corps, also in Birmingham, in March 1860—Lieutenant-Colonel John W Sanders, late of the 41st Bengal Native Infantry was in command. The corps comprised twelve companies recruited from various sources. There was one formed by workers from several newspapers, one made up of gun makers, another of Scots resident in the city. In 1883 1st Warwickshire RVC became 1st Volunteer Battalion Royal

**1st Volunteer Battalion
Royal Warwickshire Regiment, 1906.**

153

Warwickshire Regiment. Four new companies were added in 1891, the battalion then being divided into two: 'A' to 'H' Companies (1st Battalion) and 'I' to 'Q' (2nd Battalion). A Cyclist Section was formed in 1894, this being increased to a full company in 1900. At Birmingham University in the same year, 'U' Company was formed from staff and students and this, in 1908, became part of the Senior Division OTC. *Territorials: 5th and 6th Battalions Royal Warwickshire Regiment.*

A cadet corps was formed in 1864 which, according to the published history of the corps, was raised by 'The Grammar School'. No mention of this unit, however, was made in the Army List after 1866. Another cadet corps appeared in 1883, this disappearing by the end of the following year having had no officers appointed to it. Next, in 1904, came the company formed at Solihull Grammar School, then in 1907, that raised by King Edward's School. Both schools became part of the OTC in 1908.

Mr J W Reddyhoff writing in *The Bulletin of the Military Historical Society* in November 1997 notes that the Freemason's Leigh Lodge of Rifle Volunteers No.1189 (later No.887) was formed from within the battalion on 1 November 1861.

**2nd (1859-1880)**—Formed as one company at Coventry with Captain John William Hartopp, late of the 17th Light Dragoons (Lancers), and Lieutenant Josiah Yeomans Robins commissioned on 8 November 1859. Richard Caldicott, Jun joined them as ensign on 2 January 1860. Absorbed the 6th and 7th Corps, also at Coventry, in 1862 and became 'A' to 'D' Companies of the new 2nd Corps in 1880.

**2nd (1880-1908)**—The 1st Admin Battalion was formed with headquarters at Coventry in May 1860 and consolidated in 1880 as the new 2nd Corps. There were twelve companies: 'A', 'B', 'C' and 'D' Coventry

**Officers, 1st Volunteer Battalion Royal Warwickshire Regiment.**

(late 2nd Corps), 'E' and 'F' Rugby (late 3rd Corps), 'G' Warwick (late 4th Corps), 'H' Stratford-on-Avon (late 5th Corps), 'I' Nuneaton (late 8th Corps), 'K' Saltley College (late 9th Corps), 'L' and 'M' Leamington (late 10th Corps).

Re-designated 2nd Volunteer Battalion Royal Warwickshire Regiment in 1883 and increased to thirteen companies in 1900. There was a reduction, however, to eleven by the end of the following year. The King's Grammar School, Warwick provided a cadet corps in 1885, as did Leamington College in 1900 and King's County School, Warwick in 1905. King's Grammar, which was renamed Warwick School in 1894, was not seen in the *Army List* after 1906, the Leamington cadets disappearing after a few months having had no officers appointed to it. *Territorials:* 7th Battalion Royal Warwickshire Regiment. Rugby and King's County Schools joined the OTC.

**3rd (1859-1860)**—Formed at Birmingham on 8 November 1859 and amalgamated with the 1st Corps in March 1860.

**3rd (1861-1880)**—Formed as the 4th Corps at Rugby with James Atty, late major of the 2nd Warwick Militia and 52nd Regiment of Foot, as captain, George Charles Benn, lieutenant and T Mave Wratislaw, ensign. All three held commissions dated 26 November 1859. Renumbered as 3rd in May 1861 and absorbed the 12th Corps, also at Rugby, as its No 2 Company in 1868. Much of the corps was recruited from within Rugby School which, in 1873, provided a cadet corps. Became 'E' and F' Companies of the new 2nd Corps in 1880.

**4th (1859-1861)**—See 3rd Corps (1861-1880).

**4th (1861-1880)**—Formed as the 5th Corps at Warwick with John Machen, late captain with the South Devon Militia, as captain; Richard Child Heath, lieutenant and Eugene Muntz, ensign. All three held commissions dated 13 February 1860. Renumbered 4th in 1861 and became 'G' Company of the new 2nd Corps in 1880.

**5th (1860-1861)**—See 4th Corps (1861-1880).

**5th (1861-1880)**—Formed as the 7th Corps at Stratford-on-Avon with Henry Perrott, late of the 59th Regiment of Foot, commissioned as captain on 9 February 1860. Edward Flower joined as lieutenant and William Henry Hunt, ensign in the same month. Renumbered 5th in 1861 and became 'H' Company of the new 2nd Corps in 1880.

**6th (1860)**—Formed at Birmingham on 8 February 1860 and amalgamated with the 1st Corps in March 1860.

Rugby School Cadet Corps.

Sergeant H Bates, 1st Volunteer Battalion Royal Warwickshire Regiment.

Lieutenant-Colonel J W Sanders, 1st Warwickshire Rifle Volunteer Corps.

**6th (1861-1862)**—Formed as the 8th Corps at Coventry with Captain Josiah Y Robins and Lieutenant James S Whittern commissioned on 15 June 1860. Alexander Rotherham joined them as ensign in July. Renumbered 6th in 1861 and absorbed into the 2nd Corps in 1862.

**7th (1860-1861)**—See 5th Corps (1861-1880).

**7th (1861-1862)**—Formed as the 9th Corps at Coventry with Richard Caldicott as captain, Thomas Darlington, lieutenant and David Hitchin, ensign. All three held commissions dated 31 October 1860. Renumbered 7th in 1861 and absorbed into the 2nd Corps in 1862.

**8th (1860-1861)**—See 6th Corps (1861-1862).

**8th (1861-1880)**—Formed as the 10th Corps at Nuneaton with Henry Dewes as captain, Craddock Towie, lieutenant and Thomas J Craddock, ensign. All three held commissions dated 1 December 1860; John B Nason was appointed as surgeon at the same time. Renumbered 8th in 1861 and became 'I' Company of the new 2nd Corps in 1880.

**9th (1860-1861)**—See 7th Corps (1861-1862).

**9th (1861-1880)**—Formed at the Saltley Training College with Captain Henry Harvey Chattock and Lieutenant Henry Howell commissioned on 29 June 1861. Became 'K' Company of the new 2nd Corps in 1880.

**10th (1860-1861)**—See 8th Corps (1861-1880).

**10th (1861-1880)**—Formed at Leamington with James Laurie Brown as lieutenant and Phillip Lant Parsons, ensign. Both held commissions dated 15 July 1861. Absorbed the 11th Corps, also at Leamington, as No. 2 Company in 1862 and became 'L' and 'M' Companies of the new 2nd Corps in 1880.

**11th**—Formed at Leamington on 3 April 1862 with John Machen as captain, Nathaniel Merridew, lieutenant and William R. Magrath, ensign. Absorbed into the 10th Corps as its No 2 Company in 1862.

**12th**—Formed at Rugby on 22 May 1868 with James S Phillpotts as captain, Francis E Kitchener, lieutenant and Henry L Warner, ensign. Absorbed into the 3rd Corps as its No 2 Company in 1868.

**1st Cadet Battalion Royal Warwickshire Regiment**—Formed as four companies at Birmingham in June 1886 and disbanded in 1893.

# Westmorland

## Rifle Volunteers

All corps joined 1st Admin Battalion which in 1880 became the new 1st Corps.

**1st (1860-1880)**—Formed as one company and a sub-division at Kirkby Lonsdale with Captain William Moore, who received his commissioned dated 29 February 1860, Lieutenants George Washington Ireland and Francis Fenwick Pearson, and Ensigns, Daniel Harrison and John Preston. Also appointed were Thomas Harper Whitaker as surgeon, and the Rev Edward Pigot who became chaplain. Became 'A' Company of the new 1st Corps in 1880.

**1st (1880-1908)**—The 1st Admin Battalion was formed at Kirkby Lonsdale in May 1860, headquarters moving to Kendal in 1861, and was consolidated as the new 1st Corps of nine companies in 1880: 'A' Kirkby Lonsdale (late 1st Corps), 'B' Appleby (late 2nd Corps), 'C' to 'E' Kendal (late 3rd Corps), 'F' Stavely (newly formed), 'G' Windermere (late 4th Corps), 'H' Ambleside (late 5th Corps), 'J' Grasmere (late 6th Corps)/

Re-designation as 2nd (Westmorland) Volunteer Battalion Border Regiment was notified in General Order 181 of December 1887. The Sedbergh School Cadet Corps was formed and affiliated in 1901 and the Kirkby Lonsdale Cadet Company in April 1902. *Territorials:* Four companies of 4th Battalion Border Regiment. Sedbergh School joined the OTC.

**2nd (1860)**—No location is given for the 2nd Corps which first appeared in the Army List for April 1860 with John Whitwell commissioned as captain on 6 March 1860. Captain Whitwell is later joined by

Lieutenant Harry Arnold, Ensign Cartmell Harrison, Chaplain, the Rev Frederick T Raikes, and Surgeon Robert Walker, all having been gazetted on 27 March. In September the five officers are now shown as a second company to the 3rd Corps at Kendal.

**2nd (1878-1880)**—Formed as one company at Appleby on 7 August 1878 and became 'B' Company of the new 1st Corps in 1880.

**3rd**—A two-company corps at Kendal appears in the Army List for the first time with a single officer, Captain William Wilson, having a commission dated 28 February 1860. George W Ireland and David Harrison are later shown as lieutenant and ensign respectively. The remaining officers required to complete the establishment are shown by September 1860 and were in fact those previously listed as forming the 2nd Corps. Later increased to three companies and became 'C' to 'E' Companies of the new 1st Corps in 1880.

**4th**—Formed as one company at Windermere with Captain George J M Ridehaigh commissioned on 29 February 1860. He was later joined by Edward W Yeeles as lieutenant and Thomas G Postlethwaite, ensign. Became 'G' Company of the new 1st Corps in 1880.

**5th**—Formed as one company at Ambleside with John R Peddar commissioned as captain on 28 February 1860. He was later joined by Lieutenant Robert Jefferson and Ensign John Bolton who were both gazetted on 30 March. Became 'H' Company of the new 1st Corps in 1880.

**6th**—The first officer recorded as belonging to the 6th Corps at Grasmere was Captain Augustus Ruxton who is shown with a commission dated 17 April 1860. Provisions are made in the Army List for one company and a sub-division. By August, however, Ruxton has been removed and his place taken by Captain Jasper Selwyn who has been joined by Lieutenant J Bousfield and Ensign Joseph F Green. The remaining two officers required to comply with a one-and-a-half-company establishment were not to appear and by the end of 1861 the 6th Westmorland Corps is shown as a single company. Became 'J' Company of the new 1st Corps in 1880.

# Wiltshire

## Mounted Rifle Volunteers

**1st**—Formed in April 1860 at Maiden Bradley with Captain Edward Adolphus Frederick in command. The corps had been raised from tenants of the Duke of Somerset's estate, Edward Frederick (Lord Seymour) being the Duke's eldest son. When disbanded in July 1861, what remained of the volunteers were absorbed into the 6th Wiltshire Rifle Volunteer Corps.

## Rifle Volunteers

The Wiltshire RVC were placed into two administrative battalions, these forming the new 1st and 2nd Corps in 1880.

**1st (1859-1880)**—It was at a meeting held at Salisbury's White Hart Hotel in May 1859, that the decision to form a body of Riflemen, to be called the Salisbury Rifle Corps, was taken. On 28 May the *Salisbury and Winchester Journal* gave notice that the names of those wishing to enrol were being taken, the paper also pointing out that all members would be expected to pay a sum not exceeding £3/10/0 for uniform. Subsequently, John Henry Jacob Esq was appointed as captain commandant with commission dated 10 August 1859. The War Office had sanctioned one company and a sub-division, the later having its headquarters near Downton and in August 1860 was increased to the strength of a full company with Captain Beverley Robinson in command. Drills were carried out in the Market Hall, Salisbury. The rifle range used by the corps was some distance from the city on the London Road. As part of the 1st Admin Battalion, 1st Wiltshire RVC became 'A' and 'B' Companies of the new 1st Corps in 1880.

**1st (1880-1908)**—The first Admin Battalion of Wiltshire Rifle Volunteers was formed with

**Pouch-belt plate, 2nd Volunteer Battalion Wiltshire Regiment.**

headquarters at Salisbury on 8 March 1861. In command was Lieutenant General P Buckley, MP for Salisbury, ex Guards officer and veteran of Waterloo. Headquarters moved to Warminster in 1879 and consolidation in 1880 was as the new 1st Corps with eight companies: 'A' and 'B' Salisbury (late 1st Corps), 'C' and 'D' Trowbridge (late 2nd Corps), 'E' Bradford-on-Avon (late 9th Corps), 'F' Warminster (late 10th Corps), 'G' Westbury (late 13th Corps), 'H' Wilton (late 14th Corps).

Became a volunteer battalion (without change in title) of the Wiltshire Regiment in 1881. A new company ('I') was formed from around the Tisbury and Mere areas in 1892 and 'K' (Cyclist) was raised at Bradford-on-Avon in 1900. A cadet corps was formed at Salisbury and affiliated to the corps in 1890, but this had disappeared from the Army List by the end of 1897.

*Territorials:* Headquarters and five companies of the 4th Wiltshire Regiment.

**2nd (1859-1880)**—Formed at Trowbridge with Mr Thomas Clark of Bellefield receiving his commission as captain on 16 February 1860. The 2nd Wiltshire RVC had received notification of its acceptance of service during the first week of December 1859. Captain Clark's brother, William Perkins Clark, became lieutenant and John Graham Foley, ensign. On 14 February 1861, Mr W Stancomb was commissioned as captain of a second company at Rood Ashton. Stancomb soon resigned, however, the Rood Ashton contingent being dispersed, and a new No 2 Company raised in its place at Trowbridge. As part of the 1st Admin Battalion, 2nd Wiltshire RVC in 1880 became 'C' and 'D' Companies of the new 1st Corps. The Trowbridge companies were chiefly made up of mill hands employed in the woollen industry.

**2nd (1880-1908)**—The 2nd Admin Battalion was formed with headquarters at Swindon in March 1861. Headquarters moved to Chippenham in 1864, a cadet corps was formed and affiliated at Marlborough College in 1870, and consolidation in 1880 was as the new 2nd Corps with twelve companies: 'A' Malmesbury (late 3rd Corps), 'B' Chippenham (late 4th Corps), 'C' and 'D' Devizes (late 5th Corps), 'E' Market Lavington (late 7th Corps), 'F' and 'G' Swindon (late 11th Corps), 'H' Melksham (late 12th Corps), 'I' Wootton Bassett (late 15th Corps), 'K' Swindon (late 16th Corps), 'L' Marlborough (late 17th Corps), 'M' Highworth (late 18th Corps), There was also a Sub-Division at Calne.

Reduced to eleven companies in 1882 and designated 2nd Volunteer Battalion Wiltshire Regiment under General Order 181 of December 1887. *Territorials:* Transfer to the Territorial Force in 1908 was as three companies of 4th Battalion Wiltshire Regiment. Marlborough College at the same time became a contingent of the OTC.

**3rd (1859-1880)**—Formed at Malmesbury on 28 January 1860 with William T Keene as captain, Charles Richard Luce, lieutenant and John Alex Handy, ensign. Joined the 2nd Admin Battalion and became 'A' Company of the new 2nd Corps in 1880.

**4th**—Formed at Chippenham on 16 February 1860 with Captain Daniel Hugh Clutterbuck in command. Joined the 2nd Admin Battalion and became 'B' Company of the new 2nd Corps in 1880.

**5th**—Formed at Devizes on 3 March 1860 with Captain J H Grubb as captain, Robert A Cochrane, lieutenant and John E Hayward, ensign. Joined the 2nd Admin Battalion and became 'C' and 'D' Companies of the new 2nd Corps in 1880.

**6th**—Robert Dwarris Gibney in his history of the 1st Wiltshire Volunteers records how the 6th Corps at Maiden Bradley was raised from among the tenants of the Duke of Somerset and was composed of men of a 'good position socially, and, as a rule, of means.' The duke's eldest son, Edward Adolphus Frederick,

Lord Seymour, was commissioned as captain commandant on 2 April 1860. He soon resigned, however, and was replaced in July 1861 by his brother Lord Edward Percy St Maur. It was at a meeting held at the Somerset Arms that the decision to form a corps in Maiden Bradley (to be called 'The Maiden Bradley Irregulars') was adopted. As previously mention, the recruits came entirely from the Duke of Somerset's Estate at Maiden Bradley. There were also members from his properties at Witham Friary, five miles distant, and seven miles off at Silton in Dorsetshire. In December 1865 Captain Lord Edward St Maur was killed by a wounded bear while hunting in India, his command later being taken by Lieutenant H B Festing. The 6th Corps formed part of the 1st Admin Battalion and absorbed the 1st Wiltshire Mounted RVC in July 1861. This had been associated with the 6th Corps since its formation. It was also located at Maiden Bradley and is referred to by Gibney in a manner that suggests at times both formations were one and the same. It would seem that after the death in September 1869 of Earl Seymour, interest in the 6th Corps fell off. Captain Festing later resigned his command, the accounts wound up, and an application for disbandment tendered. The corps was last seen in the Army List for January 1873.

**7th**—Formed at Market Lavington on 2 March 1860 with Simon W Taylor as captain, Charles Hitchcock, lieutenant and John B Wheeler, ensign. Joined the 2nd Admin Battalion and became 'E' Company of the new 2nd Corps in 1880.

**8th**—Formed at Mere, four miles north of Gillingham, with Captain William Chafyn Grove in command—the company's letter of acceptance of service being received on 16 April 1860. The Groves of Zeals House, whose estates included the town of Mere, were prominent in the raising of the corps and were responsible for the provision of its uniforms and equipment. Indeed, the 8th Wiltshire was recruited almost entirely from workers on the Grove lands, or its tenants. Captain Grove's commission was dated 1 May 1860 and the 8th Corps was included in the 1st Admin Battalion. Robert Dwarris Gibney in his history of the 1st Wiltshire Rifle Volunteers tells how interest in the corps began to fall off, the death of its founder and commander, William Grove, doing much to hasten its disbandment in 1875.

**9th**—Formed at Bradford-on-Avon after a public meeting held on 19 December 1859, the 9th Wiltshire had its first drill at Mr Spackman's Dye Works on 24 January 1860. The officers—Captain Henry S Pickwick, Lieutenant Burton W Foster and Ensign Alfred Bevan—were not commissioned until the 17 May 1860, this day coinciding with the first parade held by the company in uniform. As part of 1st Admin Battalion, the 9th Wiltshire RVC became 'E' Company of the new 1st Corps in 1880.

**10th**—The public meeting that led to the formation of the 10th Corps took place at Warminster Town Hall on 10 December 1859. Subsequently the services of the corps as one company were accepted, and in due course the Marquis of Bath took command with a commission dated 5 March 1860. William Davis, late of the 8th Light Dragoons, became lieutenant, Mr John Scott, ensign. Drills were usually held in the Corn Market, at other times on the town's cricket field—the first to be held in the blue-grey uniform of the corps taking place on 30 May 1860. For musketry the first range used was at Knapper's Hole on Parsonage Farm, but in 1861 better facilities were found about a mile outside of Warminster at Mancomb. The armoury was at the Town Hall to begin with, but this was later moved: first to a room at the Market, then to premises on the High Street. On 16 May 1860 the ladies of Warminster presented the corps with a silver bugle and a complete set of drums and fifes. In March of the same year a sub-division was authorised at Codford, John Ravenhill and Herbert Ingram being gazetted lieutenant and ensign respectively on 31 May. As part of the 1st Admin Battalion, the 10th became 'F' Company of the new 1st Corps in 1880. Always popular in Warminster, the corps were known locally as the Jolly Tenth.

**11th**—Formed as two companies at Swindon on 31 March 1860 with William F Gooch as captain, John S Fisher, lieutenant and William Batt, ensign. Joined the 2nd Admin Battalion and became 'F' and 'G' Companies of the new 2nd Corps in 1880.

**12th**—Formed at Melksham on 1 March 1860 and joined the 2nd Admin Battalion. Became 'H' Company of the new 2nd Corps in 1880.

**13th**—Formed at Westbury, four miles north-west of Wells, on 12 March 1860 with Ralph L Lopes as captain, Augustus Yockney, lieutenant and Justly William Awdry, ensign. Joined the 1st Admin Battalion and became 'G' Company of the new 1st Corps in 1880.

**14th**—Formed at Wilton, chiefly from tenants of the Earl of Pembroke, with Charles Penruddocke of Compton Park in command, his captain's commission being dated 24 April 1860. George Lapworth was appointed his lieutenant and J Woodcock his ensign, both with commissions dated 1 May 1860. The company's drills were, among other places, often held in the Riding School at Wilton. Musketry was carried out at a local area known as the 'Punch Bowl'. A feature of the company's badge was a representation of the shrine of St Edith of Wilton taken from the town seal. As part of the 1st Admin Battalion, the 14th became 'H' Company of the new 1st Corps in 1880.

**15th**—Formed at Wootton Bassett, six miles west of Swindon, on 18 June 1860, with Richard Bradford as lieutenant and Walter F Pratt, late of the 7th Lancashire Militia, ensign. Joined the 2nd Admin Battalion and became 'I' Company of the new 2nd Corps in 1880.

**16th**—Formed at Old Swindon on 13 July 1860 with James E G Bradford as lieutenant and Edwin R Ing, ensign. Joined the 2nd Admin Battalion and became 'K' Company of the new 2nd Corps in 1880.

**17th**—Formed at Marlborough, many of the members were from Marlborough College, on 27 July 1860 with Thomas B Merriman as captain; Francis E Thompson, lieutenant and Henry J Hillier, ensign. Joined the 2nd Admin Battalion and became 'L' Company of the new 2nd Corps in 1880.

**18th**—Formed at Highworth, six miles north-east of Swindon, on 24 November 1860 with William H Hitchcock as captain, Jeffery G Grimwood, lieutenant and Henry C Crowdy, ensign. Joined the 2nd Admin Battalion and became 'M' Company of the new 2nd Corps in 1880.

# Worcestershire

## Artillery Volunteers

**1st**—With headquarters at Worcester the 1st Corps was formed on 6 June 1865 and placed into the 1st Cheshire Admin Brigade. In 1866, however, the corps was transferred to the 1st Staffordshire Brigade. But this formation was short-lived and by August 1867 the Worcestershire Artillery Volunteers were back with Cheshire. In 1869 an admin brigade was formed for Shropshire and included in it was the 1st

Worcestershire AVC. That is until 1874 when it became attached, together with the 1st Monmouthshire AVC, to that in Monmouthshire. By 1878 the strength of the 1st Monmouthshire AVC was down to just two batteries and with this in mind it was decided to rename the Monmouthshire Brigade as 1st Worcestershire. The brigade had its headquarters in Worcester and in March 1880 was consolidated as the 1st Worcestershire AVC. The reorganisation went as follows: Nos 1 and 2 Batteries Worcester (late 1st Worcestershire), No 3 Battery Malvern (late 1st Worcestershire), No 4 Battery Worcester (late 1st Worcestershire), Nos 5 and 6 Balsall Heath (late 1st Worcestershire), Nos 7 and 8 Griffithstown (late 1st Monmouthshire). A cadet corps was affiliated in June 1884 having been formed at Malvern College that year.

Over the next few years several new batteries were raised in Monmouthshire and by 1890 that county's artillery volunteers were sufficient in numbers to form its own corps. In August 1890 the 1st Monmouthshire AVC was once again seen in the Army List. With the loss

**Worcestershire Artillery Volunteers.**

of the Monmouthshire batteries new recruits were then found from the Warwickshire area and from 1892 the corps appeared in the Army List as the 1st Worcestershire and Warwickshire. In 1897 the existing eight garrison companies were reorganised into four position batteries. But in 1900 the corps once again became known as the 1st Worcestershire, the Warwickshire batteries having grown large enough to form their own. *Territorials*: 2nd South Midland Brigade RFA. The Malvern College Cadets joined the OTC.

## Rifle Volunteers

Two admin battalions were formed which became the new 1st and 2nd Corps in 1880.

**1st (1859-1880)**—Formed as one company at Wolverley with Frederick Winn Knight as captain, Alfred John Hancocks, lieutenant and Augustus Talbot Hancocks, ensign. All three held commissions dated 1 November 1859. Joined the 1st Admin Battalion and became 'A' Company of the new 1st Corps in 1880.

**1st (1880-1908)**—The 1st Admin Battalion was formed with headquarters at Hagley on 24 April 1860 and to it were added the 1st to 9th, 16th and 20th Corps. Consolidated in 1880 as the new 1st Corps with eleven companies: 'A' Wolverley (late 1st Corps), 'B' Tenbury (late 2nd Corps), 'C' Kidderminster (late 3rd Corps), 'D' Kidderminster (late 4th Corps), 'E' Bewdley (late 5th Corps), 'F' Halesowen (late 6th Corps), 'G' Dudley (late 7th Corps), 'H' Stourport (late 8th Corps), 'I' Stourbridge (late 9th Corps), 'K' Oldbury (late 16th Corps), 'L' Kidderminster (late 20th Corps).

In 1882 a new company was added at Dudley and in the following year the corps was designated as 1st Volunteer Battalion Worcestershire Regiment. Headquarters were transferred to Stourbridge between 1885-1886, then to Kidderminster in 1891, 'A' Company moving to Dudley sometime before 1908. *Territorials*: 7th Battalion Worcestershire Regiment.

**2nd (1859-1880)**—Formed as one company at Tenbury with Anthony Charles Lowe as captain, William Norris, lieutenant and William McLaughin, ensign. All three held commissions dated 18 November 1859. Joined the 1st Admin Battalion and became 'B' Company of the new 1st Corps in 1880.

**2nd (1880-1908)**—Worcester was the headquarters of the 2nd Admin Battalion which was formed on 17 August 1860 with the 10th to 15th, 17th, 18th, 19th and 21st Corps. The battalion was consolidated in 1880 as the new 2nd Corps with eight companies: 'A' Worcester (late 13th Corps), 'B' Worcester (late 14th Corps), 'C' Great Malvern and Upton-on-Severn (late 11th and 19th Corps), 'D' Evesham (late 12th Corps), 'E' Droitwich (late 18th Corps), 'F' Pershore (late 10th Corps), 'G' Bromsgrove (late 21st Corps), 'H' Redditch (late 17th Corps).

The 2nd Worcestershire RVC was re-designated as 2nd Volunteer Battalion Worcestershire Regiment in 1883. A new company was sanctioned in 1900, but the battalion's establishment was back to eight companies in 1905. A cadet corps was formed and affiliated at the Victoria Institute, Worcester in 1903. *Territorials*: 8th Battalion Worcestershire Regiment.

**3rd**—Formed as one company with headquarters at Franche House, Kidderminster with Alfred Talbot as captain, John Dixon, lieutenant and Alfred Brinton, ensign. All three held commissions dated 17 January 1860. Joined the 1st Admin Battalion and became 'C' Company of the new 1st Corps in 1880. The Volunteer Drill Hall was in Birmingham Road.

**4th**—Formed as one company at Kidderminster with William Thomas Knapp as captain, George Adam Bird, lieutenant and Henry Goddard Mottram, ensign. All three held commissions dated 24 January 1860. Joined the 1st Admin Battalion and became 'D' Company of the new 1st Corps in 1880.

**5th**—Formed as one company at Bewdley with William N Marcy as captain, John Bury, Jun, lieutenant and George Beddoe, ensign. All three held commissions dated 2 March 1860. Joined the 1st Admin Battalion and became 'E' Company of the new 1st Corps in 1880.

**6th**—Formed as one company at Halesowen with Ferdinando D L Smith as captain and James P Hunt, lieutenant. Both held commissions dated 2 March 1860. The third officer, Ensign Jeston Homfray, was gazetted later in the month. Joined the 1st Admin Battalion and became 'F' Company of the new 1st Corps in 1880.

**7th**—Formed as one company at Dudley with Henry Money Wainwright as captain, Francis Sanders, lieutenant and Charles C Hewitt, ensign. All three held commissions dated 2 March 1860. Joined the 1st Admin Battalion and became 'G' Company of the new 1st Corps in 1880.

**8th**—Formed as one company at Stourport with Joshua Rogers as captain, Charles Harrison, lieutenant and Benjamin Danks, ensign. All three held commissions dated 2 March 1860. Joined the 1st Admin Battalion and became 'H' Company of the new 1st Corps in 1880.

**9th**—Formed as one company at Stourbridge with former 1st Dragoon Guards officer James Foster as captain, M P Grazebrook, lieutenant and Frank Evers, ensign. All three held commissions dated 2 March 1860. Joined the 1st Admin Battalion and became 'I' Company of the new 1st Corps in 1880.

**10th**—Formed as one company at Pershore with Henry Scales Scobel as captain, Thomas Skekell, lieutenant and Edwin Bail, ensign. All three held commissions dated 13 March 1860. Joined the 2nd Admin Battalion and became 'F' Company of the new 2nd Corps in 1880.

**11th**—Formed as a sub-division at Great Malvern with Sir Henry E F Lambert commissioned as lieutenant on 9 March 1860. Former Royal Navy officer L C H Tongue became ensign on 20 April. Joined the 2nd Admin Battalion and became part of 'C' Company of the new 2nd Corps in 1880.

**12th**—Formed as one company at Evesham with Benjamin Workman as captain, George Smythe, lieutenant and Thomas Nelson Foster, ensign. All three held commissions dated 13 March 1860. Joined the 2nd Admin Battalion and became 'D' Company of the new 2nd Corps in 1880. The corps also drew recruits from neighbouring Bengeworth who would have crossed the old stone bridge over the Avon to get to headquarters. Evesham is fifteen miles south-east of Worcester.

**13th**—Formed as one company at Worcester with James A Macnaught, lieutenant and Thomas L Smith, ensign the first to be commissioned on 10 April 1860. Their captain, Royal Navy lieutenant H McLeod, was gazetted three days later. Joined the 2nd Admin Battalion and became 'A' Company of the new 2nd Corps in 1880.

**14th**—Formed as one company at Worcester with John Parker commissioned as captain on 13 April 1860. His junior officers, Lieutenant John De Poise D Tyrel and Ensign Edward Green, were gazetted a week later. Joined the 2nd Admin Battalion and became 'B' Company of the new 2nd Corps in 1880.

**15th**—Formed at Ombersley with Lieutenant Robert Bourne and Ensign Charles Gardiner commissioned on 13 April 1860. Joined the 2nd Admin Battalion and disbanded in 1868.

**16th**—Formed as one company at Oldbury with Pynson W Bennett commissioned as captain on 13 April 1860. His junior officers, Lieutenant John Chambers and Ensign Arthur Wright, were gazetted in the following week. Joined the 1st Admin Battalion and became 'K' Company of the new 1st Corps in 1880.

**17th**—Formed as one company at Redditch with Robert Smith Bartlett as captain, William Baulton, lieutenant and Victor Milward, ensign. All three were commissioned on 4 May 1860. Joined the 2nd Admin Battalion and became 'H' Company of the new 2nd Corps in 1880.

**18th**—Formed as one company at Droitwich with Harry F Vernon as captain, John Blick, lieutenant and William H Clay, ensign. All three were commissioned on 15 June 1860. Samuel Rodenm MD joined them as surgeon in July. Joined the 2nd Admin Battalion and became 'E' Company of the new 2nd Corps in 1880.

**19th**—Formed as one company at Upton-on-Severn with George Tennant as captain, John W Empson, lieutenant and Charles Brandon, ensign. All three held commissions dated 6 November 1860. Joined the 2nd Admin Battalion and became part of 'C' Company of the new 2nd Corps in 1880.

**20th**—Formed with headquarters at Greatfield House, Kidderminster with John Dixon commissioned as lieutenant on 16 November 1860. Ensign Charles J Dixon was gazetted later in the same month. Joined the 1st Admin Battalion and became 'L' Company of the new 1st Corps in 1880.

**21st**—Formed at Bromsgrove with Captain Robert Bourne, late of the 54th Regiment of Foot, commissioned on 20 August 1861. His junior officers, Lieutenant Edward Dodd and Ensign Arthur B Shaw, were gazetted in the following October. Joined the 2nd Admin Battalion and became 'G' Company of the new 2nd Corps in 1880.

# Yorkshire East Riding

## Artillery Volunteers

The 1st Admin Brigade of Yorkshire (East Riding) Artillery Volunteers was formed with headquarters at Scarborough on 11 May 1860 and, in addition to the East Riding corps, later also included the 2nd and 3rd North Riding and 3rd West Riding. Brigade headquarters moved to Bridlington in 1866, then back to Scarborough three years later. Consolidation in 1880 was as the new 1st Corps.

**1st (1859-1869)**—Formed at Bridlington on 9 December 1859, this corps disappeared from the Army List and instead was shown as 6th. Headquarters of the 6th were also at Bridlington and one of its officers was previously listed with the 1st Corps. Provided No 2 Battery of the new 1st Corps in 1880.

**1st (1880-1908)**—Formed in 1880 by the consolidation of the 1st Admin Brigade. Headquarters remained at Scarborough and the batteries were organised as follows: No 1 Filey (late 2nd East Riding), No 2 Bridlington (late 6th East Riding), No 3 Flamborough (late 7th East Riding), Nos 4 and 5 Whitby (late 2nd North Riding), Nos 6 and 7 Scarborough (late 3rd North Riding), Nos 8 and 9 York (late 3rd West Riding). Headquarters were moved to York in 1888 but were again

**Waist-belt clasp, Yorkshire (East Riding) Artillery Volunteers.**

situated at Scarborough from 1895. *Territorials:* North Riding Battery of the 2nd Northumbrian Brigade RFA and the West Riding RGA.

**2nd (1860-1880)**—First appeared in the Army List for February 1860 as the 1st Section of Yorkshire (East Riding) AVC at Filey. The commission of the first officer was dated 9 February. In the next List (that for March) 2nd Corps is the title given. Provided No 1 Battery of the new 1st Corps in 1880.

**2nd (1880-1908)**—See 4th Corps.

**3rd**—Formed on 28 March 1860 from employees of the Hull Dock Company. The corps was later disbanded and last seen in the Army List for November 1860.

**4th**—Formed at Hull on 12 May 1860. A section of the 4th Corps was located at Hornsea and in 1865 this was removed to form a 5th. The 4th was not included in the admin brigade and at first consisted of eight batteries. In 1877 four new batteries were raised of which one was formed at the Old Foundry and another by the Hull Gymnastic Society. The corps was renumbered as 2nd in 1880. *Territorials:* 1st and 2nd East Riding Batteries and Ammunition Column of 2nd Northumbrian Brigade RFA.

**5th**—Formed 17 March 1865 from the Hornsea section of the 4th Corps. Disbanded towards the end of 1875.

**6th**—See 1st (1859-1869).

**7th**—Formed at Flamborough on 28 June 1869 and provided No 3 Battery of the new 1st Corps in 1880.

## Rifle Volunteers

It was originally intended to group the corps formed in Hull into an admin battalion numbered as 1st and those from outside the city to be grouped as 2nd. Both 1st and 2nd Admin Battalions did in fact exist, but by the end of 1860 the Hull companies had been merged as 1st Corps. At the same time 2nd Admin became 1st.

**1st**—Formed at Hull on 9 November 1859 and absorbed the 2nd, 3rd, 4th, 7th and 9th Corps, also in Hull, before the end of 1860. The Hull Rifles, as the 1st Corps became known, now comprised eight companies with Joseph Walker Pearce appointed as lieutenant-colonel on 11 August. Colonel Pearce was to hold his position for the next sixteen years, Walter Richards noting that the 1st Corps to him owed much, in particular the use of the Cyclops Foundry, in which he had an interest, for drill purposes. The 1st Corps was re-designated as 1st Volunteer Battalion East Yorkshire Regiment under General Order 63 of May 1883. The Hymers College Cadet Corps was formed and affiliated in 1900. *Territorials:* Transfer to the Territorial Force in 1908 was as 4th Battalion East Yorkshire Regiment. Hymers College at the same time joined the OTC.

**2nd (1859-1860)**—Formed at Hull on 24 November 1859 and absorbed into the 1st Corps in March 1860.

**2nd (1880-1908)**—Beverly was the headquarters of the 1st Admin Battalion which was formed in May 1860 and including all East Yorkshire corps outside of Hull. The battalion was consolidated as the new 2nd Corps in 1880 with six companies: 'A' Howden (late 3rd Corps), 'B' Bridlington (late 5th Corps), 'C' Beverley (late 6th Corps), 'D' Driffield (late 8th Corps), 'E' Market Weighton (late 9th Corps), 'F' Pocklington (late 11th Corps).

Re-designated as 2nd Volunteer Battalion East Yorkshire Regiment by General Order 63 of May 1883. *Territorials:* Four companies of 5th Battalion East Yorkshire Regiment.

**3rd (1860)**—Formed at Hull on 12 January 1860 and absorbed into the 1st Corps in March 1860.

**3rd (1860-1880)**—Formed at Howden, the first to be appointed to the 3rd Corps was Surgeon John Hartley whose commission was dated 28 March 1860. Captain Eric W Clarke, Lieutenant Thomas Carter and Ensign Edwin Storry joined him in the following June. Became 'A' Company of the new 2nd Corps in 1880.

**4th**—Formed at Hull with Charles Morgan Norwood as captain, John Joseph Thorney, lieutenant and George Hall Ringrose, ensign. All three held commissions dated 5 January 1860. John Fearne Holden was appointed surgeon. Absorbed into the 1st Corps by the end of the year.

**5th**—Formed at Bridlington with Thomas Prickett as captain, Thomas Harland, lieutenant and Joshua Barugh, ensign. All three held commissions dated 19 January 1860. Also appointed were John Allison as surgeon and the Rev Henry F Barnes, MA as chaplain. Became 'B' Company of the new 2nd Corps in 1880.

**6th**—The first officers to be appointed to the 6th Corps at Beverley were Captain Harold Barkworth, Lieutenant Richard Hodgson, Ensign Henry W Bainton and Surgeon Robert G Boulton. All four held commissions dated 28 February 1860. Became 'C' Company of the new 2nd Corps in 1880.

**7th**—Formed at Hull with Captain William Thomas White, Lieutenant Robert Blyth, Jun and Ensign Richard Glover. All three held commissions dated 3 March 1860. Henry Gibson was appointed as surgeon. Absorbed into the 1st Corps before the end of 1860.

**8th**—Formed at Driffield with Captain D Conyers, Lieutenant Thomas Hopper and Ensign Richard Botterill commissioned on 11 May 1860. At the same time the Rev James Skinner was appointed as chaplain and Alfred Scotchburn, surgeon. Became 'D' Company of the new 2nd Corps in 1880.

**9th (1860)**—Formed at Hull on 12 May 1860 and absorbed into the 1st Corps by the end of the year.

**9th (1860-1880)**—Formed as a sub-division at Market Weighton with William Langdale as lieutenant and John S W Kirkpatrick as ensign. Both officers held commissions dated 12 May 1860. Increased to a full company in June 1865 and became 'E' Company of the new 2nd Corps in 1880.

**10th**—Formed at Hedon with William Raines as captain, Arthur Iveson, lieutenant and Robert C Metcalfe, ensign. All three officers were commissioned on 8 November 1860. Disbanded in 1876.

**11th**—Formed at Pocklington with Lord Muncaster as captain, John Vade, lieutenant and John Kilby, ensign. All three officers held commissions dated 8 August 1868. Became 'F' Company of the new 2nd Corps in 1880.

# Yorkshire North Riding

## Artillery Volunteers

**1st**—Formed at Guisborough on 27 January 1860 with eight batteries, moving its headquarters to Middlesbrough in 1881. *Territorials:* Northumbrian (North Riding) RGA.

**2nd**—Formed at Whitby on 27 March 1860 and in the following year was attached to the 1st Admin Brigade of Yorkshire (East Riding) Artillery Volunteers. Provided Nos 4 and 5 Batteries of the new 1st Yorkshire (East Riding) AVC in 1880.

**3rd (1860)**—A 3rd Corps with headquarters at Middlesbrough appeared in the Army List for one month only, that for February 1860. No officers were shown.

**3rd (1861-1880)**—Formed at Scarborough on 20 May 1861 and attached to the 1st Admin Brigade of Yorkshire (East Riding) Artillery Volunteers. Provided Nos 6 and 7 Batteries of the new 1st Yorkshire (East Riding) AVC in 1880.

**Waist-belt clasp, 1st Yorkshire (North Riding) Artillery Volunteers.**

## Engineer Volunteers

**Tees Division Submarine Miners/Electrical Engineers**—Formed in 1886, the first officers being commissioned 27 November. Designated as Electrical Engineers in 1907. *Territorials:* North Riding Fortress Engineers.

## Rifle Volunteers

Two admin battalions were formed which provided the new 1st and 2nd Corps in 1880.

**1st (1860-1880)**—Formed as one company at Malton with William C Copperthwaite as captain, Thomas Walker, Jun, lieutenant, Thomas R Etty, ensign and Richard Junes as surgeon. All four held commissions dated 18 February 1860. Joined the 2nd Admin Battalion and became 'A' Company of the new 2nd Corps in 1880.

**1st (1880-1908)**—Headquarters of the 1st Admin Battalion, formed in July 1860, were at Richmond and to it were added the 2nd, 4th, 5th, 7th, 8th, 9th, 11th, 12th, 14th, 15th, 18th, 19th and 20th Corps. The battalion was consolidated in 1880 as the new 1st Corps with nine companies: 'A' Thornton Rust (late 4th Corps), 'B' Bedale (late 8th Corps), 'C' Stokesley (late 9th Corps), 'D' Catterick (late 14th Corps), 'E' Richmond (late No 1 Company, 15th Corps), 'F' Reeth (late No 2 Company, 15th Corps), 'G' Skelton (late 18th Corps), 'H' Northallerton (late 19th Corps), 'K' Guisborough (late 20th Corps).

Headquarters moved to Northallerton in 1883 and in the same year General Order 14 of February notified re-designation as 1st Volunteer Battalion Yorkshire Regiment. After a number of relocations, amalgamations, disbandments, and in 1884 the formation of a new company, by 1893 company locations were: Leyburn, Bedale, Stokesley, Catterick, Richmond, Skelton, Northallerton, Thirst, Guisborough and Wensleydale. The coming years saw further of the same, the companies by 1898 being at: Middleham, Bedale, Stokesley, Catterick, Richmond, Redcar, Skelton, Northallerton, Thirsk and Guisborough, and by 1908: Bedale, Eston, Stokesley, Catterick, Richmond, Redcar, Skelton, Northallerton, Thirsk and Guisborough. *Territorials:* 4th Battalion Yorkshire Regiment.

Although not actually serving with the battalion at the time, mention should be made of Colonel John Gerald Wilson, CB who died in South Africa on 9 March 1902 from wounds received the previous day. Colonel Wilson had commanded the 1st Admin Battalion from 1871 to 1883 and was with the 3rd Battalion York and Lancaster Regiment when he died. Both his son and brother also lost their lives in South Africa.

**2nd (1860-1863)**—Formed as one company at Swaledale on 18 February 1860 with Sir George William Denys of Draycott Hall, Richmond as captain, Edward Leopold Denys, lieutenant and J Simm Metcalf, ensign. John George McCollah was also appointed as surgeon. Joined the 1st Admin Battalion and was disbanded in 1863.

**2nd (1880-1908)**—The 2nd Admin Battalion was formed with headquarters at Malton in July 1860 and included the 1st, 3rd, 6th, 10th, 13th, 16th and 17th Corps. Headquarters were transferred to Scarborough in 1876 and in 1880 the battalion was consolidated as the new 2nd Corps with seven companies: 'A' Malton (late 1st Corps), 'B' and 'C' Hovingham (late 3rd Corps), 'D' and 'E' Scarborough (late 6th Corps), 'F' Helmsley-in-Ryedale (late 10th Corps), 'G' Pickering (late 16th Corps).

Under General Order 14 of February 1883 the 2nd Corps was re-designated as 2nd Volunteer Battalion Yorkshire Regiment. *Territorials:* Four companies of 5th Battalion Yorkshire Regiment.

**3rd**—Formed as one company at Hovingham with William Cayley Worsley as captain, Arthur Stevens, lieutenant and George Legard, ensign. All three held commissions dated 10 February 1860. Joined the 2nd Admin Battalion and became 'B' and 'C' Companies of the new 2nd Corps in 1880.

**4th**—Formed as one company at Leyburn with Simon Thomas Scrope, Jun as captain, Nathaniel Surtees, lieutenant, Thomas Mitchell Fryer, ensign and Thomas E Cockcroft as surgeon. All four held commissions dated 29 February 1860. Joined the 1st Admin Battalion, absorbed the 12th Corps at Thornton Rust in 1874, and became 'A' Company of the new 1st Corps in 1880.

**5th (1860-1871)**—Formed as one company at Forcett with John Mitchell as captain, William Swire, lieutenant, Charles R Robinson, ensign and William Walker as surgeon. All four held commissions dated 27 February 1860. Joined the 1st Admin Battalion and was disbanded in May 1871.

**5th (1871-1875)**—Formed at Gilling on 19 June 1871 from No 3 Company of the 15th Corps. Joined the 1st Admin Battalion and was disbanded in 1875.

**6th**—Formed as a sub-division at Scarborough, the first officers to be commissioned were Lieutenant Tindall Hebden and Ensign Harcourt Johnstone on 28 February 1860. Also appointed was William Taylor as surgeon. Joined 2nd Admin Battalion, increased to a full company in June 1860, two in 1867, and became 'D' and 'E' Companies of the new 2nd Corps in 1880.

**7th**—Formed as one company at Startforth with William Sawrey Morritt as captain, Morley Headlam, lieutenant and Arthur Brown, ensign. All three held commissions dated 29 February 1860. Joined the 1st Admin Battalion, transferring to the 4th Durham Admin in November 1863. In the following month the corps moved to the 2nd Durham Admin Battalion and at the same time was re-designated as 21st Durham RVC.

**8th**—Formed at Bedale with Lipton H Potts as lieutenant, Christopher Clarke, ensign and Robert Fothergill as surgeon. All three held commissions dated 19 March 1860. Joined the 1st Admin Battalion and became 'B' Company of the new 1st Corps in 1880.

**9th**—Formed as one company at Stokesley on 6 March 1860 with George Marwood as captain, James Emerson, lieutenant and John P Sowerby, Jun, ensign. Appointed at the same time was John H Handyside as surgeon. Joined the 1st Admin Battalion and became 'C' Company of the new 1st Corps in 1880.

**10th**—Formed as one company at Helmsley-in-Ryedale on 9 March 1860 with the Hon William Ernest Duncombe as captain, John Bower, lieutenant and John R Phillips, ensign. Joined the 2nd Admin Battalion and became 'F' Company of the new 2nd Corps in 1880. In the market place at Helmsley there was unveiled in 1869 a marble effigy of the second Lord Feversham, father of Captain Duncombe.

**11th**—Formed as one company at Masham on 17 March 1860, the first officers to be commissioned being Lieutenant Thomas Smurthwaite, Ensign James D R Fisher and Surgeon Midgley Cockcroft. Joined the 1st Admin Battalion, disappearing from the *Army List* in October 1866.

**12th**—Formed as one company at Carperby with Christopher Other as captain, Francis Chapman, lieutenant and James C Winn, ensign. All three were commissioned on 10 March 1860. Joined the 1st Admin

Battalion, moving headquarters to Thornton Rust in 1869, and was absorbed into the 4th Corps in 1874.

**13th**—Formed as one company at Thirsk, the first officers to be commissioned being Lieutenant Archibald Macbean, Ensign Edward D Swarbreck and Surgeon Thomas Haymes. All three were gazetted on 27 March 1860. Joined the 2nd Admin Battalion and was disbanded in 1868.

**14th**—Formed as one company at Catterick with Thomas C Booth as captain, John B Booth, lieutenant and John Feyer, ensign. All three held commissions dated 19 April 1860. Joined the 1st Admin Battalion and became 'D' Company of the new 1st Corps in 1880.

**15th**—Formed as one company at Richmond with Roper S D R Roper as captain, Leonard Jacques, lieutenant and William Robinson, ensign. All three held commissions dated 16 April 1860. Joined the 1st Admin Battalion and added No. 2 Company at Reeth, to the west of Richmond, on 9 March 1865; No. 3 at Gilling to the north, on 28 December, and No. 4 at Richmond in February 1868. No. 3 Company was made independent as 5th Corps in June 1871, the 15th becoming 'E' and 'F' Companies of the new 1st Corps in 1880.

**16th**—Formed as a sub-division at Pickering Lythe with James A Legard as lieutenant and John Hill, ensign. Both held commissions dated 4 May 1860. Later increased to a full company, the senior officer then listed as John R Hill who was gazetted as captain on 29 December 1860. Joined the 2nd Admin Battalion and became 'G' Company of the new 2nd Corps in 1880.

**17th**—Formed as one company at Pickering Lythe East on 28 April 1860 with Edward S Cayley, Jun as captain, Escricke J Inman, lieutenant and Reginald A Cayley, ensign. Also appointed was Archibald Meggett as surgeon. Joined the 2nd Admin Battalion, moving headquarters to Brompton west of Pickering on the road to Scarborough, in 1861. Disbanded in 1865.

**18th**—Formed as one company at Skelton with John T Wharton as captain, Thomas L Yeoman, lieutenant, Edward B Hamilton, ensign and Charles C E Hopkins as surgeon. All four held commissions dated 30 May 1860. Joined the 1st Admin Battalion and became 'G' Company of the new 1st Corps in 1880.

**19th**—Formed at Northallerton, the first officers to be appointed being Lieutenant Henry Rutson and Ensign William Fowle. Both held commissions dated 20 August 1860. Joined the 1st Admin Battalion and became 'H' Company of the new 1st Corps in 1880.

**20th (1860-1861)**—A 20th Corps with headquarters given as Whitby appeared in the Army List towards the end of 1860 but disappeared from the Army List in April 1861 having had no officers appointed.

**20th (1863-1880)**—Formed as one company at Guisborough with William Weatherill as captain, William O Garbutt, lieutenant, William K Weatherill, ensign and George S Morris as surgeon. All four held commissions dated 3 February 1863. Joined the 1st Admin Battalion and became 'K' Company of the new 1st Corps in 1880.

**21st**—Formed as two companies at Middlesbrough on 13 October 1877 with Captain Walter Johnson, late of the 2nd Dragoons, in command. Joined the 4th Durham Admin Battalion and became 'G' and 'H' Companies of the new 1st Durham RVC in 1880.

# Yorkshire West Riding

## Artillery Volunteers

The 1st Admin Brigade was formed with headquarters at Bradford on 21 March 1864 with all but the 3rd Corps included. The brigade was consolidated as the new 1st Corps in 1880.

**1st**—Formed at Leeds on 2 August 1860. *Territorials: 1st West Riding Brigade RFA.*

**2nd (1860-1880)**—Formed at Bradford on 10 October 1860 and also included batteries at Bowling and Heckmondwike. In 1864 the Bowling Battery was removed to form a 5th Corps. Heckmondwike was also to leave, this time to form a 6th Corps in 1867. Upon disbandment of the 6th Corps in 1875, the

Heckmondwike personnel were returned to the 2nd. Provided Nos 1 to 6 Batteries of the new 2nd Corps in 1880.

**2nd (1880-1908)**—Formed in 1880 by the consolidation of the 1st Admin Brigade. Headquarters remained at Bradford and the batteries were organised as follows: Nos 1 to 4 Bradford (late 2nd Corps), Nos 5 to 6 Heckmondwike (late 2nd Corps), Nos 7 and 8 Halifax (late 8th Corps). *Territorials:* 2nd West Riding Brigade RFA.

**3rd**—Formed at York on 9 February 1861 and included in the 1st East Yorkshire Admin Brigade. Became Nos 8 and 9 Batteries of the new 1st East Riding AVC in 1880.

**4th**—Formed at Sheffield on 6 February 1861 and was allowed to include the name of its headquarters in its title from 1864. *Territorials:* 3rd West Riding Brigade RFA.

**5th**—Formed from the Bowling Battery of the 2nd Corps in 1864. A new battery was raised at Batley in 1866 and this was removed in the following year to form a 7th Corps. The 5th was disbanded in 1874.

**6th**—Formed at Heckmondwike from members of the 2nd Corps and was first seen in the Army List for June 1867. Absorbed back into the 2nd in 1875.

**7th**—Formed on 2 October 1866 as No 2 Battery of the 5th Corps and was removed to form the 7th in the following year. Disbanded in August 1877.

**8th**—Formed at Halifax on 19 May 1871 and provided Nos 7 and 8 Batteries of the new 2nd Corps in 1880.

**1st Yorkshire (West Riding) Artillery Volunteers.**

## Engineer Volunteers

**1st**—Formed at the Sheffield School of Art 8 November 1860, 'Sheffield' forming part of the title from 1884. A cadet corps was formed and attached which appeared in the Army List between September 1872 and September 1880. Another was formed in 1883, but this also disappeared, making its last appearance before the end of 1884. Wesley College provided a cadet corps in 1890, the college being renamed as the King Edward VII College in 1907.

**2nd Yorkshire (West Riding) Engineer Volunteers.**

*Territorials:* 1st and 2nd West Riding Field Companies and West Riding Divisional Telegraph Company.

**2nd**—Formed at Leeds 25 March 1861, 'Leeds' being permitted as part of the title from 1864. *Territorials:* Northern Wireless, Air-Line and Cable Telegraph Companies, 10th and 11th West Riding Batteries, Royal Field Artillery and the Yorkshire Mounted Brigade Transport and Supply Column, Army Service Corps.

## Rifle Volunteers

Five Admin Battalions were formed which, in 1880, became the new 1st, 5th, 6th, 8th and 9th Corps. There was also a 1st Sub-division which became the 15th Corps.

**1st (1859-1880)**—The services of the 1st Corps at York were accepted on 5 September 1859, a former major of the 1st Dragoons Guards, George Briggs, being appointed as captain commandant with commission dated 10 February 1860. Four companies were soon formed, the last of which was raised by St Peter's School. Joined the 1st Admin Battalion, a No 5 Company being raised in the early part of 1862. For details of this corps, and others in the West Riding, a reliable source comes in the form of *West York Rifle Volunteers 1859-1887* by K D Pickup. In the 1st Corps section he records how in the early days drills were held at three separate locations, St Leonard's Place, Parliament Street and Lowther Street. At a cost of £1,700, the old Sand Hill Hotel in Colliergate was purchased in 1871 and after much building work, a new drill hall was opened there in December 1872. Became 'A' to 'E' Companies of the new 1st Corps in 1880.

**1st (1880-1908)**—York was the headquarters of the 1st Admin Battalion which was formed in May 1860 and included the 1st, 16th, 17th, 27th, 31st, 33rd and 38th Corps. The battalion was consolidated in 1880 as the new 1st Corps with eleven companies: 'A', 'B', 'C', 'D' and 'E' York (late 1st Corps), 'F' Harrogate (late 16th Corps), 'G' Knaresborough (late 17th Corps), 'H' and 'J' Ripon (late 27th Corps), 'K' Tadcaster (late 31st Corps), 'L' Selby (late 38th Corps).

Under General Order 181 of December 1887 the 1st Corps was re-designated as 1st Volunteer Battalion West Yorkshire Regiment. A new company was added in 1900 and by 1908 companies were located at: York (5), Harrogate (2), Knaresborough (1), Ripon (2), Pateley Bridge (1) and Selby (1). *Territorials:* 5th Battalion West Yorkshire Regiment.

**2nd (Hallamshire)**—According to Bartholomew's *Survey Gazetteer of the British Isles,* Hallamshire is an 'ancient lordship of the West Riding of Yorkshire'. It is mentioned in the *Doomsday Book* and is represented by the parishes of Sheffield and Ecclesfield. It was in Sheffield on 30 September 1859 that three separate

Shako badge,
3rd Yorkshire (West Riding)
Rifle Volunteer Corps.

7th Yorkshire
(West Riding) Rifle
Volunteer Corps.

Glengarry badge,
2nd Volunteer Battalion
West Yorkshire Regiment.

companies were formed and designated as 2nd, 3rd and 4th Yorkshire West Riding RVC, the three being amalgamated by the end of the year under the new title of 2nd Yorkshire West Riding (Hallamshire) RVC and the command of Major Wilson Overend—his commission dated 22 December 1859. At the same time as the merger took place an additional company was raised, yet another being added when No 5 was formed from employees of the Atlas Works. The establishment of the 2nd Corps would reach seven companies by the end of 1861. Re-designation as 1st (Hallamshire) Volunteer Battalion York and Lancaster Regiment was notified by General Order 14 of February 1883. *Territorials:* 4th Battalion York and Lancaster Regiment.

**3rd (1859)**—Formed at Sheffield on 30 September 1859 and by end of year had amalgamated with the 2nd Corps as its No 2 Company.

**3rd (1859-1908)**—On 27 September 1859 two independent companies were formed in Bradford and designated as 5th and 6th Corps. In February of the following year, together with other Bradford companies hitherto un-numbered, the two were merged as 5th Corps. By April 1860, however, the new corps had been numbered as 3rd, its establishment being four companies with Major Commandant Samuel Cunliffe Lister in command. Absorbed the 24th Corps at Eccleshill as No.5 Company in October 1860. Now eight companies strong, in 1887, under General Order 181 of December, the 3rd Corps was re-designated as 2nd Volunteer Battalion West Yorkshire Regiment. A Cyclist company was added in 1900, the first Volunteers from the battalion in that year sailing for South Africa and active service in the Boer War. Captain J L McLaren, who was commissioned on 27 January 1897, died of phthisis on 12 March 1902 while serving with the Imperial Yeomanry. *Territorials:* 6th Battalion West Yorkshire Regiment.

**4th (1859)**—Formed at Sheffield on 30 September 1859 and by end of year had amalgamated with the 2nd Corps as its No 3 Company.

**4th (1860-1908)**—The original 7th and 8th Corps were both formed at Halifax on 13 October 1859. These were shortly followed by the 13th and 14th, also in Halifax, and on 24 February 1860 the four companies were amalgamated as 7th Corps, but renumbered, however, as 4th on 27 April. Major Commandant Edward Akroyd of Bank Field, Harley Hill, took command. A No 5 Company was added at Sowerby in 1861 and new companies later following at Brighthouse, Hebden Bridge and Upper Shibden Hall. Reduced now to six companies, the 4th Corps was designated as 1st Volunteer Battalion Duke of Wellington's Regiment in 1883 and by 1908 located: four companies at Halifax and one each at Brighthouse and Check Heaton. *Territorials:* 4th Battalion Duke of Wellington's Regiment.

The Akroyd Museum and Art Gallery at Harley Hill was opened in 1886 in the former seat of

Edward Akroyd, the first commanding officer.

**5th (1859-1860)**—See 3rd Corps (1860-1908).

**5th (1860-1880)**—Formed as the 9th Corps at Wakefield with J Hulme Holdsworth as captain, John Barff Charlesworth, lieutenant and George William Alder, ensign. All three held commissions dated 17 November 1859. They were later joined by Edward Waddington, MD who had been appointed as surgeon. Joined the 3rd Admin Battalion and renumbered as 5th by July 1860, the corps soon comprised three companies: the 1st was formed by tradesmen, the 2nd by clerks and the 3rd by working men. A 4th was later added and in 1880 the old 5th Corps became 'A' to 'D' Companies of the new 5th Corps.

**5th (1880-1908)**—Formed in June 1860 with headquarters at Wakefield, the 3rd Admin Battalion included the 5th, 28th, 29th, 30th, 37th, 38th and 43rd Corps and was consolidated in 1880 as the new 5th with ten companies: 'A', 'B', 'C' and 'D' Wakefield (late 5th Corps), 'E' Goole (late 28th Corps), 'F', 'G' and 'H' Dewsbury (late 29th Corps), 'J' and 'K' Batley (late 43rd Corps).

Re-designated as 1st Volunteer Battalion King's Own Light Infantry (South Yorkshire Regiment) in February 1883, the regiment itself being re-designated King's Own Yorkshire Light Infantry in 1887. Company locations by 1908 were: Wakefield (3), Normanton (1), Goole (1), Dewsbury (2), Ossett (1) and Batley (2). *Territorials:* Transfer to the Territorial Force in 1908 saw the Wakefield, Dewsbury, Ossett and Batley companies as 4th Battalion King's Own (Yorkshire Light Infantry), while those from Normanton and Goole provided part of the 5th.

**6th (1859-1860)**—See 3rd (1860-1908).

**6th (The Huddersfield) (1860-1880)**—The services of a corps at Huddersfield were accepted on 3 November 1859, the number received being 10th, but this was changed to 6th Corps in July 1860. The corps, which joined the 5th Admin Battalion, soon comprised four companies with Captain Henry Frederick Beaumont in command. No 5 was added in 1864 followed in 1868 by No 6 at Outlane, four miles north-west of Huddersfield, No 7 at Lindley and No 8 at headquarters. The Lindley company was recruited mostly from the several manufacturing firms in the area. Also in 1868, The Huddersfield was added to title. Sometime during the 1870s four companies were lost, leaving the 6th to provide 'A' to 'D' Companies of the new 6th Corps in 1880. The woollen trade employed many in Huddersfield, the machinery for those mills, as well as locomotive boilers, being made in the town's several foundries. Silk spinning also went on, No 3 Company of the corps being almost entirely recruited from workers at three firms: Leonard & Sons, Day & Sons, and E T Monk & Co.

**6th (1880-1908)**—Formed with headquarters in Huddersfield on 18 September 1862, the 5th Admin Battalion included the 6th, 32nd, 34th, 41st and 44th Corps. The battalion was consolidated in 1880 as the new 6th Corps with ten companies: 'A', 'B', 'C' and 'D' Huddersfield (late 6th Corps), 'E' Holmfirth (late 32nd Corps), 'F', 'G', 'H' and 'J' Saddleworth (late 34th Corps), 'K' Mirfield (late 41st Corps).

Designated as 2nd Volunteer Battalion Duke of Wellington's Regiment in February 1883, headquarters at this time being at The Armoury in Ramsden Street. A new company was raised at Huddersfield in 1900. *Territorials:* Part of both the 5th and 7th Battalions Duke of Wellington's Regiment.

**7th (1859-1860)**—See 4th Corps (1860-1908).

**7th (Leeds) (1860-1908)**—On 17 November 1859 the first company of the Leeds Rifle Volunteers was formed within the city. This was numbered as the 11th Corps, which by March 1860 consisted of five companies with Major William J Armitage in command. In May 1860 the 22nd Corps, also in Leeds, was absorbed, but this brought about no increases in establishment. By 1861, however, an additional four companies had been raised. Of these No 6 was provided by the Monkbridge Steel Company (one of its directors, Frederick W Kitson becoming commanding officer), No 7 by Fairbairn's Wellington Foundry (Andrew Fairburn as captain), No 8 from men at Messrs Greenwood & Bailey (Thomas G Greenwood as captain, George G Greenwood, ensign) and No 9, which was recruited from Messrs Joshua Tetley's Brewery (Francis W Tetley in command). The last company to be formed was in August 1875, this brining the

establishment up to ten companies which remained the strength of the corps until 1908.

As a result of the amalgamation during the early part of 1860 between the Halifax Corps, the 7th position in the West Riding list became vacant. This was filled by the 11th Corps on 3 July 1860. In 1864 the additional title Leeds was added, the next change being as 3rd Volunteer Battalion West Yorkshire Regiment in December 1887. Of the Volunteers from the battalion that saw active service in South Africa, Lieutenant Sydney Arthur Slater died from enteric fever while serving with the Imperial Yeomanry on 29 January 1901. For an action at Bultfontein in September 1900, he was awarded the Distinguished Service Order. There is a plaque in his honour at Giggleswick School near Settle. *Territorials:* 7th and 8th Battalions West Yorkshire Regiment.

**8th (1859-1860)**—See 4th Corps (1860-1908).

**8th (1880-1908)**—Formed with headquarters at Doncaster in August 1860, the 4th Admin Battalion included the 18th, 19th, 20th, 21st, 36th, 37th and 40th Corps. Consolidated in 1880, the battalion formed the new 8th Corps with nine companies: 'A' Pontefract (late 18th Corps), 'B' Rotherham (late 19th Corps), 'C' Doncaster (late 20th Corps), 'D' Doncaster (late 21st Corps), 'E' Rotherham (late 19th Corps), 'F' Barnsley (late 37th Corps), 'G' Wath-upon-Dearne (late 40th Corps), 'H' Barnsley (late 37th Corps), 'J' Rotherham (late 36th Corps).

Re-designated as 2nd Volunteer Battalion York and Lancaster Regiment in February 1883. A new company was added in 1884 and a cadet corps was affiliated at Rotherham in 1894. This, however, had disappeared from the Army List during 1899. Two new companies were added in 1900, and company locations by 1908 were: Pontefract, Rotherham (3), Doncaster (5), Barnsley (2) and Wath-upon-Dearne. *Territorials:* Transfer to the Territorial Force in 1908 saw the Rotherham, Barnsley and Wath-upon-Dearne personnel to the 5th Battalion York and Lancaster Regiment, while those from Doncaster and Pontefract formed part of the 5th Battalion King's Own Yorkshire Light Infantry.

**9th (1859-1860)**—See 5th Corps (1860-1880).

**9th (1880-1908)**—Formed with headquarters at Skipton-in-Craven in June 1860, the 2nd Admin Battalion included the 12th, 15th, 23rd, 25th, 26th, 35th, 42nd and 45th Corps. The battalion was consolidated as the new 9th Corps in 1880 with eight companies: 'A' Skipton-in-Craven (late 12th Corps), 'B' Settle (late 15th Corps), 'C' Burley (late 23rd Corps), 'D', 'E' and 'F' Keighley (late 35th Corps), 'G' Haworth (late 42nd Corps), 'H' Bingley (late 45th Corps).

Re-designated as 3rd Volunteer Battalion Duke of Wellington's Regiment in February 1883, new companies being added in 1884 and 1900. *Territorials:* 6th Battalion Duke of Wellington's Regiment.

**10th**—See 6th Corps (1859-1880).

**11th**—See 7th Corps (1860-1908).

**12th**—Formed as one company at Skipton-in-Craven with Matthew Wilson as captain, George Robinson, lieutenant and Henry Alcock, Jun, ensign. All three held commissions dated 8 February 1860. Joined the 2nd Admin Battalion and became 'A' Company of the new 9th Corps in 1880. Matthew Wilson became the commanding officer of the 2nd Admin Battalion in August 1860.

**13th**—See 4th Corps (1860-1908).

**14th**—See 4th Corps (1860-1908).

**15th**—Formed with Walter Morrison as lieutenant and John Ingleby, ensign. Their commissions were dated 17 November 1859 and the corps was known as the 1st Sub-division until March 1860. James J Luce was appointed as surgeon about the same time. Joined the 2nd Admin Battalion and became 'B' Company of the new 9th Corps in 1880. The early Army Lists show the 15th Corps as being at North Craven; later issues, however, give the more accurate headquarters location of Settle.

**16th**—Formed as one company at Harrogate on 21 February 1860 with John James Harrison as captain, J Holt, lieutenant and Henry Drury, ensign. All three held commissions dated 21 February 1860. In March, William H England was appointed as surgeon. Joined the 1st Admin Battalion and became 'F' Company of the new 1st Corps in 1880. K D Pickup notes how the 16th and the 17th Corps were both unofficially referred to as the Claro Rifles. Harrogate, Knaresborough and Wetherby (33rd Corps) were within the Claro 'Wapentake'—a northern and midland term for a sub-division of a county, rather like a 'hundred' elsewhere.

**17th**—Formed as one company at Knaresborough with Samuel James Brown as captain, Charles John Radcliffe, lieutenant and Ralph O Hodgson, ensign. All three held commissions dated 27 February 1860. Joined the 1st Admin Battalion and became 'G' Company of the new 1st Corps in 1880.

**18th**—Formed as one company at Pontefract with Richard T Lee as captain, Charles C Templer, lieutenant and James Robson, ensign. All three held commissions dated 3 March 1860 and they were joined by Joshua H Simpson, who was appointed as surgeon, and the Rev Richard Stainforth who was appointed as chaplain. Joined the 4th Admin Battalion and became 'A' Company of the new 8th Corps in 1880.

**19th**—Formed as one company at Rotherham with George Wilton Chambers as captain, Arthur Hirst, lieutenant and William Hirst, ensign. All three held commissions dated 29 February 1860. Joined the 4th Admin Battalion and became 'B' and 'E' Companies of the new 8th Corps in 1880. K D Pickup in his book *West York Rifle Volunteers 1859-1887* shows a plan for a drill hall at Rotherham, the work being completed in 1873 at Wharncliffe Street. According to a letter signed by the commanding officers of the 19th and 36th Corps (the latter also at Rotherham) it would seem that both companies were using, prior to the new hall being opened, the Court House and Corn Exchange.

**20th**—Formed at Doncaster with Archibald Sturrock as captain, James Payne, lieutenant and Richard C Hornby, ensign. All three held commissions dated 5 March 1860. Joined the 4th Admin Battalion and became 'C' Company of the new 8th Corps in 1880. K D Pickup notes how Captain Sturrock of Elmfield Park House was a railway official at Doncaster [the Great Northern Railway Company then] and that the majority of the 20th were recruited from his staff.

**21st**—Formed at Doncaster with Henry F Pilkington as captain, William E Smith, lieutenant and John W S Collinson, ensign. All three held commissions dated 5 March 1860. Joined the 4th Admin Battalion and became 'D' Company of the new 8th Corps in 1880.

**22nd**—Formed at Leeds on 29 February 1860 and absorbed into the 11th Corps in the following May.

**23rd**—Formed as one company at Burley-in-Wharfedale, ten miles north of Bradford, with William Edward Foster as captain, William Macleod, lieutenant and Edward Hirst Hudson, ensign. All three held commissions dated 20 February 1860. Thomas Scott, MD was appointed as surgeon. The company was requited from employees at Captain Foster's mill. Joined the 2nd Admin Battalion and became 'C' Company of the new 9th Corps in 1880.

**24th**—Formed at Eccleshill, ten miles west of Leeds, with Benjamin Farrer as lieutenant and William Yewdall, ensign. Both held commissions dated 27 February 1860. Absorbed into the 3rd Corps as its No 5 Company in October 1860.

**25th**—Formed as one company at Guiseley with Matthew William Thompson as captain, Henry G Baker, lieutenant and Jasper L White, ensign. All three held commissions dated 5 March 1860. Joined the

2nd Admin Battalion and was disbanded in August 1876. Standing on high ground between the Aire and the Wharfe, Guiseley's mills gave employment to many from the area.

**26th**—Formed as one company at Ingleton with John Thomas Coates as captain and Richard Brown, lieutenant. Both held commissions dated 21 March 1860. Ensign Joseph Hunter, Chaplain Richard Denny and Surgeon Richard Elletson were included in the corps before the end of 1860. Joined the 2nd Admin Battalion and is last seen in the Army List for January 1874.

**27th**—Formed as one company at Ripon with J Rhodes as captain, R Kearsley, lieutenant, T Wood, ensign and C Husband as surgeon. All four held commissions dated 13 April 1860. Joined the 1st Admin Battalion. A No 2 Company was raised in 1870 and became 'H' and 'J' Companies of the new 1st Corps in 1880. K D Pickup records how the Earl de Grey and Ripon gave permission for 'Red Bank' to be used as a drill ground, Masterman Crag, adjacent, being converted to a rifle range.

**28th**—Formed as one company at Goole with John Egremont as captain, John H Rockett, lieutenant, Robert S Best, ensign and John Stone, MD as surgeon. All four held commissions dated 2 May 1860. Joined the 3rd Admin Battalion and became 'E' Company of the new 5th Corps in 1880.

**29th**—Formed as one company at Dewsbury with Thomas H Cook as captain, John Wormald, lieutenant, Charles E Rhodes, ensign and George Fearnley as surgeon. All four held commissions dated 3 May 1860. Joined the 3rd Admin Battalion, but on reaching the strength of six companies in 1867 was removed. The establishment was reduced to three, however, in 1873 and the 29th Corps then returned to 3rd Admin. Became 'F' to 'H' Companies of the new 5th Corps in 1880.

**30th**—Formed as one company at Birstal in April 1860, is first officers being commissioned on 1st September 1860: Lieutenant Frederick H Knowles, Ensign Arthur Knowles and Surgeon Robert Rayner. Joined the 3rd Admin Battalion and disappeared from the Army List in October 1873.

**31st**—The 31st Corps, with headquarters at Tadcaster, first appeared in the Army List for July 1860. Officers were appointed—Captain Charles Shann, Lieutenant John A Bromet, surgeon Thomas S Upton—but their commissions were not issued until 16 February 1864. Joined the 1st Admin Battalion in the following September and became 'K' Company of the new 1st Corps in 1880.

**32nd**—Formed as one company at Holmfirth with J Earnshaw Morehouse as captain, John Harpin, lieutenant, George H Hinchliff, ensign and Charles J Trotter as surgeon. All four held commissions dated 2 June 1860. Joined the 5th Admin Battalion and became 'E' Company of the new 6th Corps in 1880. The Volunteer Drill Hall was built in 1891.

**33rd**—Formed as one company at Wetherby with Captain Thomas Broadbent and Lieutenant James Coates commissioned on 24 December 1860. Ensign John Hannam made up the establishment on 1 March 1861. Joined the 1st Admin Battalion and was disbanded in 1863.

**34th (Saddleworth)**—The 34th Corps was formed as one company at Saddleworth with Francis F Whitehead as captain, Joshua Hirst, lieutenant and George F Buckley, ensign. All three held commissions dated 10 September 1860. A second company was formed in May 1861, the command of which was given to Captain James Bradbury. The Bradbury family, records K D Pickup, provided four officers to the Saddleworth Corps, one Beckett Bradbury being its first surgeon. In April 1862 'Saddleworth' became part of the 34th's full title. By 1869 the establishment stood at eight companies, these being located at Saddleworth, Delph, Lydgate, Slaithwaite, Marsden, Golcar, Woodsome and Kirkburton. Reduced to four companies, however, in 1877 and at same time included in the 5th

**2nd Volunteer Battalion York and Lancaster Regiment.**

Admin Battalion. Became 'F', 'G', 'H' and 'J' Companies of the new 6th Corps in 1880. A busy wool manufacturing town, one large employer at Saddleworth was the Royal George Mills, one of its officials being Captain Francis F Whitehead.

**35th (Airedale)**—Formed as one company at Keighley with William Ferrand as captain, William L Marriner, lieutenant and Joseph Craven, ensign. All three held commissions dated 27 October 1860. Also appointed were the Rev William Busfield as chaplain and Angus Cameron who became surgeon. Joined the 2nd Admin Battalion in 1865, Airedale being added to the title in 1862. The 35th was increased to two companies in November 1861, three in 1876, and became 'D' to 'F' Companies of the new 9th Corps in 1880.

**36th**—Formed as one company at Rotherham with Edward Robinson as captain, Fretwell W Hoyle, lieutenant and Matthew E Chambers, ensign. All three held commissions dated 19 October 1860. Joined the 4th Admin Battalion in 1862 and became 'J' Company of the new 8th Corps in 1880.

**37th**—Formed as one company at Barnsley with Walter S Stanhope as captain, Robert C Clarke, lieutenant, William A Potter, ensign and John Blackburn as surgeon. All four held commissions dated 2 November 1860. Joined the 3rd Admin Battalion in March 1862, transferring to 4th Admin in April 1863. Became 'F' and 'H' Companies of the new 8th Corps in 1880.

**38th**—Formed as one company at Selby with Robert Parker as captain, John Marshall, lieutenant and William Liversidge, ensign. All three held commissions dated 1 January 1861. Also appointed at the same time were the Rev Francis W Harper as chaplain and Thomas W Burkitt who became surgeon. Joined the 3rd Admin Battalion, transferring to 1st Admin in 1863, and became 'L' Company of the new 1st Corps in 1880. At Selby Abbey a large six-light window in the south transept shows various scenes from the Bible along with portraits of Ensign William Liversidge and his wife who gave the glass.

**39th**—Formed as one company at Bingley with William Ellis as captain, John Benjamin Popplewell, lieutenant and George Henry Townend, ensign. All three held commissions dated 8 April 1861. A second company was formed in August 1869, the command of which was given to Titus Salt, Jun. It was no doubt due to his influence that the headquarters of the 39th Corps were moved in August 1871 to Saltaire. The industrial town with the biggest mills in Yorkshire and 800 houses for its workers which had been entirely built by the enterprise of his father Sir Titus Salt. The corps was disbanded in April 1875.

**40th**—Formed at Hoyland Nether with George K Day as captain, Joshua H Dawes, lieutenant and Joshua Biram, ensign. All three held commissions dated 19 March 1863. Appointed at the same time were the Rev J Cordeaux, who became chaplain to the corps, and Robert Adamson its surgeon. Joined the 4th Admin Battalion, moving headquarters to Wath-upon-Dearne in 1866, and became 'G' Company of the new 8th Corps in 1880.

**41st**—Formed as one company at Mirfield with Edward Day as captain, Joseph S Hurst, lieutenant and Thomas Wade, ensign. All three held commissions dated 23 November 1864. Joined the 5th Admin Battalion and became 'K' Company of the new 6th Corps in 1880.

**42nd**—Formed as one company at Haworth with George Merrall as captain; John Sugden, lieutenant and George H Merrall, ensign. All three held commissions dated 9 April 1866. Appointed at the same time were Amos Ingham as surgeon and the Rev Joshua B Grant who became chaplain. Joined the 2nd Admin Battalion and became 'G' Company of the new 9th Corps in 1880.

**43rd**—The services of the 43rd Corps at Batley were accepted on 22 June 1867, Benjamin Sherd being commissioned as captain on 16 October 1867. Joined the 3rd Admin Battalion, was later increased to two companies, and became 'J' and 'K' Companies of the new 5th Corps in 1880.

**44th**—Formed at Meltham with Captain Edward C Goody and Lieutenant Thomas J Hurst commissioned on 29 August 1868. The Rev Edward C Watson was appointed as chaplain to the corps at the same time. Joined the 5th Admin Battalion and was disbanded in 1876.

**45th**—Formed at Bingley on 30 June 1875 largely from former members of the recently disbanded 39th Corps. Joined the 2nd Admin Battalion and became 'H' Company of the new 9th Corps in 1880.

# FURTHER RESEARCH

**The Army List**—By far the most comprehensive record of officers who served in the Volunteer Force is the War Office Monthly Army List. These record every officer serving as of date of publication—although a List dated, e.g., January 1860, will be correct up to the previous month. Here we have names, ranks, dates of commissions which enable the researcher to compile a full record of a man's journey through the officer ranks from his entry into the Volunteer Force, through to such time that he retires, resigns or dies. Later on, as volunteer officers were required to pass as efficient in various subjects, these qualifications are also shown.

**Muster Rolls**—Although other ranks do not appear in the Army List their names were recorded in muster rolls complied by individual volunteer corps. Here we will usually find name, rank, date of enrolment into the corps, address and occupation. Sadly, these precious references are now few and far between. Look for them in county record offices, local and regimental museums, and the National Archives which have a good number.

**Published Unit Records**—If there is any printed matter connected with the Volunteer Force scarcer than the muster roll, it is the published 'Regimental History'. There are a dozen or so what might be termed as 'full' records at best, and these I have mentioned in my own list of sources and throughout the text. There have been, however, a good number of short booklets, or lengthy magazine articles, published over the years which are well worth tracking down. Again, county record offices should have these to hand. But knowing what to ask for is always a problem and I recommend—what the military historian anyway has come to term as his 'bible' on such matters—Arthur S White's *A Bibliography of Regimental Histories of the British Army*. For many years out of print, it is thankfully now available as a reprint from publishers Naval & Military Press, ISBN 9781843421559.

**Local Newspapers**—Local newspapers are a must. Items notifying meetings to discuss the formation of volunteer corps, who joined them, where they drilled, what they wore, where they camped and what parades they took part in, were regular features.

**National Archives**—As previously mentioned, there are muster rolls to be seen here. Also recommended are the useful, but incomplete Pay Lists for Volunteer Staff (WO 13/4622-4675), Registers of the Volunteer Officers' Decoration (WO330/3-4) and Registers for Other Ranks Volunteer Long Service Medal (WO 102/21). Those all important Army Lists are available on open shelves.

# REFERENCES

Beckett, Ian F W. *Riflemen Form*. Ogilby Trust, Aldershot, 1982.

Dooner, Mildred G. *The 'Last Post'*. Southgate, Rochester 1903.

Hart, Colonel Charles J. *The History of the 1st Volunteer Battalion The Royal Warwickshire Regiment*. The Midland Counties Herald Ltd, Birmingham, 1906.

Hayhurst, T H. *A History and Some Records of the Volunteer Movement in Bury, Heywood, Rossendale and Ramsbottom*. Thomas Crompton & Co, Bury 1887.

Igglesden, Charles. *History of the East Kent Volunteers*. The Kentish Express Ltd, Ashford, 1899.

Kellerher, Jim. *The Paddington Rifle 1860-1912*. Privately published, London 1984.

Pickup, K D. *West York Rifle Volunteers 1859-1887*. Cavendish Press, Leicester.

Richards, Walter. *His Majesty's Territorial Army*. Virtue & Co. 1910/11.

Rodney Wilde, Colonel E T. *Tower Hamlets Rifle Volunteers*. Coningham Bros, Limehouse, 1910.

Sargeaunt, B E. *A Military History of the Isle of Man*. T Buncle & Co Ltd, Arbroath, 1947.

Sturmey Cave, Colonel T. *A History of the First Volunteer Battalion Hampshire Regiment 1859 to 1889*. Simkin & Co, London 1905.


*Bulletin of the Military Historical Society,* various issues, 1948 to date.

*Journal of the Society for Army Historical Research,* various issues.

*London Gazette* 1859-1908.

*Monthly Army List* 1859-1908.

*Territorial Year Book 1909.*

*Volunteer Service Gazette*. Various issues.

*Volunteer Service Magazine*. Six Vols. May 1892 to June 1898.

*Illustrated London News*. Numerous issues 1859-1890.

Local newspapers.

Regimental histories, magazines and journals—more than 250 consulted.

Lightning Source UK Ltd.
Milton Keynes UK
UKHW050813110619
344177UK00004B/29/P